WALT DISNEY WORLD

Expert Advice from the Inside Source

THE
OFFICIAL
GUIDE

Wendy Lefkon EDITORIAL DIRECTOR

Jill Safro EDITOR

Jessica Ward ASSOCIATE EDITOR

Pam Brandon CONTRIBUTING EDITOR

Alexandra Mayes Birnbaum CONSULTING EDITOR

Stephen Birnbaum FOUNDING EDITOR

 DISNEY EDITIONS

NEW YORK

Contents

What's New?

To spotlight attractions making their debut, listings are marked with the stamp shown here. Look for it throughout the book. Here are a few highlights:

For Steve, who merely made all this possible

ISBN 978-1-4231-3861-7
G942-9090-6-11231

Printed in the United States of America

Other 2012 Birnbaum's Official Disney Guides

Disney Cruise Line
Disneyland
Walt Disney World Dining
Walt Disney World For Kids
Walt Disney World Pocket Parks Guide

A Word from the Editor

For some of us, our first Walt Disney World experience dates back to 1971, the year this new "Disneyland in Florida" made its debut. At that time, the Magic Kingdom was the only theme park, and it could be explored easily in a few days. Nonetheless, for those who came, it was love at first sight, and we've returned again and again.

Never before has there been so much incentive to visit (and revisit) the memory-making capital of the world. Star Tours—The Adventures Continue, the Studios' amazing new 3-D attraction—has shot to the top of most "must-see" lists. A show known as Disney Junior—Live on Stage! lights up legions of little faces. And perennial favorite Fantasmic! never fails to impress with its clever mix of music, fantasy, and pyrotechnic

Editor Jill Safro consults with Mickey and Minnie, the ultimate Disney insiders.

flair. Over at Epcot, the high-flying Soarin' attraction continues to delight, while Captain EO dazzles a new generation with his intergalactic musical magic. The Epcot International Food & Wine Festival gets bigger and better each year. And the Magic Kingdom wows visitors with that splendid blast from the past known as the Main Street Electrical Parade. Of course, that's just the tip of the iceberg, as so much of Walt Disney World has grown and evolved since our last edition. We are privileged and proud to provide readers with our extensively researched, insider look at some of the most cherished attractions, resorts, and restaurants on Earth.

When Steve Birnbaum launched this guide back in 1981, he made it clear what was expected of anyone who worked on it. The book would be meticulously revised each year, leaving no attraction untested, no snack or meal untasted, no hotel untried. First-hand experiences like these, accumulated over the years, make this book the most authoritative guide to the World. Our expertise, however, is not achieved by being escorted through back doors of attractions (although we would thoroughly enjoy that). Instead, we wait in lines with everyone else, always hoping to have a Disney experience like that of any other guest. Happily, logistical pickles are uncommon, leaving us time to investigate all the nooks and crannies of Walt's vast World.

After 41 fun-filled years, the World has vastly expanded—and so has our knowledge of the most popular vacation destination on the planet. On some occasions we've encountered sweltering weather and swelling crowds—times when even the happiest of travelers can turn into Grumpy for a moment or two. Had we known then what we know now, we could have spared ourselves some trying experiences. In one case, a staffer waited more than an hour to take a tour at the Studios. Standing in line with a notebook, she was asked by another guest if there was a quiz at the end. When she explained what she was doing, he expressed surprise to learn that she was waiting with the masses. But that's always been our strategy. We believe the best way to gather useful advice for a Walt Disney World guest is to be one. Over and over again!

Take Our Advice

We've done our best to keep you from making any tactical mistakes. We realize that even the most meticulous vacation planner needs *detailed, accurate, and objective information* to prepare a successful itinerary. To achieve that goal, we encourage the sharing of insight and information from Walt Disney World staffers—but the decision of whether or not to use such information is entirely up to the discretion of this book's editor.

To that end, we have packaged handy bits of advice in the form of sample itineraries and "hot tips" throughout the book. This advice comes directly from the copious notes we've taken during our thousands of days spent in Walt Disney World. We've also used our "Birnbaum's Best" stamp of approval wherever we deemed it appropriate, highlighting our favorite attractions and restaurants—the crowd-pleasers we believe stand head, shoulders, and ears above the rest.

You, the reader, benefit from the combination of our many years of experience that, together with our access to current insider information, makes this guide unique. We like to think it's indispensable, but we'll let you be the judge of that a few hundred pages from now.

Credit Where Credit Is Due

Enormous thanks to the teams of dedicated, detail-conscious Walt Disney World cast members from Guest Communications, the Disney Reservation Center, Food & Beverage, Merchandise, Resort Operations, Sports & Recreation, Attractions Operations, Disney Cruise Line, Disney Vacation Club, Marketing, and Disney Parks Synergy.

Kudos to Michelle Olveira for her skilled fact-checking, and to Carolyn Brunetto for her meticulous proofreading. Thanks also to designer Clark Wakabayashi, copy editor extraordinaire Erika Nein, and to Nisha Panchal and Jennifer Eastwood for their editorial support and production panache.

Heartfelt thanks to our photo shoot team: Stacey Cook, Michael Carroll, Brendan Carroll, Joan Peterson, Irene Ferdinand, Ana Rivera, and Lori Loftis—and, of course, Mickey Mouse and Minnie Mouse.

Hats off to those for whom doing Walt Disney World research is truly a labor of love. The "volunteer" class of 2012 includes Irene Safro, Roy Safro, the Henning family (Amy, Chris, Avery, and Elle), the Weigel family (Joy, Hayden, and Delaney), the Lagano family (Judy, Chris, Jessica, Max, and Kyle), Linda Verdon, Margaret Verdon, Trace Schielzo, Regan Flynn, and Christina Fontana.

Of course, no list of acknowledgments would be complete without mentioning our founding editor, Steve Birnbaum, whose spirit, wisdom, and humor still infuse these pages, as well as Alexandra Mayes Birnbaum, who continues to be a guiding light—to say nothing of being a careful reader of every word.

The Last Word

Finally, it's important to remember that every worthwhile travel guide is a living enterprise; the book you hold in your hands is our best effort at explaining how to enjoy Walt Disney World at this moment, but its text is in no way etched in stone. Disney is constantly changing and growing, and in each annual edition we refine and expand our material to serve your needs even better. For this year's edition, though, this must be the final word.

Have a great visit!

Jill Safro

—Editor

Don't Forget to Write

No contribution is of greater value to us in preparing the next edition of this book than your comments on what we have written and on your own experiences at Walt Disney World. Please share your insights with us by writing to:

Jill Safro, Editor
Birnbaum's Walt Disney World 2012
Disney Editions
114 Fifth Avenue, 14th Floor
New York, NY 10011

Getting Ready to Go

The key to a fabulous vacation at Walt Disney World is advance planning. This remarkably varied complex is too vast and diverse to allow a spontaneous visit to be undertaken with much success—especially when you consider the rapid rate at which the World has expanded. That does not mean that even the most casual visitors can't have some significant fun, but they are bound to have regrets about things they missed because of time pressures or a simple lack of information. The purpose of this guide is to eliminate potential frustration while getting the biggest bang for your vacation buck.

What follows, then, is meant to provide a sensible scheme for planning a satisfying visit to Walt Disney World, one that will offer the most fun and the least amount of disappointment. But how do you know which of the countless activities will be the most enjoyable for you and your family? Do your homework. The best strategy is to make sure you have a clear idea of all that is available long *before* you arrive in the Orlando area.

When to Go

When talk finally turns to the best time to make a trip to Walt Disney World, Christmas and Easter are often mentioned, as well as the traditional summer vacation period—especially if there are children in the family. But there is also good reason to avoid these periods, namely the tremendous crowds they attract. And when Disney World is crowded, it can be very crowded, indeed. On the busiest days, visitors may wait as much as two hours to experience the more popular attractions when waiting in lines. That's at least twice as long as during less busy times of the year. Weekends, in general, are quite popular with locals. Monday through Wednesday are generally quieter.

Considering seasonal hours, weather, crowd patterns, and Disney resort rates, optimal times to visit Walt Disney World are usually mid-January through early February, late April through late May, and September through December (except Thanksgiving and Christmas weeks).

Note that during some of the less crowded times of the year—particularly during the winter —some attractions are closed for renovations. In addition, water parks are often closed for refurbishment during cooler months. Call 407-824-4321, or check *www.disneyworld.com* for a current schedule, updated each season.

Mid-November through December is a festive time of year the world over, and Disney World is no exception. The theme parks are decorated to the nines for the holiday season. Epcot holds nightly tree-lighting ceremonies, and the Magic Kingdom drapes Cinderella Castle in thousands of sparkling lights. Many other special events are held during this period, including Mickey's Very Merry Christmas Party in the Magic Kingdom (a separate admission ticket is required). The party

brings a dusting of "snow" to Main Street from about 7 P.M. to midnight for several days between mid-November and the first three weeks of December. It also features holiday shows around the park, including Mickey's Once Upon a Christmastime Parade, plus a unique fireworks show: Holiday Wishes. Select performances from Mickey's Very Merry Christmas Party are also staged in the park during regular hours on the days leading up to, including, and following Christmas. Note that this event is popular and usually sells out way ahead of time. Get tickets in advance by calling 407-W-DISNEY (934-7639). It's usually easier to snag tickets for dates earlier in the season.

Animal Kingdom gets into the spirit of the season with Mickey's Jingle Jungle Parade. Epcot celebrates with Holidays Around the World, including the nightly Candlelight Processional, complete with a mass choir, 50-piece orchestra, and a reading of the story of Christmas by a celebrity narrator. Dinner packages are available for some World Showcase restaurants. (We recommend the dinner package: It guarantees seating for dinner as well as preferred seating at the Candlelight Processional. Without a package, you should arrive at least one hour before showtime or risk being shut out of your preferred performance.) Disney's Hollywood Studios features the Osborne Family Spectacle of Dancing Lights, a display of millions of lights depicting holiday scenes. For updated information regarding the dates and location of this perennially popular, sparkly spectacular, visit *www.disneyworld.com*.

There are holiday decorations at each Walt Disney World hotel, too, including a Victorian Christmas at the Grand Floridian, a seaside party at the Yacht and Beach Club, and a Cajun holiday at Port Orleans Riverside.

For reservations, call 407-W-DISNEY (934-7639), a travel agent, or the Walt Disney Travel Company at 407-828-8101. Visit *www.disneyworld.com*, or call 407-939-7630 for information. Special-event tickets are sold separately.

HOT TIP!

The period of time between the end of Thanksgiving weekend and the week before Christmas is one of the least crowded and most festive times of the year. It's a wonderful time to visit.

Crowd Patterns

Day-to-Day Trends

In general, the weekends tend to be among the most crowded days at Walt Disney World theme parks, followed by Thursdays and Fridays. Morning through early afternoon is a bustling time for the theme parks and their respective "E-ticket" attractions. Days that offer Extra Magic Hours tend to be more crowded at their respective theme parks (see page 21). When the weather's steamy, the water parks tend to pack them in—so be sure to get an early start if you're headed to Blizzard Beach or Typhoon Lagoon.

When the time comes to plot an itinerary, it's helpful to know about crowd patterns beyond the four theme parks as well. As a rule, Downtown Disney and Disney's water parks host their largest throngs on weekends. Of course, in these circles, a bigger crowd could possibly mean a better time. Golfers should note that weekend tee times are typically in the highest demand, while Monday and Tuesday tee times are the easiest to come by.

Seasonal Shifts

The chart below indicates the density of crowds in the theme parks throughout the year. Though it's tough to generalize about a property as vast and ever-changing as Walt Disney World—special events (such as the Disney Marathon and Epcot's Food and Wine Festival) and package deals can swell park attendance during a period typically marked by smaller crowds—the chart highlights historic trends.

Least Crowded means that there will be lines, but most attractions can be visited without much waiting.

Average Attendance refers to times when there are lots of people around, but lines are relatively manageable.

Most Crowded reflects times when lines at popular attractions can mean a wait of as much as two hours. As a rule, when school is out, the crowds are most definitely in at Walt Disney World.

Least Crowded

- 2nd week of January through 1st week of February (excluding Marathon Weekend)

- Week before Labor Day until the start of Epcot's Food & Wine Festival

- Period after Food & Wine Festival ends until Thanksgiving week

- Week after Thanksgiving through week before Christmas

Average Attendance

- 1st week of January

- 2nd week of February until Presidents' week

- End of February through 2nd week of March

- Last week of April through May

- Thanksgiving week (excluding Thanksgiving Day)

Most Crowded

- Major holidays

- Presidents' week

- Marathon Weekend

- 3rd week of March through 3rd week of April

- June through the 3rd week of August

- Epcot Food & Wine Festival

- Christmas through New Year's Day

- Any time school's out for vacation

Holidays and Special Events

Special affairs are staged throughout the year, not only to mark holidays but also to celebrate other interests. *The dates and details below are subject to change without notice*; call 407-824-4321 to confirm, or check out *www.disneyworld.com* for up-to-the-minute information about specific events.

JANUARY

Walt Disney World Marathon Weekend (January 5–8): Some 20,000 entrants run through several theme parks and many other areas of the World during this 26.2-mile race (January 8). Characters and cast members are on hand to inspire runners. Similar hoopla surrounds the half marathon (January 7). There's also a 5K family run on January 6. (It's okay to walk the 5K, but you must maintain a 16-minute mile.) Packages are available. Call 407-939-4786 for package details or to book. For marathon weekend event information and schedules, call 407-938-3398, or visit *www.rundisney.com* for details. Note that hotel rooms are in high demand for this event. Reserve yours as early as possible.

MARCH–JUNE

Saint Patrick's Day (March 17): Everyone is Irish on Saint Patrick's Day—especially at Raglan Road, Downtown Disney's Irish pub. Epcot's United Kingdom pavilion marks the day with Irish dining and dancing.

   Atlanta Braves Spring Training (Late February–March): Play ball! Having weathered a long winter, giddy baseball fans flock to the ESPN sports complex to enjoy a dose of America's favorite pastime. For information, visit *www.espnwwos.com/atlantabraves*.

   Easter (April 8): Most of the Disney theme parks stay open late during the two weeks straddling the Easter holiday. Keep in mind

that this is an extremely busy time to visit.

   Epcot International Flower & Garden Festival (March 7–May 20): Epcot is blooming with elaborate gardens (including more than 30 million fragrant blossoms) and topiary displays, behind-the-scenes tours, gardening workshops, concerts, and guest speakers. Learn from the experts how to create a gorgeous garden.

   Star Wars Weekends (May and/or June): Disney's Hollywood Studios salutes *Star Wars* with actors and characters from the movies, plus photo ops, trivia contests, and more. Visit *www.disneyworld.com/starwars* for details.

JULY

Fourth of July Celebration: Double-size fireworks over the Magic Kingdom, Epcot, and Disney's Hollywood Studios make for a very colorful night. This is an exceptionally busy time to visit Disney World.

SEPTEMBER–NOVEMBER

Night of Joy (September): Two nights of celebration highlight contemporary Christian music presented live in the Magic Kingdom. For dates and tickets, call 407-827-7200. This popular event attracts a bit of a rowdy crowd (of mostly teens and young adults).

   Children's Miracle Network Golf Classic (October): Top PGA Tour players compete alongside amateurs in this big tourney, played on the Palm and Magnolia golf courses. Packages are available. For more information, visit *www.childrensmiraclenetworkclassic.com*.

   Epcot International Food & Wine Festival (September 28–November 11): World Showcase celebrates the flavors of different countries (even those not usually represented around the lagoon) through tastings ($2 to $8 per sample), demos from top chefs, and wine and cooking seminars. It's a satisfying way in which to wander World Showcase.

   Halloween (late September–October): The festivities vary a bit from year to year.

Here's a sampling of what to expect:

Fort Wilderness Resort and Campground generally hosts a pumpkin-carving contest and a children's costume contest, followed by a screening of a scary movie. It also offers Halloween-themed wagon rides with storytelling and surprises along the way.

Downtown Disney has hosted kids' costume contests and trick-or-treating. Grown-ups have been known to don costumes, too. Animal Kingdom also invites guests to trick-or-treat.

The Magic Kingdom will play host to its Halloween spectacular, **Mickey's Not-So-Scary Halloween Party**, September through October. The special-ticket activities include a costume parade, dancing, appearances by Disney villains, trick-or-treating, and Halloween fireworks. This is an extremely popular Magic Kingdom event. Purchase your tickets as far in advance as possible. And don't forget to wear a costume. As a spooky bonus, **Mickey's Boo-to-You Halloween Parade** makes its way through the Kingdom during the Halloween party. For information about dates on which the not-so-scary party takes place, call 407-827-7200.

Festival of the Masters (early November): This three-day fine arts show draws more than 150 of the world's top artists to Downtown Disney. For additional information, visit *www.disneyworld.com/art*.

NOVEMBER–DECEMBER

Disney's Magical Holidays: Decorations and festivities abound in Walt Disney World's parks and resorts. The Magic Kingdom hosts **Mickey's Very Merry Christmas Party** on several nights from mid-November through the first three weeks of December, complete with snow flurries on Main Street and hot cocoa. Entertainment for the special-ticket party includes **Mickey's Once Upon a Christmas-time Parade** and a special edition of the Wishes fireworks show; select performances are staged during regular hours just before Christmas. Animal Kingdom presents the **Mickey's Jingle Jungle Parade** during the holiday season, too.

Epcot's **Holidays Around the World** (November 23–December 30) features the Christmas Candlelight Processional, including a choral concert, plus a celebrity narrator who reads the story of Christmas. The event is included with park admission, but seating is limited and it is extremely popular. Arrive at least an hour before showtime, or book a dinner package (which combines dinner at a World Showcase eatery with guaranteed Processional seating). For details, call 407-939-3463.

The Osborne Family Spectacle of Dancing Lights (November–January) is a big crowd-pleaser. This dazzling light display brightens Disney's Hollywood Studios with millions of lights "performing" in synchronized motion with music. It's presented in the Streets of America backlot area.

New Year's Eve Celebration (December 31): There are extra-large fireworks displays over the Magic Kingdom, Epcot, and Disney's Hollywood Studios (though there are no fireworks at all at Animal Kingdom—imagine the stampede!). These parks stay open until about 1 A.M. (It varies from year to year.) Many of the resort restaurants, as well as the nightspots at Downtown Disney, also welcome the new year Disney style. La Nouba by Cirque du Soleil features a festive finale to ring in the new year (Downtown Disney, West Side).

A Tisket, A Tasket . . .

. . . a "Welcome to Walt Disney World Basket." The Disney Florist can deliver this and a striking array of themed surprises to any room on Disney property (and many that aren't). There's no occasion they can't rise to—from a birthday to Earth Day, from engagements to golden wedding anniversaries—a call to the Disney Florist (the only one serving WDW) can yield custom-tailored bouquets, baskets, and even Christmas trees. (They also have a division dedicated exclusively to Walt Disney World engagements.)

Not satisfied with a simple delivery to a resort room? The Florist folks encourage creativity. Got a favorite Disney character? Into the basket he or she goes! One package known as "The Glass Slipper" (complete with slipper and tiara) can actually be delivered to guests enjoying a romantic carriage ride.

For more information or to place an order, call 407-827-3505 (daily from 8 A.M. to 6 P.M.), or visit *www.disneyflorist.com*.

Keeping WDW Hours

Since operating hours fluctuate quite a bit, call 407-824-4321 or visit *www.disneyworld.com* for current schedules.

THEME PARKS: Theme park hours vary seasonally. In May, September, October, parts of November and December, and all of January, the Magic Kingdom is usually open from 9 A.M. to 8 P.M.; Epcot is open from 9 A.M. to 9 P.M. (Some Future World attractions close at 7 P.M.); Disney's Hollywood Studios is open from 9 A.M. until about an hour after sunset; and Animal Kingdom is open from 9 A.M. until about 5 P.M. The parks take turns offering Extra Magic Hours throughout the week. That is, on any given day, one of the parks may allow Disney World resort guests to enter an hour early or stay in the park for up to three hours after it closes to the public. All participating WDW resorts have schedules at the front desk.

The Magic Kingdom keeps later hours through summer and other busy periods, including Christmas and Easter. The parks may be open until 1 A.M. on New Year's Eve.

Disney's Hollywood Studios often stays open until 10 or 11 P.M. in the summer, too.

DOWNTOWN DISNEY MARKETPLACE: Shops are open from about 9:30 A.M. until 11 P.M. Sunday through Thursday; 11:30 P.M. on Friday and Saturday. Restaurant hours vary.

DOWNTOWN DISNEY PLEASURE ISLAND: Restaurant and lounge hours vary. Note that parts of this zone will be under construction in 2012. The name of this area was correct at press time, but it may change. For updates, visit *www.disneyworld.com*.

DOWNTOWN DISNEY WEST SIDE: At the AMC cineplex, movies begin as early as 10 A.M. Restaurants are open from about 11:30 A.M. to midnight. Shops are usually open from 10:30 A.M. to 11 P.M. (midnight on Friday and Saturday).

WATER PARKS: Water parks are open from about 10 A.M. to 5 P.M. Check for Extra Magic Hours on select "peak" days.

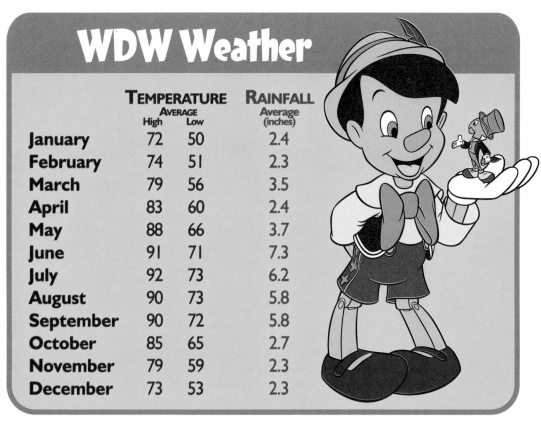

WDW Weather

| | TEMPERATURE | | RAINFALL |
| | AVERAGE | | Average |
	High	Low	(inches)
January	72	50	2.4
February	74	51	2.3
March	79	56	3.5
April	83	60	2.4
May	88	66	3.7
June	91	71	7.3
July	92	73	6.2
August	90	73	5.8
September	90	72	5.8
October	85	65	2.7
November	79	59	2.3
December	73	53	2.3

How to Get There

By Car

While most visitors to the Orlando area fly in, some prefer to drive. If you opt for a road trip, figure on logging no more than 350 to 400 miles a day—a distance that won't wear you down so much that you can't enjoy your trip.

Contact state tourist boards to inquire about the availability of free maps; for a Florida map and guide, call 888-735-2872, or pick up a copy of *Rand McNally Road Atlas* or the *AAA North American Road Atlas*; both are sold in bookstores. Driving directions from most cities are also available on the Internet. One site to try is *www.mapquest.com*.

From Orlando International Airport*

By car: During rush hour, take the airport's South Exit to the Central Florida Greeneway (Route 417) to Route 536, which leads to Walt Disney World. The tolls run about $2.

For the shortest route, take the North Exit to Route 528, going west toward Tampa. Pick up I-4 west, and go to a WDW exit. Tolls are about $2. The route is usually heavily trafficked, but manageable during non-rush periods of the day. It's busiest on weekday mornings and evenings and any time when a theme park is scheduled to open or close.

By Disney's Magical Express: This tailor-made, complimentary transportation program is available to guests staying at select Disney resorts. For more information, turn to page 15.

By car service: Florida Towncar offers efficient, congenial, direct service to Disney area resorts. And they offer our readers a special rate, too! Simply mention the Birnbaum Guide when you book your ride and expect a round-trip rate of about $85 for up to 5 passengers (that's $15 off the regular rate). Call 407-277-5466 or 800-525-7246 up to 24 hours ahead, or visit *www.florida-towncar.com*. Online reservations should be made at least 72 hours ahead.

Reliable towncar service is also available from Crown Noris Limousine. Drivers take guests directly to their resort. The company also offers a special round-trip rate for Birnbaum readers— mention this book and expect to pay about $120 for up to four passengers for a towncar, or about $215 for a limo for up to 7 passengers. Reservations are required and cancellations must be made at least 48 hours ahead. Call 407-240-4533, or visit *www.norislimousine.com*. Prices may increase if there is a significant jump in prices at the pump.

By shuttle: At Orlando International Airport, Mears Motor Shuttle offers vans and buses 24 hours a day. It serves the Swan and Dolphin, Hotel Plaza Blvd. properties, and other non-Disney area hotels. Shuttles make multiple stops; a trip can take an hour or more. On the return trip, Mears requires guests be picked up at least 3–4 hours prior to flight times. Reservations should be made 24 hours ahead. There is often a long wait at the airport (even with a reservation), and employee attitudes fluctuate wildly. This is not our preferred mode of transit.

The shuttle cost to most hotels is $21 one way, $34 round-trip per adult; $17 one way, $27 round-trip per child ages 4 through 11; free for children under 4. Fares to International Drive properties are a little lower. There may be a long wait to get on a shuttle at the airport, and service is not direct. Call 407-423-5566 for information, or visit *www.mearstransportation.com*.

By taxi: Metered cabs may cost between $60 and $70 each way, depending on the destination—and the integrity of the driver. Some taxis can accommodate up to 9 people (for the price of one). Bell services can call for a cab at any WDW resort. Note that many drivers do not have SunPass, so it'll cost you 55 cents a minute while waiting to pay each toll. What's more, many drivers do not know the area streets (or pretend not to)—resulting in bigger fares than necessary. Until cabs offer a flat rate to and from the airport, we are sticking with Magical Express or towncars.

*Gratuities are not included in any of the transfer rates. It is customary to tip for good service.

Reputable automobile clubs offer help with breakdowns; towing; insurance that covers personal injury, accidents, arrest, bail bond, and lawyers' fees for defense of contested traffic cases; and travel-planning services, including free maps and route mapping. Services vary from one club to the next, and membership fees range widely, from about $50 to $120 a year.

By Air

When it comes to airfares, there is no real trick to unearthing the most economical ones: Simply shop around. Call a travel agent, browse the Internet, and keep these tips in mind:

- Watch your local newspapers for ads announcing short-term promotional fares. When a deal presents itself, grab it.

- The more flexible you can be in your dates and duration of stay, the more money you're likely to save.

- Take advantage of advance-purchase fares (lower rates that apply if a ticket is bought at least two to three weeks prior to the scheduled departure).

- Keep in mind that the lowest airfares usually carry a penalty if you have to revise your flight schedule, and that certain discounted tickets are nonrefundable.

Did You Know?

It's perfectly legal to make a right turn at a red light on roads throughout the state of Florida.

Resources for Road Trippers

There are a variety of reputable national automobile clubs to choose from. Among the leading clubs:

- **Allstate Motor Club**
  Customer Service Center
  P.O. Box 3094
  Arlington Heights, IL 60006
  800-998-8697
  www.allstatemotorclub.com

- **American Automobile Association (AAA)**
  1000 AAA Dr. #28
  Heathrow, FL 32746
  407-444-7000 or 800-564-6222
  www.aaa.com

- **Ford Auto Club**
  Customer Relationship Center
  P.O. Box 6248
  Dearborn, MI 48126
  800-392-3673

- **Gulf Motor Club**
  929 N. Plum Grove Rd.
  Schaumburg, IL 60173
  800-633-3224

- **Signature Nationwide Auto Club**
  Attention: Customer Service
  P.O. Box 968008
  Schaumburg, IL 60196
  800-323-2002
  www.autoclub.com

- **Auto Club of America**
  P.O. Box 21443
  Oklahoma City, OK 73156
  800-411-2007
  www.autoclubofamerica.com

Travelers may also check with state tourist boards for free maps. Other map sources are the *AAA North American Road Atlas* and the *Rand McNally Road Atlas*; they are sold in many bookstores.

- When you call to make a reservation, ask about any fare restrictions, including an obligatory Saturday night stay-over.

- Fly when most people don't: For vacation destinations, that usually means leaving the ground on Tuesday or Wednesday.

- Visit airline Web sites. They may e-mail details about discounted fares. Some offer a discount for purchasing tickets online.

By Train

Amtrak serves the Orlando area twice daily to and from New York City, with various stops made along the way. The trip takes approximately 22 hours and costs from about $250 to $400 round-trip, coach. (Book early for lower fares; discounts are often available, so be sure to ask.) If you're staying at Walt Disney World, plan to take a cab or shuttle to the area hotels; the cost varies, depending on the destination. Rental cars are also available. They are not on-site, but are easily reached by shuttle.

For reservations and information on this and other routes, call 800-USA-RAIL (872-7245), visit the Amtrak Web site at *www.amtrak.com*, or contact a travel agent.

By Bus

Greyhound provides frequent direct service to Orlando and Kissimmee (the latter is closer to Walt Disney World). From either destination, you can take a taxi to your hotel, but first check if your hotel offers shuttle service. For more information, contact Greyhound at 800-231-2222, or visit *www.greyhound.com*.

Disney's Magical Express Service

Disney's Magical Express service is for guests planning a stay at a Walt Disney World-owned-and-operated resort and arriving at Orlando International Airport. Meant as a money-saver as well as a convenience, the service lets guests check luggage at their airport of origin, bypass baggage claim, and board a bus to their WDW resort. The luggage, which guests affix with special tags before leaving home, is usually delivered to the resort room within several hours of arrival. On the final day of a trip, prior to boarding the bus back to the airport, guests who fly participating airlines (at press time, that included Air Canada, Aer Lingus, AirTran, Alaska, American, Delta, JetBlue, United, and US Airways) check their luggage at their resort and receive a boarding pass for their airline. (Luggage fees may apply.) Once at the airport, they can skip the airline check-in counter and proceed directly to the line for security. If you'd prefer to schlep your own bags, you can still hitch a free ride on the bus. Here are some specifics:

- Magical Express service is booked when you book your resort and must be done at least 10 days prior to arrival. (Have flight information handy when you make the call.) We recommend making the reservation as early as possible—preferably five to six weeks ahead.

- Reservations may be made via *www.disneyworld.com*, 407-W-DISNEY, or a travel agent.

- Tip the driver as you would had you paid for the trip: $1–$2 per bag is appropriate.

- Special luggage tags will be sent to the party that makes the reservation. These tags must be put on all bags that will be checked at the airport.

- Upon landing at Orlando International Airport, skip baggage claim (if you tagged your bags) and proceed to the Disney Welcome Center, located in the Main Terminal Building on the B side, Level 1. Don't forget to have your transfer vouchers and a photo ID handy. Check in at the desk. Note that one person may check in the whole party, so there's no need for everyone to stand in the check-in line.

- On the return trip, expect to be picked up at least three hours before your scheduled flight departure time. Consider that when you make your air arrangements.

- Guests who require wheelchair-accessible transportation should make their needs known when making the reservation. Confirm reservations before you leave home.

- Guests flying on "non-participating" airlines are entitled to the free shuttle service, too.

The good news? It is a money-saver. In fact, a family of four can shave at least $100 off their total vacation cost by taking the Magical Express shuttle as opposed to other forms of transportation. It's also handy to bypass check-in at the airport on the return trip. The downside? Well, to call any service "magical" is to elevate expectations. It's not really "express," either—as most buses make multiple stops at Disney resorts. So if time is of the essence, it might not be the best choice. Same goes for the transportation of luggage. It may take an hour to arrive at your resort room, but it may also take three to six. So if you'll need anything right away—bathing suits, pajamas, sunscreen, medication, etc.—pack it in a day bag, carry it onto the plane, and transport it to the resort yourself.

Planning Ahead
Logistics

Organizing a trip properly takes time, but most travelers find the increased enjoyment well worth the effort. The fact is, planning can become a pleasant sort of "armchair" exercise, and kids will enjoy their visit to Disney all the more if they, too, are involved in the process.

To assist in that effort, we immodestly recommend *Birnbaum's Walt Disney World For Kids*, a colorful look at the World, written for readers ages 7 through 14. For those planning to pair a Disney cruise with a Walt Disney World visit, *Birnbaum's Disney Cruise Line* is the definitive source.

HOT TIP!
So you've used this book to plan your trip to Walt Disney World. What are you going to do now? Go to *www.disneyworld.com*! Here you can get WDW news and park hours, purchase tickets, and more.

Information Sources

For information about Walt Disney World, call 407-W-DISNEY (407-934-7639) or visit *www.disneyworld.com*. Lots of current specifics, such as park hours, ticket prices, refurbishment schedules, and directions are available through an automated system 24 hours a day. For information by mail, write to: Walt Disney World, P.O. Box 10000, Lake Buena Vista, FL 32830-1000.

Internet users can tap into updates about happenings in the World, get information on trip planning, reserve a room, order tickets, and get theme park hours and special-events listings by entering *www.disneyworld.com*. Disney Cruise Line vacation packages may be booked at *www.disneycruise.com*.

For information and discounts on area attractions, restaurants, and hotels, contact the Official Visitor Information Center, 8723 International Drive, Suite 101, Orlando, FL 32819 (a satellite office of the Orlando Convention & Visitors Bureau); 407-363-5872,

or 800-551-0181; *www.orlandoinfo.com*.

For details about other Central Florida attractions, contact Visit Florida; 888-735-2872 (to request a complimentary visitors guide and map) or 850-488-5607; *www.visitflorida.com*.

On-site Resources: Those staying at a Walt Disney World resort should consider their hotel's lobby concierge desk the primary resource. Resort guests also receive Walt Disney World information via their room's television (it runs in a continuous loop). Fort Wilderness campers are advised to stop at the Pioneer Hall Information and Ticket Window, call extension 2788, or touch 11 on a phone near any restroom.

What to Pack

While there is hardly a dress code at Walt Disney World, neat, casual clothing is the rule, with few exceptions. Most notably, jackets are required for men at Victoria & Albert's restaurant in the Grand Floridian resort. More generally, T-shirts and shorts are perfectly acceptable during the day. For evening, slacks, jeans, or Bermuda length shorts are appropriate. Bathing suits are a must, along with the appropriate attire for any sport you want to pursue.

Lightweight sweaters are necessary even in summer—to wear indoors when the air-conditioning gets chilly. From November through March, warmer clothing is a must for evening. Pack for weather extremes so you'll be comfy should it become unseasonably warm or cool. Always bring plenty of sunscreen, and don't forget the bug spray. If possible, pack lightweight rain gear (a poncho is best). The most important item of all? Comfortable walking shoes (two pair).

Guests at the resorts on Hotel Plaza Boulevard may access a tourist-information TV program of their own. Some other area hotels also show a version of the program, usually aiming to provide an overview of all Central Florida attractions.

For Day Visitors: When purchasing one-day admission to a given theme park, guests receive a complimentary guidemap and entertainment Times Guide for that park. Ticket holders may receive all four park guides upon request. Extra guidemaps are available at City Hall (in the Magic Kingdom) and at Guest Relations (in Epcot, Disney's Hollywood Studios, and Animal Kingdom), as well as in many shops and restaurants throughout the park.

Package Pointers

The sheer number and diversity of packages offering vacations in Central Florida are enough to bewilder even the savviest traveler. Still, such plans are worth exploring. Most offer the convenience of a vacation that's completely organized in advance, and one that will generally cost less than the sum of the same transportation, accommodations, and admission elements purchased separately. In addition, since most package providers purchase blocks of Disney resort rooms, they are an excellent source for securing a room on Walt Disney World property when the hotel of your choice is booked.

American Airlines Vacations (800-321-2121), US Airways Vacations (800-455-0123), Southwest Vacations (800-243-8372), *www. expedia.com*, *www.travelocity.com*, and the Walt Disney Travel Company (407-939-6244 or *www.disneyworld.com*) all offer packages that feature WDW on-site hotels, as well as choice off-property accommodations. Many packages include the added attraction of low-cost air transportation. The American Automobile Association (call 407-444-7000 or visit *www.aaa.com*) offers AAA Vacations and other travel packages, which include certain perks and discounts. For other possibilities, consider GOGO Worldwide Vacations (*www.gogowwv.com*), check the travel section of your local newspaper, or consult with a travel agent.

Walt Disney Travel Company offers six vacation plans. They are: Magic Your Way base package, Magic Your Way Plus Dining package, Magic Your Way Plus Quick Service Dining package, Magic Your Way Plus Deluxe Dining package, Magic Your Way Premium package, and the Magic Your Way Platinum package. (Visit *disneyworld.com/dvd* to order a complimentary vacation planning DVD.)

Travel agents may design packages around a specific type of vacation: say, a golf getaway, honeymoon, or family reunion. They may include extra elements such as unlimited tee times or a carriage ride. Still others are tied to an annual event, such as the Walt Disney World Marathon (see Holidays and Special Events on page 10 of this chapter). Finally, Disney's Sand and Castle package combines a Disney World vacation with a stay at Disney's Vero Beach Resort or other Florida beach resorts. (See page 89 in *Transportation & Accommodations* for details on the Disney Vacation Club.) Air transportation, rental car, or airport transfers can be added to packages.

The value of a package depends on your needs. Before considering options, use this book to help determine which of the accommodations, activities, and attractions most appeal to you. There's real value in some package elements, such as airport transfers and meal discounts. Several packages also include meals with the Disney characters, tennis lessons, golf greens fees, spa treatments, boat rentals, and the like.

Never choose a package that includes elements you don't want or won't have time to enjoy. While extras such as welcoming snacks may sound appealing, their cash value is negligible. Also beware of any packages that tout certain services as selling points that are actually available to every Disney guest.

HOT TIP!
When purchasing a Walt Disney World package, pay attention to the type of WDW ticket that's included—and make sure you are able to customize the ticket to meet your needs. See page 20.

"Magic Your Way" Packages

"Magic Your Way" is the name of the game when it comes to Disney World vacation planning. The phrase, meant to reflect each individual's freedom to customize a vacation, covers quite the gamut of options. Most of all, it covers six vacation packages: Magic Your Way, Magic Your Way Plus Dining, Magic Your Way Plus Quick Service Dining, Magic Your Way Plus Deluxe Dining, Magic Your Way Premium, and Magic Your Way Platinum. They can be booked through the Walt Disney Travel Company (407-939-7675), travel agents, and *www.disneyworld.com*.

The packages have some elements in common. For starters, they're all intended to be flexible and include a Walt Disney World resort stay and a theme park ticket of some kind. They must be paid for in full. All packages must be canceled at least 45 days before the trip to avoid a penalty. Everyone staying in the room must have the same package and ticket options. Finally, they all come with the following:

• Extra Magic Hours benefit: WDW resort guests may enjoy exclusive access to theme parks select mornings and evenings. For details on Extra Magic Hours, see page 21.

• Disney's Magical Express service: complimentary transportation to and from Orlando International Airport, plus baggage delivery to your resort room. See page 15 for details.

• Complimentary use of the Walt Disney World transportation system (buses, boats, and the ever-popular monorail).

Magic Your Way Package: This "package" is, quite simply, a stay at any Walt Disney World-owned-and-operated resort paired with a theme park ticket. The big decisions to be made here are (1) which resort to reserve, and (2) the number of days and add-ons you want on your park ticket. (For more on Walt Disney World theme park ticket structures and pricing, turn to pages 20–25.)

Magic Your Way Plus Dining Package: Take the above description of the Magic Your Way package, throw in a Disney Dining Plan, and you've got a vacation plan with the freedom to dine at more than 100 different eateries—not to mention the potential to shave a few bucks off your dining budget. The package includes one quick-service meal, a snack, and one meal at a table-service restaurant per person, per night of your vacation. (For more information on the Dining Plan, see the box on page 19.) The package also includes a Magic Your Way base ticket. (See pages 20–25 for ticket specifics.)

Magic Your Way Plus Quick Service Dining Package: This plan includes two meals and two snacks per day, per guest—but all meals are of the quick-service variety. It includes a refillable mug for each member of the party participating in this package.

Magic Your Way Plus Deluxe Dining Package: Similar to the two aforementioned packages, but this plan comes with three meals a day, all of which can be cashed in at any eatery that is a Dining Plan participant (regardless of whether it is quick service or table service).

Magic Your Way Premium Package: It's called "premium" because it includes many of the World's most popular features:

- A stay at a Disney-owned-and-operated resort
- Magic Your Way ticket with "add-ons" (see page 20 for details).
- Premium Dining Plan: breakfast, lunch, and dinner per person, per night. For details on the WDW Dining Plan, see sidebar and visit *www.disneyworld.com*, or call 407-WDW-DINE (939-3463).
- Unlimited access to select recreation opportunities, including golf, guided fishing excursions, water sports, and more. (Restrictions apply, and advance reservations may be required.)
- Admission to Cirque du Soleil's La Nouba show (one admission per person).
- Admission to a Disney Children's Activity Center at a select Walt Disney World resort (ages 4–12).
- Unlimited admission to select Theme Park tours: Magic Kingdom's Family Magic Tour, The Magic Behind Our Steam Trains, and Keys to the Kingdom; Epcot's

Behind the Seeds, Simply Segway Experience, and The Undiscovered Future World; and Animal Kingdom's Backstage Safari and Wild By Design. See pages 218–220 for tour details.

- Special dining experiences, including meals with Disney characters, "signature" dining experiences, and dinner shows.
- One resort refillable soft drink mug per person (good for the length of your stay).

Magic Your Way Platinum Package: An upgrade from the Premium Package, the Platinum version features a stay at a deluxe Disney resort, plus extra options such as spa treatments and high-end dining opportunities.

Disney Dining Plan

The Disney Dining Plan is popular for a reason: Forget the flexibility of dining at more than 100 different eateries for a moment, and ponder the notion of saving up to 30 percent on rations for your trip. We're salivating at the prospect. What follows was accurate at press time, but details are likely to change in 2012:

Each day of the plan—which starts at about $44 a day and is offered as part of the Magic Your Way Plus Dining package—includes:

- One table-service meal, including entrée, dessert (lunch or dinner), and non-alcoholic beverage.

- One quick-service meal, including entrée, dessert, and non-alcoholic beverage.

- One snack, such as ice cream, popcorn, or a medium soft drink at select quick-service spots or snack carts.

- The option of exchanging two table-service meals for one meal at a high-end "signature restaurant" or a dinner show, such as the Hoop-Dee-Doo Musical Revue.

To sum up: Say your family of four were to purchase a five-night package. Together you'd be entitled to 20 quick-service meals, 20 table-service meals, and 20 snacks. And you are free to use them in any way you want. That is, if you want to skip a meal one day or have five meals in a single day, by all means go for it. (Just remember that you have a finite number of meals allotted.) Usage is tracked electronically via your room key. Taxes are included, gratuities are not. Be sure to tip your servers. Hold on to your receipts, as they show your remaining meal balance.

In addition to the traditional table-service establishments, certain "character dining" experiences are available to Dining Plan participants, as are select Downtown Disney locations. Note that kids ages 3–9 are required to order from the children's menu where available.

To find out which restaurants are participating, turn to our *Good Meals, Great Times* chapter. For updates, call 407-939-3463 or go to *www.disneyworld.com*.

The Dining Plan must be purchased at the same time you book your WDW resort stay. Finally, if you get the Dining Plan, you still need to make reservations. We recommend doing so as far ahead as possible (180 days).

All About Theme Park Tickets

Buying a park ticket can be very simple. Plan on visiting one park on one day? Just pick up a One-Day Base Ticket. Perhaps you are a frequent visitor, and expect to pass through theme park turnstiles dozens of times over the next calendar year. In that case, an Annual Pass is what you're looking for. Now, if your park-going plans lie somewhere in between (and most do), you will have to be a little more strategic.

When it comes to selecting the perfect type of admission ticket, it pays to do some homework. Study all the options, evaluate your priorities, and make no hasty decisions. For starters, there are four major factors to consider: (1) total number of days you'd like to visit theme parks, (2) to park-hop or not to park-hop, (3) whether you want to pre-pay (and

HOT TIP!

At the end of your visit, note the number of unused days on a multi-day ticket. Write it on the ticket itself. (Make sure you purchase the No Expiration add-on within 14 days of first use.)

save some time) for "extras" such as admission to water parks, DisneyQuest, etc., and (4) should you invest in the No Expiration option for your ticket.

The following information was correct at press time and is meant to help you make wise choices. Keep in mind that *Disney ticket prices are likely to change in 2012* (they always do!), so call 407-824-4321 for up-to-the-minute information.

Did You Know?

The phrase "E-ticket ride" is American slang for "the ultimate in thrills." It comes from the early days of Disney parks, back when tickets were used for each attraction. E-tickets were reserved for the most exciting rides of all.

Magic Your Way Tickets

Base Tickets: Available for 1 to 10 days. Valid for admission to one park per day—the Magic Kingdom, Epcot, Disney's Hollywood Studios, or Disney's Animal Kingdom. (The base ticket does not allow for park-hopping.) Unused days expire 14 days after the ticket is activated, which is the first day a park is visited.

(For pricing, see page 24.) The ticket is called a base ticket because, with the exception of Annual Passes, all other tickets begin as such. Guests may customize base tickets to fit their own vacation needs.

Park Hopper Option: This option lets guests visit more than one theme park on a single day. The privilege extends through the length of the ticket. It costs $55 to add to all base tickets (regardless of the number of days).

Water Park Fun & More Option: This option covers entry to Blizzard Beach and/or Typhoon Lagoon water parks, DisneyQuest (arcade), Disney's sports complex, or a round of golf at Disney's Oak Trail golf course. For $55, you'll get between two and ten visits to these spots. The number of visits depends on the number of days on your base ticket—the more days, the more visits.

HOT TIP!

Want to maximize your theme-park-ticket dollar? Buy more days than you plan to use and get the No Expiration option. You can save unused days for a future trip and save a lot on your per-day admission price.

No Expiration Option: Remember when we used to say that your Walt Disney World tickets "don't expire until you do?" Alas, that's no longer the case. Now, multi-day base tickets expire 14 days after the first day they are used. That's the bad news. The good? You can add the No Expiration peace of mind for a fee: $25 for 2-day tickets; $35 for 3-day tickets; $75 for 4 days; $115 for 5 days; $130 for 6 days; $160 for 7 days; $195 for 8 days; $220 for 9 days; and $225 for 10 days.

Extra Magic Hours

How'd you like to visit a Disney theme park before it opens to the public? Or stick around for hours after it's officially closed for the day—at no extra cost? Well, if you're a guest staying at a Walt Disney World-owned-and-operated resort, the Swan, Dolphin, Shades of Green, or the Hilton on Hotel Plaza Boulevard, you can. It is one of the major perks that comes with staying on Disney property.

Here's how it works: One park opens its doors an hour early or stays open three hours late on any given day. Basically, the park becomes something of a members-only private playground for Walt Disney World resort guests. So, provided that you have a WDW resort ID and a park ticket, you're in! No secret password necessary. Keep in mind that you will need park-hopping privileges if you plan to visit a park other than the one offering extra hours on any given day. If you don't plan to park-hop, you must visit the theme park offering Extra Magic Hours on that particular day. The Blizzard Beach water park may offer Extra Magic Hours on select "peak" days.

When a theme park opens early in the morning, guests are admitted starting exactly one hour prior to the official opening time. Transportation to the park starts about 30 minutes before that. Be sure to have your WDW resort ID handy. Flash it and you'll be allowed to visit some (but not all) attractions and mingle with Disney characters.

Ask your resort's lobby concierge for a schedule, or visit *www.disneyworld.com*.

PHOTO BY JILL SAFRO

Theme Park Annual Pass: This pass offers admission to the four theme parks for a year. It can be used in more than one park on the same day (also known as park-hopping), and includes use of Disney transportation, as well as free parking at the theme parks. Annual passes can be purchased at the entrance to any of the theme parks (they can be renewed there or by mail). A photo ID must be presented for purchase by adults and may be required for future use of the pass. Passes are non-transferable. At press time, the cost was $519 for adults, $478 for kids.

Annual pass-bearers qualify for many Walt Disney World discounts and benefits, such as reduced rates at select Disney resorts at certain times of year. A special newsletter called the *Mickey Monitor* keeps passholders up to date regarding discount offers. The pass expires one year after it is first used. A discounted renewal rate applies if the pass is renewed before expiration. (The old pass must be presented in order to receive the discounted renewal rate.) A pass may be renewed by mail or at the entrance to any theme park.

Premium Annual Pass: This pass has everything the Theme Park Annual Pass has to offer and more—namely, admission to the water parks, ESPN Wide World of Sports complex (non-premium events only), and DisneyQuest for a year, plus one round of golf at the Oak Trail golf course. Premium Annual Passholders are eligible for the same discounts and benefits as Theme Park Annual Passholders. Premium Annual Passes can be purchased at the entrance to any of the four theme parks (they can be renewed there or by mail). A photo ID must be presented for purchase by adults and may be required for future use. Premium Annual Passes are non-transferable. These passes expire one year after first use. The cost is $649 for adults, $598 for kids.

HOT TIP!

Do you have old (unused) Walt Disney World theme park tickets squirreled away for a rainy day? Well, feel free to dig 'em out! If the tickets were purchased prior to January 2, 2005, they will be honored for admission at any theme park. (The exception to this rule? Length of Stay passes. These, by definition, expired at the end of your stay.) Note that unused one-day park tickets never expire, regardless of when they were purchased.

Premier Annual Pass: This pass provides admission to all Disney theme parks and water parks on both U.S. coasts (including Disneyland Park and Disney California Adventure) for one year. It also includes admission to WDW's DisneyQuest, ESPN Wide World of Sports complex (non-premium events only), and the Oak Trail golf course. Unlimited park-hopping and parking are included, as are the same discounts offered with Disney's other annual passes (select merchandise, food, and resort discounts). The Premier Pass costs about $749, plus tax. Guests already bearing Walt Disney World or Disneyland Resort Annual Passes may upgrade to the Premier Pass at any time. For details, visit *www.disneyparks.com/Premier*, or call 407-824-4321.

Deciding Factors

Choosing the Right Ticket: Before you make your decision, it helps to map out your vacation. Remember, all tickets start as Base Tickets. They are a bare-bones, admission-to-one-theme-park-at-a-time deal. That's ideal

Ticket Tag System

As a means of enforcing the non-transferability aspect of all Walt Disney World tickets, Disney has devised a system to trace each ticket to its rightful owner. The procedure is as follows: Take your ticket (after signing the back of it) and slip it into the machine beside the turnstile at any park entrance. While the machine is crunching the data encrypted on the ticket's magnetic strip, gently press the tip of your forefinger onto the glowing gizmo perched above the ticket-grabbing device. Remove your finger and presto! Your ticket should pop out the other side, giving you the green light to enter. Grown-ups have to do this every time they use the ticket. Kids are spared the hassle. Though simple, the system tends to cause bottlenecks at the turnstiles. Be sure to allow extra time to get into the park.

for some folks—especially those planning a relatively short stay. Still, the first step for every potential guest is to decide just how many days they plan to spend in the theme parks. Keep in mind that as days are added, the average price per day drops a little. After four days, the daily rate drops significantly. Any unused days expire 14 days after the ticket is activated, unless the No Expiration option is purchased. Once the length of stay is determined, it's time to customize the ticket. Do you want to park-hop? Add $55. Want to add the Water Park Fun and More package? For an extra $55, you can do so. Finally, if you're

HOT TIP!
To expedite your party's "ticket tag" finger scan experience, make sure each adult is holding his or her own ticket before getting in line at the turnstiles.

not certain that you'll use all the days on your pass, you can add on the No Expiration option. That starts at $25. It may seem like a lot to think about, but it makes for a very organized Walt Disney World vacation. And it can save you a chunk of change, too.

If you are planning a longer visit, or two trips in a year, we recommend a 10-day Park Hopper with No Expiration or an Annual Pass. In addition to unlimited admission to the parks, an Annual Pass entitles bearers to discounts on

HOT TIP!
If your child "outgrows" his or her park ticket (by turning 10), you can upgrade the ticket at any of the theme parks.

everything from dinner shows to room rates.

Note: Only one person per party need possess an Annual Pass to net a discount on a resort rate. This option is great for travelers with flexible vacation schedules, as the discounts do vary and are often announced just weeks before they go into effect.

Tickets with Unused Days: Prior to 2005, WDW tickets never expired. That is no longer the case. Remaining days on any multi-day admission ticket now expire 14 days after the ticket is first activated *unless* the No Expiration option is purchased.

Attractions Outside the Theme Parks: For Typhoon Lagoon or Blizzard Beach, prices are about $49 for one day and about $100 for an annual pass for adults; $41 for one day and about $81 for an annual pass for kids (ages 3–9). At DisneyQuest, adults pay $43 per day or $89 for an annual pass, while the price for kids is $37 per day or $71 for an annual pass. There is also a DisneyQuest/Water Parks annual pass. Cost is about $129 for adults, $99 for kids. The ESPN Wide World of Sports complex runs about $14 for adults, about $10 for kids. Cirque du Soleil's La Nouba is $71–$124 for adults, $57–$99 for kids. Prices are likely to change in 2012.

How Do You Book a Room? Let Us Count the Ways.

You're ready to reserve a room at a resort on Walt Disney World property. How nice for you! But, before you dial 407-W-DISNEY (934-7639) or a travel agent, know this: There are three different ways to book your WDW stay. It's best to know what you want in advance. It will save you time and spare confusion while on the phone. Here's the scoop:

• **Room Only Reservation**—What you hear is what you get: a hotel room only. It requires an advance deposit and allows you to cancel up to 5 days prior to the start of the reservation (penalty-free). It comes with a 12-digit confirmation number.

• **Walt Disney World Travel Company Basic Plan**—A package that includes room, luggage tags, a round of mini-golf for the entire party, and trip insurance. Must be paid in full up front and must be canceled at least 45 days prior to check-in to avoid a penalty. (The confirmation number has 8 digits.)

• **Magic Your Way Base Package**—Includes room and theme park tickets. It may be customized in many ways, such as adding the Disney Dining Plan, Water Park admission, and more (see page 18). Must be paid in full upon reserving and may be canceled up to 45 days ahead (any later and there will be hefty penalties). Once reserved, expect to get an 8-digit confirmation number.

Ticket Prices

Base Ticket*		10-Day	9-Day	8-Day	7-Day	6-Day	5-Day	4-Day	3-Day	2-Day	1-Day
	Ages 10 & up	$291 ($29.10/ day)	$283 ($31.45/ day)	$275 ($34.38/ day)	$267 ($38.14/ day)	$259 ($43.17/ day)	$251 ($50.20/ day)	$243 ($60.75/ day)	$232 ($77.34/ day)	$168 ($84.00/ day)	$85
	Ages 3–9	$272 ($27.20/ day)	$264 ($29.34/ day)	$256 ($32.00/ day)	$248 ($35.43/ day)	$240 ($40.00/ day)	$232 ($46.40/ day)	$224 ($56.00/ day)	$214 ($71.34/ day)	$155 ($77.50/ day)	$79
ADD: Park Hopper**		$55	$55	$55	$55	$55	$55	$55	$55	$55	$55
ADD: Water Park Fun & More***		$55 10 visits	$55 9 visits	$55 8 visits	$55 7 visits	$55 6 visits	$55 5 visits	$55 4 visits	$55 3 visits	$55 2 visits	$55 2 visits
ADD: No Expiration****		$225	$220	$195	$160	$130	$115	$75	$35	$25	Not available

*Base Ticket admits guest to one theme park each day of use. Park choices are: Magic Kingdom, Epcot, Disney's Hollywood Studios, and Disney's Animal Kingdom.

**Park Hopper option entitles guest to visit more than one theme park on each day of use. Park choices are any combination of theme parks on each day of use.

***Water Park Fun & More option entitles guest to a specified number of visits to a choice of entertainment and recreation venues. Choices include Disney's Blizzard Beach water park, Disney's Typhoon Lagoon water park, DisneyQuest, and ESPN Wide World of Sports complex.

****No Expiration means unused admissions on a ticket have no expiration date. All multi-day tickets expire 14 days after first use unless No Expiration is purchased.

Save Time in Line!

For those of us who'd prefer not to waste time standing in line for theme park attractions, Disney's Fastpass is nothing short of a miracle. Basically, the system allows guests to forgo the task of waiting in an actual line for a number of theme park attractions. How? Simply by walking up to the Fastpass booth (located near the entrance of participating attractions) and slipping their park ticket into the Fastpass machine. In return, guests get a slip of paper with a time period printed on it (in addition to the safe return of their park ticket). That time—for example, 4:05 P.M. to 5:05 P.M.—represents the window in which guests are invited to return to the attraction and practically walk right in—without standing in a long line.

Once you use your Fastpass to enter an attraction (or the time on it has passed), you can get a new Fastpass time for another attraction. It may be possible to get another Fastpass within 45 minutes or sooner (depending on availability). To find out, read the fine print on your current Fastpass ticket. For example, if one pass was issued at 2 P.M., you can get a Fastpass for another attraction at 4 P.M. (possibly sooner). Sound confusing? It won't be once you've tried it.

Disney's almost-too-good-to-be-true Fastpass service is free and available to everyone bearing a valid theme park ticket. It should be available during peak times of the day and all peak seasons. Fastpass assignments are limited and tend to go quickly on busy days. Always start the day with your "must-see" attraction. We've placed the Fastpass logo (**FP**) beside the listing for all of the attractions that were participating at press time. However, since attractions may be added or dropped, check a park map for a complete listing of Fastpass attractions.

Note that all Disney attractions offer the option of standing in a traditional line. If you enjoy the standing-in-line experience, go for it. Otherwise, Fastpass is the way to go!

Purchasing Tickets

Admission tickets are sold at park entrances, WDW resorts, the resorts on Hotel Plaza Boulevard, Orlando International Airport, the Transportation and Ticket Center (TTC), and Downtown Disney Guest Relations. Cash, traveler's checks, personal checks (with ID), American Express, Visa, MasterCard, Diner's Club, Discover, JCB Card, Disney Visa, Disney Dollars, and Disney gift cards are accepted. Not all tickets are available at each location, so call 407-934-7639 to confirm.

We recommend buying tickets in advance from a travel agent, or in one of these ways:

Tickets by Phone: All tickets can be purchased by phone; call 407-W-DISNEY (934-7639). There is a $5 handling fee for standard home delivery (allow 15 days); $15 for express delivery (allow 7 days); and $25 for international delivery (allow 12 days). There is no fee for pick-up at a WDW Will Call window.

Tickets Online: Tickets can be bought through *www.disneyworld.com*. The fees for delivery are the same as those listed above.

Tickets at the Disney Store: Select multi-day theme park tickets are available for purchase at any local Disney Store.

Tickets by Mail (3- to 7-day Magic Your Way tickets only): Allow at least three to four weeks for processing and include a return address. Send a money order (for the exact amount, plus $4 for handling), payable to Walt Disney World Company, to: Walt Disney World, Box 10140, Lake Buena Vista, FL 32830-0030. Attention: Ticket Mail Order.

HOT TIP!

Prior to your visit, call 407-939-7639 or visit *www.disneyworld.com* for current ticket information. You will be able to save a bit of time buying tickets before you arrive at a Walt Disney World park.

Money-Saving Tips

A Walt Disney World vacation can be an exceptionally expensive undertaking, but it is possible to keep costs down a bit. When budgeting for your trip, keep in mind that WDW prices are comparable to those in a large city. Here are a few tips to help you conserve cash.

Lodging

- When it comes to saving money on accommodations, timing is truly the key. While off-season dates tend to vary, depending on the hotel, value season for most Walt Disney World resorts generally means January through mid-February, late August through late September, and early November through late December.

- The Swan and Dolphin resorts often have rate specials when other WDW resorts have peak rates. Check *www.swandolphin.com*.

- Consider how much time you will actually spend at your hotel, and don't pay for a place with perks you won't have time to enjoy. Hotels often allow kids to stay free in parents' rooms, but the cutoff age varies.

- When considering the cost-effectiveness of off-property lodging, factor in the time, money, and inconvenience of commuting to and from attractions.

- Realize, too, that the advantages of staying on-property (tops among them the Extra Magic Hours perk, Disney's Magical Express, and access to Walt Disney World's transportation system) also apply to those staying in the least expensive rooms in Disney's hotels. The most important addresses for budget-watching Disney fans, the All-Star and Pop Century resorts, offer the lowest rates on Disney property. Rooms at Caribbean Beach, Port Orleans French Quarter and Riverside, Disney's

Art of Animation, and Coronado Springs are slightly higher priced. Also, note that the only difference between the least and most expensive rooms in a hotel is often the view. Consider how often you'll be looking out that window.

Food

- Visit costlier establishments at lunchtime (if you so desire) rather than at dinner; entrées often cost a bit less at the midday meal.

- While Club Level accommodations can absorb the cost of some meals and snacks, the best way to stretch your dining dollar is to get the Disney Dining Plan.

- Carry snacks and sandwich fixings and enjoy them picnic-style wherever possible.

- Look for lodging with kitchen facilities: The savings on food may be more than the extra accommodations expense.

- Small refrigerators are available for free at Walt Disney World deluxe and moderate resorts and for about $10 a day at Disney's value resorts.

- A souvenir mug can be purchased at most resorts, good for refills during your stay at the resort. (Similar mugs are sold in the parks, but don't come with free refills.)

- The Trail's End Restaurant at Fort Wilderness has inexpensive yet satisfying, all-you-can-eat breakfast and dinner buffets.

- Pack kid-friendly snacks, such as fruit, cereal, or even a lollipop. (Snack stands are plentiful, but not always handy or cost-efficient.)

- Don't plan on eating three big table-service meals a day. It gets expensive—and filling!

- The Magic Your Way vacation package with the basic Dining Plan can control meal costs. It provides two meals and a snack per day. The fixed price (starting at about $44 a day for guests ages 10 and up and $11 for kids between 3 and 9) includes tax, but not gratuity. It is customary to tip for good service.

Satisfying Substitutes

Fewer frills rarely mean less fun at Walt Disney World. Here are money-saving alternatives to two of Disney's higher-priced treats.

If you'd rather not spring for admission to Downtown Disney West Side venues, consider taking a trip to the BoardWalk resort. Among other diversions, you'll find Jellyrolls (a sing-along piano bar with a cover of about $10), Atlantic Dance (a nightclub with no cover charge), and ESPN Club (a cover-free sports bar). A short walk will take you to the Swan hotel, home to the karaoke-friendly Kimonos Lounge.

If the Grand Floridian ($460–$1,630 a night) doesn't quite fit into your budget, consider staying in a Mansion room at Port Orleans Riverside ($159–$240 a night). Southern hospitality replaces Victorian splendor, and, though the guestrooms aren't quite as spacious, the air of sophistication makes for a most satisfying stay. And for a sweet deal on a suite, consider the colorful new resort called Disney's Art of Animation (it will open in late 2012).

Discounts

- Theme Park Annual and Premium Annual Passholders receive so many discounts on meals, dinner shows, tours, room rates, and more that it may be worth purchasing an Annual Pass for longer visits or if you plan to take more than one trip within a year.

- WDW resorts that offer Annual Passholder discounts vary from month to month, and discounted rooms aren't always available for booking very far in advance. It's best to be flexible with travel dates. For additional information, call 407-560-7277 or 407-W-DISNEY. Passholders can save 20 percent at many WDW eateries by joining the Tables in Wonderland program. For info, call 407-WDW-DINE (939-3463).

- Discounts on Disney World resort rates and theme park tickets are available to Florida residents, and seasonal promotions occur. Call 407-W-DISNEY (939-7639) for specifics.

- The Swan, as well as some off-property hotels, offer discounts to seniors and AAA or AARP members as well. Some AAA branches offer discounts on some park passes, as well as discounts on rooms and select packages with the AAA Disney Magic

Moments Savings Program. Contact your local branch for more information.

- Web-based *travelocity.com* offers a variety of Disney vacation packages. Vacation Outlet sometimes offers packages at a reduced rate. Visit *www.vacationoutlet.com*, or call 800-825-3633 for details.

HOT TIP!
Bring inexpensive, light rain gear from home. You'll need it—especially in summer.

- For a free Orlando Magicard, visit *www.orlandoinfo.com/magicard*, or call 800-643-9492. Cardholders net discounts at Orlando-area hotels, restaurants, shops, and more.

- Disney Rewards Visa holders earn reward dollars when they use the card. These dollars can be redeemed at Disney World, the Disney Cruise Line, and Disneyland. If you're not a Disney Visa cardholder and would like to become one, flip to the back page of this book. Our coupon can help you get a special Birnbaum bonus.

- Okay, so it's not exactly a discount, but we think the 10-day Magic Your Way ticket with the No Expiration add-on is a great value. It brings down the daily cost of visiting a theme park. Plus, the tickets "don't expire until you do," so unused days can be saved for another trip.

- Go to *disneyworld.disney.go.com/special-offers/* to find out if any discounts apply for your WDW visit.

HOT TIP!
It may be cheaper to spread out over two rooms in a "value" or "moderate" resort than to have everyone stay in one room at "deluxe" Disney digs.

GETTING READY TO GO

Making a Budget

A stay at Disney's kingdom need not cost a king's ransom (though it easily can). In fact, with a well-planned budget, money at Disney World can stretch relatively far.

Vacation expenses tend to fall into five major categories: (1) transportation (which may include any combination of costs for airfare, airport transfers, train tickets, car rental, gas, parking, and taxi service); (2) lodging; (3) theme park tickets; (4) meals; and (5) miscellaneous (recreational activities, souvenirs, postcards, film, toiletries, and home expenses such as pet boarding, etc.).

When planning your budget, first consider what level of service suits your needs. Some people prefer to spend fewer days at Disney but stay at a deluxe hotel or dine at pricier restaurants, while others would rather make their money cover a longer vacation that includes a value-priced resort and less expensive meals. The choice is up to you. Once you've established your spending priorities, determine your price limit. Then make sure you don't exceed it when approximating your expenses—without a ballpark figure to work around, it's easy to get carried away.

Sample Budget

The following is an example of a low- to moderately-priced budget designed for a family of four (two adults and two kids planning to stay at WDW for five nights and six days). Totals do not include tax.

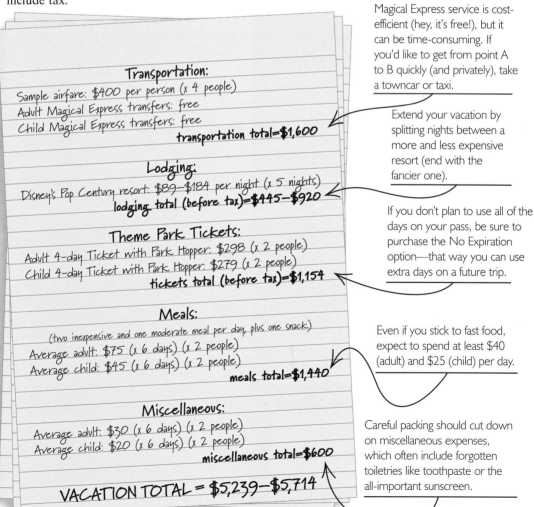

Transportation:
Sample airfare: $400 per person (x 4 people)
Adult Magical Express transfers: free
Child Magical Express transfers: free
transportation total=$1,600

Lodging:
Disney's Pop Century resort: $89–$184 per night (x 5 nights)
lodging total (before tax)=$445–$920

Theme Park Tickets:
Adult 4-day Ticket with Park Hopper: $298 (x 2 people)
Child 4-day Ticket with Park Hopper: $279 (x 2 people)
tickets total (before tax)=$1,154

Meals:
(two inexpensive and one moderate meal per day, plus one snack)
Average adult: $75 (x 6 days) (x 2 people)
Average child: $45 (x 6 days) (x 2 people)
meals total=$1,440

Miscellaneous:
Average adult: $30 (x 6 days) (x 2 people)
Average child: $20 (x 6 days) (x 2 people)
miscellaneous total=$600

VACATION TOTAL = $5,239–$5,714

Magical Express service is cost-efficient (hey, it's free!), but it can be time-consuming. If you'd like to get from point A to B quickly (and privately), take a towncar or taxi.

Extend your vacation by splitting nights between a more and less expensive resort (end with the fancier one).

If you don't plan to use all of the days on your pass, be sure to purchase the No Expiration option—that way you can use extra days on a future trip.

Even if you stick to fast food, expect to spend at least $40 (adult) and $25 (child) per day.

Careful packing should cut down on miscellaneous expenses, which often include forgotten toiletries like toothpaste or the all-important sunscreen.

Planning Your Itinerary

A Timeline

First Things First

- Make hotel and transportation arrangements as far ahead as possible. Note that many Disney hotels fill up more than six months in advance. Call 407-W-DISNEY (934-7639) to book a room at a Disney hotel; your confirmation should arrive within two weeks. Log it and other pertinent information in your Birnbaum Trip Planner at the end of this book.

- Check park hours for your planned visit. (Hours are available up to 7 months ahead; Call 407-824-4321, or visit *www.disneyworld.com*.) Closing times will be particularly helpful when making evening plans. Create a day-by-day schedule, deciding which area of WDW to visit on each day of your trip.

6 Months

- Choose dining spots from those listed in the *Good Meals, Great Times* chapter. Call 407-WDW-DINE (939-3463) to make restaurant reservations. *Guests with a confirmed reservation at a WDW-owned-and-operated resort may call 180 days before scheduled check-in date and book dining reservations for up to 10 days of their planned stay. Have your hotel confirmation number handy when you make the call.*

- Character meals such as those at Cinderella's Royal Table must be booked 180 days ahead. Call 407-WDW-DINE and have a credit card handy.

- Dinner-show reservations may be secured up to 180 days in advance. Consult page 270 for details, and call 407-WDW-DINE for reservations.

- Unless you purchased a package that includes theme park admission, it's time to order tickets. Refer to pages 20–25 for details, and call 407-824-4321; tickets should arrive within four weeks. Keep in mind that you will save money by purchasing select tickets in advance.

- Specialty cruises (see page 217) may be booked by calling 407-WDW-PLAY (939-7529).

- If you have purchased a Magic Your Way Premium or Platinum package and plan to play golf, or will be staying at a WDW resort or a resort on Hotel Plaza Boulevard, you may book a tee time on one of WDW's golf courses now (see pages 222–223 for details on the courses). Golf lessons may also be reserved at this time. Call 407-WDW-GOLF (939-4653) for reservations. Those not staying on WDW property may make reservations 60 days ahead.

- Fishing excursions (see pages 226–227) may be booked by calling 407-WDW-BASS (939–2277).

- Tennis lessons may be reserved by calling 407-621-1991. Turn to page 224 for information.

- Parasailing and waterskiing excursions (for details, see pages 225–226) may be booked by calling 407-939-0754 or visiting *www.sammyduvall.com*.

- Trail-ride reservations may be made up to 180 days in advance. Call 407-WDW-PLAY.

- If you'd like to add a behind-the-scenes tour to your vacation, now is the time to make a reservation. See pages 218–220 for details, and call 407-WDW-TOUR (939-8687).

3 Months

- Double-check park hours for your stay, as they may have changed.
- Some attractions may be closed for refurbishment during your visit. An updated refurbishment schedule is released each season. Call 407-824-4321.

10 Days

- Airline confirmation and travel-package vouchers should have arrived by now. Contact your travel agent or the travel company if they have not.

- Will you be staying at a WDW-owned-and-operated resort? If so, check in online! (See page 53.)

1 Week

- Reconfirm all reservations. Finalize your day-by-day schedule, including all confirmation numbers. Make one copy for your suitcase and one to carry with you in the parks.

STEP-BY-STEP

SAMPLE SCHEDULES

Many visitors have a deep desire to cover each and every inch of Walt Disney World in the span of a few short days. While we hesitate to discourage these most ambitious of travelers, we feel the need to enlighten them: Walt Disney World is a staggeringly large place. In fact, it's nearly as big as San Francisco and jam-packed with about as many diversions as you'd expect from a city that size. You could spend two full weeks on Disney property and still not have time to do it all. The theme parks alone require every bit of four days just to see the major attractions.

What's the best strategy for organizing a Walt Disney World visit? Make a list of the parks, attractions, and activities you *most* want to see and use it to create an itinerary. Don't forget to allow time for swimming, boating, or relaxing in a hammock. This is, after all, a vacation.

Assuming you've narrowed your "must-do" list to the barely manageable, we recommend a stay of at least four to five days. This allows for a visit to each of the theme parks and some time to enjoy many of the recreational activities at your resort. Longer stays can include water parks, Downtown Disney, a dinner show, and more. When planning your days (which you should do before leaving home), be sure to take into account theme park hours and seasonal temperatures in Central Florida.

The following sample schedules assume that you eat breakfast at your resort (unless otherwise stated) and arrive up to 20 minutes before the official opening time. These schedules, though tirelessly tested and proven successful by Birnbaum's editors, are not carved in stone. Use them as a guide, tailoring the itineraries to suit your family's individual tastes. And use them in conjunction with complimentary theme park Times Guides (available at park entrances).

Note that we have not included specific instructions with regard to Fastpass in our sample itineraries. It's not because we don't love the service. In fact, we highly recommend using Fastpass, even if working it into a daily schedule is an inexact science. When it is offered, it makes it much easier to breeze through the turnstiles and tackle the theme parks in a highly organized (and time-saving) manner. By all means, take advantage of the Fastpass opportunity every chance you get—especially first thing in the morning for the über-popular attractions. Not only will it make you feel like a VIP, but it will free up time in your schedule for things you otherwise might not have gotten to.

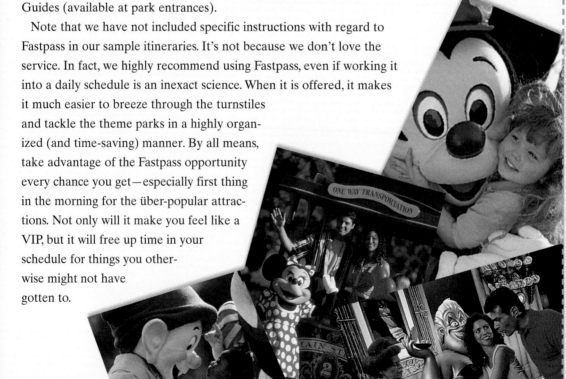

Magic Kingdom
ONE–DAY SCHEDULE

❤ Begin the day with a brisk stroll down Main Street, U.S.A. Cut through Adventureland on your way to Splash Mountain and Big Thunder Mountain Railroad. Backtrack to Pirates of the Caribbean, Jungle Cruise, The Magic Carpets of Aladdin, or The Enchanted Tiki Room.

❤ Access Frontierland via the path near the Enchanted Tiki Room. Consider lunching at Pecos Bill Cafe or Columbia Harbour House. Be sure to check out the Hall of Presidents while in Liberty Square.

❤ If time allows, squeeze in The Haunted Mansion before the afternoon parade. Watch the parade and move on to Fantasyland.

❤ See as much of Fantasyland as possible, including Mickey's PhilharMagic, It's a Small World, Peter Pan's Flight, and The Many Adventures of Winnie the Pooh.

❤ If the timing's right, head to the front of the Castle for a live stage show.

❤ Haven't seen Haunted Mansion or the Country Bear Jamboree? Go for it!

❤ If the Main Street Electrical Parade is scheduled to run twice, explore Tomorrowland during the earlier showing. See Space Mountain, Buzz Lightyear's Space Ranger Spin, Stitch's Great Escape, and the race cars at the Tomorrowland Speedway.

❤ View Wishes, a truly impressive fireworks display, from the middle of Main Street.

❤ Watch the Main Street Electrical Parade from Frontierland.

❤ If there's time, revisit a favorite attraction (guests are usually admitted right up until closing time).

Continued on page 32

LINE BUSTERS

Even when the park is packed, there are some attractions with shorter or faster moving lines. Among them are: Tomorrowland Transit Authority PeopleMover, Walt Disney World Railroad, The Enchanted Tiki Room, Carousel of Progress, Country Bear Jamboree, It's a Small World, and Tom Sawyer Island.

Magic Kingdom

ONE–DAY SCHEDULE

IF YOU HAVE YOUNG CHILDREN

- Head directly to Fantasyland (walk right through the Castle) and ride Dumbo, Peter Pan, Mickey's PhilharMagic, and The Many Adventures of Winnie the Pooh.

- Stop for a spin in a teacup on the way to Frontierland. Sing along with Big Al and the gang at the Country Bear Jamboree.

- Check the schedule for the Castle stage show before riding the carousel and It's a Small World.

- Line up for the afternoon parade about 30 minutes early. Or skip the parade, finish up Fantasyland, and take a magic carpet ride in Adventureland. If it's hot (and your tot has waterproof diapers), head to the tiki statues near Jungle Cruise. They spit water!

- Most little ones enjoy the Walt Disney World Railroad, too.

FASTPASS ATTRACTIONS

Space Mountain

Splash Mountain

Big Thunder Mountain Railroad

Buzz Lightyear's Space Ranger Spin

Jungle Cruise

The Many Adventures of Winnie the Pooh

Peter Pan's Flight

Town Square Theater

MAGIC KINGDOM MUSTS

Here's a list of the attractions that put the *magic* in the Magic Kingdom:

Splash Mountain • **Big Thunder Mountain Railroad**
The Haunted Mansion • Pirates of the Caribbean
Peter Pan's Flight • **It's a Small World** • Space Mountain
Buzz Lightyear's Space Ranger Spin
The Many Adventures of Winnie the Pooh • **Mickey's PhilharMagic**
The Main Street Electrical Parade • Wishes (fireworks show)

GETTING READY TO GO

Epcot

ONE–DAY SCHEDULE

- ❤ Start the day by making a beeline for Future World's Soarin' and Test Track. (If the Test Track line is long, consider jumping on the "single riders" line. It moves a bit faster.) If you have no health issues and no susceptibility to motion sickness whatsoever, experience the out-of-this-world adventure known as "highly intense" Mission: SPACE. (Otherwise, ride "Mission: SPACE-lite"—the less intense, non-spinning version.) Follow it up with The Seas with Nemo & Friends. Keep in mind that World Showcase doesn't open until 11 A.M.

- ❤ Stop for lunch at The Land's Sunshine Seasons, The Electric Umbrella, or Coral Reef in The Seas pavilion.

- ❤ After exploring The Land, consider a viewing of *Captain EO* in the Imagination pavilion. Save time to enjoy ImageWorks, a small, high-tech playground. Little kids love it.

- ❤ If you're in the mood for some serious pin trading (or shopping), stop by Pin Central in Innoventions Plaza. (Workers who are wearing pins are always willing to swap Disney pins.)

- ❤ Check out Spaceship Earth before heading to Innoventions. If the Universe of Energy is open for business, pay it a visit.

- ❤ Make your way to World Showcase by early evening and start your circular tour of the world at Canada. Proceed counter-clockwise around the lagoon. Don't miss the *Impressions de France* movie in the France pavilion, the American Adventure show, and Maelstrom in Norway. Take in as much live entertainment as you can—World Showcase has a lot to offer!

- ❤ After dinner, scope out a spot to watch IllumiNations—Reflections of Earth. (We enjoy the areas near Italy and Japan, but there are excellent viewing locations all around World Showcase Lagoon.)

TIMING TIP: If you have reservations for dinner at World Showcase, give yourself 30 to 40 minutes to get there from the front gate. Taking a *FriendShip* water taxi can shave a few minutes off your trip (although it isn't much faster than brisk walking).

Continued on page 34

LINE BUSTERS

Tired of long lines? Go to: The Circle of Life movie in The Land, Universe of Energy, Impressions de France in the France pavilion, or The American Adventure. The Spaceship Earth line thins out in the afternoon, as does the line for the attractions inside The Seas with Nemo & Friends.

Continued from page 33

Epcot

ONE-DAY SCHEDULE

IF YOU HAVE YOUNG CHILDREN

- Begin the day by thoroughly exploring The Seas with Nemo & Friends. Then head over to Imagination! to experience Journey Into Imagination with Figment and the ImageWorks interactive playground.

- At World Showcase, head to Mexico's boat ride and, for braver tots, Norway's Maelstrom.

- Visit the Kidcot Fun Stop in each country. Don't miss the koi pond in Japan, and Germany's tiny village.

- If the weather is warm, let little ones splash in the interactive fountain on the pathway joining Future World with World Showcase or the spray zone in front of Test Track.

FASTPASS ATTRACTIONS

Mission: SPACE

Test Track

Captain EO

Living with the Land

Maelstrom (in Norway)

Soarin'

EPCOT ESSENTIALS

There is a lot to see and do at Disney's discovery park. Don't leave without investigating these outstanding attractions:

Universe of Energy • **Captain EO**
Test Track • Living with the Land • **Soarin'**
IllumiNations—Reflections of Earth • **Turtle Talk with Crush**
The Seas with Nemo & Friends • The American Adventure show
Mission: SPACE ("non-spinning" version)

Disney's
Hollowood Studios

ONE-DAY SCHEDULE

- ♥ Some attractions open later in the morning; consult a park Times Guide for exact times. Also, many shows here run on a schedule (e.g., the American Idol™ Experience and Beauty and The Beast—Live on Stage); check for times throughout the day. Note that this park is not the easiest to navigate. Keep your park map handy at all times.

- ♥ Toy Story Mania is wildly popular. Get there early for a Fastpass.

- ♥ Daredevils should begin the day with Rock 'n' Roller Coaster, followed by some eye-opening drops at The Twilight Zone™ Tower of Terror.

- ♥ If Beauty and the Beast is playing soon, grab a seat. Otherwise, plan to come back later and go to The Magic of Disney Animation, Voyage of The Little Mermaid, and the American Idol Experience.

- ♥ Pause for lunch at the 50's Prime Time Cafe, Sci-Fi Dine-In Theater, or Starring Rolls Cafe.

- ♥ Line up 20 to 30 minutes early to watch the popular Pixar Pals Countdown to Fun parade. (Note that if you skip the parade, it is an excellent time to visit Voyage of The Little Mermaid, or The Great Movie Ride.)

- ♥ Be sure to see Muppet*Vision 3-D, followed by the Studio Backlot Tour, Star Tours—The Adventures Continue, Lights, Motors, Action—Extreme Stunt Show, and the Indiana Jones Epic Stunt Spectacular.

- ♥ Take tots to the Honey, I Shrunk the Kids Movie Set Adventure and Disney Junior—Live on Stage.

- ♥ If you missed Beauty and the Beast—Live on Stage, go now and, if you haven't hit it yet, be sure to experience The Great Movie Ride.

- ♥ If Fantasmic is being presented today, you want to get a spot in line at least 50 minutes before showtime. Note that if you choose to skip Fantasmic, plan to exit the park before the last performance breaks. If you do stay for the show, know that you can meander through select shops while the throngs file through the turnstiles at the exit.

Continued on page 36

LINE BUSTERS

When lines abound at Disney's Hollywood Studios, we suggest the following: The Magic of Animation, Indiana Jones Epic Stunt Spectacular (the theater accommodates 2,000 guests at a time), Honey, I Shrunk the Kids Movie Set Adventure, Studio Backlot Tour, American Idol Experience (this theater also has enormous seating capacity), American Film Institute Showcase, Walt Disney: One Man's Dream, and Sounds Dangerous Starring Drew Carey.

GETTING READY TO GO

Continued from page 35

Disney's Hollywood Studios

ONE-DAY SCHEDULE

IF YOU HAVE YOUNG CHILDREN

- Begin with Toy Story Mania, followed by the Voyage of The Little Mermaid attraction (but warn kids about moments of darkness and a thunderstorm), and Muppet*Vision 3-D.

- Have lunch at Pizza Planet, then watch the parade. Romp in the Honey, I Shrunk the Kids Movie Set Adventure, catch Disney Junior—Live on Stage, and see Beauty and the Beast—Live on Stage. Skip Fantasmic—it tends to terrify tots.

- Catch up with Disney characters at Animation Courtyard and on Pixar Place.

FASTPASS ATTRACTIONS

Rock 'n' Roller Coaster
  Starring Aerosmith

Toy Story Mania!

Star Tours—The Adventures Continue

The Twilight Zone Tower of Terror

Voyage of the Little Mermaid

STUDIOS STANDOUTS

If you're short on time, be sure to catch as many of the following four-star attractions at Disney's Hollywood Studios as possible:

The Twilight Zone Tower of Terror • **Rock 'n' Roller Coaster**

Beauty and the Beast—Live on Stage

The Great Movie Ride • Toy Story Mania!

Muppet*Vision 3-D • **Star Tours—The Adventures Continue**

Fantasmic! • American Idol Experience

GETTING READY TO GO

Disney's
Animal Kingdom
ONE-DAY SCHEDULE

❤ Guests who arrive at park opening may enjoy a good-morning greeting from Disney characters. Many shows here run on a schedule, so check for times throughout the day. Make a point of seeing Festival of the Lion King and Finding Nemo—The Musical. They appeal to all ages. If you want to experience Expedition Everest (and you should), now's the time to get the Fastpass.

❤ As you enter the park, pass through the Oasis and head toward DinoLand U.S.A. After riding Dinosaur, catch Finding Nemo—The Musical (arrive early). Take young children to the Boneyard before leaving the area.

❤ In Asia, tackle Expedition Everest, ride Kali River Rapids, then visit the tigers at the Maharajah Jungle Trek, and see the delightful Flights of Wonder show at the Caravan Stage.

❤ Check a park Times Guide for the Festival of the Lion King schedule. Plan to arrive in Camp Minnie-Mickey at least 45 minutes before it starts (it's a wildly popular show). If possible, mingle with Disney characters before seeing Festival of the Lion King.

❤ Stop at Yak & Yeti or Tusker House for lunch. Then jump aboard the Wildlife Express train to Rafiki's Planet Watch. Don't miss the Song of the Rainforest and the Affection Section petting farm.

❤ After experiencing Africa's Kilimanjaro Safaris, take a relaxing hike on the animal-laden Pangani Forest Exploration Trail.

❤ Wander the Discovery Island Trails around the Tree of Life, taking time to search for animals carved into the tree and its roots.

❤ Finish off the day with a screening of It's Tough to be a Bug and revisiting your favorite attractions.

Continued on page 38

LINE BUSTERS

When herds of guests mob Disney's Animal Kingdom attractions, there are a few places to escape the stampede: The Oasis, Pangani Forest Exploration Trail, Maharajah Jungle Trek, Discovery Island Trails, The Boneyard playground, and Rafiki's Planet Watch. (You'll need to take the Wildlife Express train to Rafiki's Planet Watch.)

GETTING READY TO GO

Continued from page 37

Disney's Animal Kingdom

ONE-DAY SCHEDULE

IF YOU HAVE YOUNG CHILDREN

- We recommend lingering a bit in the Oasis on your way into the park. Then make a left and head straight to Camp Minnie-Mickey. Visit with some Disney characters, and watch Festival of the Lion King. (Warn sensitive youngsters that the music may be a bit loud.)

- Stop by the Tree of Life to notice all of the animal carvings in its trunk. (Note that the show inside the tree, It's Tough to be a Bug, is very intense and may frighten young children.)

- Eat lunch at Pizzafari or head to DinoLand's Restaurantosaurus. Be sure to see The Boneyard playground, Finding Nemo—The Musical, and Chester and Hester's Dino-Rama.

- In Asia, go to the Maharajah Jungle Trek. Consider riding Africa's bumpy Kilimanjaro Safaris. See the Pangani Forest Exploration Trail. Then take the train to Rafiki's Planet Watch.

FASTPASS ATTRACTIONS

Primeval Whirl

Kilimanjaro Safaris

Dinosaur

Kali River Rapids

Expedition Everest

ANIMAL KINGDOM ACES

An abbreviated visit to Disney's Animal Kingdom is enough to make anybody growl. The following attractions should help soothe the savage beast, er, guest:

Dinosaur • Kali River Rapids • **Kilimanjaro Safaris**
Pangani Forest Exploration Trail • **Expedition Everest**
Finding Nemo—The Musical • Maharajah Jungle Trek
Flights of Wonder • **Festival of the Lion King**
It's Tough to be a Bug!

Magic Kingdom*

HALF–DAY SCHEDULES

Morning at the Magic Kingdom

- Where to begin? It's a big decision. Know that the area you postpone may have long lines by the time you get there. We like to start by heading to Adventureland.

- Visit Pirates of the Caribbean, then head to Splash Mountain and Big Thunder Mountain Railroad.

- Visit The Haunted Mansion and then grab a spot for the afternoon parade.

- Watch the parade in Frontierland. Or skip the parade and go to Peter Pan's Flight, Winnie the Pooh, It's a Small World, and Mickey's PhilharMagic.

- Head to Tomorrowland to experience Space Mountain. Follow it up with Buzz Lightyear's Space Ranger Spin. Take youngsters for a trip on the Tomorrowland Speedway (but warn them that there will be moments of total darkness).

The Magic Kingdom After Lunch

- Check a Times Guide and choose a time to take in the Castle stage show.

- Explore Town Square Exposition Hall. If the wait to meet Mickey Mouse is more than 45 minutes, consider coming back in the late evening.

- Start in Adventureland. Ride the Jungle Cruise and Pirates of the Caribbean.

- Head to Frontierland. Do Splash Mountain and Big Thunder Mountain Railroad. Then see the Country Bears or Tom Sawyer Island (the latter closes at dusk).

- Take a spin at the Mad Tea Party, and see the highlights of Fantasyland, including It's a Small World, Peter Pan, Mickey's PhilharMagic, and The Many Adventures of Winnie the Pooh.

- Pop in at The Haunted Mansion and The Hall of Presidents before dinner.

- Now it's time for Tomorrowland. (If you have the energy and the evening parade is running twice, stay in Tomorrowland during the early run. See the parade later.) Go directly to Space Mountain or Buzz Lightyear's Space Ranger Spin.

- If it's offered, catch the Main Street Electrical Parade. And don't miss the fireworks!

- Shop on Main Street, U.S.A., while the exiting throngs file out.

* For details on where to meet Disney characters, see page 132.

HALF DAY WITH YOUNG CHILDREN

Start at Town Square Exposition Hall. Meet Mickey and Minnie inside! If it's parade time, grab a spot on the curb. After fully exploring Fantasyland (do not miss It's a Small World), consider a visit to the Country Bear Jamboree. Soar on a magic carpet in Adventureland, then head to Tomorrowland. Cap off the day by a spin with Buzz Lightyear, followed by the Main Street Electrical Parade and the fireworks.

Epcot

HALF–DAY SCHEDULES

Morning at Epcot

❥ Head right to Soarin' and Test Track. If you're up for the "intense" Mission: SPACE, go for it. (We prefer the "less intense," non-spinning version of the attraction.) Then move on to The Seas with Nemo & Friends, followed by *Captain EO* in the Imagination pavilion.

❥ See Universe of Energy and all of The Seas with Nemo & Friends before moving on to World Showcase—it opens at 11 A.M. Save Spaceship Earth for later, when the line dies down a bit. When hunger calls, stop for lunch. See the countries that interest you most, making sure to see the show inside the American Adventure and the boat rides in Norway (Maelstrom) and Mexico (Gran Fiesta Tour Starring the Three Caballeros).

Epcot After Lunch

❥ If you don't have restaurant reservations and would like to have dinner at a World Showcase restaurant, stop by Guest Relations to make them. If not, consider dining at the nearby BoardWalk resort (it's a short stroll or *FriendShip* boat ride away).

❥ See as much of Future World as possible before heading to World Showcase. (Future World usually closes at 7 P.M., while World Showcase stays open until 9 P.M.)

❥ Spend the evening touring World Showcase. Keep an eye on the clock so you can secure a good spot around the lagoon to watch the evening's presentation of IllumiNations—Reflections of Earth.

❥ Avoid the crush of exiting crowds by browsing the wares in the Mouse Gear shop in Future World.

HALF DAY WITH YOUNG CHILDREN

Begin with a visit to the Epcot Character Spot, followed by The Seas with Nemo & Friends to take a ride in a "clam-mobile," see Turtle Talk with Crush, and romp in Bruce's Shark World. Follow it up with a visit to Spaceship Earth. Check out the Kidcot Fun Stops throughout the park and stop by the miniature village in Germany. If there's time, check out ImageWorks in Imagination.

WHERE TO MEET THE CHARACTERS*

Epcot Character Spot (Mickey, Minnie, Goofy, Donald); **Germany** (Snow White, Pinocchio); **France** (Beast and Belle); **United Kingdom** (Mary Poppins); **China** (Mushu); **Morocco** (Jasmine and Aladdin); **Showcase Plaza** (Duffy the Disney Bear)
*Characters subject to change.

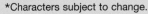

Disney's Hollywood Studios

HALF-DAY SCHEDULES

Morning at Disney's Hollywood Studios

❤ Kick-start the day with a visit to Toy Story Mania, followed by trips to Rock 'n' Roller Coaster and Tower of Terror (just don't do the thrill rides on a full stomach). From there, move to Muppet*Vision 3-D.

❤ Before lining up for the parade, see The Magic of Disney Animation; Beauty and the Beast—Live on Stage; Lights, Motors, Action—Extreme Stunt Show; and The Great Movie Ride.

Disney's Hollywood Studios After Lunch

❤ Begin with Tower of Terror, Rock 'n' Roller Coaster, and Beauty and the Beast—Live on Stage.

❤ See Voyage of The Little Mermaid; Star Tours; Muppet*Vision 3-D; The Great Movie Ride; Lights, Motors, Action—Extreme Stunt Show; Toy Story Mania (expect a wait of at least an hour); the Indiana Jones Epic Stunt Spectacular, and the Studio Backlot Tour.

❤ If there's time, see Walt Disney: One Man's Dream and the Magic of Animation before grabbing a spot in line for Fantasmic (if the nighttime spectacular is being presented today).

HALF DAY WITH YOUNG CHILDREN

Start with Toy Story Mania!, followed by Disney Junior—Live on Stage, the Honey, I Shrunk the Audience Movie Set Adventure, and Beauty and the Beast—Live on Stage. Skip Fantasmic—it is just too intense for most tykes.

WHERE TO MEET THE CHARACTERS*

Park Entrance at park opening time (Mickey, Donald, Chip, Dale, and more); **Animation Courtyard** (Playhouse Disney friends such as Jojo and Goliath, plus Mickey Mouse); **Pixar Place** (Woody, Jessie, Bullseye, or other *Toy Story* characters); **Streets of America** (friends from *Monsters, Inc.* and *Cars*)

*Characters subject to change.

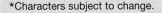

Disney's Animal Kingdom

HALF-DAY SCHEDULES

Morning at Disney's Animal Kingdom

- Go to Asia to ride the thrilling Expedition Everest and Kali River Rapids, and hike the Maharajah Jungle Trek.

- Experience the Flights of Wonder show on the way to Kilimanjaro Safaris and the Pangani Forest Exploration Trail.

- Check a Times Guide for the next Festival of the Lion King show. Arrive at least 45 minutes ahead of time (it's wildly popular).

- Finish up with Finding Nemo—The Musical; Dinosaur; and It's Tough to be a Bug—though the last two may be too intense for tots.

Disney's Animal Kingdom After Lunch

- Check a Times Guide for Festival of the Lion King and Finding Nemo— The Musical schedules. Arrive 45 minutes early during peak times of year. Then visit Disney characters in Camp Minnie-Mickey.

- If there is entertainment or a parade scheduled, stick around Discovery Island to enjoy it. Otherwise, head to the Kilimanjaro Safaris ride. Do the Pangani Forest Exploration Trail, and take the train to Rafiki's Planet Watch.

- Ride Expedition Everest and Kali River Rapids, and experience the Maharajah Jungle Trek. Try to catch Flights of Wonder, too.

- Wander the Discovery Island Trails and see It's Tough to be a Bug.

- Before dinner, dodge dastardly dinos on Dinosaur.

HALF DAY WITH YOUNG CHILDREN

Scope out animal life in The Oasis before heading to Camp Minnie-Mickey. Meet Disney characters and see The Festival of the Lion King before visiting DinoLand U.S.A. Explore The Boneyard and ride TriceraTop Spin. If time allows, take the train to Rafiki's Planet Watch, where kids can bond with live animals (mostly goats) in the Affection Section. And the Flights of Wonder bird show captivates guests of all ages.

WHERE TO MEET THE CHARACTERS*

Park Entrance at park opening (characters vary); **Camp Minnie-Mickey Greeting Trails** (Minnie, Mickey, Tigger, Pooh, Pluto, Goofy, Rafiki, and Terk); **Donald's Safari Breakfast in Tusker House** (Donald, Mickey, and Goofy)

*Characters subject to change.

Making the Most of Longer Visits

Longer stays allow the chance to sample some of the World's myriad offerings. Spend another day in the one park you most enjoyed. Lounge by the pool, go biking, or play tennis or golf. Go shopping at Downtown Disney. Cool off at one of Disney's innovative water parks. Have lunch at a WDW resort, and try a special dinner at Victoria & Albert's in the Grand Floridian, or at California Grill in the Contemporary. Check out the restaurants at Pleasure Island and Downtown Disney West Side, or spend the evening at the BoardWalk. Take golf or tennis lessons. Go fishing, waterskiing, or horseback riding. Visit a spa. Participate in a behind-the-scenes program. Play a round of miniature golf. See a game at the ESPN Wide World of Sports complex. For even more ideas, see our *Sports*; *Everything Else in the World*; and *Good Meals, Great Times* chapters.

How to Save a Rainy Day

Florida rain showers come and go with such regularity that you could set your watch by them, especially during summer months. They're usually brief, though torrential. Of course, there are times when gray clouds linger longer. Here are some ways to make the most of a soggy day:

- Head for DisneyQuest, a huge interactive play zone at Downtown Disney West Side. It'll keep the whole family entertained (and dry) for hours.

- See a movie on one of AMC Theatres' many screens at Downtown Disney.

- Check out Cirque du Soleil's La Nouba.

- Consider taking in an indoor event at the ESPN Wide World of Sports complex. For information, call 407-939-1500.

- Don your rain gear and go to Epcot. The pavilions in Future World house a bounty of sheltered diversions. (Ponchos are sold throughout WDW for about $8 each.)

Customized Travel Tips
Traveling with Children

Tell youngsters that a Walt Disney World vacation is in the works and the response is apt to be overwhelming. Our guide, *Birnbaum's Walt Disney World For Kids*, written for children ages 7 through 14, can be a useful resource for getting them involved in the planning from the outset. Filled with information about the World from a kid's perspective, it can be used as a reference before and during the trip, and as a souvenir afterward.

Walt Disney World ranks among the easier spots on earth for families with children. Keep in mind, however, that kids under 7 must be accompanied by an adult to enter the theme parks; kids under 10 must be accompanied at the water parks. With most teens, however, it is enough to establish a meeting place and time inside the Magic Kingdom, Epcot, Disney's Hollywood Studios, or Animal Kingdom.

Child Care: In-room child-care service can be summoned to all Disney-owned resorts. The service is available 24 hours a day, seven days a week, though it is not run by Disney. For pricing and to make a reservation with Kid's Nite Out, visit *www.kidsniteout.com*, call 407-828-0920 or 800-696-8105, or inquire at your resort's lobby concierge. Another company, Super Sitters, offers this child-care service as well. In addition to resort babysitting, they can accompany a party during theme park visits. This allows parents to take older kids on attractions while the sitter keeps an eye on the younger ones. To reach them, call 407-382-2558 or visit *www.super-sitters.com*.

Children's Activity Centers: The Polynesian, Grand Floridian, Animal Kingdom Lodge, Wilderness Lodge, Yacht and Beach Club, and Dolphin resorts each have an on-site children's activity center. These centers accept (potty-trained) kids ages 3 through 12. For details and availability, phone 407-939-3463 for all but the Dolphin. "Camp Dolphin" operates daily from 5:30 P.M. to midnight and accepts children ages 3 through 12. Camp Dolphin costs $10 per hour, per child. For information, call 407-934-4241.

Baby Care Centers: Located in all theme parks, these centers are for parents with young kids. They are not meant as day care. All kids must be accompanied by a parent or guardian. There are rooms with rocking chairs and couches in feeding rooms for nursing mothers, and screenings of Disney films for young children. Centers have facilities for changing diapers, preparing formula, warming bottles, and washing bottles. Diapers, bottles, formula, pacifiers, and baby food are among the supplies for sale. Baby Care Center locations are listed on theme park guidemaps. There are changing areas in most women's and in some men's restrooms.

Lost Children: Disney employees (aka "cast members") will know what to do if a child starts to call for his or her parents. If your child wanders off, stop in at the Baby Care Center or City Hall in the Magic Kingdom; at Guest Relations or the Baby Care Center in Epcot; at Guest Relations at Disney's Hollywood Studios; or at Guest Relations in Animal Kingdom. A computerized system allows for a detailed description of the child and his or her status, helping to reunite families quickly. There are no paging systems, but in emergencies an all-points bulletin can be put out among cast members. The Guest Relations staff of each park can help, too.

Parental Perk

Families with babies or small children should know about the "rider switch" policy (aka "baby swap") at the theme parks. At attractions with age or height restrictions, a parent who waits nearby with a young child while the other parent rides the attraction can go right on soon after the first parent comes off. Be sure to ask the attendant at the attraction's entrance. They'll tell you how to proceed.

It helps to prepare your child for the possibility of an accidental separation. Direct him or her to contact an employee (anybody wearing a name tag) and ask for help.

Refrigerators: For parents of young children, an in-room fridge is not a mere luxury, it's a necessity. Disney's deluxe, moderate, and Vacation Club accommodations generally come equipped with a small refrigerator. (If your room does not have one, request it. And make sure you are not charged.) Guests in "value" resorts can rent one for about $10 per day. Request the fridge when you make your reservation, and be sure to confirm that request shortly before you arrive.

Baby Food: Many parents choose to ship a box of food and baby supplies to their resort before they leave home. It is possible to purchase jars of baby food at most Disney resorts, but the selection isn't huge. For a wider variety of foodstuffs to choose from, make a trip to the Winn-Dixie at 11957 Apopka-Vineland Road (just beyond the Crossroads shopping center) or Gooding's at the Crossroads, near Hotel Plaza Boulevard. For directions, inquire at your resort's front desk.

Winn-Dixie and Gooding's, as well as nearby convenience stores, are also within a reasonable cabbing distance. Be sure to hire an authorized cab for the trip (one with regulated rates). Your resort staff can make the arrangements and give you an estimate of the cost.

If you have a milk (or other food-supply) emergency after hours, know that these Walt Disney World resorts have 24-hour snack bars: Grand Floridian, Polynesian, Dolphin, and Buena Vista Palace.

Cribs: Most Walt Disney World resort rooms come with a small, playpen-like crib. (Look for it in the closet. If it's not there, call to request one.) They're free, but somewhat flimsy. If you'd like something a little bigger or sturdier, consider renting a crib from Orlando Crib Rental (407-433-7770).

Diapers: Each Disney resort has at least one shop in which to pick up diapers. If you're brand loyal, pack your own. Be sure to throw a few waterproof diapers into your bag each morning. You never know when you'll run into an interactive fountain on Disney property. They're necessary for pool use, too.

Tips for Teens

When it comes to teens at Disney World, The Little Mermaid's Ariel has plenty of company. Of course, be they of the fish or human variety, teenage guests have special needs all their own. Here are some tips, courtesy of Amy Newcomer, Birnbaum's WDW teen expert:

- Bring your own music. It's perfect for the trip to Disney World and for sitting poolside at your resort. But don't wear your earphones for your whole trip.

- Have some of your own money on hand. If it's your hard-earned cash, you won't spend it as fast as you would Mom and Dad's!

- Pack a hat. Why? It's much easier to throw a hat on than waste time doing your hair.

- Try to get along with your brothers and sisters—even if it isn't always easy. Don't bug them to do the things you want to do all the time. Offer to do things they want to do, too.

- One of the coolest things for teens to do is an Extra Magic Hours evening at a theme park. They let you stay in a park after hours and ride all the best rides with basically no wait! Another good thing to do at night is to go shopping, especially at Downtown Disney Marketplace.

- *Attention, parents!* Try to include your teens in planning your trip. If they get a say during planning, they will be much happier when they arrive at Walt Disney World. Also, don't make them get up every morning at 6 A.M. Try to give them a day or two to wake up late and lounge around the pool or a water park.

Resort Fun: All WDW resorts have at least one arcade. Most of the hotels have little playgrounds as well as toddler-friendly pools. For information on special children's activities at Disney resorts, turn to page 216.

Strollers: Available for $15 for one day and $13 per day of a multi-day rental at stroller rental areas at each of the theme parks. (Strollers are not available for rent at the water parks.) Double strollers cost $31 for one day and $27 per day of a multi-day rental. Deposits are no longer required for stroller rentals at the theme parks.

HOT TIP!

If you have a baby, you'll need a stroller during your Walt Disney World visit. Although they may be rented at the theme parks, consider bringing one from home. It'll save you money and the hassle of getting one each time you visit a park. Plus, there's the convenience of using it all over WDW property. (Disney rents strollers at the theme parks and Downtown Disney, but they can't leave the place from which they are rented.)

Keep in mind that strollers are not permitted inside the attractions (they can be parked near each attraction entrance). If a stroller disappears while you're in an attraction, a replacement may be obtained. Ask a park worker for the nearest replacement location. Guests have to pay only once a day for a stroller. If you rent one in the morning and plan to spend the afternoon at another park, just present your receipt for a stroller there.

If you'll need a stroller for several days, consider purchasing the Length of Stay rental ticket. It'll save you two dollars off the daily price and it should cut down on time spent in the rental line. Simply buy the ticket on your first visit to a theme park and put your receipt in a safe place—that's what you'll need to show to get a stroller on the remaining days of your stay.

Downtown Disney Marketplace and West Side rent single strollers for $10 a day, plus a refundable deposit (there are no doubles available here). You may also bring your own stroller into the parks.

Note: You will be asked to remove the child and fold your stroller before boarding Walt Disney World buses and boats.

Traveling Without Children

Walt Disney World has become an extremely popular destination for adults without children, appealing to singles, couples, and empty-nesters alike. Disney has responded to the demand with an entertainment and dining selection for grown-ups without kids in tow.

Couples

There is a place for lovebirds at Walt Disney World. Actually, there are many spots in the World perfectly suited to those with romantic intentions.

- Grown-ups love to roam the parks unencumbered by little ones and strollers. The Magic Kingdom's carousel-and-castle combo invokes the enchantment in true fairy-tale tradition. Epcot's World Showcase has the aura of a whirlwind tour (and the inspiration for a future trip?), with countries as exotic and far-reaching as Japan and Morocco. Disney's Hollywood Studios recaptures an era of starry-eyed elegance. And what could be more enjoyable than sharing a safari through Africa at Animal Kingdom?

  By day, there is romance in the theme parks for couples who are already inclined to hold hands; by night, the parks sparkle with an intensity that inspires sudden mushiness in those who never considered themselves the type, and that's before the fireworks.

- As Disney's themed resorts go about transporting guests to various times and places, they make quite a few passes through settings straight out of everyone's fantasy escape textbook—from the Victorian charms of the Grand Floridian to the exotic island getaway that is the Polynesian resort. You won't find a more inspirational backdrop than that at the rustic Wilderness Lodge, marked by geysers, waterfalls, steamy hot springs, and a grand stone fireplace. At the

The Most Romantic Places in the World

WDW RESORTS

- Animal Kingdom Lodge
- Coronado Springs
- Grand Floridian
- Polynesian
- Port Orleans Riverside
- Wilderness Lodge
- Yacht and Beach Club

WDW RESTAURANTS

- Artist Point
- Bistro de Paris
- California Grill
- Cinderella's Royal Table
- Citricos
- Le Cellier Steakhouse
- Narcoossee's
- Sanaa
- Victoria & Albert's
- Yachtsman Steakhouse

WDW LOUNGES

- Belle Vue Lounge at BoardWalk
- Bongos' Pineapple Bar at Downtown Disney West Side
- Citricos Lounge at Grand Floridian
- Il Mulino New York Trattoria Lounge at the Swan
- Rix Lounge at Coronado Springs
- The Lounge at The Wave . . . of American Flavors at Contemporary resort
- Victoria Falls at Animal Kingdom Lodge

WDW THEME PARK SPOTS

- All of Epcot's World Showcase
- Castle rose garden in the Magic Kingdom

nostalgic BoardWalk resort, surrey bikes are available for romantic rides along the waterfront. And a peaceful stroll around Crescent Lake is a lovely way to cap off the day.

- The myriad of recreational activities that couples may enjoy at Walt Disney World include tennis, golf, water-skiing, sailing, horseback riding, couples' treatments at one of four on-property spas, and more.

Older Travelers

Disney World can sometimes be challenging for older travelers. And the heat, particularly in summer, can be hard to take. But with the proper planning and precautions, it's just as delightful for older visitors as for kids.

- For slower times, visit the parks Monday through Wednesday. (Thursdays through Sundays tend to attract lots of locals.)

- Try to eat early or late to avoid the meal-time crowds. In the Magic Kingdom, select restaurants such as Tony's Town Square Restaurant and Columbia Harbour House. Or take the monorail to the peaceful Polynesian, Contemporary, or Grand Floridian resorts, where pleasant dining

Vacation Insurance

No one books a vacation expecting to cancel it at the last minute—yet sometimes life intervenes and it's simply unavoidable. So it may be worth working travel insurance into your vacation budget (we do). It may include coverage for trip cancellation and interruption, travel delay, loss of baggage, medical expenses, and more. Be sure to ask about travel insurance when you reserve your trip.

options abound (check ahead to find out which restaurants serve lunch). In Epcot, the Coral Reef restaurant and La Hacienda are pleasant spots. At Disney's Hollywood Studios, the Hollywood Brown Derby offers a relaxing meal, as does Mama Melrose's Ristorante Italiano.

- If you need to refrigerate medicine, know that all small refrigerators are included with the room rate at WDW "deluxe" and "moderate" resorts. They can be provided at "value" resorts for a daily fee.

- The Florida sun tends to be brutal year-round. Always wear sunscreen and a hat.

- Don't underestimate distances at Epcot or Animal Kingdom; you may need to walk more than three miles in a day. If that's daunting, consider renting a wheelchair.

- Pace yourself. It's smart to head back to your hotel for a swim or a nap in the afternoon and then return to the parks later on.

HOT TIP!

Even the fittest of seniors may want to avoid some of Walt Disney World's more physically challenging attractions. Do heed all warning signs at attraction entrances to thrill rides and consider steering clear of high-activity level experiences such as the Magic Kingdom's Swiss Family Treehouse (seemingly endless stairs!), the Maharajah Jungle Trek, and Pangani Forest Exploration Trail at Animal Kingdom (lots of walking and few places to rest).

The hotels connected by monorail are particularly convenient for this.

- Many Orlando-area hotels and attractions offer discounts to seniors and AARP members. Contact the Official Visitor Information Center (407-363-5872) for details.

Solo Travelers

Those who travel alone (be it for business or just for fun) can have as memorable a time here as they would anywhere else.

- Solo travelers with extra time should consider taking a behind-the-scenes tour.

- Many of the finer restaurants now have counters at which to eat—perfect for chatting with other diners.

- Sometimes, being a solo traveler can mean shorter wait times at attractions. Test Track is among those with "single rider" lines.

- Other opportunities for unencumbered travelers include parasailing and water-skiing (at the Contemporary), horseback riding (at Fort Wilderness), taking a spin in a racecar (at the Richard Petty Driving Experience), bass fishing (407-WDW-BASS; 939-2277), surfing lessons (407-939-7873), and watching a pro baseball game (at ESPN Wide World of Sports). Call 407-939-7529.

- Downtown Disney's lounges and restaurants can prove to be fertile meeting places. The BoardWalk is another lively destination. Sports fans find its ESPN Club most inviting. And suds fans appreciate the home-brewed libations at Big River Grille & Brewing Works. Sushi lovers fit right in at the California Grill sushi bar.

- The lounges at Walt Disney World hotels are relaxed and welcoming. The same atmosphere prevails at the Tune-In Lounge in the 50's Prime Time Cafe at Disney's Hollywood Studios, at the Rose & Crown Pub (in the United Kingdom pavilion), and the lovely lounge at Contemporary resort's The Wave . . . of American Flavors.

Important WDW Telephone Numbers

AMC Theatres (Downtown Disney):
888-262-4386

Behind-the-Scenes Tours:
407-WDW-TOUR (939-8687)

Central Reservations:
407-W-DISNEY (934-7639)

Dining Reservations:
407-WDW-DINE (939-3463)

Dr. P. Phillips Hospital:
407-351-8500

ESPN Wide World of Sports Complex:
407-939-1500

Florida Hospital Celebration Health: 407-303-4000

Golf Reservations:
407-WDW-GOLF (939-4653)

Recreation:
407-WDW-PLAY (939-7529)

Theme Park Lost and Found:
407-824-4245

Walt Disney Travel Company:
407-828-8101

Walt Disney World Information:
407-824-4321

Weather: 407-824-4104

Tips for International Travelers

Visitors from outside the U.S. need not feel like strangers in a strange land when they arrive at Walt Disney World—even if they speak a language other than English. Information is readily available in many different languages. These tips may also be helpful:

- Free park maps can be found in Spanish, French, German, Portuguese, and Japanese at the entrance to all parks, as well as at Guest Relations.

- Free translation services are available at all four theme parks and include a specially designed translation device called Ears to the World, Disney's Show Translator. The units are lightweight headsets that use wireless technology to provide synchronized narration at several popular theme park attractions. They are available in French, German, Japanese, Portuguese, and Spanish. There is no charge to use the service, but a $100 refundable deposit is required to borrow one.

- Several Disney resorts offer services for their international guests. Ask about them when you inquire about reservations.

- When making reservations through 407-WDW-DINE or WDW-PLAY, ask to speak with a foreign-language host or hostess.

- Most WDW restaurants offer menus in various languages. Some have picture menus.

- Foreign currency exchange is available at Guest Relations in each of the theme parks. Traveler's checks may be purchased at the SunTrust bank by Downtown Disney.

- Most Disney resort room keys can act as a charge card. Purchases made at WDW will be billed to a credit card that is presented at check-in.

- Many Disney employees are fluent in more than one language. Languages spoken are noted on employee name tags.

- Guests traveling long distances and through time zones should conserve their energy. It might be wise to relax by the pool on the day of arrival, instead of trying to fit in a full day at a theme park—it's never beneficial to start a vacation exhausted!

- Phone cards good for international calls can be purchased at several Disney World shops and in many resorts. Inquire at Guest Relations. Resist the urge to direct dial calls from resort rooms.

Telephone Dos and Don'ts

It's a common practice for hotels to assess a surcharge for phone calls, and Disney is no exception. To avoid whopping bills, charge calls to a phone card, and keep these tips in mind:

- A direct-dialed, long-distance call will set you back the cost of the call at the AT&T operator-assisted day rate, plus a 55 percent surcharge. The rate applies to both domestic and international long distance. Applicable taxes are included. Rates are subject to change.

- Prepaid phone cards are available for purchase in most WDW resort lobbies.

- There is no longer an additional fee for guests making credit card, prepaid phone card, or any type of operator-assisted calls from a resort-room phone.

- There is no charge to call an 800 number from a WDW resort room.

- Calls made between most WDW resorts are local (and toll-free) calls.

- Directory assistance 411 phone calls cost $.85 each; a 555-1212 call costs $1.40.

- There is no charge to call from room to room within a resort.

- Cell-phone users, check with your carriers to avoid tallying up "roaming" charges.

- All Disney-owned-and-operated resorts support mobile computing through a data-port connection on the guestroom telephone, with applicable charges.

Travelers with Disabilities

Disney tends to get high marks from travelers with disabilities because of attention paid to special needs. Here is an overview:

GETTING AROUND: Special parking is available for guests at the theme parks; ask for directions at the Auto Plaza upon entering. From the Transportation and Ticket Center (TTC), the Magic Kingdom is accessible by ferry or by monorail. All monorail stations are accessible to wheelchairs. The ramps are lengthy and a bit steep, but manageable.

Wheelchairs: Guests are welcome to bring their own wheelchairs or Electric Convenience Vehicles (ECVs). They also have the option of renting them at a theme park, BoardWalk resort, or from a local vendor. Wheelchairs may be rented in theme parks for $12 per day ($10 per day with a Length of Stay rental). In the Magic Kingdom, they are available at the Stroller and Wheelchair Rental. Epcot's rental areas are inside the main turnstiles and at the International Gateway entrance. Oscar's Super Service rents wheelchairs at the Studios. At Animal Kingdom, wheelchairs are available to rent at Garden Gate Gifts.

If you plan to visit the parks for several days, consider getting a multi-day wheelchair rental. Called a Length of Stay ticket, it comes at a $2-per-day discount. You'll pay for the entire stay when you first visit a theme park. Simply show your receipt the next time you visit a rental location.

The water parks have a small number of wheelchairs to borrow. There's no charge, but the supply is limited. Guests must leave a valid "ID" as deposit. Downtown Disney Marketplace Strollers & Wheelchairs and DisneyQuest rent wheelchairs for $15 a day, plus a $100 deposit. ECVs are available at Marketplace Strollers & Wheelchairs for $45 per day with a $100 deposit. Wheelchairs at ESPN Wide World of Sports may be borrowed for free.

HOT TIP!
The theme park disability parking areas are quite a distance from the wheelchair rental areas. If you require assistance, seek out a parking lot attendant and request a chair to get you to the park entrance. There you can rent a chair or ECV for park use.

Resorts with zero-depth-entry pools may have a small number of wheelchairs available to assist guests entering the pools.

Electric Convenience Vehicles (ECVs) are available for rent in every theme park. They cost $50 for one day, plus a $20 refundable deposit. They usually sell out early. A word of

HOT TIP!
Elderly, ill, or injured guests who do not ordinarily use a wheelchair may benefit by using one here. There is a lot of ground to cover. And standing in line for attractions requires strength and stamina.

advice for first-time users: Practice makes perfect. So, before you head into a thicket of park guests, take it for a test drive.

Equipment rented at a park *cannot leave that park*. If you'd like to hold on to yours for the whole trip, call a company that rents standard and electric wheelchairs, as well as scooters. It makes for a much less harried experience—but keep in mind that you will have to transport the wheelchair or scooter. (Monorails and buses are equipped to accommodate, but some boats are not.) Three companies from which to rent are LifeAire (800-417-9496), ScootAround (888-441-7575), and Walker Mobility (888-726-6837). Pickup and delivery (often for free or with a small surcharge) are available at all hotels in the WDW area (not just those on-property). In our opinion, guests are better off renting from a local vendor or bringing their own equipment. The quality is generally better, and you don't have to worry about availability. The Walt Disney Company is not affiliated with, nor does it endorse, these companies.

Buena Vista Scooters has an on-property presence at Disney's BoardWalk resort. They have a limited number of first-come, first-served ECVs. The cost is about $32 a day. It's possible to reserve in advance; visit *www. buenavistascooters.com*, or call 407-938-0349 or 866-484-4797. These scooters may be taken anywhere and have a two-day minimum rental period. The company provides free pickup and delivery to all WDW area resorts.

There are designated areas for guests using wheelchairs to view the fireworks at Epcot and to view the parades in each of the theme parks. Check a park guidemap for locations.

Accessibility: It's relatively easy to get around the parks by wheelchair. (Although Animal Kingdom does offer the occasional challenge.) Most attractions are accessible to guests who can be lifted from chairs with assistance from a member of their party, and some can accommodate guests who must remain in wheelchairs. Consult the park's *Guidemap for Guests with Disabilities* (for a free set, write to Walt Disney World Guest Correspondence, P.O. Box 10000, Lake Buena Vista, FL 32830) for details about access, or check with the ride host or hostess. At the water parks, life jackets are available for travelers with disabilities.

All Disney hotels have accommodations equipped for guests with disabilities, including roll-in showers. Other features—which vary, depending on the resort—include: wheelchair-accessible bathrooms, bed accessories, strobe-light smoke detectors, in-room Text Typewriters (TTYs), and more. The following resorts have zero-depth-entry pools: Animal Kingdom Lodge, Caribbean Beach, the Contemporary's Bay Lake Tower, Grand Floridian, Polynesian, and Saratoga Springs. For assistance in choosing a hotel that best fits your requirements, ask for the Special Reservations Department when you call Central Reservations (Voice: 407-939-7807; TTY: 407-939-7670).

RESOURCES: Visual Disabilities: Guests can get a handheld device that verbally describes each park as well as many attractions. Each requires a $25 refundable deposit. Braille guides and maps are also available.

Hearing Disabilities: Pay phones with Text Typewriters (TTYs) are available throughout Disney World. For more information, call 407-824-4321 or 407-827-5141. Sign language is available for some shows. Call at least two weeks ahead for arrangements.

Assistive-listening devices that amplify attraction audio are available at City Hall in the Magic Kingdom and at Guest Relations in Epcot, Animal Kingdom, and Disney's Hollywood Studios. A $25 refundable deposit is required. Sites with assistive-listening systems are listed on park guidemaps.

Attraction Access

Most park attractions are accessible to guests who are able to get out of their wheelchairs (with or without assistance). And a growing number have queues that can be navigated in a wheelchair or ECV. When that's the case, guests are urged to do so. If a wheelchair or ECV cannot be accommodated in the queue area, ask an attendant to direct you to an auxiliary entrance. Such entrances are intended for guests using wheelchairs or with service animals. For specifics on this policy, guests should visit any Guest Relations location.

Captioning systems, including reflective and handheld devices, are available at theme park Guest Relations windows. The former project show dialogue onto panels; the latter provide captioning on personal devices at certain attractions. A $25 deposit is required.

Note: *Trained service animals are welcome in all Disney parks.*

Booking the Trip: These organizations specialize in assisting disabled travelers:

• The Society for Accessible Travel & Hospitality (347 Fifth Ave., Suite 605, New York, NY 10016; 212-447-7284; *www.sath.org*)

• Accessible Journeys (35 W. Sellers Ave., Ridley Park, PA 19078; 610-521-0339 or 800-846-4537; *www.accessiblejourneys.com*)

• Flying Wheels Travel (143 W. Bridge St., Owatonna, MN 55060; 507-451-5005 or 877-451-5006; *www.flyingwheelstravel.com*)

Vehicles: Wheelchair Getaways (*www.wheelchair-getaways.com*; 800-642-2042) and Rainbow Wheels of Florida (800-910-8267; *www.rainbowwheels.com*) both rent wheelchair-accessible vans and offer pickup and delivery for most area hotels.

WDW Weddings & Honeymoons

Believe it or not, Walt Disney World is one of the most popular honeymoon destinations in the United States. Why the appeal? The resorts offer some romantic stretches of white-sand beaches for evening strolls, fine restaurants for candlelight dinners, and a host of activities to rival almost any European or Hawaiian destination. Add to that the fantasy of the Magic Kingdom, the wonder of Epcot, the glamour of Disney's Hollywood Studios, and the majesty of Animal Kingdom—plus Downtown Disney and BoardWalk nightlife, water parks, and the Disney Cruise Line—and it's not hard to see why Disney is tops with newlyweds.

After years of fending for themselves, folks looking to honeymoon here now have help at hand. A variety of packages cater specifically to newly married couples. For information, call toll-free: 877-566-0969.

The folks at Walt Disney World have also received oodles of requests from couples who wanted to actually get married at one of the theme parks. They responded by creating a program known as Disney's Fairy Tale Weddings. Today, couples can tie the knot in evening ceremonies at some parks during seasons when they close early. (The area in front of Cinderella Castle in the Magic Kingdom is one of Walt Disney World's wedding hot spots, as are several Epcot sites.)

The Yacht and Beach Club, BoardWalk, Polynesian, and Wilderness Lodge resorts also host their share of weddings. The Wedding Pavilion, on the grounds of the Grand Floridian Resort and Spa, offers a Victorian-style indoor setting with a prime view of Cinderella Castle and the Seven Seas Lagoon. A combination of stained glass, sage green and soft pink florals, and benches with heart-shaped cutouts (seating around 250 guests) creates the romantic ambience. Couples can fill their wedding albums with photos taken at Picture Point, under a trellis of climbing white roses, with the faraway castle prominently in the background.

Weddings range from elegant affairs, without a hint of Disneyana, to ceremonies in which the bride arrives in Cinderella's coach and Mickey and Minnie Mouse are among the guests at the reception.

At Franck's Bridal Studio, Walt Disney World specialists work with couples to customize each wedding. Among the services offered are cakes, photography, flower arranging, and musical entertainment. Franck's specialists can help secure accommodations, rehearsal dinners, bachelor parties, and more.

For information about planning a Walt Disney World wedding, call 407-566-7633 or visit *www.disneyweddings.com*; for honeymoon packages, call 877-566-0969 or visit *www. disneyhoneymoons.com*.

Honeymoon Registry

Launched, appropriately, on Valentine's Day, happy couples can create a gift registry for their honeymoon. Gifts include theme park tickets, resort accommodations, spa treatments, and more. For more information or to sign up for the Disney Honeymoon Registry, visit *www.disneyhoneymoonregistry.com* or call 407-939-7776.

Online Resort Check-in

Headed to a Walt Disney World-owned-and-operated resort? If you have access to the Internet, you can take advantage of Disney's new online resort check-in service. It'll help get you into your room quicker upon arrival, adding precious minutes to your Disney vacation.

Here's how it works: Within 10 days of your arrival date (45 days for Disney Cruise Line packages), grab your resort reservation number and go to *www.disneyworld.com*. That's where you'll provide the info usually supplied at the front desk of a resort, plus give Disney a heads-up regarding your room preferences (which can't be guaranteed), and estimated arrival time.

When you cross the resort's threshold, make a beeline for the Online Check-in Services area in the lobby. There you'll be handed a special welcome packet including a Key to the World card (room key). Simply present a valid photo ID to pick up the ready-made folder and complete the check-in process.

For more information, call 407-939-7639.

MAGICAL MILESTONES

1971–1982

1971
Magic Kingdom

1973
Pirates of the Caribbean, Tom Sawyer Island

1974
Star Jets (now Astro Orbiter)

1983–1990

1983
Journey into Imagination pavilion (now Imagination!)

1984
Morocco pavilion

1986
The Living Seas (now The Seas with Nemo & Friends)

1991–1997

1991
Muppet*Vision 3-D, Beauty and the Beast—Live on Stage, SpectroMagic

1992
Splash Mountain, Voyage of The Little Mermaid

1994
Innoventions (replaced Communicore), Honey, I Shrunk the Audience, The Twilight Zone™ Tower of Terror

1998–2011

1998
Disney's Animal Kingdom, Buzz Lightyear's Space Ranger Spin, Fantasmic!, DisneyQuest, Disney Cruise Line

1999
Sounds Dangerous Starring Drew Carey, Kali River Rapids, Test Track, Rock 'n' Roller Coaster, The Many Adventures of Winnie the Pooh

2003
Mission: SPACE, Mickey's PhilharMagic, Wishes (fireworks show)

Even frequent visitors have trouble keeping up with all the changes at Walt Disney World. The timeline below will help you determine which major attractions have opened since your last visit.

1975
Space Mountain, WEDway PeopleMover (now Tomorrowland Transit Authority PeopleMover)

1980
Big Thunder Mountain Railroad

1982
Epcot

1988
Epcot's Norway pavilion and IllumiNations

1989
Disney-MGM Studios (now Disney's Hollywood Studios), Typhoon Lagoon

1990
Star Tours (original version), Honey, I Shrunk the Kids Movie Set Adventure

1995
California Grill, Blizzard Beach

1996
Ellen's Energy Adventure, Fantasia Gardens mini golf, BoardWalk

1997
Downtown Disney West Side, ESPN Wide World of Sports complex

2005
Soarin', Lights, Motors, Action!—Extreme Stunt Show, Crushin' Gusher (at Typhoon Lagoon)

2006
Expedition Everest (and Captain Jack Sparrow joins the Pirates of the Caribbean!)

2007
Finding Nemo—The Musical, Monsters, Inc. Laugh Floor

2008
Toy Story Mania!

2009
The American Idol Experience

2011
Star Tours—The Adventures Continue makes its debut at Disney's Hollywood Studios

Fingertip Reference Guide

BARBERS AND SALONS

One of the most amusing places to get a haircut is the Magic Kingdom's old-fashioned Harmony Barber Shop. It's located beside the Car Barn in the Town Square section of Main Street. Cost is about $18 for adults and $15 for kids. Hours are 9 A.M. to 5 P.M. daily. Reservations may be made by calling 407-939-3463. Walk-ins are accommodated on a first-come, first-served basis.

Haircuts, coloring, manicures, and other services are available at the American Beauty Shoppe/Captain's Chair in the Contemporary (407-824-3411), Periwig Beauty and Barber Shop at the Yacht and Beach Club (407-934-3260), Ivy Trellis at the Grand Floridian (407-824-3000, ext. 2581), the Mandara Spa at the Dolphin (407-934-4772), the salon at the Buena Vista Palace (407-827-3200), and the Casa de Belleza at Coronado Springs (407-939-3965).

BUSINESS SERVICES

Disney provides a range of services for those who simply must mix business with pleasure. Photocopiers, fax machines (also found at Guest Relations in the theme parks), and FedEx materials are available at the lobby concierge at any Walt Disney World resort. In addition, the Contemporary, Grand Floridian, Animal Kingdom Lodge, Yacht and Beach Club, Swan, Dolphin, and Coronado Springs resorts provide computers, printers, and Internet access for a fee. A video-conferencing center is located near Downtown Disney. For information, call 407-827-2000.

CAMERA NEEDS

Photo spots around the theme parks can help you capture the best shots. Hoping to photograph fireworks with a digital camera? A tripod will help.

Flash photography is not permitted inside any Walt Disney World attraction. One-time-use cameras are available at many shops throughout the World. The best selection can be found at the camera shops in each park. Also, when capturing moments with Disney characters on videotape, refrain from using camera lights. (The lights are too bright for the characters' sensitive eyes.)

Camera Supplies: If you need a battery or a memory card for your camera, head to Town Square Exposition Hall in the Magic Kingdom; the Camera Center near Spaceship Earth or World Traveler at International Gateway in Epcot; The Darkroom on Hollywood Boulevard in Disney's Hollywood Studios; or Garden Gate Gifts in Animal Kingdom. If you're traveling by plane, pack film in a carry-on bag. (Checked-baggage screening equipment will damage film.)

CAR CARE

Three gas stations with convenience stores are on the property, all of which are open 24 hours a day. One is on Buena Vista Drive across from Pleasure Island; another is on Floridian Way near the Magic Kingdom Auto Plaza. The third, near the BoardWalk resort on Buena Vista Drive, also has a car wash.

Breakdowns happen, but they don't spell disaster. All WDW roads are patrolled by security vehicles equipped with radios that can be used to call for help. If you need a tow or other services, call the AAA Car Care Center (407-824-0976). Located in the Magic Kingdom Auto Plaza, the AAA Car Care Center offers full mechanical services and free towing on-property, Monday through Saturday, 7:30 A.M. to 10 P.M. After hours, call 407-827-4777. For off-property car care, rely on Riker's Wreckers (407-855-7776 for towing; 407-238-9800 for repairs); or AAA (if you're a member).

DRINKING LAWS

In Florida, the legal drinking age is 21. Minors are permitted to accompany their parents to WDW lounges and bars, but may not sit or stand at the bar. No alcohol is served in the Magic Kingdom, but alcoholic beverages are sold in Epcot, Disney's Hollywood Studios, Animal Kingdom, and Downtown Disney.

Spirits are sold in at least one shop at most Disney resorts. Liquor may be purchased from room service at the Polynesian, Animal Kingdom Lodge, Contemporary, Grand Floridian, Yacht and Beach Club, BoardWalk, Swan, and Dolphin resorts; beer and wine are usually available for delivery at other resorts.

LOCKERS

Lockers can be found in the following theme park locations: to the right, just inside the Magic Kingdom entrance, beside Spaceship

Earth in Epcot, next to Oscar's Super Service inside the main entrance at Disney's Hollywood Studios, and just inside the entrance and to the left at Animal Kingdom. Lockers are also available at the Transportation and Ticket Center (TTC).

Items too big to fit can be checked with the locker attendant at the Magic Kingdom, at Package Pickup in Epcot, and at Guest Relations at Disney's Hollywood Studios and Animal Kingdom. Cost is about $7 per day for small lockers and $9 for large ones (plus a $5 refundable deposit). Items may not be stored overnight. Lockers are cleaned out after the park closes.

Note: Be sure to save your rental receipt; it can be used again that day to secure a locker in any of the four theme parks.

LOST & FOUND

The extensive indexing system maintained by Walt Disney World's Lost and Found department is impressive, especially when a prized possession turns up missing, whether it's false teeth or a camera. (Both have been lost in the past; the dentures were never claimed.)

If you lose (or find) something, report it at any one of these Lost and Found locations: the Transportation and Ticket Center (TTC), City Hall in the Magic Kingdom, the Guest Relations lobby in Innoventions East at Epcot, at Guest Relations in Disney's Hollywood Studios, Guest Relations near the Animal Kingdom entrance, or the Concierge at any Walt Disney World resort. At Fort Wilderness, dial 7-2726 from a comfort station telephone; from outside the campground, phone 407-824-2726.

Items lost in a theme park may be claimed on the day of the loss at the park's Lost and Found, and thereafter at the Transportation and Ticket Center (TTC) Lost and Found station. To report lost items after your visit, call

HOT TIP!

Nobody starts the day expecting to lose something. But trust us, it pays to plan ahead. Put your name and contact number on your valuables, especially cameras. Disney does a good job of tracking lost items, but it's a whole lot easier to pick a labeled camera out of the heap of look-alikes than it is to find your "little silver" one. (Yes, it happened to us. D'oh!)

407-824-4245. Hats, strollers, sunglasses, and WDW merchandise are kept for one month; everything else is kept three months.

We highly recommend attaching contact information to all camera equipment. It makes it a whole lot easier for the folks at Lost and Found to pick your camera out of the giant, silver haystack!

MAIL

Postage stamps are sold at all WDW resorts; World of Disney at Downtown Disney; at the Newsstand shop in the Magic Kingdom; at shops near the lockers in Epcot, Disney's Hollywood Studios, and Animal Kingdom.

The old-fashioned mailboxes in the theme parks are not official U.S. mailboxes, but letters (with postage) can be mailed from them. Postmarks read "Lake Buena Vista," not "Walt Disney World."

Mail may be addressed to guests, in care of their hotel. The address for all WDW resorts is Walt Disney World, P.O. Box 10000, Lake Buena Vista, FL 32830.

MEDICAL MATTERS

Travelers with chronic health problems should carry copies of all prescriptions and get names of local doctors from hometown physicians. However, Walt Disney World is equipped to deal with many types of medical emergencies. In the Magic Kingdom, next to the Crystal Palace, there is a First Aid Center staffed by a registered nurse; there is another such facility at Epcot in the Odyssey Center complex. At Disney's Hollywood Studios, the First Aid Center is inside the Guest Relations building at the main entrance. The Animal Kingdom First Aid Center is located on Discovery Island near the back side of the Creature Comforts shop.

Walt Disney World resort guests and those staying at other area hotels have access to services providing non-emergency medical care. Centra Care Walk-In Urgent Care (*www.centracare.org*), owned and operated by Florida Hospital, has 18 area locations, most near pharmacies and with X-ray facilities.

The main facility is at 12500 South Apopka Vineland Road (407-934-2273; close to Downtown Disney) and is open 8 A.M. to midnight weekdays and 8 A.M. to 8 P.M. weekends. The facility at 8014 Conroy-Windermere Road (407-291-9960; near the resorts at Universal Studios Orlando) is open 8 A.M. to 8 P.M. weekdays and 8 A.M. to 5 P.M. on weekends. One location in Kissimmee is at 7848 W. Irlo Bronson Highway (407-397-7032). It's open 8 A.M. to 8 P.M. weekdays and 8 A.M. to 5 P.M. weekends. There is also a 24-hour in-room physician service (407-238-2000).

Courtesy transportation is available from most area hotels to Centra Care clinics, and there is a no-tipping policy. Waits in walk-in clinics can be lengthy, but Centra Care drivers call ahead to learn which has the shorter wait. If you prefer to do the driving, the center that's closest to Disney property is at 12500 South Apopka Vineland Rd. (SR 535)—across from the Crossroads shopping center. It's open weekdays from 8 A.M. to midnight and weekends from 8 A.M. to 8 P.M.

The most common maladies reported by Disney guests? Sunburn, blisters, colds, fevers, earaches, and injuries from falls. For emergencies, dial 911, or call nearby Florida Hospital Celebration Health (407-303-4000) or Dr. P. Phillips Hospital (407-351-8500).

For Diabetics: All Walt Disney World parks and resorts can provide refrigeration services for insulin. All "deluxe" and "moderate" accommodations have refrigerators, and small refrigerators may be rented at other resorts for about $10 a night. The fee is waived for folks who need the fridge to store medicine, but a doctor's note may be required.

Prescriptions: Turner Drugs (407-828-8125) delivers medications to many area resorts, including those on Disney property.

MONEY

Cash, traveler's checks, American Express, MasterCard, Visa, Discover Card, Disney Visa, Diner's Club, JCB Card, Disney Dollars, and Disney gift cards are accepted as payment for most WDW charges. (Personal checks are accepted for park tickets and resort stays when presented with a credit card and valid ID.)

A Disney resort guest perk: Leave a credit card imprint at check-in, and the hotel IDs may be used to cover shop purchases, lounge and restaurant charges, and recreational fees incurred inside Walt Disney World. A bill will be sent to your home for all charges made past check-out time.

ATMs: Automated teller machines are scattered throughout Walt Disney World. Theme park locations include the Magic Kingdom (near the locker rental, in City Hall on Main Street, U.S.A., in Frontierland near the Shootin' Arcade, and in the Tomorrowland arcade); Epcot (near the main entrance, on the path between Future World and World Showcase, and in Germany); Disney's Hollywood Studios (at the entrance, inside Pizza Planet, and near Keystone Clothiers); and Animal Kingdom (near the entrance and near Chester & Hester's); plus the Transportation and Ticket Center (TTC). Most Walt Disney World resorts have ATMs; the Fort Wilderness ATM is at Pioneer Hall. Three can be found in Downtown Disney: next to Tren-D in the Marketplace, and near the West Side's House of Blues and Wetzel's Pretzels. Most bank cards and credit cards are accepted; the fees range from about $2 to $3.

Banking: SunTrust, across from Downtown Disney, offers a variety of services. Guests can get cash advances up to $5,000 on Master-Card, Discover, and Visa credit cards; receive incoming wire transfers up to $3,000 (for a $50 fee); and cash, replace, or purchase American Express traveler's checks. Fees may apply. This branch is open from 9 A.M. to 4 P.M. Monday through Thursday, and until 5 P.M. Fridays (407-828-6103 or 800-786-8787).

Disney Dollars: Money bearing the image of Mickey, Goofy, or Minnie is available for purchase at City Hall (Magic Kingdom) and Guest Relations (Epcot, Disney's Hollywood Studios, and Animal Kingdom) in $1, $5, and $10 denominations. (The exchange rate is always a buck for a buck.) Disney Dollars are accepted as cash in most of the World.

Traveler's Checks: Even the most careful vacationer occasionally loses a wallet. Traveler's checks can take the sting out of that loss. Look for promotions by banks at home in the months preceding a vacation to see if one of the major brands—American Express, MasterCard, Visa,

Citibank, and Bank of America—is available free. Stash the receipt bearing the check numbers in a place separate from the checks themselves, along with a piece of identification such as a duplicate driver's license or a spare credit card to speed the refund process should your checks get lost.

To purchase, cash, or replace American Express traveler's checks, go to the SunTrust bank across from the Downtown Disney Marketplace. (If you do not have a record of the check numbers, first contact the place where you purchased the traveler's checks. Then, an American Express referral number is required; call 800-221-7282.)

Foreign Currency Exchange: Up to $50 per person in foreign currency may be exchanged daily at Guest Relations in the theme parks, and up to $500 at the Concierge desk at WDW resorts.

PETS

No pets (other than service animals) are allowed in the theme parks, Downtown Disney, or the resorts, except at certain Fort Wilderness campsites. Of course, that's no reason to leave Fifi or Fido at home—especially when you can treat them to a pampered getaway at the new Best Friends Pet Resort, a sprawling luxury facility (don't call it a kennel!) complete with cat condos, doggy suites, and special acccommodations for "pocket pets," including birds and hamsters. Cats or dogs from shared households may share quarters, but cats *and* dogs are not permitted to cohabitate.

The facility, which is now the only place to board animals at Walt Disney World, provides a full range of hospitality services, including day care (boarding in suites), grooming services, and doggy day camp (group sessions where pups play games and frolic with other dogs under the supervision of a trained animal counselor).

Best Friends Pet Resort is located at 2510 Bonnet Creek Parkway, across from Disney's Port Orleans. Its services are available to everyone, but guests staying at Walt Disney World resorts net discounts. Indoor boarding (which includes two walks) costs $34 per day for Walt Disney World resort guests; indoor/outdoor boarding (with one walk) runs $36 a day; vacation villas (one walk, play group, flat-screen TV, and a turndown biscuit) cost $53, and VIP luxury suites (two walks, two play-groups, flat-screen TV, webcam, and bedtime story) cost $69 a day (and, with a 3-day mini-

mum, they throw in a "Go Home Fresh Bath").

To prevent separation anxiety, guests are encouraged to visit their pets during regular operating hours. Though hours vary, Best Friends is usually open from about one hour before the earliest theme park opening to about one hour after the latest park closing. The center is not open to the public 24 hours, but it is staffed round the clock (a handy service for guests experiencing travel delays or other emergencies). There are several certified veterinary technicians on staff, and all associates are trained in animal first aid. For directions, details on services or to make reservations, call 877-4-WDW-PETS (493-9738), or visit *www.wdw.bestfriendspetcare.com.*

Be sure to bring along your pet's certificate of vaccinations, since Florida law requires proof of immunization for animals involved in biting incidents. Elderly pets must be in good health with bladder and bowel control, and be mobile. It's always a good idea to pack your pet's favorite blanket or toy, too. Never leave a pet in a car—it's extremely dangerous and it's against the law.

Outside Walt Disney World: A few hotels in the Orlando area, including the Rosen Inn at Pointe Orlando (for $10 plus tax per night; 407-996-8585), let pets stay with guests. Call Visit Orlando (407-363-5872 or 800-551-0181; the latter is a recording).

RELIGIOUS SERVICES

Though religious services are occasionally offered on Disney property, regular services are available at these local houses of worship:

Protestant: Sundays at 10:30 A.M. at River of Life Presbyterian, 8323 W. Sand Lake Rd. Call 407-351-4333. Sundays at 8:15 A.M., 9:30 A.M., and 11 A.M. at the Community Presbyterian Church, 511 Celebration Ave., Celebration, FL; 407-566-1633.

Muslim: Prayer takes place five times a day at the Islamic Center of Orlando, 11543 Ruby Lake Rd. Call 407-238-2700 for more details.

Catholic: The closest Catholic church is Mary, Queen of the Universe Shrine, 2½ miles southeast of Lake Buena Vista, at 8300 Vineland Ave. This church seats 2,000 people. Call 407-239-6600 for mass times.

Jewish: Reform services are held at the Congregation of Reform Judaism (928 Malone Dr., Orlando; 407-645-0444), near Winter Park, about 20 miles from Walt Disney World. Conservative services are held at Temple Ohalei Rivka, also known as the Southwest Orlando

Jewish Congregation (11200 S. Apopka Vineland Rd.; 407-239-5444), about two miles from Downtown Disney.

SHOPPING FOR NECESSITIES

Almost any everyday item can be purchased right on the property. At least one shop in every Disney resort stocks a small selection of toiletries. In addition, over-the-counter health aids, plus many other useful items, can be purchased at the Emporium on Main Street in the Magic Kingdom; they're kept behind the counter, so ask for what you want.

Aspirin, sunscreen, and sundries are also available at Island Supply in Adventureland and Mickey's Star Traders in Tomorrowland. In Epcot, sundries are sold in at least one shop in each World Showcase pavilion and at all Future World stores. At Disney's Hollywood Studios, stop by the Crossroads of the World and Movieland Memorabilia shops. At Animal Kingdom, you can pick up "the bare necessities" at Island Mercantile.

Local supermarkets include Winn-Dixie (11957 Apopka-Vineland Rd.) and Gooding's (at Crossroads shopping complex across S.R. 535 near Hotel Plaza Boulevard). Gooding's is slightly closer to WDW, but rather pricey.

SMOKING

Disney's strict nonsmoking policy became even stricter with the adoption of the Florida Clean Air Act. Smoking is prohibited in all indoor and outdoor spaces, unless specifically designated as "smoking areas." These areas are marked on park guidemaps. All eateries are smoke-free, as are clubs and lounges. Tobacco products are not sold in the theme parks. Guests may purchase tobacco products at WDW resorts and Downtown Disney.

All Walt Disney World resort hotels are nonsmoking. Designated outdoor areas are available for those who choose to smoke. Remember, this is a statewide smoking policy, so if you venture off Disney property, the same rules apply.

Lost Adults

Occasionally, traveling companions get separated in the crush of the crowds, or someone may fail to show up at a meeting spot. When this happens, it's good to know that messages can be left for fellow travelers at Guest Relations in any of the theme parks.

TELEPHONE CALLS

It takes more than the traditional seven digits to make a local call in this neck of the woods. Every time a local call is placed in Central Florida, callers must dial the area code and the seven-digit number. The rule applies to calls made within the same area code as well as for those that connect with other area codes. For local calls, it is not necessary to dial a 1 before the ten-digit number.

Local calls made from pay phones normally cost 50 cents each. Rates charged by non-Disney resorts can vary quite a bit (for local and long-distance calls alike). Ask about rates and fees *before* you make calls beyond your resort. See page 50 for more telephone tips.

HOT TIP!
The point is to escape the real world, so turn off that cell phone—or at least stick to texting. That way the magic—for you and those around you—will be uninterrupted. If you have to make a call, do so by the nearest public phone station.

If you plan to connect to the Internet via personal computer, don't forget to bring a list of local access numbers for dial-up service. And know that even if the area code is 407, it doesn't guarantee that the exchange is a local one.

TIPPING

Tips are no less valued at Disney resorts than at any other hotel—$1 per bag is appropriate for lugging luggage; $1 to $3 per person, per night for housekeeping services (include a note to avoid confusion). Gratuities of 15 to 20 percent (excluding tax) are customary at full-service restaurants. (If service is exceptional or otherwise, adjust accordingly.) Gratuity is included in the room-service bill at WDW resorts and some off-property hotels. Note that a 10 percent gratuity is added for dining at the Pepper Market at Coronado Springs (despite the self-serve set-up).

Give cab drivers a 15 percent tip for good service. Baggage handlers at the train station and airport expect about $1 per bag.

WEATHER

Call Walt Disney World Weather Information (407-824-4104), or check The Weather Channel Web site (*www.weather.com*).

Transportation & Accommodations

The popularity of Walt Disney World has made the region around Orlando one of the world's major tourism and commercial centers, and transportation facilities, from a state-of-the-art airport to an efficient network of highways, bring visitors to the area by the millions.

There's no doubt that getting to and around the Walt Disney World region can be very confusing. The only more perplexing dilemma may be choosing the best accommodations for your group from the huge assortment of hotels and motels.

The accommodations owned and operated by Disney itself range from futuristic towers to cabins buried deep in piney woods. In between are resorts that evoke striking images of Africa, the South Pacific, historic Florida, the Pacific Northwest, the Caribbean, New England, early Atlantic City, New Orleans, the Southwest, Mexico, and the sports, movie, and music worlds, plus a sprawling, well-maintained campground. And that list doesn't include the many villas or the studios and homes with one, two, and three bedrooms that can be "purchased" through a special vacation-ownership system. What follows should help travelers sort out the broad range of lodging options within the borders of Walt Disney World. Regardless of where you plan to stay, we offer this advice: Book your room as far in advance as possible. You won't regret it.

Getting Oriented

Orlando, the Central Florida city of more than one million residents, is the municipality with which Walt Disney World is most closely associated. Walt Disney World, however, is in a far smaller community called Lake Buena Vista, 15 miles from Orlando's business center. A number of hotels and restaurants are located in Lake Buena Vista, though there are many more in Orlando.

HOT TIP!

Parking spaces are cleverly labeled throughout Walt Disney World. Yet, many drivers still misplace their vehicles. Avoid being dopey: Always write down your parking location!

ORLANDO-AREA HIGHWAYS: The most important Orlando traffic artery is I-4, which runs diagonally through the area from southwest to northeast, cutting through the southern half of Walt Disney World. It then angles on toward Orlando and Winter Park, ending near Daytona Beach at I-95, which runs north and south along the Atlantic coast.

All the city's other important highways intersect I-4, and each has a name as well as a number. From south to north, they include U.S. 192 (aka Irlo Bronson Memorial Highway), which takes an east-west course that crosses the Walt Disney World entrance road and leads into downtown Kissimmee on the east; S.R. 528, aka the Beachline Expressway (formerly the Beeline), which shoots eastward from I-4; S.R. 435 (aka Kirkman Road), which runs north and south and intersects International Drive, where many motels catering to WDW visitors are located; U.S. 17-92-441 (aka Orange Blossom Trail), which runs north and south, paralleling Kirkman Road on the east; and S.R. 50 (aka Colonial Drive), which runs east and west.

WALT DISNEY WORLD EXITS: The 40-square-mile tract that is Walt Disney World is roughly rectangular. I-4 runs through its southern half from southwest to northeast. The major Disney destinations are most efficiently reached by taking the I-4 exits suggested in the paragraphs that follow; off the highway, clear signage makes it easy for

visitors to get anywhere in the World. This road is congested more often than not. Keep in mind that construction work and special events will often require rerouting of traffic patterns on I-4, so it's best to follow signs as directed:

- **Exit 64A,** marked "192/Magic Kingdom," leads to the Magic Kingdom, Disney's Hollywood Studios, Fort Wilderness, Palm and Magnolia golf courses, and the Contemporary, Polynesian, Grand Floridian, and Wilderness Lodge resorts.
- **Exit 65** leads to the ESPN Wide World of Sports complex, Disney's Animal Kingdom, Blizzard Beach, Coronado Springs, All-Star Music, Sports, and Movies, Pop Century, and Disney's Animal Kingdom Lodge. It is also a good alternate route to Disney's Hollywood Studios park.
- **Exit 67,** marked "Epcot/Downtown Disney," leads to Epcot, Typhoon Lagoon, Downtown Disney, Lake Buena Vista golf course, Disney's Saratoga Springs Resort & Spa, the BoardWalk, Caribbean Beach, Swan, Dolphin, Yacht and Beach Club, Port Orleans Riverside and French Quarter, and Old Key West resorts.
- **Exit 68,** marked "S.R. 535/Lake Buena Vista," is the best route to the resorts on Hotel Plaza Blvd. and the Crossroads of Lake Buena Vista shopping center. It can serve as an alternate route to Epcot.

HOT TIP!

The cost to valet park a vehicle at any Walt Disney World-owned-and-operated resort is $12 per day (not including gratuity). There is no charge for self-parking for guests at any of the resorts.

WDW Transportation

Walt Disney World transportation is extensive, with boats, buses, and the monorail all doing their part to shuttle guests around. Visitors staying at WDW hotels should receive a detailed brochure about transportation options at check-in. (If you don't, just ask.) For transportation information, call 407-824-4321.

One of the system's hubs is called the Transportation and Ticket Center (TTC), located near the Magic Kingdom. Monorail, bus, and ferry service connect the TTC to points throughout the World. Day visitors must park here before taking a monorail or ferry to the Magic Kingdom. (Most Disney resort guests can bypass the TTC via direct buses.)

The monorail runs along a circular route near the Magic Kingdom, stopping at the TTC, Polynesian, Grand Floridian, Magic Kingdom, and Contemporary resorts. A separate extension of the monorail system connects the TTC to Epcot. Bus service is the cornerstone of the WDW transportation system. It is efficient (though less than it used to be), if a bit confusing. With occasional exceptions, buses arrive every 25–30 minutes or so, from one hour before park opening until about an hour after closing; bus stops are clearly marked. Travel times vary, depending on the route.

Although Disney resort guests are provided with complimentary transportation to all sites on-property, that transportation is not always direct. *Build in extra time for travel*, especially if you have made reservations at a restaurant.

Should You Rent a Car?

If you plan to spend all of your time on WDW turf, you can spare yourself the expense. Towncar and shuttle service from the airport to all area hotels is available around the clock, and taxis are another option. Within the World, an exhaustive network of transportation brings guests from point to point (if not always directly). Most area hotels offer their own bus service to and from Disney theme parks (inquire in advance about schedules and costs, if any).

However, for those planning to visit Orlando-area restaurants and any attractions outside Walt Disney World, a rental car is a must. It is easiest to rent from one of the companies at the airport: National (800-227-7368), Alamo (800-327-9633), Avis (800-331-1212), Budget (800-527-0700), or Dollar (800-800-4000). Other rental agencies provide shuttles from the airport, so it may be worth the extra time if you get a good deal. For day trips, consider Alamo or National at the Disney Car Care Center (407-824-3470; complimentary shuttle service is available), or one of the rental agencies that have desks at the resorts on Hotel Plaza Blvd., or simply inquire about car rental at the front desk of your resort. It is also possible (and easy) to rent a car from National or Alamo at the WDW Dolphin resort.

Also, know that traveling between resorts can be time consuming and usually requires at least one transfer.

From several Walt Disney World locales, water launches usher guests to the Magic Kingdom, Epcot, Disney's Hollywood Studios, Downtown Disney, or between resorts. Boats generally depart every 20 to 30 minutes.

TRANSPORTATION ID REQUIREMENTS:

Guests who wish to use the Disney transportation system may be asked for proof of riding privileges. Accepted IDs afford different degrees of access. WDW resort ID cards, Magic Your Way tickets with Park Hopper options or Water Park Fun & More options, and Annual Passes let guests use all Disney buses, monorails, and boats. Valid one-day theme park tickets permit guests to use monorails and the ferries running between the TTC and the Magic Kingdom, but do not allow use of buses.

TAXI SERVICE: Taxi cabs are available for about $3.85 for the first mile, $2.20 per extra mile. Stick with authorized cab services. Many unauthorized services charge outrageous rates. When we travel between resorts that aren't joined by boat or monorail and find ourselves pressed for time, we may splurge and take a cab. Inquire at the bell services desk at your resort's front entrance. They'll direct you to the nearest authorized taxi or order one on your behalf. (Pay attention to the route the driver takes—we've been driven in circles on many occasions.)

THE MONORAIL: The Disney World monorail system is an efficient (and to many, downright exciting) way to travel. There are two main loops, which converge at the Transportation and Ticket Center (TTC) stop. One loop connects the Contemporary, Polynesian, and Grand Floridian resorts with the Magic Kingdom and the TTC. The other loop links Epcot with the TTC. Note that guests staying in the aforementioned resorts have a private track on the Magic Kingdom loop, making for a hastier exit at closing time. Monorails run from about 7 A.M. until about one hour after park closing.

Did You Know?

The Walt Disney World monorail system—a 14.7-mile highway in the sky—has carried more than a billion passengers since 1971.

Timing Tip: It takes 3–5 minutes to get from stop to stop on the Magic Kingdom's resort monorail loop, making for a grand circle total of about 15 to 25 minutes. Note that he monorail does not run during Extra Magic Hours.

Transportation Tips

• If you are staying at a Disney resort, be sure you get the "Your Guide to the Magic" brochure at check-in.

• Most buses are equipped with wheelchair lifts. Such buses have a blue emblem on the windshield and rear door.

• When using the WDW transportation system to travel between your resort and a theme park, or from one park to another, allow an extra 45 minutes to get to your destination.

• The interval between the arrivals of most Disney buses is about 20–25 minutes.

• Be forewarned: It takes a long time to travel by bus from resort to resort. Plan on a trip of up to 90 minutes and at least one transfer (at a park or at Downtown Disney).

• Monorails usually run until two hours after the latest park closing time (one hour after Magic Kingdom Extra Magic Hours).

• Note that there is no direct transportation between Disney's BoardWalk and most other resorts. You must first travel to Downtown Disney or a park and transfer to the appropriate bus. (Or take a cab.)

• Try to avoid vacating a theme park just as it closes. Instead, plan to linger a bit in a shopping area, or grab a seat and watch the crowds crawl toward their respective buses, boats, cars, and monorails.

• It is not uncommon, especially at park opening and closing times, for guests to be asked to stand on the bus or monorail.

• Keep in mind that the most obvious mode of transportation may not be the quickest. For example, it is often faster to walk to the Magic Kingdom from the Contemporary resort than it is to take the monorail.

• It's possible to rent a car from any Disney resort. For details, inquire at the Lobby Concierge desk, or contact the front desk.

• WDW resort guests who arrive with a car receive a complimentary parking permit upon check-in. The permit, good for the length of your stay, allows you to park most places on property for free.

WDW Accommodations

With hundreds of resorts in the Orlando area to choose from, it's definitely a challenge to select a hotel. Here's our advice.

Weigh the Options: First decide whether to stay on or off Disney property. Many opt for a Disney resort because the conveniences and perks offered to resort guests are appealing (see page 66). Given that, there are still two major factors that tend to lure guests off property: vacation budget and itinerary.

Travelers on a tight budget may find off-property options that are quite reasonable. However, Disney offers rooms as low as about $89–$184 per night (depending on hotel and season), so choose off-property digs only if the price difference is substantial.

Guests who will spend only part of their trip exploring Disney may also prefer an off-property hotel—one that's closer to the other attractions on their itinerary.

There's also the issue of what one may or may not consider deluxe. Disney-owned-and-operated "deluxe" resorts do tend to provide more amenities and services than their "moderate" and "value" counterparts, but do not often rival comparably priced accommodations in the real world.

Deciding Factors: Once the on- or off-property decision has been made, it's time to look at hotels. The big differences among on-property accommodations are in the size of the rooms and bathrooms, attention to decor, level of service, dining options, transportation options, recreational facilities, landscaping, location, and, of course, cost.

Consider how much time you'll spend in the room, whether you'd like to return to the hotel during the day, and if you'll have time to use all the amenities that are included in the price. Parties with five or more members have an additional concern: how best to accommodate their group. It may be less expensive to reserve adjoining, value-priced rooms instead of one luxe room or villa. Kids age 17 and under stay free at Disney resorts, but there is a fee for each adult beyond two staying in a room.

Ask the Right Questions: Once a hotel that meets all basic criteria is selected, it's best to do one last round of research, so there will be no surprises at check-in.

For example, ask about any possible hidden costs, like shuttle service to and from Walt Disney World (which can be more than $20 per person, round-trip) or taxes that may not be included in the quoted price. Though most off-property hotels offer transportation to WDW, the frequency and number of buses vary significantly. Find out the exact schedule and the number of stops made. Ask where the bus picks up and drops off, too. Try to avoid those that stop in busy parking lots.

Some hotels advertise a misleading proximity to Disney. While a hotel may be a short distance from the border, the commute to the parks may be considerable. Get specifics. (Distance from your favorite park is also a factor to consider when staying on-property.)

Reserve a Room: Found the perfect hotel? Book it before someone else does, and don't forget to ask about any special discounts, seasonal promotions, and cancellation policies.

A Room with a View

There's a lot to be said for throwing back the curtains and gazing at a breathtaking view, provided you have the time to appreciate it and your view is within your price range. The following is a breakdown of different "views" you may select from at the various WDW resorts. It will help you determine the best view for your budget.

Although the categories vary, depending on the resort type, the "standard view" is always the lowest rate available.

Value Resorts

Standard View = Parking lot, pool, garden, and everything else

Moderate Resorts

Standard View = Parking lot or landscaping

Water View = Pool, marina, lake, river

Deluxe Resorts

Standard View = Parking lot

Garden View = Landscaping

Water View = Pool, lake, or other water

Lagoon View = Seven Seas Lagoon

Savanna View = Animal pastures (at Animal Kingdom Lodge)

Walt Disney World Resorts

Walt Disney World hotels fall into two categories: Disney-owned-and-operated and non-Disney-owned resorts. Of all the WDW properties, the Swan and Dolphin and the resorts on Hotel Plaza Boulevard don't belong to Disney. Services and benefits in these resorts are slightly modified (see pages 85 and 102).

On-Property Perks: WDW resorts offer guaranteed admission (with ticket) to the parks —even when they're filled to capacity and closed to the general public; use of the WDW transportation system; the convenience of charging most purchases to their hotel bill; and the Extra Magic Hours benefit, which allows extra time in a select park on select days. Guests who stay at a Disney-owned-and-operated resort and arrive via air at Orlando International Airport are entitled to Disney's Magical Express service (see page 15).

Room Amenities: Disney rooms have alarm clocks, a small safe, shampoo, voice mail, and TVs. There are hair dryers, irons, small refrigerators (in deluxe and moderate resorts), and coffeemakers (with coffee) in many rooms. Laundry facilities, dry cleaning, and room service are offered in most resorts (for a fee).

Resort Primer

Payment Methods: Hotel bills and room deposits may be paid by credit card, Disney Dollars and gift cards, traveler's check, money order, cash, or personal check. Checks must bear the guest's name and address, be drawn on a U.S. bank, and be accompanied by proper photo ID (a valid driver's license or government-issued passport will do the trick).

Room Deposit Requirements: When booked through Central Reservations, a deposit equal to one night's lodging (or campsite rental) is required *within 14 days* of the time that a reservation is made. Reservations are automatically canceled if deposits are not received by the 14-day deadline. (Reservations booked less than 30 days prior to arrival will receive special instructions for deposits.) Reservations booked through the Walt Disney World Travel Company are subject to a substantial cancellation fee. Ask about the cancellation policy when you book your room.

When booking by phone, guests may pay the deposit with a major credit card. Those who wish to use another payment method may do so by mailing it with the payment stub that comes with the reservation confirmation.

Cancellation Policy: With the exception of Magic Your Way packages, deposits for resort stays will be fully refunded if the reservation is canceled at least five days before the scheduled arrival. Magic Your Way packages must be canceled at least 45 days ahead.

Additional Charges: When more than two adults (age 18 and up) occupy a standard room, the added per-day fee for each extra adult is $2 at Fort Wilderness campsites; $5 at Fort Wilderness Cabins; $10 at the Pop Century and All-Star resorts; $15 at Caribbean Beach, Port Orleans French Quarter and Riverside, and Coronado Springs; and $25 at all other WDW resorts. Note that in some resorts, an extra bed may be required to sleep an extra adult. If so, beds cost $15 per night.

Check-in and Check-out: The early checkout time (11 A.M. at all WDW-owned-and-operated lodgings) and the late check-in times (1 P.M. at the campsites, 3 P.M. in most hotels, 4 P.M. at Disney Vacation Club accommodations) often come as a surprise. Guests who arrive before check-in time can pre-register, store luggage at Bell Services (without fee), and head to the parks or relax by the pool.

WDW ID Cards: Issued on guests' arrival at Disney resorts, the cards (which double as room keys) entitle guests to use of WDW transportation (through the last day of your stay) and charge privileges (provided you leave a credit card number with the hotel) to cover purchases in shops and restaurants, as well as recreational fees incurred in the World.

Note: Charges incurred on a hotel ID after check-out will be reflected in a revised bill, which will be sent by Disney. Swan and Dolphin guests may use their IDs to charge meals inside the two hotels only.

HOT TIP!

The following WDW resorts can accommodate up to 5 guests in a standard room: Grand Floridian, Yacht and Beach Club, Contemporary, Polynesian, BoardWalk, Port Orleans Riverside, and Fort Wilderness Cabins.

WALT DISNEY WORLD RESORT

DELUXE

Name & Location	Setting/Theme	Favored By	Romantic Hideaways	Kids Adore	Dining Tip	Resort Category & Amenities
Animal Kingdom Lodge* Animal Kingdom area (page 95)	African wildlife preserve	Animal lovers—nearly every room affords a view of wandering wildlife; Art aficionados—authentic African artwork abounds; Disney Vacation Club members	Private balconies by moonlight; Sunset lounge overlooking the savanna	The kopje, a rocky outcropping from which to spy on critters; Story time beside the lobby fireplace; Rustic bunk beds (on request)	Sample the exotic eats and atmosphere of Boma while savoring the sights of the savanna.	Full-service restaurants, fast-food spots, room service
BoardWalk* Epcot area (page 87)	Turn-of-the-20th-century Atlantic City	Night owls—the entertainment options are numerous and right in the backyard; Epcot lovers, who will appreciate the short commute; Disney Vacation Club members	Moonlight strolls along the boardwalk; A special fireworks cruise	The Keister Coaster, a 200-foot waterslide at the main pool; The face-painting booth on the boardwalk at night	Snack on saltwater taffy, cotton candy, or old-fashioned sticky buns while strolling along the boards.	Luggage service; Valet parking; Swimming pools; Beach access‡
Contemporary* Magic Kingdom area (page 72)	Retro-futuristic exterior, thoroughly modern interior	Families—the monorail whisks through it, and the Magic Kingdom is a short walk away; Professionals, who can take advantage of the hotel's many business services; Disney Vacation Club members	The rooftop lookout (available only to California Grill patrons) helps make up for the resort's otherwise less-than-romantic atmosphere	The "party" held every 45 minutes at Chef Mickey's fabulously fun character meals; Watching the monorail whoosh through the resort	Reserve California Grill for a time that's likely to coincide with the Magic Kingdom's Wishes fireworks show. The view is amazing.	On-site recreation, such as boat rentals‡; On-site kids' activities; Most rooms sleep five guests
Grand Floridian Magic Kingdom area (page 76)	Victorian seaside resort	Honeymooners—who will love spending much of their vacation basking in the resort's unebbing romantic atmosphere; Magic Kingdom and monorail fans	Manicured rose gardens; Honeymoon suites; The Grand Lobby for a cocktail while an orchestra performs on the balcony	Nightly marshmallow roasts and alfresco Disney films; Having dinner with Cinderella and her friends at 1900 Park Fare; Zero-depth-entry pool	Have a spot of traditional afternoon tea, accompanied by a scone, at the Garden View Lounge.	Monorail, bus, or boat transport to all parks
Polynesian Magic Kingdom area (page 74)	South Pacific	Romantics—the white-sand beaches and lush, tropical setting may make you swoon; Vacationers looking for a hotel with a real resort feel; Magic Kingdom and monorail fans	Beach coves for two, Sunset Pointe	The Tuesday–Saturday torch-lighting ceremony in the Great Ceremonial Hall; The slide- and waterfall-endowed volcano pool	The Spirit of Aloha dinner show is favored by many for its entertainment and revamped menu.	‡Except Disney's Animal Kingdom Lodge

❣ This resort hosts character meals.   * Animal Kingdom Lodge, Beach Club, BoardWalk, Contemporary, and Wilderness Lodge also have Vacation Club accommodations.   **Wilderness Cabins are considered "moderate."   ‡Except Disney's Animal Kingdom Lodge

DELUXE   DISNEY VACATION CLUB

Name & Location	Setting/ Theme	Favored By	Romantic Hideaways	Kids Adore	Dining Tip	Resort Category & Amenities
Swan & Dolphin Epcot area (page 85)	Beachfront whimsy	Guests who want many of the Disney perks but not necessarily the Disney hotel Bargain hunters—when WDW resorts are "peak," these resorts may offer discounts	A secluded area behind the grotto pool waterfall	The swan-shaped pedal boats The giant swan and dolphin statues perched atop their respective resorts	The Swan's Kimonos Lounge serves sushi with a side of karaoke.	Full-service restaurants, fast-food spots, room service Luggage service Valet parking Swimming pools Beach access‡ On-site recreation, such as boat rentals‡ On-site kids' activities Many rooms sleep five guests Monorail, bus, or boat transport to all parks ‡Except Disney's Animal Kingdom Lodge
Wilderness Lodge* Magic Kingdom area (page 78)	America's grandest national parks	Sweethearts—love is always in the air at this resort Winter visitors—the warm, cozy atmosphere is even more inviting when the many fireplaces are roaring Disney Vacation Club members	Steamy, bubbling "hot springs" whirlpools The cozy alcoves hidden on each floor of the main building	Totem poles, an erupting geyser, and countless Hidden Mickeys—there's even a free tour to help guests find them	Sample berry cobbler or the cedar plank salmon—Artist Point signature dishes Savor morning coffee from a fireside rocking chair	
Yacht & Beach Club* Epcot area (page 82)	Martha's Vineyard and Nantucket Island	Ambitious guests—those who plan to see and do everything Disney has to offer will like the central location Everyone—deluxe atmosphere and amenities appeal to all Disney Vacation Club members	The Yacht Club's peaceful gazebo Secluded whirlpools The beach—perfect for twilight strolls	Stormalong Bay—the sand-bottomed, three-acre pool, with a waterslide and a shipwreck to play on	Cape May Cafe's bountiful nighttime clambake has many a surf-and-turf fan lining up for more	
Disney's Old Key West Downtown Disney area (page 93)	Key West	Guests looking for a homey, village atmosphere Disney Vacation Club members Those who appreciate roomy rooms	Private whirlpool tubs—they come with all accommodations but the studios	The weekly Tiny Tot Tea Parties and Un-Birthday Parties with snacks, games, and treats, held at Community Hall One super pool slide	Olivia's pleases all palates with a nice mix of pastas and fresh fish. The conch chowder is a yummy way to start a meal.	Kitchens, restaurants, pizza delivery Luggage service Swimming pools On-site recreation, such as boat rentals Front-door parking Villas sleep 4–12 Bus or boat transport to all parks Washers and dryers Boat to Downtown Disney
Disney's Saratoga Springs Resort & Spa Downtown Disney area (page 92)	Historic Saratoga Springs, New York	Peace seekers—the atmosphere is meant to soothe Disney Vacation Club members Space seekers. The accommodations are generally more spacious than at other resorts.	Pretty gardens and meandering pathways Private whirlpool tubs—they come with all accommodations but the studios	The kids-only water-spray area near the pool Kid-oriented activities at Community Hall	Turf Club is a low-key, local dining room. Downtown Disney's tempting array of eateries is a mere stone's throw away.	

MODERATE (amenities)
- Restaurant, food court, limited room service
- Luggage service
- Swimming pools with slides
- On-site recreation, such as bikes and boat rentals
- Rooms sleep four guests
- Bus transport to all parks

VALUE (amenities)
- Food court, pizza delivery
- Luggage service
- Swimming pools
- Bus transport to all parks

FT. WILDERNESS (amenities)
- Recipient of perfect ratings from *Trailer Life* and *Woodall's* magazines
- Bus transport to all parks

Caribbean Beach — Epcot area (page 81)
Theme: Tropical islands

Families—the colorful design, themed pool, and beach setting make this hotel ideal for families. Pirate fans! The main pool and about 400 rooms have a buccaneer theme.

- Aruba beach—the hotel's longest, most secluded strip of sand
- The fortress pool and Caribbean Cay Island. The coconut postcards sold at the Calypso shop (real coconuts!)
- Try a food court kid's meal—it's served in a sand bucket with a shovel.

Coronado Springs — Animal Kingdom area (page 97)
Theme: Mexico and Southwest USA

Conventioneers—which means more business services (and a health club), higher food prices, and slightly less family entertainment than at the other moderate resorts

- The waterfront in the peaceful Casitas area. The gazebo-style boat-rental dock at twilight
- The Dig Site—which encompasses the resort's playground and main pool with its Mayan temple waterslide
- Carry-out items at the Pepper Market food court are spared the 10 percent gratuity charge.

Port Orleans French Quarter and Riverside — Downtown Disney area (pages 90–92)
Theme: New Orleans French Quarter and Antebellum South, respectively

Lovebirds on a budget—the Riverside decor is like many of Disney's deluxe hotels, as is the romance factor, but the price is considerably less. The French Quarter provides a peaceful, urban alternative

- Any room in Magnolia Bend's stately mansions. The peaceful gardens scattered about the Riverside quarters
- The pool, fishing hole, and playground at the Riverside's Ol' Man Island. The French Quarter's Doubloon Lagoon—a sea serpent-themed family pool
- Sample the fresh beignets from the food court. You'll think you're in Jackson Square.

All-Star Movies, Music, & Sports — Animal Kingdom area (page 94)
Theme: Comic book

Penny savers of all ages—these resorts offer fun, colorful theming, plus all the WDW perks, at a much lower price than at other Disney resorts. Space cravers adore the Family Suites at All-Star Music

- All-Star Music's Jazz and Broadway areas (note that Music tends to attract more couples without kids than the other two themes)
- Awe-inspiring, super-size icons—the movie and sports themes score the highest points. Extra-large arcades
- Pick up a pizza at the pickup window in the food court and have a pizza party.

Pop Century — Animal Kingdom area (page 98)
Theme: American pop culture

Budget watchers and nostalgia buffs—this sprawling resort celebrates pop history with bright colors and big icons. Young athletes and their families—ESPN Wide World of Sports is located nearby

- Sipping specialty cocktails poolside
- The state-of-the-art arcade. Wildly oversize cell phones, yo-yos, bowling pins, and more. The interactive water fountain near the playground
- The refillable mug, good for use at the food court and throughout your stay, definitely scores points as far as bargains go.

Fort Wilderness Cabins** and Campground — Magic Kingdom area (page 79)
Theme: Rustic woods

Seasoned RV enthusiasts—Disney's hookups are considered top-notch. Families—who appreciate the modern amenities of the cabins, which fit six and fall into Disney's "moderate" category

- The Fort Wilderness beach at night—perfect for viewing the Electrical Water Pageant on Bay Lake
- Pony rides, wagon rides, a blacksmith's shop, and campfire marshmallow roasts
- Join the nightly campfire circle and roast marshmallows with Chip and Dale.

---

* Animal Kingdom Lodge, Beach Club, BoardWalk, Contemporary, and Wilderness Lodge also have Vacation Club accommodations.   **Wilderness Cabins are considered "moderate."

❤ This resort hosts character meals.

Rates* at WDW Properties

	Value	Regular	Peak*
DELUXE‡			
Animal Kingdom Lodge			
Rooms (sleep 4 to 5)	$265–$440	$330–$515	$390–$580
Rooms–Club Level (5)	$385–$420	$460–$495	$535–$570
BoardWalk Inn			
Rooms (5)	$345–$485	$400–$540	$475–$610
Rooms–Club Level (5 to 6)	$500–$735	$570–$820	$650–$900
Contemporary			
Rooms–Garden Building (5)	$315–$450	$365–$505	$390–$560
Rooms–Tower (5)	$440–$525	$495–$585	$565–$665
Rooms–Club Level (4)	$580–$670	$665–$765	$790–$1,630
Grand Floridian Resort & Spa			
Rooms (5)	$460–$585	$505–$655	$595–$780
Rooms–Club Level (5)	$570–$1,250	$665–$1,390	$790–$1,630
Polynesian			
Rooms (5)	$405–$595	$465–$650	$535–$780
Rooms–Club Level (5)	$545–$725	$610–$805	$725–$930
Swan & Dolphin (Rates were accurate at press time, but are likely to change. Call 800-227-1500 for updates.)			
Rooms–Standard View (4)	$159–$409	$169–$429	$179–$469
Rooms–Upgraded View (4)	$184–$485	$194–$505	$204–$545
Suites (5 to 10)	$309–$4,000	$319–$4,000	$329–$4,230
Wilderness Lodge			
Rooms (4)	$265–$390	$325–$445	$390–$520
Rooms–Club Level (4)	$425–$615	$495–$720	$570–$1,270
Yacht & Beach Club‡			
Rooms (5)	$335–$480	$390–$530	$465–$580
Rooms–Club Level (5)	$475–$725	$545–$815	$615–$875
DISNEY VACATION CLUB			
Animal Kingdom Lodge Villas			
Studios (4)	$300–$445	$335–$495	$410–$565
Villas (4–12)	$435–$1,690	$500–$1,935	$595–$2,165
Beach Club Villas			
Studios (4)	$345–$355	$400–$410	$475
Villas (4–8)	$500–$710	$565–$925	$660–$1,150
BoardWalk Villas			
Studios (5)	$345–$370	$400–$410	$475
Villas (4–12)	$500–$1,735	$565–$1,980	$580–$2,195
Bay Lake Towers (at Contemporary)			
Studios (4)	$415–$495	$475–$560	$550–$630
Villas (4–8)	$515–$1,900	$575–$2,160	$670–$2,405
Disney's Old Key West			
Studios (4)	$315–$330	$355–$365	$415
Vacation Homes (4–12)	$435–$1,340	$490–$1,495	$565–$1,675

* Rates for Friday and Saturday night stays are generally higher than other days. Call 407-939-7639 for specifics.

	Value	Regular	Peak*
DISNEY VACATION CLUB (continued)			
Disney's Saratoga Springs Resort & Spa			
Studios (4)	$315–$330	$355–$365	$415
Villas (4–8)	$435–$1,340	$490–$1,495	$565–$1,675
The Villas at Wilderness Lodge			
Studios (4)	$355–$365	$405–$415	$490
Villas (4–8)	$485–$720	$555–$925	$680–$1,090
MODERATE			
Caribbean Beach			
Rooms (4)	$159–$234	$180–$255	$204–$279
Coronado Springs‡			
Rooms (4)	$164–$219	$180–$240	$209–$264
Port Orleans French Quarter and Riverside			
Rooms (4)	$159–$189	$180–$210	$204–$234
Fort Wilderness Cabins			
Cabins (6)	$285–$315	$340–$355	$375–$405
VALUE			
All-Star Movies, All-Star Music‡, and All-Star Sports			
Rooms (4)	$84–$117	$107–$149	$134–$174
Family Suites (6)	$198–$229	$254–$294	$305–$355
Art of Animation			
Rooms (4)	$94–$112	$119–$139	$144–$169
Suites (6)	$248–$279	$304–$344	$355–$405
Pop Century			
Rooms (4)	$89–$127	$114–$159	$139–$184
FORT WILDERNESS CAMPGROUND			
Fort Wilderness Campsites			
Sites with partial hookup (10)	$48–$52	$66	$78
Sites with full hookup (10)	$64–$68	$83	$100
Preferred/Premium sites (10)	$70–$83	$92–$105	$108–$119

2012 Value rates apply: January 2 to February 15 and August 5 to September 27 for all Value and Moderate resorts; January 2 to February 15 and August 5 through October 4 for Campsites; January 2 to February 15 and August 19 to September 27 for all other WDW properties. **2012 Regular rates apply:** February 26 to March 8 and April 15 to May 31 for all Value and Moderate resorts; April 15 to August 4 for Campsites; February 26 to March 8 and April 15 to July 14 for all other WDW properties (except Swan and Dolphin). **2012 Peak rates apply:** February 16 to February 25 and March 9 to April 14 for all WDW properties (except Swan and Dolphin). **2012 Pre-holiday rates apply:** October 5 to December 20 (Campsites only). **2012 Holiday (higher than peak) rates apply:** December 21–31. **2012 Summer rates apply:** June 1 to August 4 (Value and Moderate resorts only). **2012 Fall rates apply:** September 28 to December 20 for all Value and Moderate resorts; October 21 to December 20 for all other WDW properties (except Swan and Dolphin and Fort Wilderness Campsites).

Room capacity: Numbers in parentheses reflect maximum occupancy based on existing beds. A trundle bed (for one) can be rented at some properties for $15 a day. Playpen-like cribs can be requested for free in most resorts. Rates include up to two adults. There is an additional charge for each extra adult in a room.

CALL 407-934-7639 FOR RESERVATIONS

Note: The prices provided here were correct at press time, but rates are likely to change. Charge is for one-day, single or double occupancy. ‡ For information about suites, call 407-934-7639.

Magic Kingdom Area

Contemporary & Bay Lake Tower

Watching the monorail trains disappear into the Contemporary's 15-story A-frame tower never fails to impress. The sleek trains look like long spaceships docking as they glide inside the resort.

Passengers, for their part, are impressed by the cavernous lobby, with its tiers of balconies and, at its center, the soaring 90-foot-high, floor-to-ceiling tile mural depicting scenes from the Southwest. (Look carefully and you may spot the five-legged goat.)

This imposing structure has 655 rooms in its main tower and garden building, plus those in Bay Lake Tower—one of the newest additions to the Disney Vacation Club. There are shops, restaurants, snack bars, lounges, a marina, beach, health club, and more. The pool area incorporates two whirlpools and a waterslide. The convention center offers business services. One of the resort's most notable features is its 15th-floor observation deck. From here, guests dining at the resort's California Grill can enjoy a bird's-eye view of the Magic Kingdom. Another bonus: a walking path to the Magic Kingdom (it's a 10- to 15-minute stroll away).

The 14th floor boasts more than 20 new "health and wellness" suites—featuring environmentally friendly design elements, relaxing scents, a custom menu featuring organic food for the concierge lounge and private dining, in-suite cardio fitness equipment, and more. Other amenities include express check-in and check-out, complimentary continental breakfast, evening refreshments, and nightly turn-down service. The 12th floor also provides guests with special club-level privileges. To contact the Contemporary, call 407-824-1000.

ROOMS: Boasting a sleek and truly contemporary design, the rooms here are evenly apportioned among the main tower and garden building. All rooms located in the tower have private balconies and views of Bay Lake or the Magic Kingdom. Most rooms can accommodate five guests (plus a child under 3). Typical units have a daybed and two queen-size beds; some rooms have a king-size bed and a daybed. The bedding is a cut above most Disney resorts.

PHOTO BY JILL SAFRO

And every room has a flat-screen TV.

Business-minded folks rejoice over the desk space and high-speed Internet connection (for a fee). While the ceiling fans have gone away, room temperature may be set as low as 65 degrees. Note that the bathrooms here, though elegant in design, are a bit baffling. There's not much shelf or counter space, the flat sinks tend to stay damp, and the sliding doors don't lock.

Connecting rooms may be requested, though not guaranteed. A variety of suites, consisting of a living room and one or two bedrooms, can accommodate 4 to 8 people. There is free weekday newspaper delivery. Other amenities include hair dryers and coffeemakers.

Warning: The monorail can be heard from lower rooms in the main tower. For maximum quiet, request a park view on a higher floor or stay in the garden wing. Of course, all rooms get serenaded by the nightly fireworks at the nearby Magic Kingdom park.

The 15-story Bay Lake Tower, a Disney Vacation Club property that sits next to the Contemporary and is connected by a covered walkway, mimics the colors and strong horizontal lines of its neighbor (one of the original resorts on Walt Disney World property). The tower's crescent shape hugs a lakeside pool.

Studios sleep up to four and offer a kitchenette, queen-size bed, and double sleeper sofa. Sleeping up to five, the one-bedroom villas have full kitchens, two bathrooms, a king-size bed in the master bedroom and queen sleeper sofa, and a sleeper chair in the living room. Two-bedroom villas sleep up to nine, and the two-story grand villas sleep up to 12. All configurations feature a flat-panel TV.

WHERE TO EAT: In addition to the many restaurants and snack spots, 24-hour room service provides a wide range of offerings.

California Grill: On the 15th floor. The specialty is California fare—flatbreads, grilled meats, seafood, and market vegetables. An added treat: the spectacular view of the Magic Kingdom fireworks for dining guests.

Chef Mickey's: Located on the fourth floor. Mickey and his friends host daily buffets. Breakfast features Mickey Mouse waffles as well as more traditional items. Dinner offers carved meats, nightly specials, and a variety of entrées, plus a sundae and dessert bar.

Contempo Cafe: A quick-service spot with freshly prepared fare (there's a "grab and go" selection, too), this snack bar is on the fourth floor, next to Chef Mickey's.

The Wave . . . of American Flavors: A snazzy spot on the first floor, this eatery offers healthy and creative fare all day.

WHERE TO DRINK: The Magic Kingdom's no-alcohol policy does not trickle over to its nearest neighbor.

California Grill Lounge: On the resort's 15th floor, adjoining the California Grill. Picture windows provide a dramatic backdrop for sipping California wines and other drinks, and nibbling on appetizers. Seating is limited.

Contemporary Grounds: This lobby coffee bar serves cappuccino, espresso, latte, and other gourmet coffees, plus pastries and snacks.

Outer Rim: On the fourth-floor concourse, overlooking Bay Lake. Serves appetizers, cocktails, and specialty drinks.

Sand Bar and Cove Bar: These poolside spots offer drinks, fruit plates, and light snacks from the grill.

The Wave . . . of American Flavors Lounge: Inside The Wave restaurant, this hip spot serves a vast array of wine, cocktails, beer, and appetizers.

WHAT TO DO: Volleyball nets may be set up on the beach. Waterskiing, wakeboarding, parasailing, and fishing excursions may be arranged (see *Sports* for details).

Arcade: Game Station, a spacious arcade, can be found on the resort's fourth floor.

Bass Fishing: See page 226.

Boating: Sea Raycer motorboats, Boston Whaler Montauks, and other boats may be rented at the resort's marina.

Health Club: The Olympiad Fitness Center has strength machines, bicycles, sauna, treadmills, lockers, and massage (by appointment). Equipment use is free to WDW resort guests.

Parasailing: Supervised excursions are offered at the marina. Cost is about $95 per person, or $170 for two to ride tandem. Reservations are necessary; call 407-939-0754.

Salon: Contemporary Resort Salon on the third floor of the tower provides haircuts, facials, manicures, and other services.

Shopping: The fourth-floor concourse is home to several shops. Fantasia sells character merchandise, including plush animals and clothing for kids. Fantasia Market has newspapers, magazines, books, snacks, and liquor. Bay View Gifts (BVG) carries character merchandise and apparel for adults, items with the Contemporary resort logo, jewelry, souvenirs, home decor items, kitchenware, and candy.

Swimming: In addition to a round, lakeside pool, the free-form pool features a 17-foot-high curving slide, interactive squirt zone for little ones, and a whirlpool or two. Life jackets may be borrowed at no cost. Private cabanas can be rented at Bay Lake pool near the marina. Call 407-W-DISNEY for pricing and to make reservations.

Tennis: Two tennis courts are available to guests of the Contemporary resort and Bay Lake Tower. No charge.

Watercraft Excursions: Guided excursions on personal Jet Ski-like watercraft are offered for $80 per half hour or $135 per hour. Call 407-939-0754.

Waterskiing, Wakeboarding, Tubing: Ski boats with instructors may be rented for $85 per half hour or $165 per hour at the marina. Call 407-939-0754 for reservations and pricing.

TRANSPORTATION: The Contemporary resort is connected to the Transportation and Ticket Center (TTC) and the Magic Kingdom by monorail. From the TTC, Epcot can be reached by transferring to another monorail. Buses take guests to Disney's Hollywood Studios, Animal Kingdom, Blizzard Beach, Typhoon Lagoon, and Downtown Disney. Watercraft travel from the marina to Fort Wilderness and Wilderness Lodge.

Polynesian

The Polynesian resort is as close an approximation of the real thing as Walt Disney World's designers could create. The vegetation is lush, and the architecture summons the tropics. The mood is set by a three-story garden that occupies most of the lobby. Water cascades over craggy volcanic rocks, while coconut palms tower over about 75 different species of tropical and subtropical plants.

The structure that contains this mass of greenery, the Great Ceremonial House, is the central building in the Polynesian complex. The front desk, shops, and most of the restaurants are located here. Flanking the Ceremonial House on either side are 11 two- and three-story village longhouses named for various Pacific islands. These structures house the resort's 847 rooms. The monorail stops at this hotel, making it a convenient place to stay; in fact, it's just a short ride to the Magic Kingdom.

Club-level service offers such amenities as

Did You Know?

The white sand on the beaches near the Polynesian and Grand Floridian resorts and along the Seven Seas Lagoon actually came from the bottom of Bay Lake, located behind the Contemporary resort.

express check-in, continental breakfast, cookies and soft drinks every afternoon, hors d'oeuvres and desserts in the evening, and a lounge with a prime view of the Seven Seas Lagoon and Cinderella Castle (not to mention the nightly fireworks displays in the Magic Kingdom). Club-level rooms and suites are located in the Tonga and Hawaii buildings. The telephone number for the Polynesian is 407-824-2000.

ROOMS: Many of the rooms have balconies, and most have a view of the gardens, Seven Seas Lagoon, or one of the resort's swimming pools; rooms in the Tokelau, Tahiti, and Rapa Nui buildings are the largest. Many rooms have two queen-size beds and a daybed, and can accommodate five guests (plus a child under age 3). Adjoining rooms may be requested. The resort's suites—located exclusively in the Tonga building—can accommodate four to nine guests. Some have a king-size bed in the bedroom and one queen-size bed in the parlor. Amenities include a flat-screen TV, high-speed Internet access (for a fee), coffeemaker (with coffee), hair dryer, small refrigerator, and ceiling fans. This is one of a few Walt Disney World resorts to offer snacks and soft drinks via vending machines.

WHERE TO EAT: A variety of specialties are available from room service between 6:30 A.M. and midnight. Also, some interesting eating spots are located here.

Capt. Cook's: On the lobby level of the Great Ceremonial House. This is a good spot for light fare 24 hours a day. In addition to packaged salads and sandwiches, look for items such as sushi and fresh fruit. There is a made-to-order section—not to mention a high-tech ordering system. This is the place to head when you wish to fill your Polynesian Resort Refillable Mug. (For a one-time purchase fee of about $15, you're entitled to unlimited soft-drink refills at this location for the length of your stay.)

Kona Cafe: On the second floor of the Great Ceremonial House. This family restaurant serves lunch and dinner with an Asian flair, while the breakfast menu is filled with traditional American selections.

Kona Island: A coffee bar by day, this spot delivers one of the best cups of coffee you'll get in all of Walt Disney World. The coffee bar is usually open until about noon. Come 5 P.M., this casual corner morphs into a surprisingly satisfying sushi bar. Kona coffee is proffered

in the evenings, too—as are bags of freshly ground coffee beans.

'Ohana: On the second floor of the Great Ceremonial House. 'Ohana serves family-style dinners roasted in a large fire pit. Disney characters host a breakfast every morning.

WHERE TO DRINK: The Polynesian theme has inspired a whole raft of deceptively potent potables. As might be expected, both the drink offerings and the settings in which they are served are as tropical as they come.

Barefoot Bar: Adjoining the volcano pool zone; open seasonally.

Tambu Lounge: There's a tropical air about this lounge adjoining 'Ohana. The bar serves appetizers and exotic specialty drinks. Sporting events are shown on a large TV.

WHAT TO DO: A wide range of activities is available at the Polynesian, including a jogging path. Fishing excursions can also be arranged.

Arcade: Located near Capt. Cook's, this small spot offers a variety of games.

Bass Fishing: See page 226 or call 407-WDW-BASS (939-2277).

Boating: Several types of sailboats, Sea Raycer boats, Boston Whaler Montauks, and pontoon boats may be rented at the marina. Specialty cruises are available.

Children's Program: The Never Land Club is a supervised activity program for (potty-trained) kids ages 3 through 12. It's offered between 4 P.M. and midnight. The cost is about $12 per hour. Reservations are necessary; call 407-WDW-DINE (939-3463).

Shopping: BouTiki is the place for swimwear, resort-wear, souvenirs, and more. Trader Jack's sells Disney souvenirs, toys, newspapers, magazines, and fashions. It's also stocked with food, spirits, soft drinks, snacks, and other fixings for an impromptu room party. Wyland Galleries of Florida features art with a marine-life motif.

Swimming: There are two pools here: the unguarded elliptical East Pool, in the shadow of the Tokelau, Hawaii, Tuvalu, Rapa Nui, and Tahiti buildings; and the larger free-form Nanea Volcano pool, found closer to the marina and main beach. The latter is a popular volcano-themed watering hole, complete with slide and zero-depth entry. It appeals to swimmers of all ages. Note that a limited number of wheelchairs are available to borrow for use in the pool. Guests often get waterlogged into the wee hours of the morning in these parts (though the lifeguards go home at night). Toddlers have their own sprinkler area nearby. The beaches are strictly for sunbathing, sandcastle-building, and snoozing.

TRANSPORTATION: The Polynesian resort is on the monorail line to the Magic Kingdom and the Transportation and Ticket Center (TTC). From the TTC, Epcot can be reached by transferring to another monorail. Buses take guests to Disney's Hollywood Studios, Animal Kingdom, Blizzard Beach, Typhoon Lagoon, and Downtown Disney. Watercraft travel from the marina to Magic Kingdom.

Category Conundrum

Value vs. Moderate vs. Deluxe—which resort category is best for you? Categories reflect the price of a room, the style of the accommodation, and the level of service.

• Deluxe properties (the most expensive) are defined by their larger, practically appointed rooms, several restaurants, and such amenities as extended room service hours. This category generally includes Disney Vacation Club properties.

• Fort Wilderness Camping covers campsites, but not Wilderness Cabins (which fall into the Moderate resort category).

• Moderate properties (in the middle range, price-wise) feature comfortably sized rooms, full-service restaurants and food courts, and bellhop luggage service.

• Value properties (the least expensive resort category) offer fewer frills and smaller quarters. Meals are provided at food courts. Recreation and transportation options at these resorts are limited.

Grand Floridian Resort & Spa

At the turn of the century, Standard Oil magnate Henry M. Flagler saw the realization of his dream: The railroad he had built to "civilize" Florida had spawned along its right-of-way an empire of grand hotels, lavish estates, prominent families, and opulent lifestyles. High society blossomed in winter, as the likes of John D. Rockefeller and Teddy Roosevelt checked into the Royal Poinciana in Palm Beach, enjoying the sea breezes from the oceanside suites.

The hotel later burned to the ground, and Florida's golden era faded with the Depression. But nearly a century after Flagler first made Florida a fashionable resort destination, Walt Disney World opened a grand hotel—an 867-room Victorian structure with gabled roofs and carved moldings—on 40 acres of Seven Seas Lagoon shorefront, between the Magic Kingdom and the Polynesian.

Like its late-19th-century predecessors, the Grand Floridian resort boasts abundant verandahs, ceiling fans, intricate latticework and balustrades, turrets, towers, and red-shingle roofs. And yet, it offers all the advantages of modern living, including monorail service. With five restaurants, two lounges, five shops, and an arcade, plus a kids' activity center, convention center, two pools, a marina, and full-service health club and spa, the Grand Floridian is not only a grand hotel but a complete resort.

The main building houses the Grand Lobby, a palatial space soaring five stories to a ceiling of stained-glass domes and glittering chandeliers. Palms and an aviary decorate the sitting area; an open-cage elevator carries guests to the shops and restaurants on the second floor.

The turn-of-the-20th-century theme is everywhere, from the costumes worn by the employees to the shop displays, restaurants, and room decor. The telephone number for the Grand Floridian resort is 407-824-3000.

ROOMS: The rooms are filled with charm, decorated as they might have been a century ago—with printed wall coverings, marble-topped sinks, ceiling fans, and Victorian woodwork. Amenities include hair dryer, bathrobes, mini fridge, flat-panel TV, clock radio with iPod dock, nightly turndown service, coffeemaker, weekday newspaper delivery, and high-speed Internet service (for a fee).

The main building houses club-level rooms and suites; lodge buildings, each four and five stories high, contain standard rooms, slightly smaller "attic" chambers, and suites. Most rooms measure about 400 square feet and include two queen-size beds, plus a daybed, to accommodate up to five people. Many rooms have terraces. Suites include a parlor, plus one, two, or three bedrooms; there are queen-size beds in the bedrooms. Most of the 15 Deluxe King Rooms, located on the second, third, fourth, and fifth floors, enjoy wonderful views.

On the third floor, the club-level desks offer such services as reservations and information. The fourth floor features a quiet seating area where continental breakfast and evening refreshments are served. Club-level service is also available in the Sugarloaf building.

WHERE TO EAT: Most restaurants and lounges are located on the first two floors of the main building. Room service is available 24 hours a day.

Citricos: The largest of the hotel's restaurants is also the newest. It features market-fresh cuisine from southern Europe. Open for dinner only. Some seating affords excellent views of the nightly fireworks presentation at the Magic Kingdom.

Gasparilla Grill & Games: This 24-hour snack bar offers light items for all-day dining and snacking, plus a selection of video games.

Grand Floridian Cafe: Its peaches-and-cream color scheme and verandah-like feel make this a great place for a quick sit-down meal. All meals are served.

Narcoossee's: This casual restaurant and bar has a romantic shoreline location. The ever-changing menu includes such delectables as roast lamb chops and seafood. Guests may sip cocktails on the verandah.

1900 Park Fare: A buffet restaurant decorated with carousel horses, plants, and Big Bertha, the carnival organ. Characters host breakfast and dinner daily.

Victoria & Albert's: The eatery is named after the former queen and prince consort of England. Meals are served to no more than 60 guests (ages 10 and up) per seating. Jackets are required for men, and reservations are a must.

WHERE TO DRINK: Guests will find the refined lounges here to be lovely escapes. Citricos and Narcoossee's both have bars, complete with a full menu for dining. Drinks (bought in Mizner's Lounge) may also be enjoyed in the majestic lobby.

Citricos: Proof that good things come in small packages (seven barstools and 10 or so tables), this lounge has an extensive wine list, specialty coffees, and full menu.

Garden View Tea Room: This pretty spot offers a view of the hotel's lush, landscaped garden and pool area. Afternoon tea is served (as are finger sandwiches and small desserts).

Mizner's Lounge: Named after the eccentric, wildly prolific architect who defined much of the flavor of Florida's Palm Beach County, this bar is on the second floor.

Narcoossee's: Located in the heart of the restaurant, this lounge offers more than 40 wines by the glass, plus a full bar and menu.

Pool Bar: The place for pool and beachside refreshments, this spot features a variety of snacks and beverages.

WHAT TO DO: The Grand Floridian offers all the recreational facilities of a beach resort. Fishing excursions can be arranged (refer to the *Sports* chapter for details).

Arcade: Gasparilla Grill & Games is on the first floor of the main building.

Bass Fishing: See page 226.

Boating: Sailboats, Boston Whaler Montauks, pontoon boats, and Sea Raycer speedboats are available for rent (by the hour or half hour) at Captain's Shipyard Marina. The *Grand 1* yacht (including a captain and first mate) can be rented for $450 an hour and accommodates up to 18 guests.

Campfire and Sing-a-long: Guests are invited to gather round the campfire on a nightly basis and join in a "campy" sing-a-long on the shores of Seven Seas Lagoon. Marshmallows and s'mores kits may be purchased. Afterward, everyone is treated to a screening of a Disney film on the beach.

Children's Programs: The Mouseketeer Club is a supervised program for (potty-trained) kids ages 3 through 12. It's open from 4:30 P.M. to midnight; the cost is about $12 per hour for each child. Reservations are required; call 407-WDW-DINE (939-3463). Kids may also embark on a special Pirate Adventure or enjoy a princess tea. (See page 216 of the *Everything Else in the World* chapter.) For additional information call 407-WDW-DINE (939-3463).

Golf: The resort is conveniently close to Disney's Magnolia, Palm, and Oak Trail golf courses. Call 407-WDW-GOLF (939-4653), or visit *www.disneyworldgolf.com* for information or to reserve tee times.

Health Club: The health club has exercise machines, saunas, whirlpools, and steam rooms.

Salon: The Ivy Trellis salon offers a full line of hair-care services.

Shopping: On the first floor of the main building is Summer Lace, specializing in women's resort-wear and swimwear, and Sandy Cove, for gifts, sundries, and home decor. One level up is the cheerful M. Mouse Mercantile character shop, Basin for bath supplies, and Commander Porter's, a men's shop.

Spa: The spa offers massage, herbal wraps, and aromatherapy; *www.relaxedyet.com*. There are some spa treatments for children.

Swimming: There are two large pools and a kiddie pool for guests to splash in. The pool nearest the spa is a zero-depth-entry pool and features a 181-foot slide.

Tennis: There are two clay courts. Cost is about $13 per hour, per person. Lessons are available. For reservations, call 407-621-1991.

TRANSPORTATION: The Grand Floridian is connected to the Transportation and Ticket Center (TTC) and Magic Kingdom by monorail. From the TTC, Epcot can be reached by transferring to another monorail. Buses take guests to Disney's Hollywood Studios, Animal Kingdom, Blizzard Beach, Typhoon Lagoon, and Downtown Disney. Watercraft travel from the marina to Magic Kingdom.

Wilderness Lodge & Villas

This resort recalls the spirit of the early American West and the feeling of the National Park Service lodges built during the early 1900s. These grand structures architecturally unified the elements of the unspoiled wilderness parks, kept harmony with nature, and incorporated the culture of Native Americans. The Wilderness Lodge artfully recaptures this rustic charm.

The resort is located between the Contemporary resort and Fort Wilderness on Bay Lake. The lobby, which is shared by the lodge and villas, is in an eight-story, log-structured building. Massive bundled log columns support a series of trusses, while two Pacific Northwest totem poles soar 55 feet into the air. Four levels of corridors surround the lobby, providing access to guestrooms, sitting nooks, and terraces. The monorail does not stop here. Club-level service is available on the top floor. The telephone number for the Wilderness Lodge and Villas is 407-824-3200.

ROOMS: Most of the 727 guestrooms have two queen-size beds and a balcony. Some have a queen-size bed and bunk beds. The bathrooms have separate vanity areas with double sinks. The wallpaper has a Native American-motif border, and the colorful bedspreads and plaid curtains add to the decor. Images of wildlife complete the theme. Rooms include an iron (with board), hair dryer, coffeemaker (with coffee), mini fridge, high-speed Internet access (for a fee), flat-screen TV, and weekday newspaper delivery.

The 114 two-bedroom equivalents (villas) are housed in a five-story building adjoining Disney's Wilderness Lodge. This tribute to turn-of-the-20th-century design is also one of the Disney Vacation Club properties. The style of the villas building was inspired by the grandeur of Rocky Mountain geyser country. Villas are available to all guests when not occupied by Disney Vacation Club members.

Each studio has a queen-size bed and a double sleeper sofa, plus a kitchenette with microwave, coffeemaker, and mini refrigerator. Larger (one- and two-bedroom) villas sleep four to eight and have dining areas, kitchens, laundry facilities, master baths with whirlpool tubs, and DVD players. They include a king-size bed in the master bedroom, a living room with a queen sleeper sofa, and either two queen-size beds or a queen-size bed and a double sleeper sofa in extra bedrooms.

WHERE TO EAT: The Northwest theme is carried out with flair in the hotel's eateries. Room service runs from 7 A.M. to 11 A.M. and 4 P.M. to midnight.

Artist Point: Decorated with art representing painters who first chronicled the Northwest landscape, this fine-dining spot features salmon, game, steak, and other seafood, as well as wines from the Pacific Northwest.

Roaring Fork: Fast food and light snacks are available at this snack bar. This is also the resort's "refillable mug" station. Purchase a mug for about $15 and refill it with soft drinks —for free—for the length of your stay.

Whispering Canyon Cafe: A boisterous, family-style restaurant with all-day dining.

WHERE TO DRINK: Two spots are available for a relaxing break.

Territory Lounge: This lounge honors the survey parties who led the move westward. In addition to specialty drinks, microbrewed beer, espresso, and snacks are served.

Trout Pass: The poolside bar features a variety of specialty drinks and snacks.

WHAT TO DO: The resort offers many recreational activities. Teton Boat & Bike Rental is in the Colonel's Cabin by the lake. Fishing

of clothing with the Wilderness Lodge logo and Disney character merchandise. There is a small selection of grocery items, too. The shop is usually open until about 11 P.M. There's also a pin-trading cart in the lobby.

Swimming: The main pool looks as if it were carved from the rockscape. A beach, a kiddie pool, two whirlpools, and a geyser complete the design. Fire Rock Geyser erupts on the hour from early morning until 10 P.M. The Hidden Springs pool and whirlpool spa near the Villas provide a quieter alternative.

TRANSPORTATION: Boats go to the Magic Kingdom, Contemporary, and Fort Wilderness. Buses go to Magic Kingdom, Epcot, Disney's Hollywood Studios, Animal Kingdom, Blizzard Beach, and the Transportation and Ticket Center (TTC). Buses go directly to Typhoon Lagoon and Downtown Disney. (The Fort Wilderness bus does not stop here.)

excursions may be arranged (refer to the *Sports* chapter for details).

Arcade: The Buttons and Bells Arcade has about 30 different games to keep kids (and grown-ups) busy.

Bass Fishing: See page 226.

Biking: Bikes may be rented for scenic rides around the resort. A three-quarter-mile path leads to Fort Wilderness.

Boating: A variety of watercraft may be rented for trips around Bay Lake and the Seven Seas Lagoon.

Carolwood Pacific Room: A fireplace and railroad memorabilia add atmosphere to this relaxing room, equipped with comfy seating, tables, and games. It is located in the Wilderness Lodge Villas building.

Children's Program: The Cub's Den is a supervised dining and entertainment club for (potty-trained) kids ages 3 through 12. Supervised activities, including Disney movies and Western-themed arts and crafts, keep kids entertained from 4:30 P.M. to midnight. Cost is about $12 per hour, per child. Dinner and a snack are included. Call 407-939-3463 for reservations.

Health Club: The only thing rustic about the Sturdy Branches health club is the structure it's housed in. Open 24 hours, it features modern cardio and strength equipment, bicycles, sauna, and more. Massage therapy is available.

Shopping: Wilderness Lodge Mercantile stocks necessities and sundries as well as a line

Fort Wilderness Resort & Campground

The very existence of this canal-crossed expanse—with more than 750 acres of cypress and pine—always surprises visitors who come to Walt Disney World expecting to find nothing more than theme parks.

Tucked among the campsites are hundreds of Wilderness Cabins for rent, complete with housekeeping service. The cost is comparable to that of some of the more expensive rooms at Disney resorts, but each sleeps up to 6 guests and offers about 500 square feet of space. The phone number for the Fort Wilderness resort and campground is 407-824-2900.

WHERE TO EAT: There are a couple of dining options, but many people cook their own meals here. A small selection of supplies is sold at the Meadow Trading Post and the Settlement Trading Post. Ask about nearby grocery stores when you check in.

Trail's End: This log-walled spot in Pioneer Hall serves home-style fare three times a day. Pizza is an option from 4:30 P.M. to 10 P.M. Spirits are available. The breakfast buffet delivers a hefty bang for the buck.

WHERE TO DRINK: Cocktails are served at Crockett's Tavern in Pioneer Hall.

FAMILY ENTERTAINMENT AFTER DARK: The Hoop-Dee-Doo Musical Revue is quite popular. It's offered year-round. Another crowd-pleasing dinner show, Mickey's Backyard Barbecue, is offered seasonally. Reservations are recommended; call 407-939-3463. There's also a free nightly campfire program held near the Meadow Trading Post. (For details, see the *Everything Else in the World* and *Good Meals, Great Times* chapters.)

WHAT TO DO: There's a plethora of free activities to choose from, including two pools (the Fort Meadows pool has an aquatic play zone for tots and a slide), tennis courts, and campfire sing-alongs. For a fee, guests can enjoy wagon rides, pony rides, carriage rides, guided fishing trips, Segway tours, archery, boats, bikes, and more. Activities are described in *Everything Else in the World* and *Sports*.

TRANSPORTATION: Buses circulating at 15- to 30-minute intervals provide transportation within the campground, while buses and boats connect Fort Wilderness to the rest of the World. The Magic Kingdom, Contemporary, and Wilderness Lodge are best reached via water-craft that depart from the marina. Buses to Wilderness Lodge, and the TTC depart from the Settlement stop only. Buses to Epcot, Animal Kingdom, Disney's Hollywood Studios, Blizzard Beach, Typhoon Lagoon, and Downtown Disney leave from the Outpost stop.

Electric golf carts and bikes may be rented outside the Reception Outpost as an alternative means of getting around within the campground. Call 407-934-7639 for golf cart reservations. Available to Fort Wilderness guests only, golf carts cost about $59 per day, $378 per week.

CAMPSITES: Fort Wilderness has 799 traditional sites. They feature electricity hookups (30/50-amp), water, sanitary disposal, high-speed Internet access (for a fee), and cable television. Partial-hookup campsites supply electricity and water hookups only. All campsites feature a paved driveway pad, picnic table, and charcoal grill. Most loops have at least one air-conditioned comfort station with restrooms, private showers, an ice machine, phones, and a laundry room. A site allows for occupancy by up to ten. Each site has room for one car (in addition to the camping vehicle). Other cars may be parked in the main lot.

The various campground areas are designated by numbers. The 100–500 loops are closest to the beach, the Settlement Trading Post, and Pioneer Hall. The 1500–2000 loops are farthest away from the beach and many other Fort Wilderness activities, but they are quieter and more private. Premium campsites are big-rig friendly and are wider and deeper to accommodate large vehicles. Pets are welcome at certain campsites for a nightly charge of $5. They can frolic at Waggin' Tails Dog Park, the new "off leash" pet play area.

WILDERNESS CABINS: These woodland dwellings offer a rustic escape (with all the comforts of home, plus housekeeping). Falling into WDW's "moderate" resort category, the interiors of the six-person, log cabin-like buildings are decorated with wilderness accents. Each one is shaded by a pine canopy. Cabins include air-conditioning, a full kitchen, two TVs, a DVD player, full bath, hair dryer, iron, a deck, picnic table, and charcoal grill.

Note: No extra camping equipment allowed; all guests must be accommodated in a cabin.

Epcot Area

Caribbean Beach

This colorful hotel is set on 200 acres southeast of Epcot and near Disney's Hollywood Studios. It is composed of five brightly colored "villages" surrounding a 45-acre lake called Barefoot Bay. Each village is identified with a different Caribbean island—Martinique, Barbados, Trinidad, Aruba, and Jamaica—and features pastel walls, white railings, and vividly colored metal roofs. There are 2,112 rooms in all, making Caribbean Beach one of the largest hotels in the United States.

The villages consist of a cluster of two-story buildings, a swimming pool, a guest laundry, and a lakefront stretch of white-sand beach. Guests check in at the Custom House, a reception building that projects the feeling of a tropical resort. Decor, furnishings, and staff costumes all reflect the Caribbean theme. Old Port Royale, a complex located near the center of the property, evokes images of an island market. Stone walls, pirates' cannons, and tropical birds and flowers add to the atmosphere. The area houses the resort's food court, restaurant and lounge, arcade, and two shops.

The lakeside recreation area includes a pool with waterfalls and a slide; the main beach; the Barefoot Bay Boat Yard and Bike Works, where boats and bicycles may be rented; and a 1.4-mile promenade around the lake that's perfect for biking, walking, or jogging. Kids

HOT TIP!

Avast ye hearties! About 400 rooms at Caribbean Beach resort were redesigned to appeal to the swashbuckler in all of us. The pirate-pleasing parlours are perfect for swapping sea stories.

love it here. The telephone number for the Caribbean Beach resort is 407-934-3400.

ROOMS: Rooms are located in two-story buildings in each island village. A typical 340-square-foot room has two double beds and can sleep up to four. The rooms here are a bit larger than standard rooms at Disney's other moderate resorts. Rooms are decorated in tones softer than the colors found on the exterior. Many have *Finding Nemo* touches or a pirate motif. Each room has a small refrigerator, coffeemaker (with coffee), and high-speed Internet service (for a fee). A note for the budget-conscious: All rooms here are identical in terms of size and comfort, and the only difference between the most and least expensive is the view. To minimize time spent walking, request a room nearest the lobby or bus stop when you check in.

WHERE TO EAT: A full-service eatery called Shutters and the Old Port Royale food court are located in Old Port Royale. Limited room service is available from 4 P.M. to 11:30 P.M.

Bridgetown Broiler: Omelets, biscuits, and French toast are offered for breakfast. Dinner brings rotisserie chicken and other items.

Grab-N-Go Market: Open from early morning until about 11 P.M., this spot sells sandwiches and salads, plus an assortment of pastries, bagels, cheesecake, pies, and more.

Montego's Deli: Breakfast items such as pancakes, sausage, and oatmeal are served in the morning. Salads and deli sandwiches are offered for dinner.

Old Port Royale Hamburger Shop: Sandwiches, cheeseburgers, and fries are served for lunch and dinner. Mickey waffles are offered for breakfast.

Royale Pizza & Pasta Shop: Pizza is available in individual portions, along with pasta dishes and salads.

TRANSPORTATION & ACCOMMODATIONS

81

Shutters at Old Port Royale: This full-service Old Port Royale restaurant features items such as prime rib and a catch of the day. Cocktails and soft drinks are served, too.

WHERE TO DRINK: The tropical theme is carried out in the specialty drinks found at Banana Cabana. Light snacks are also available at this poolside spot.

WHAT TO DO: There are many recreational opportunities here. The promenade around the lake is ideal for walking, biking, or a jog.

Arcade: Goombay Games at Old Port Royale offers a selection of amusements.

Biking: Bikes may be rented at the Barefoot Bay Boat Yard and Bike Works.

Boating: Sailboats, Sea Raycer boats, Boston Whaler Montauks, canoes, pedal boats, and pontoon boats are available for rent at the Barefoot Bay Boat Yard and Bike Works for use on the resort's scenic 45-acre lake.

Fishing: Guided fishing excursions are offered on Barefoot Bay. Call 407-WDW-BASS for updates.

Playgrounds: Playgrounds are located on the Barbados, Jamaica, and Trinidad beaches.

Shopping: Calypso Straw Market carries swimwear and items featuring the resort's logo. Calypso Trading Post has Disney character merchandise and sundries.

Swimming: Each village has its own pool, and one of the pools has a waterfall and a slide in a Caribbean-themed setting, conjuring up images of high-seas adventures. Kids simply adore it.

PHOTO BY MIKE CARROLL

TRANSPORTATION: Buses go to the Magic Kingdom, Epcot, Disney's Hollywood Studios, Animal Kingdom, and Blizzard Beach. Other bus routes lead to Downtown Disney and Typhoon Lagoon. Getting around within the resort is done via buses bearing an "Internal Resort Shuttle" sign.

Yacht & Beach Club and Beach Club Villas

The New England seaside exists at Disney World in the form of the Yacht and Beach Club, and the Beach Club Villas. Situated beside Epcot, the resorts, designed by noted architect Robert A. M. Stern, are set around a 25-acre lake. The adjacent properties share most facilities—including a convention center offering access to business services—and transportation options.

The Yacht Club's design evokes images of the New England seashore hotels of the 1880s. Guests enter the five-story beige clapboard building along a wooden-planked bridge. Hardwood floors and brass enhance the nautical theme. A lighthouse on the pier serves as a beacon to welcome guests back to the hotel from WDW attractions. To reach the Yacht Club by telephone, call 407-934-7000.

Distance from the ocean is irrelevant over at the sand-and-surf-focused Beach Club resort, approached along an entrance drive flanked by oak trees. A walkway leads past a croquet court to beachside cabanas on the white-sand shore. Guests are met by hosts and hostesses dressed in colorful beach resort costumes of the 1870s. The telephone number for the Beach Club resort is 407-934-8000.

ROOMS: Yacht Club rooms are decorated in a nautical motif. The Beach Club's rooms are also amply sized and, naturally, reflect a beach motif. In each room, the furniture is white, and (at the Yacht Club) the headboard design on the one king-size bed or two queen-size beds incorporates small ships' wheels. Some rooms have daybeds. Most of the suites have a king-size bed as well as two sleeper sofas. In the bathrooms, there is a separate vanity with double sinks. Each room has a ceiling fan, iron (with board), hair dryer, weekday newspaper delivery, mini fridge, makeup mirror, a small safe, and a comfy chair. Club-level rooms are available.

A five-story building beside the Beach Club is home to 177 two-bedroom equivalents. The villas are available to Disney Vacation Club members. (They are available to all guests when not occupied by Vacation Club members.) Each studio has a queen-size bed and a double sleeper sofa, plus a kitchenette with a microwave, coffeemaker, and mini fridge, as well as a DVD player. Larger villas sleep four to eight, and all have a dining area, kitchen, laundry room, and a master bath with whirlpool tub. They include a king-size bed in the master bedroom, living room with queen sleeper sofa, and either two queen-size beds or a queen-size bed and a double sleeper sofa.

WHERE TO EAT: The themes of yachting and the sea play an important role in the restaurants that are found at their respective resorts. A wide variety of menu items is available from room service 24 hours a day.

Beach Club Marketplace: Stop here for hot and cold breakfast items such as cheese omelet croissants or pastries, (made-to-order) salads, sandwiches, and snack selections.

Beaches and Cream Soda Shop: A small, classic soda fountain where shakes, malts, and sundaes are the prime lure. Burgers and sandwiches are served as well. The shop is located between the two resorts.

Cape May Cafe: An indoor clambake is held here at the Beach Club each night. The varied and bountiful buffet features several types of clams and mussels, plus beef ribs and chicken. A character breakfast is presented daily.

Captain's Grille: There is a breakfast buffet, as well as an à la carte menu for breakfast, lunch, and dinner. Located at Yacht Club.

Hurricane Hanna's Grille: Burgers, sandwiches, salads, hot dogs, and other snacks are served here. A full bar is also located here, and poolside beverage service is available.

Yachtsman Steakhouse: Select cuts of aged beef are the specialty of the house. Fresh seafood and poultry are also offered.

WHERE TO DRINK: The lounges in both resorts offer a variety of specialty drinks in relaxing seaside settings.

Ale and Compass: This Yacht Club lobby lounge, featuring specialty coffees and drinks, provides a nice respite after a long day. Mornings bring a selection of continental breakfast items.

Crew's Cup: The place to try beer shipped in from the world's seaports before dining at Yachtsman Steakhouse next door.

Martha's Vineyard: This quiet lounge at the Beach Club offers selections from American and international vineyards, served by the glass or bottle, as well as a full bar and appetizers.

WHAT TO DO: There is enough to do here to fill an entire vacation. A sand volleyball court may be found on the Beach Club side of the property. Equipment is available at no cost at the Ship Shape health club. Bikes and boats may be rented.

The Fantasia Gardens Miniature Golf complex is close by, and guided fishing excursions may be arranged (see *Sports*). And last but not

HOT TIP!

Playpen-like cribs that accommodate one child under age 3 are available at all Disney resorts. Ask about them when you call to reserve your room. They're free. (If you'd like a more substantial sleeping apparatus for your toddler, refer to page 45 of the *Getting Ready to Go* chapter.)

least, the BoardWalk entertainment district is a short walk around the lake.

Arcade: Lafferty Place Arcade has about 60 video games and pinball machines.

Boating: Pontoons, Boston Whaler Montauks, Sea Raycers, and other boats are available for rent at the Bayside Marina.

Children's Program: The Sandcastle Club, for potty-trained kids ages 3 through 12, is available from 4:30 P.M. to midnight. Cost is about $12 per hour for each child. Reservations are required; call 407-939-3463. Toys, videos, games, and computers help keep children entertained. Dinner and a snack are included.

Health Club: The Ship Shape health club has strength and cardio machines, sauna, whirlpool, steam room, and massage. It's open 24/7 to resort guests ages 14 and older.

Salon: The Periwig salon for men and women is located in the central area.

Shopping: At the Yacht Club, Fittings & Fairings Clothes and Notions is an all-purpose shop offering character merchandise and sundries. At the Beach Club, the Beach Club Marketplace has a similar selection of goods.

Swimming: Between the marina and the beach is the centerpiece of the dual resort—Stormalong Bay, a three-acre pool that's like a mini water park. There is a lagoon expressly for relaxed bathing, and another with currents, jets, and sand-bottomed areas. Several whirlpools are scattered throughout the area. Adjacent to the main pool is a shipwreck, where guests can enjoy a waterslide. There is one unguarded pool and whirlpool at the far end of each hotel. There is also an unguarded pool by the Beach Club Villas. Guests may also opt to sunbathe on the beach, though swimming is not permitted.

Tennis: There is one lighted tennis court on the Yacht Club side of the property. Rental equipment is available at the Bayside Marina.

TRANSPORTATION: Guests travel to Epcot and Disney's Hollywood Studios via ferryboats or walkways. Buses go to the Magic Kingdom, Animal Kingdom, Downtown Disney, Typhoon Lagoon, and Blizzard Beach.

Meetings & Conventions

Convention centers at Walt Disney World range in size from 20,000 to 200,000 square feet. The Dolphin's center, featuring an exhibit hall and an executive boardroom, is the largest; the Swan provides additional space. The Contemporary has three ballrooms and a spacious pre-function area with lots of natural light. The convention center at the Yacht and Beach Club is reminiscent of a grand turn-of-the-century New England town-meeting hall. The Grand Floridian Resort and Spa has a lavish center with silk brocade walls. The BoardWalk offers a smaller conference area with a lakeside gazebo for outdoor events. And Coronado Springs, the first moderately priced Disney resort to offer convention facilities, boasts one of the largest hotel ballrooms in the U.S.

Among the unique services available to Disney conventioneers is the use of Disney characters and performers for events. Special events can even be held in the parks. Resort business centers have clerical staffs and computers, in addition to faxing and photocopying equipment. (These services are available to all resort guests.)

Those interested in scheduling a convention should call 321-939-7221. Organizers are advised to book their events six months in advance, especially for large groups.

Swan & Dolphin

These sister resorts, situated on the shores of Crescent Lake, can easily be distinguished by the 47-foot swan and 56-foot dolphin statues that top them. The waterfalls, rows of palm trees, and beachfront location all reflect the tropical Florida landscape that was their inspiration. Both hotels were designed by noted architect Michael Graves as examples of "entertainment architecture." The turquoise waves on the colored facade of the Swan's 12-story main building and two 7-story wings are clearly evidence of this design, as is the Dolphin's exterior mural, which features a banana-leaf pattern. The soaring 27-story triangular tower at the center of the Dolphin is flanked by four 9-story guestroom wings.

The resorts share extensive convention facilities, many recreational options, and a host of restaurants. The Swan and Dolphin are operated by Westin and Sheraton, respectively, but are treated as Walt Disney World resorts; guests here enjoy most WDW resort benefits. One notable difference involves room key-charging privileges: Guests cannot use their room keys to charge purchases on Disney property, with the exception of within the Swan and Dolphin resorts themselves. The direct line for the Swan and Dolphin is 407-934-3000. Reservations for either resort may be made by calling 800-227-1500 or by visiting *www.swandolphin.com*.

ROOMS: The rooms at both resorts have been redesigned with a fresh, contemporary look. Amenities include free weekday newspaper delivery, safes, mini bars, irons and boards, two dual-line telephones, and wireless Internet access (for a fee). Rooms equipped for guests with disabilities are available. Valet parking is $18 per day.

There are 756 rooms and 55 suites at the Swan, each of which comes with one king-size or two queen-size beds. At the Dolphin, the 1,509 rooms and 112 suites feature two double beds or one king-size bed. Dolphin rooms also include a separate vanity and dressing area.

WHERE TO EAT: In addition to many restaurant choices, 24-hour room service provides an extensive all-day dining menu. (The room service here is considered among the best at Walt Disney World.)

Cabana Bar & Beach Club: This full-service poolside spot near the Dolphin serves jerk-spiced chicken wings, salads, crab cakes, and more. The full bar serves specialty drinks.

The Fountain: Homemade ice cream is the specialty at this Dolphin eatery. Huge sundaes, shakes, malts, and burgers are also offered.

Fresh: Designed to resemble a cheerful marketplace, this Dolphin spot serves breakfast and lunch only. Items may be chosen from a menu or made to order.

Garden Grove Cafe: This Swan eatery, which features a park-like atmosphere, serves breakfast, lunch, and dinner daily. A buffet breakfast with the characters is held on Saturdays and Sundays, while a character dinner takes place nightly.

Il Mulino New York Trattoria: The highly acclaimed Italian restaurant is located on the first floor of the Swan. The setting, which is reminiscent of an old-world trattoria, is relaxed yet vibrant. Features such as *Piatti per il Tavolo* (family-style dining) and wood-fired pizzas complement Il Mulino New York's family-friendly Walt Disney World locale.

Picabu: A cafeteria with a bit of flair. The 24-hour convenience store here sells snacks and sundries. It has Starbucks coffee, too.

> ### HOT TIP!
> The Swan and Dolphin resorts run seasonal promotions throughout the year. For information, call 800-227-1500 or visit *www.swandolphin.com*.

Shula's: An upscale celebration of two American favorites: steak and football. It's a bit pricey, but the steaks are superb and the side orders are big enough to share.

Splash Terrace: A poolside cafe near the Swan serving lunch and snacks. A full-service bar is also located here.

Todd English's bluezoo: This eatery features coastal cuisine, beef, and chicken dishes with international and domestic influences.

WHERE TO DRINK: It's easy to find a nice cocktail spot in this neck of the woods.

Java Bar: This spot at the Swan offers a respite from the hubbub. Enjoy gourmet coffees with pastries in the morning, and wine and specialty drinks at night.

Kimonos: The Asian decor makes this Swan lounge an inviting place for sake, sushi, and other Japanese selections. Karaoke is a house specialty. This place is generally hopping a bit later than most other Walt Disney World resort lounges.

Lobby Lounge: A cozy Dolphin area featuring wine and specialty drinks.

Shula's Steak House Lounge: Settle into a comfy chair and sip a drink in this lounge adjacent to Shula's dining room.

WHAT TO DO: The Swan and Dolphin share many recreation options. Volleyball nets and hammocks are set up on the beach. The Fantasia Gardens Miniature Golf complex and BoardWalk are nearby (the proximity to BoardWalk and Epcot is a big plus). Disney's Hollywood Studios is a boat ride (or about a 20-minute walk) away.

Boating: Watercraft are available for rent on the beach between the Swan and Dolphin.

Children's Program: Camp Dolphin welcomes children (potty-trained) ages 4 through 12 and has supervised activities from 5:30 P.M. to midnight. The cost is $10 per child, per hour.

Health Clubs: There is a fitness center near the pool area at the Dolphin. State-of-the-art equipment is available, as are personal trainers. This site has a sauna and a large whirlpool. There's also a smaller health club with basic exercise equipment near Splash Terrace at the Swan.

Playground: A sandy play area with swings and jungle gyms is located on the beach near the grotto pool.

Shopping: Disney Cabanas, located in the lobby of the Swan, features character merchandise and sundries. Four shops are located at the Dolphin. Sugar[3] allows chocolate lovers the chance to sample some tasty concoctions. Lamont's offers resort-wear for men and women. Daisy's Garden is the place to find character goods at the Dolphin. Galleria Sottil is the Dolphin's art gallery. Expect to find paintings, sculptures, and other assorted works of art. The Cabana Beach Hut, by the Dolphin pool, specializes in "pool-fun" essentials, while the 24-hour convenience store within Picabu sells grocery items and sundries.

Spa and Salon: The Mandara Spa features full-service body treatments, plus hairstyling, manicures, pedicures, and more.

Swimming: In addition to a shared children's wading pool, there are two lap pools, and a themed grotto pool with slides between the Swan and Dolphin. Several whirlpools are scattered around the area.

Tennis: Hard-surface tennis courts are located behind the pool area closest to the Swan resort. They are open 8 A.M. to 10 P.M.

Arcades: A room full of cutting-edge video games is located near Picabu at the Dolphin. Another can be found in Splash Terrace at the Swan.

TRANSPORTATION: Guests travel to Epcot and Disney's Hollywood Studios via ferryboats or walkway. (It takes about 10 minutes to walk to Epcot's back entrance and about 20 minutes to reach Disney's Hollywood Studios on foot. Ferryboats don't move much faster—and they make multiple stops—so allow plenty of time to reach either destination.) Buses go directly to the Magic Kingdom, Animal Kingdom, Downtown Disney, Typhoon Lagoon, and Blizzard Beach.

BoardWalk Inn & Villas

The enchantment of a bygone era is recaptured in the BoardWalk. The resort combines a waterside entertainment complex with deluxe hotel accommodations and vacation villas. Dining, recreation, shopping, and entertainment venues line the boardwalk, and twinkling lights trim the buildings. The ambience continues throughout, with detailed architecture featuring sherbet-colored facades, flagged turrets, and striped awnings, all reminiscent of the turn of the 20th century. The BoardWalk resort is adjacent to Epcot's International Gateway and connected to it via walkway. The phone number for BoardWalk is 407-939-5100.

ROOMS: Accommodations here evoke the charm of early Eastern-seaboard inns. Most have private balconies or patios. The Board-Walk Inn has 371 deluxe hotel rooms decorated with cherrywood furniture, boardwalk postcard-print curtains, and light green accents. Guestrooms at the Inn sleep up to five, and feature two queen-size beds (or one king-size bed) and a child's daybed. Romantic two-story garden suites each have a private garden enclosed by a white picket fence. They sleep four, and have a living room on the first floor and a king-size bed in the bedroom loft. The Inn also has club-level rooms and suites.

The 282 two-bedroom equivalents are collectively called BoardWalk Villas. These are Disney Vacation Club villas, available when not occupied by members. Each studio has a queen-size bed and double sleeper sofa, plus a kitchenette with microwave, coffeemaker, and small refrigerator. Larger (one-, two-, and three-bedroom) villas sleep 4 to 12 people, and feature dining areas, fully equipped kitchens, laundry facilities, master baths with whirlpool tubs, and VCR/DVD players. They also include a king-size bed in the master bedroom, living room with a queen sleeper sofa, and a queen-size bed plus a double sleeper sofa in any additional bedrooms.

Rooms at the BoardWalk Inn include weekday newspaper delivery. All rooms have an iron (with board), hair dryer, and high-speed Internet access (for a fee).

WHERE TO EAT: This resort has a wealth of dining and snacking options. A variety of vendors along the boardwalk tempt with hot dogs, crêpes on a stick, gourmet coffee, and more. For those looking to eat in, room service is available.

Big River Grille & Brewing Works: This working brewpub features a full menu, complemented by fresh specialty ales. View the on-site brewmaster through floor-to-ceiling glass walls.

BoardWalk Bakery: A popular stop that offers fresh baked goods, sandwiches, espresso,

Resort Roundup

What's the best place to stay at Walt Disney World? It's a tough question—and one that Birnbaum editors are asked all the time. The answer? Well, it depends. Do you have a favorite park? What's your price range? Will a clown's tongue that doubles as a pool slide make your day? All factors to consider. That said, here are our favorites in each of Disney's price categories:

BIRNBAUM'S ★BEST★ DELUXE

Yacht Club: In addition to a picturesque setting, this resort is all about location. For starters, you can walk to Epcot (and the Studios if you're feeling ambitious). Of course, you can always take a water taxi. You're a stone's throw from the excitement of the bustling BoardWalk entertainment district, but get to enjoy the relative peace of life on the quieter side of Crescent Lake. Excellent dining options abound. And the pool is to die for. We enjoy the Beach Club, too, but prefer to stay here. It's a bit quieter, and there are more rooms with full balconies.
Very honorable mentions: Grand Floridian and Polynesian

BIRNBAUM'S ★BEST★ MODERATE

Port Orleans Riverside: One need not be a Southern aristocrat to live like one. Many of the guest buildings at this resort, formerly known as Dixie Landings, were designed to look like historic mansions. Even the food court has a certain Southern ambience. There's a table-service restaurant and a cozy lounge (which may offer entertainment). Kids enjoy dropping their hooks in the fishing hole (strictly catch-and-release) and splashing in the free-form pool on Ol' Man Island. Pretty gardens and a relatively reasonable price add to the appeal.
Honorable mention: Caribbean Beach

BIRNBAUM'S ★BEST★ VALUE

Pop Century: This, the newest of the "value" properties, has some of the boldest and brightest theming around, but what really sets it apart is the food court: Everything Pop's mix of made-to-order and grab-and-go selections makes for a pleasant and efficient dining experience.
Honorable mention: All-Star Movies

and cappuccino. Huge display windows allow passersby to watch bakers at work. "Bun rises" are held here every morning. Note that the line moves slowly.

BoardWalk Carts: Stands along the boardwalk offer snacks and coffee.

ESPN Club: A serious sports bar for serious sports fans, it provides sports video entertainment and all-day dining.

Flying Fish Cafe: This restaurant has a show kitchen, and its dinner menu emphasizes seafood, steak, and fresh seasonal items.

Kouzzina by Cat Cora: Mediterranean cuisine with a Greek emphasis is the focus here. A window dispenses pizza and breakfast items.

Seashore Sweets': An old-fashioned sweet shop that serves candies, saltwater taffy, ice cream, frozen yogurt, and specialty coffees.

WHERE TO DRINK: Guests have a multitude of options right in their backyard.

Atlantic Dance: This waterfront club is an elegantly designed dance spot. You must be at least 21 to enter. There usually isn't a cover charge, but that may change.

Belle Vue Lounge: Listen to old-time tunes on antique radios and play board games in this cocktail lounge near the lobby.

Jellyrolls: Dueling pianos provide live entertainment in a casual warehouse atmosphere. The cover charge is generally about $10 nightly. You must be at least 21 to enter Jellyrolls and able to prove it.

Leaping Horse Libations: The carousel-themed pool bar at Luna Park serves a variety of cocktails, as well as snacks.

WHAT TO DO: The three-quarter-mile pathway encircling Crescent Lake (en route to Epcot) provides a ready venue for walkers and joggers. BoardWalk guests may rent boats from Yacht and Beach Club's Bayside Marina. The Fantasia Gardens Miniature Golf complex is nearby. At the resort itself, Ferris W. Eahlers Community Hall rents out equipment for many recreational pursuits, including croquet, shuffleboard, table tennis, badminton—even books and videos. Fishing excursions can be arranged.

Biking: Community Hall offers a variety of bicycles for rental. Surreys (canopied quadracycles for four) may also be rented.

Health Club: Muscles & Bustles health club has steam rooms, modern exercise machines, and circuit-training equipment, as well as massages. The health club is open 24 hours a day for BoardWalk guests.

Midway Games: This area on the Board-Walk's WildWood Landing features games of luck and skill similar to those found along traditional boardwalks. There is a charge to play these games.

Shopping: Dundy's Sundries in the lobby is the source for basic necessities. Character Carnival on the boardwalk has children's apparel as well as character merchandise. Screen Door General Store stocks groceries, dry goods, snacks, and beverages. Thimbles & Threads, also on the boardwalk, carries apparel for men and women. Wyland Galleries features marine and environmental art.

Surrey Bike Ride: A trip around the lake in a pedal-powered surrey is available for a fee.

Swimming: The BoardWalk's swimming area, Luna Park, has a pool with a 200-foot water-slide, "Keister Coaster," patterned after a wooden roller coaster. (The slide, shown at right, is a clown's tongue. Kids get a big kick out of it.) A family of elephants is found posed throughout the area; their trunks act as a shower for adults on the pool deck or children in the wading pool. The resort has two unguarded pools. There are three whirlpools, one in each pool area.

Tennis: Two lighted tennis courts are available for play. Equipment may be rented at Community Hall.

Video Arcade: Side Show Games Arcade has video games.

TRANSPORTATION: Guests may travel to Epcot and Disney's Hollywood Studios via ferryboats or walkways. (It takes about 10

minutes to walk to International Gateway, aka Epcot's back door. The stroll to Disney's Hollywood Studios takes about 20 minutes.) Buses transport guests to the Magic Kingdom, Animal Kingdom, Typhoon Lagoon, Blizzard Beach, and Downtown Disney.

Disney Vacation Club

Disney Vacation Club grants members the convenience of flexible vacations from year to year, with the ability to choose when and where to visit, how long to stay, and the type of accommodations. It starts with the purchase of a real estate interest in a Disney Vacation Club property. For a one-time purchase price and annual dues, members can enjoy vacation stays at Aulani Resort & Spa (in Oahu, Hawaii); Bay Lake Tower (at Contemporary resort), Animal Kingdom Villas, Old Key West Resort, Beach Club Villas, BoardWalk Villas, the Villas at Disney's Wilderness Lodge, and Saratoga Springs Resort & Spa at WDW; Disney's Vero Beach Resort in Florida; Disney's Hilton Head Island Resort in South Carolina; and the Villas at Disney's Grand Californian Resort & Spa in Anaheim, California; plus access to additional destinations around the globe. Through Member Getaways, members may also elect to stay at their choice of more than 500 resorts worldwide, including most Disney resorts and the Disney Cruise Line.

Disney's Vero Beach Resort is a two-hour drive from Walt Disney World. It has villa-type accommodations comparable to those at Disney's Old Key West Resort—with lush surroundings, the beach, and local sights. The proximity makes it easy to tack a beach vacation onto a WDW visit.

Disney Vacation Club information centers may be found at each of the Walt Disney World hotels and theme parks. For more information, call 800-800-9100, or visit *www.disneyvacationclub.com.*

Downtown Disney Area

Port Orleans French Quarter

This 1,008-room resort invites comparisons to the historic French Quarter of New Orleans. (Although Port Orleans French Quarter and Port Orleans Riverside [formerly known as Dixie Landings] technically function as one resort, we give them individual attention to provide guests with the information necessary to select the area that works best for them.)

Starting at the entrance gate, with its wrought-iron portal and overgrown landscape, the appeal of the Delta City surrounds arriving guests. The entry drive leads to the heart of the "city," which is Port Orleans Square. The central building was based on a turn-of-the-20th-century mint. The Mint houses check-in facilities (for Port Orleans French Quarter *only*), a shop, food court, and arcade. It has a vaulted ceiling, and the check-in desks are designed as bank-teller windows. The musical notes in the mural are the notes to "When the Saints Go Marching In."

The phone number for Port Orleans French Quarter is 407-934-5000.

ROOMS: The guestrooms are located in seven 3-story buildings (with elevators). Each room has two double beds; some king-size beds are available. The rooms are a bit smaller than the standard rooms at the more expensive Disney hotels, but they are comfortable for a family of four. The buildings are painted cream, pink, blue, purple, and yellow, and feature wrought-iron railings of varying designs. Connecting rooms may be requested but can't be guaranteed. The least expensive rooms overlook gardens or parking areas, and the most expensive rooms offer water views. All rooms have coffee-makers (with coffee), mini refrigerators, and high-speed Internet service (for a fee).

WHERE TO EAT: A counter-service food court has a variety of dining options.

Sassagoula Floatworks & Food Factory: A variety of specialty foods is available in this food court, including gumbo, chicken with red beans and rice, fresh-baked beignets, and other traditional Creole dishes. Burgers, pizza, ice cream, and baked goods are also on the menu.

WHERE TO DRINK: A pool bar operates seasonally, and guests on a quest for a cocktail may head to Port Orleans Riverside—it's a short bus ride away. Of course, there's always Downtown Disney or any theme park other than the Magic Kingdom.

WHAT TO DO: A themed pool is the highlight of the recreational opportunities here.

Biking: Bicycles and surrey bikes are available for rent at Port Orleans Riverside.

Boating: Pedal boats, kayaks, canoes, Sea Raycers, Boston Whaler Montauks, and pontoon boats may be rented at Port Orleans Riverside.

Carriage Rides: Refer to page 91 for details.

Fishing: Two-hour guided fishing excursions are available (see *Sports*).

Shopping: Jackson Square Gifts & Desires, located at Port Orleans Square, features Disney character merchandise, clothing bearing the Port Orleans resort logo, and sundries.

Swimming: Doubloon Lagoon is a free-form pool built around a bright blue sea serpent. The waterslide is actually the creature's tongue. A shower at the pool features an alligator's head, and there is a large clamshell where an all-gator band serves as the centerpiece of a fountain. There is a large whirlpool nearby. Port Orleans French Quarter guests are also invited to swim in the pool at Ol' Man Island at Port Orleans Riverside.

Video Arcade: South Quarter Games is located at Port Orleans Square. It has a selection of state-of-the art, interactive games.

TRANSPORTATION: Buses go to the Magic Kingdom, Epcot, Disney's Hollywood Studios, Animal Kingdom, Typhoon Lagoon, Blizzard Beach, and Downtown Disney. Small water taxis transport guests to Downtown Disney, too.

Port Orleans Riverside

Here, the city feel of the French Quarter gives way to the rural South. The resort is divided into "parishes." Closest to the "city," guestrooms are found in Mansion homes; farther upriver are the Bayou guestrooms, with a more rustic feel. The phone number for the Port Orleans Riverside resort is 407-934-6000.

ROOMS: The 2,048 Mansion and Bayou rooms are of the same size, and each has two double beds (some king-size beds are available); 963 of the Bayou rooms have trundle beds (designed to sleep a child) as well. There is a fee of $15 per night for a trundle bed. The Magnolia Bend Mansion rooms are situated in elegant manor homes with stately columns and grand staircases. The Alligator Bayou rooms are in rustic, weathered-wood buildings that are tucked among flora native to the area. Although all buildings have two to three floors, only the Magnolia Bend Mansions have elevators.

The Bayou rooms surround Ol' Man Island, a 3½-acre recreational area with a pool, playground, and fishing hole. Decorative touches in the rooms include wood and tin armoires and pedestal sinks with brass fittings. The closet space is not enclosed. The rooms are a bit small, but they can accommodate four guests. Rooms are equipped with a coffeemaker (with coffee), fridge, and high-speed Internet access (for a fee).

More than 500 Riverside rooms invite guests to live like royalty. These "royal guestrooms" feature special touches inspired by Disney's animated classics (all featuring regals of some sort), ornately decorated beds with fiber optic special effects, custom bed coverings and drapes, artwork featuring Princess Tiana and other regals, and more. If you want the royal treatment while residing at Port Orleans Riverside, make your wishes known when you book the room.

WHERE TO EAT: In addition to a restaurant and food court, the hotel offers limited pizza delivery from 4 P.M. until midnight.

Boatwright's Dining Hall: This 200-seat table-service eatery, next to Riverside Mill, serves Cajun specialties and American fare for dinner. Reservations are recommended.

Riverside Mill: This food court resembles an old-fashioned cotton mill with a working waterwheel that powers the cotton press inside.

The five counter-service stands here offer all sorts of choices. The basic selections are available for breakfast. **Pizza 'n' Pasta** has pasta dishes, pizza, and bread sticks; **Grill Shop** offers fried fish, chicken nuggets, and burgers; **Carving Station** serves freshly sliced turkey; **Specialty Shop** offers soup and sandwiches; and the **Bakery** serves pastries, ice cream, yogurt parfait, and more. If you buy a resort refillable mug, Boatwright's is where you fill it.

WHERE TO DRINK: Two lounges possess an enticing degree of charm.

Muddy Rivers: The poolside bar serves beer, wine, cocktails, specialty drinks, and soft drinks. Seasonal.

River Roost: Situated in a room designed as a cotton exchange, this lounge features specialty drinks and light hors d'oeuvres.

WHAT TO DO: Many of the resort activities are at Ol' Man Island, a recreation center featuring a pool, whirlpool, wading pool, interactive fountains, and a playground.

Arcade: The Medicine Show Arcade features a small selection of games.

Biking: Bicycles of all types can be rented.

Boating: Pedal boats, canoes, kayaks, Sea Raycers, Boston Whaler Montauks, and pontoon boats are available for rent.

Carriage Rides: Horse-drawn carriages take guests for 25-minute rides throughout the grounds of the resort. Carriages hold up to 4 adults or 2 adults and 3 small kids. Each trip departs from the marina. Call 407-939-7529 for reservations.

Fishing: Two-hour guided fishing excursions are available (see *Sports*). It's also possible to drop a line at the Fishin' Hole on Ol' Man Island. Catch-and-release only.

Playground: An elaborate play area is located on Ol' Man Island next to the pool.

Shopping: Fulton's General Store in the Riverside building stocks Disney character merchandise, clothing, and sundries.

Swimming: In addition to the main pool and kiddie pool at Ol' Man Island, there are five unguarded pools at the resort. Guests may also swim in the French Quarter pool.

TRANSPORTATION: Buses go from Port Orleans Riverside to the Magic Kingdom, Epcot, Disney's Hollywood Studios, Animal Kingdom, Typhoon Lagoon, Blizzard Beach, and Downtown Disney. Water taxis also ferry guests to and from Downtown Disney.

Disney's Saratoga Springs Resort & Spa

Just across the lake from the hustle and bustle of Downtown Disney, this Disney Vacation Club resort is a peaceful complement to its nearest neighbor. Disney's Saratoga Springs Resort & Spa aspires to recapture the heyday of upstate New York country retreats of the late 1800s. The resort covers 65 acres. To contact Saratoga Springs, call 407-827-1100.

ROOMS: There are studios and villas with one, two, and three bedrooms. A studio consists of a room with a queen-size bed and a double sleeper sofa, bathroom, kitchenette, microwave, and coffeemaker. All units have a porch or a balcony, access to complimentary laundry facilities, and high-speed Internet access (for a fee).

One-bedroom villas have a king-size bed in the master suite and a queen-size sleeper sofa in the living room. The one bathroom has a whirlpool tub. The full kitchen has a fridge, stove, microwave, toaster, coffeemaker, dinnerware, and dishwasher. Each unit has a washer and dryer.

Two-bedroom villas have an additional bathroom and bedroom, with either one queen-size bed and a double sleeper sofa or two queen-size beds. The three-bedroom Grand Villa has similar features as the two-bedroom models, but is about twice the size and has four bathrooms.

The resort's treehouse villas, elevated on pedestals and designed to blend into the woodsy environment, offer serene views of the surrounding treetops. Each "cabin-casual" villa has a full kitchen, flat-panel TVs, three bedrooms, two bathrooms, and sleeps up to nine.

WHERE TO EAT: There are two eateries here and dozens across the lake. Several barbecue areas are available to resort guests.

The Artist's Palette: Set in a converted artist's loft, this spot offers all meals. Among

the selections are fresh tossed salads, sandwiches, pizza, baked goods, and more.

Turf Club Bar & Grill: A cozy spot for lunch and dinner, Turf Club has a horse-racing motif.

Groceries: In these parts, in-room grocery delivery is available from Artist's Palette, and many guests cook their own meals. If you've got a car, ask for directions to a grocery store.

WHERE TO DRINK: In addition to local bars, guests imbibe at nearby Downtown Disney.

Backstretch Bar: A poolside watering hole.

On the Rocks: A pool bar serving the usual battery of cocktails.

Turf Club Bar & Grill: In addition to a pool table, this spot serves a variety of drinks.

WHAT TO DO: In addition to enjoying spa treatments, guests may rent bikes, play basketball, swim, walk, swat tennis balls, and more.

Arcade: Expect to find the usual bells and whistles at "Win, Place, or Show."

Biking: Bicycles may be rented from Horsin' Around Rentals.

Boating: Boats may be rented at Captain Jack's Marina at nearby Downtown Disney.

Golf: The resort is adjacent to the Lake Buena Vista golf course.

Health Club: This spot features strength and cardio machines and weightlifting equipment.

Playground: There is a small kids' play area near an unguarded pool. (Be sure to supervise youngsters at all times.)

Shopping: The Artist's Palette stocks a variety of souvenirs and sundries.

Spa: The award-winning spa has treatment rooms for massage, manicures, facials, aromatherapy, and more.

Swimming: High Rock Spring cascades down rugged rockwork and feeds into a free-form, heated zero-depth-entry pool. The splash zone features a waterslide, two whirlpools, and an interactive play area for kids. There are four unguarded pools, too.

Tennis: Two courts are at the ready.

TRANSPORTATION: Buses go from Saratoga Springs to all theme and water parks. Boats ferry guests to Downtown Disney.

Disney's Old Key West Resort

Escape to the spirit of the Florida Keys. Disney's Old Key West Resort is the original Disney Vacation Club property, but villas not occupied by members are available for nightly rental. It has the laid-back feel of a resort community and all the amenities that go with resort life. The homey accommodations have lots of space and the convenience of kitchen facilities, making the resort nice for longer stays. The villas, designed in a Key West theme, were completely refurbished in 2011. The telephone number for Disney's Old Key West is 407-827-7700.

VILLAS: A studio consists of a large room with two queen-size beds, a table and chairs, and a small fridge, coffeemaker, microwave, and sink. Bathrooms are spacious. Each of the one-bedroom villas has a king-size bed in the master bedroom and a queen-size sleeper sofa in the living room; the master bath has a whirlpool tub, sink, and shower.

The two-bedroom villa features a king-size bed in the master bedroom, two queen-size beds in the second bedroom, living room with queen-size sleeper sofa and DVD player, dining room, and a kitchen with a refrigerator, dishwasher, toaster, and coffeemaker, plus plates, flatware, cooking utensils, and more.

The master bathroom is divided into two rooms with an extra-large whirlpool tub and a sink in one and an oversize shower, sink and vanity, and toilet in the other. There's a porch or balcony off the living room and bedroom, and ceiling fans in each room. The configuration of the two-story, three-bedroom Grand Villas is similar to that of the two-bedroom models, but adds a third bedroom with two

double beds. As for capacity, studios and one-bedroom villas sleep 4 people, the two-bedroom villas sleep 8 guests, and the two-story, three-bedroom villas accommodate 12.

WHERE TO EAT: In addition to the restaurant here, there are grills and picnic tables.

Good's Food to Go: The perfect place to pick up fixin's for a continental breakfast, this place also offers burgers, soups, salads, sandwiches, and simple snacks.

Olivia's Cafe: This full-service restaurant serves Key West favorites, plus more traditional items, for breakfast, lunch, and dinner. Menus change seasonally.

WHERE TO DRINK: The watering holes at Old Key West are as laid-back as they come.

Gurgling Suitcase: This tiny bar serves specialty drinks, wine, beer, and soft drinks.

Turtle Shack: This poolside spot serves pizza, salads, sandwiches, and light snacks. Open seasonally.

WHAT TO DO: At Conch Flats Community Hall, table tennis, board games, a large-screen TV, DVD rentals, and planned activities are offered. There are basketball, shuffleboard, and volleyball courts, and equipment is available at Hank's Rent 'N Return.

Arcade: The Electric Eel Game Room is in the Hospitality House; the Flying Fish Game Room is by the Turtle Shack snack bar.

Biking: Bikes and surrey bikes may be rented from Hank's.

Boating: Pedal boats, Sea Raycers, Boston Whaler Montauks, and pontoon boats are available for rent at Hank's.

Health Club: The Fitness Center at R.E.S.T. Beach has a variety of exercise equipment.

Playground: A kids' play area is located by each of the resort's swimming pools.

Shopping: Conch Flats General Store has groceries, books, sundries, and more.

Swimming: The sprawling main pool, with a large whirlpool nearby, is located behind the Hospitality House. The children's pool and play area looks like a big sandcastle and features a 125-foot slide. Additional pools are found around the resort.

Tennis: There are three courts.

TRANSPORTATION: Buses go to the theme parks, water parks, and Downtown Disney. Water taxis also make the trip between the resort and Downtown Disney.

Animal Kingdom Area

All-Star Movies, Music & Sports

The All-Star resorts are among the most brightly and boldly themed at Walt Disney World. Each resort has 1,500 to 1,920 rooms housed in ten buildings devoted to five Disney movies, types of music, and sports.

Sports fans will find themselves in a world of baseball, football, tennis, surfing, or basketball at the All-Star Sports resort. Brightly colored, larger-than-life football helmets, surfboards, tennis balls, basketball hoops, and baseball bats adorn the buildings.

At the All-Star Music resort, Broadway, country, jazz, rock, and calypso are the themes. A walk-through, neon-lit jukebox; a three-story pair of cowboy boots; and a Broadway theater marquee are among the giant icons.

The All-Star Movies resort celebrates five classic Disney films: *Toy Story*, *The Mighty Ducks*, *Fantasia*, *101 Dalmatians*, and *The Love Bug*. Buildings are adorned with such icons as 40-foot Dalmatians and wildly oversize versions of Buzz Lightyear and Woody.

As value resorts, the All-Star properties offer few frills, but the service and whimsical atmosphere are pure Disney.

Guests check in at Cinema Hall for All-Star Movies, Melody Hall for All-Star Music, or Stadium Hall for All-Star Sports. To reach All-Star Movies, call 407-939-7000; to phone All-Star Music, call 407-939-6000; to contact All-Star Sports, call 407-939-5000.

ROOMS: The guestrooms, measuring 260 square feet, are rather small compared with those at Port Orleans, which are 314 square feet. Each room has two double beds (except for rooms designed for travelers with disabilities, which have one king-size bed), a vanity area with a sink, a separate bathroom, a small dresser, and a small table with chairs.

All-Star Music boasts 192 Family Suites. Each one sleeps up to six guests and has two bathrooms, a "master" bedroom with its own flat-screen TV, and a kitchenette with counter space, sink, microwave, coffeemaker, and under-counter refrigerator.

WHERE TO EAT: Three food courts—**World Premiere** in Cinema Hall, **Intermission** in Melody Hall, and **End Zone** in Stadium Hall. Each features a bakery, convenience market, and several stands geared to pizza, pasta, salads, and burgers. Each food court has a seating area with a beverage bar. The All-Star resorts all deliver pizza, salads, beer, and wine to rooms from 5 P.M. to 1 A.M.

WHERE TO DRINK: There are no lounges at the All-Star resorts; however, the **Silver Screen Spirits**, **Singing Spirits**, and **Team Spirits** pool bars serve drinks throughout the day and evening. The bars are in the main pool areas.

WHAT TO DO: Guests may swim in any of the resort pools. All-Star guests may rent boating equipment at any WDW resort marina.

Arcades: Each of the All-Star resorts has one video arcade.

Playground: A playground is located in each hotel's courtyard area.

Shopping: Maestro Mickey's in Melody Hall, Sport Goofy's Gifts and Sundries in Stadium Hall, and Donald's Double Feature in Cinema Hall all have magazines, books, character merchandise, and sundries.

Swimming: Each hotel has two pools and one kiddie pool. The main pool at All-Star Movies has a *Fantasia* theme (look for Sorcerer Mickey). The smaller Duck Pond Pool is based on *The Mighty Ducks*. At the All-Star Music resort, the Calypso Pool is in the form of a giant guitar, while the Piano Pool bears a striking resemblance to a grand piano. At All-Star Sports, Surfboard Bay has an ocean motif. The smaller Grand Slam Pool pays tribute to our national pastime.

TRANSPORTATION: Buses make pickups at All-Star's Cinema Hall, Melody Hall, and Stadium Hall for trips to each of the theme parks, water parks, and Downtown Disney. Each resort has its own bus stops.

A word about All-Star resort transportation: The bus service at these "value" resorts tends to be slightly more efficient than at other locations. The combination of fewer stops and connections is a bonus for guests staying here.

Disney's Animal Kingdom Lodge & Villas

At first glance, Disney's Animal Kingdom Lodge evokes images of a sleepy, little thatched-roof game lodge in the wilds of southern Africa. Upon closer examination, however, it's clear that the only things sleepy or little about this place are the small creatures that live in its shadow. Those animals, along with their more sizable cousins, inhabit acres of meticulously re-created African savanna that practically surround the resort. Exotic birds and all manner of hoofed animals, including giraffes, zebras, and Thomson's gazelles, call the wildlife reserve home. With the freedom to wander within a dozen or so yards of the lodge itself, these critters allow guests to go on safari without leaving their balconies.

The resort is located about a mile from Disney's Animal Kingdom park. The lobby is a huge, high-ceilinged room, richly appointed with colorful African artwork and artifacts. The biggest draw here is the four-story observation window overlooking the savanna. It's one of many portals through which to gaze upon meandering wildlife.

Like the African game lodges on which it is

based, Disney's Animal Kingdom Lodge was constructed using a semicircular design. From overhead, it looks a bit like a horseshoe. This allows for maximum animal-viewing potential. Indeed, many of the resort's guestrooms have direct views of the savanna areas. Be sure to specify your viewing preference when you book a room. The telephone number for Disney's Animal Kingdom Lodge is 407-938-3000.

ROOMS: The 972 rooms, all finished in tapestries and vibrant colors, feature handcrafted dark-wood furniture, sand-colored walls, and earth-tone-patterned carpets. Deluxe rooms are a bit more spacious than their standard counterparts. Most rooms have two queen beds (some king-size beds are available), plus a daybed to accommodate up to five people; bunk beds are available in many rooms. All rooms have balconies. Suites include a parlor,

plus one or two bedrooms; there are king-size or queen-size beds in the bedrooms. Bathrooms have a separate vanity area with double sink. All rooms include an iron (with board), hair dryer, refrigerator, and weekday newspaper delivery. Club-level service is available.

As for the Villas, the first phase, located in Jambo House, opened in 2008. The second phase, Kidani Village, began hosting guests in its thatched-roof, hewn timber homes in early 2009. Also included in this village are a pool, fitness center, shop, table-service restaurant, and more. As with all DVC resorts, the homes are available to guests when not being used by members. For information on this member of the Disney Vacation Club family, call 800-800-9100 or visit *www.disneyvacationclub.com*.

WHERE TO EAT: In addition to its restaurants, the hotel offers round-the-clock room service.

Boma—Flavors of Africa: Boma is modeled after a bustling African marketplace. The restaurant boasts many types of cuisine in what chefs describe as a "global fusion" style. Served buffet style, the fare is a mix of French, Malaysian, Indian, Chinese, and English.

Jiko—The Cooking Place: The colors of sunset are the backdrop for this sublime eatery with an African flair. Wines from South Africa are featured.

The Mara: A spacious fast-food restaurant serving such kid-pleasers as pizza, burgers, and chicken fingers.

Sanaa: This colorful, table-service eatery at Kidani Village features African- and Indian-inspired cuisine.

WHERE TO DRINK: The lounges here are rustic and inviting. Some even offer the opportunity to sip cocktails while observing wildlife.

Cape Town Lounge and Wine Bar: Located inside Jiko—The Cooking Place, this spot features wines from South Africa.

Maji and Uzima Springs: These poolside bars serve specialty and traditional drinks.

Sanaa: A new 24-seat lounge located within the restaurant of the same name.

Victoria Falls: Set alongside a soothing waterfall, this mezzanine-level lounge features coffee, tea, domestic and South African wines, and assorted cocktails.

WHAT TO DO: Spying on wildlife is the main event in these parts. However, if you can manage to pry yourself away from those hoofed exhibitionists for a bit, there are plenty of

other diversions available—including tennis, basketball, shuffleboard, and a barbecue pavilion. Note that guests are welcome to partake in activities offered at other Walt Disney World resorts.

Arcades: Pumbaa's Fun & Games and Safari So Good are both stocked with the latest video games.

Children's Program: The Simba's Cubhouse play area, for (potty-trained) kids ages 3 through 12, is open in the evenings starting at 4 P.M. It costs about $12 per hour, per child. Reservations are required; call 407-939-3463. Kids can learn about the wildlife at the resort through nature-themed activities.

Health Club: Zahanati Massage and (24-hour) Fitness Center has exercise equipment, sauna, and spa services including massage. Kidani Village's Survival of the Fittest also offers exercise equipment.

Playground: The Hakuna Matata playground is located near the pool.

Shopping: Zawadi Marketplace stocks Africa-themed gifts, Disney character merchandise, clothing with the Animal Kingdom Lodge logo, and sundries. Johari Treasures tempts shoppers at Kidani Village.

Swimming: The resort's huge main pool, Uzima, looks like a natural watering hole. More impressive than the size of the zero-depth-entry pool, however, is the view from the pool deck. In addition to a kiddie pool, there are two whirlpools nearby. Kidani Village is home to another pool (Samawati Springs) and to Uwanja Camp, a watery playground.

Tennis: There are two clay courts available to all Animal Kingdom Lodge guests.

TRANSPORTATION: Buses go to the Magic Kingdom, Epcot, Disney's Hollywood Studios, Animal Kingdom, Typhoon Lagoon, Blizzard Beach, and Downtown Disney.

Coronado Springs

This resort reveals its Southwestern U.S.-Mexican theme in such elements as a tiled stucco lobby with a fountain and a pyramid with water tumbling down from it that appears to have created the Mayan ruin-themed pool. The 1,921 rooms are found in three guest areas that stretch around Lago Dorado, a 22-acre lake. (It can take five minutes or more to walk to the farthest rooms.) The food court and restaurant are near the lobby. A convention center offers access to business services. The phone number for Coronado Springs is 407-939-1000.

ROOMS: Standard rooms are smaller than those at Disney's deluxe hotels, but adequate for up to four; each has two double beds (some king-size beds are available). In-room amenities include a coffeemaker, refrigerator, hair dryer, and dataport. Decor varies in each section but is characterized by yellow, blue, and scarlet accents. In the Casitas area, where most suites are located, terra-cotta guest buildings occupy a citylike landscape. In the pueblo-style Ranchos, scattered along a dry streambed, rooms have a rustic feel. Cabanas, located along the rocky palm-lined beach, reflect the casual feel of their namesake.

WHERE TO EAT: In addition to a full-service restaurant and food court, limited room service is available for breakfast and dinner.

Cafe Rix: A quick-service eatery, Rix has offerings for breakfast, lunch, and dinner.

Maya Grill: Open for breakfast and dinner, this spot offers seafood, steak, lamb, and pork cooked over an open-pit, wood-fired grill.

Pepper Market: High ceilings make this nontraditional food court feel like an open-air market. The fare includes tacos, tostadas, pizza, pasta, and omelets made to order. Note that there is an automatic ten-percent gratuity for dining in the Pepper Market.

WHERE TO DRINK: There are three places to wet your whistle at Coronado Springs.

Laguna Bar: A lagoonside lounge outside the lobby, this spot serves drinks during pool hours.

> ## HOT TIP!
> Coronado Springs' La Marina operates on a seasonal basis. If it isn't open during your stay, know that Coronado guests may rent boats, bikes, and enjoy other recreational experiences offered at any Walt Disney World resort.

Rix Lounge: This colorful lounge provides cocktails, appetizers, and evening entertainment, and is located in the main building.

Siestas: In the Dig Site area, this poolside bar lets swimmers and archaeologists enjoy a variety of cocktails and light snacks.

WHAT TO DO: There is an array of water sports in which to participate, as well as volleyball and a short nature trail.

Arcades: Iguana Arcade is in the Dig Site area.

Biking: Bikes and surrey bikes may be rented at La Marina.

Boating: A selection of equipment, including pedal boats and motorboats, is available for rent at La Marina.

PHOTO BY JILL SAFRO

Fishing: Two-hour, guided fishing excursions are offered on the 22-acre Lago Dorado. Call 407-WDW-BASS. Fishing excursions are offered seasonally.

Online Check-in

Planning a stay at a Disney owned-and-operated resort? If so, you can take advantage of Disney's online check-in service.

Meant to streamline the actual check-in experience, the virtual service is available 10 days in advance of and up through your arrival day.

Online check-in expedites the arrival experience by getting the pesky paperwork out of the way prior to arrival. Before you log on, know that you'll be asked to provide the following: the credit card that will be used for room charges, mobile phone number, address, arrival and departure times, the names of all guests, and room requests (but know that special requests are subject to availability).

With all that info already in the system, guests just need to show up at the resort and present a valid government-issued photo ID. In return, they receive a welcome packet including room keys and WDW information. There should be clear signs indicating the spot for packet pick-up.

How does one check in via the Internet? Simply visit *www.disneyworld.com* and click on the checking-in section under My Disney Vacation. Note that this service is available for all WDW resort categories. And know that checking in online does not mean you can check in early. (Unless, of course, there is a room available—a happy surprise that has been known to happen.)

Health Club: La Vida fitness center offers a full range of strength and cardio equipment 24/7, plus spa services (by day).

Playground: The Explorer's Playground is part of the Dig Site play area and includes a huge sandbox, complete with Mayan carvings waiting to be excavated.

Salon: The Casa de Belleza salon is located near La Vida Fitness Center. A full-service facility, Casa de Belleza offers hair cuts, sets, coloring, beard and mustache trim, manicures, pedicures, facials, and more. Operating hours are generally from 9 A.M. until 6 P.M. daily. To make an appointment, call 407-939-3965.

Shopping: Panchito's Gifts & Sundries is where you will find souvenir items with a Southwestern flavor, Disney merchandise, film, and necessities.

Swimming: The main pool is in the Dig Site area. It surrounds a Mayan pyramid and features a towering 123-foot waterslide. There is a whirlpool and a kiddie pool. Each guest-room area features an unguarded pool.

TRANSPORTATION: Buses go to the Magic Kingdom, Epcot, Disney's Hollywood Studios, Animal Kingdom, Typhoon Lagoon, Blizzard Beach, and Downtown Disney.

Pop Century

What do you get when you mix decades of American pop culture with a Disney resort? Pop Century! Like the All-Star resorts, Pop Century is a vivid celebration of Americana. The 2,880-room resort represents the second half of the twentieth century. The resort's larger-than-life "time capsules" commemorate the toys, fads, dance crazes, and catchphrases that swept the nation from the 1950s through the 1990s. It's groovy . . . you dig?

As a WDW value resort, the Pop Century property offers few frills, but the service is good, the atmosphere's colorful, and the transportation is efficient. Guests check in at Classic Hall, which also features a food and merchandise location, arcade, and guest services desk. To reach Pop Century resort, call 407-938-4000.

ROOMS: The guestrooms, measuring 260 square feet, are a bit on the small side compared with those at Port Orleans, which are 314 square feet. Each room has two double beds (with the exception of rooms designed for travelers with disabilities, which have one king-size bed), a vanity area with a sink, a bathroom, a small dresser, a table with chairs, and a dataport.

WHERE TO EAT: The food court features a bakery and a convenience market, plus several stands geared to pizza, pasta, and burgers. The Pop Century resort delivers pizza to guestrooms from about 4 P.M. to midnight.

WHERE TO DRINK: Petals is a bar located near the Hippy Dippy pool.

WHAT TO DO: Guests may swim in any of the Pop Century resort pools. They may rent boating equipment at any WDW resort.
   Arcade: Revisit classic video games or discover some new ones at Fast Forward arcade.
   Playground: There is a soft-surface playground with, among other compelling features, an interactive water fountain.
   Shopping: The Everything Pop shop has a selection of books, character merchandise, sundries, and snacks.
   Swimming: The hotel has three pools (in the shapes of a bowling pin, computer, and a flower), plus a kiddie pool.

TRANSPORTATION: Buses stop at Classic Hall for trips to each of the four theme parks, Blizzard Beach, Typhoon Lagoon, and Downtown Disney.

Art of Animation Resort

The Walt Disney World resort landscape is getting a serious burst of color with the addition of this vibrant celebration of Disney animation. A brand-new "value" resort, Disney's Art of Animation makes its debut in the middle of 2012.

   Pop Century's next-door neighbor (the resorts share access to Hourglass Lake), Art of Animation boasts colossal figures from classic animated films. It also has three themed pools (Flippin' Fins, Cozy Cone, and The Big Blue Pool), playgrounds, courtyards, an arcade, and an interactive splash zone featuring everyone's favorite clownfish, Nemo.

   Standard rooms, which are housed in *The Little Mermaid*-themed buildings, sleep up to 4 and come with the usual amenities afforded to Walt Disney World's "value" resorts (see page 65 for details).

   Suites are spread among *The Lion King*, *Cars,* and *Finding Nemo* buildings. Each unit sleeps up to 6 guests (in 3 separate sleeping areas), a kitchenette, and 2 bathrooms.

   A food court known as Landscapes Cafe serves three meals a day (and is the place to fill up refillable mugs for the length of your stay). Choices here include salads, sandwiches, burgers, pizza, and pasta. There is also a "grab and go" market with pre-packaged selections, and in-room pizza delivery. Sundries and souvenirs are offered at the Ink and Paint shop. Spirits are available at the pool bar near The Big Blue pool.

   The resort also offers high-speed Internet access, babysitting and childcare services, laundry, and dry cleaning. (Fees apply.)

   At press time, the resort was expected to open by June 1, 2012. For reservations, visit *www.disneyworld.com* or call 407-W-DISNEY (934-7639).

Disney Cruise Line

Disney Cruise Line ships—*Disney Wonder*, *Disney Magic*, *Disney Dream*, and the brand-new *Disney Fantasy*—rank among the world's finest oceangoing vessels. The onboard experience is essentially the same on all Disney ships, but some restaurants, entertainment, and theming differ—as do the lengths of the cruises and the destinations. The *Dream* and *Fantasy* primarily take guests on cruises to the Caribbean, the *Magic* takes guests to Nova Scotia and the Caribbean, and the *Wonder* journeys to Alaska and the Mexican Riviera.

From the ships' design to entertainment options, families, teens, and adults all have their own comfort zones—without ever having to say good-bye to Mickey. (In addition to the Mouse, the usual cast of characters is onboard.) Caribbean cruises depart from Port Canaveral, Florida; Galveston, Texas; and New York, New York. Cruises to the Mexican Riviera start at the Port of Los Angeles. And Alaskan cruises depart from Seattle and Vancouver. When transfers are purchased, guests travel to the port by motor coach. They then board a Disney ship for their journey. For specifics on these departure points, visit *www.disneycruise.com* or call 800-910-3659.

Since U.S. government passport requirements continue to change, a valid passport is strongly recommended for everyone planning to sail on a Disney cruise.

The ships' classic exteriors recall the majesty of early ocean liners. For example, *Disney Magic* guests enter a three-story atrium, where traditional definitions of elegance expand to include a bronze statue of Mickey as helmsman and subtle cutout Disney character silhouettes along the grand staircase. There's even a 15-foot, topsy-turvy statue of a "goofy" painter hanging off the *Disney Magic*'s stern.

Vacations can be booked through a travel agent, or by calling 800-910-3659 or visiting *www.disneycruise.com.*

ROOMS: All staterooms aboard the ships are a cut above the standard cruising cabin. On average, staterooms offer about 25 percent more space, most have a bath and a half, and the majority are outside rooms with ocean vistas —many with verandahs. All feature telephones with "land lines," TVs, hair dryers, and safes. There are rooms equipped for guests with disabilities. Interior rooms on the *Dream* and *Fantasy* have "magical portholes" with live video feed from the bridge. All staterooms are nonsmoking (though smoking is permitted on stateroom verandahs).

Shipboard accommodations, meals, and entertainment are included, as are meals on Disney's private island, Castaway Cay.

Note: Some names and theming differ from ship to ship, but the experiences are comparable.

WHERE TO EAT: There are several themed dining rooms (with one adults-only restaurant alternative on the *Magic* and *Wonder* and two on the *Dream* and *Fantasy*); guests dine in each of the main rooms, enjoying a different culinary experience each night.

WHERE TO DRINK: Among the options are several lounges, including a sports bar and several poolside spots. Beat Street is a colorful, adults-only cluster of nighttime entertainment venues located on the *Magic*. The *Wonder* equivalent is known as Route 66. On the *Dream* and *Fantasy* it's The District and Europa, respectively. Each area is zoned for grown-ups and offers a variety of environments for guests to play, party, or just relax.

WHAT TO DO: Recreational zones on each ship, as well as at ports of call, are strategically located to attract families, teens, and adults to different areas, with nearly an entire deck devoted to kids. A cruise director keeps guests apprised of the options. Shore excursions may be booked ahead at *www.disneycruise.com* or once aboard the ship.

Activities for Grown-ups: Adults-only activities range from wine tasting to guest lectures. There is an adults-only pool onboard and a secluded beach for grown-ups at Castaway Cay.

Buena Vista Theater: A state-of-the-art cinema, this movie theater offers new and classic feature films.

Children's Programs: A huge area dedicated exclusively to kids offers supervised, age-specific programs for kids ages 3 through 12 from 9 A.M. until midnight. Teens can enjoy special programs at Vibe. These spots can be found on all Disney Cruise ships. Ocean Quest is a *Magic*-only area that lets young sailors experience a scaled replica of the ship's bridge.

Deck Parties: Guests may dance to live music, sip cocktails, and nibble snacks at informal, swinging shindigs at sea. With the exception of the Alaska itinerary, most cruises feature a popular pirate-themed party complete with fireworks.

Shopping: In addition to the shipboard shops, guests may indulge their shopping fantasies while exploring the various ports of call. Shops on the ship are duty free.

Spa and Salon: Adult guests get in ship-shape at this bright, modern facility, which offers exercise equipment and spa treatments (with indoor and outdoor treatment rooms), educational and enrichment programs, sauna, steam room, whirlpool, and massage. The salon offers many services, including haircuts, manicures, and pedicures (fees apply). Note that appointments fill up fast—book in advance at *www.disneycruise.com* or as soon as possible once aboard the ship.

Sports: Guests play volleyball and basketball on the sports deck and at Castaway Cay. (Each ship has its own sports deck.)

Swimming: There are several whirlpools and three swimming pools on each ship: a family pool, a kids' pool, and an adults-only pool. Guests may also swim off the sandy shores and lagoon of Castaway Cay.

Teen Entertainment: On all ships, a place called Vibe is where teens (and teens only) may hang out, watch movies, and listen to music. There are also teen-oriented activities on the ship, as well as on Castaway Cay. Activities are for teens ages 13 through 17.

Walt Disney Theatre: A tribute to the grand theatrical palaces of long ago. Guests see an original live production each night.

Castaway Cay

Every Disney Cruise Line trip that departs from Port Canaveral, Florida, wraps up with a visit to Castaway Cay (pronounced *key*). Disney has maintained the island's natural beauty while providing a host of outdoor activities, including snorkeling, biking, and boating. The island has a beach for families, a beach for teens, and a mile-long stretch of sand—complete with massage cabanas—for adults only.

As guests awaken at the island, they find their ship docked at Castaway Cay's private pier. The pier allows for easy access to and from the ship.

Castaway Cay, a 1,000-acre tropical island, is in the Bahamas, east of Fort Lauderdale. Trams are available for guests who wish to explore the island. All of the architecture, including a bar, restaurant, market, and even a post office, is in traditional Bahamian style.

Resorts on Hotel Plaza Blvd.

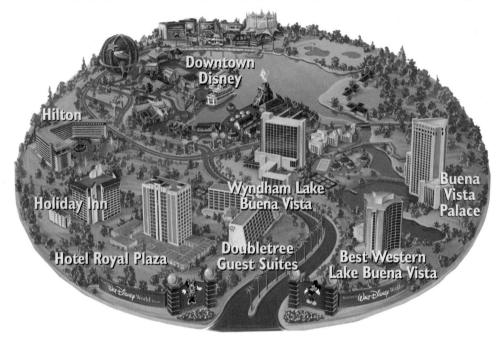

These seven hotels—Best Western Lake Buena Vista, Doubletree Guest Suites, Wyndham Lake Buena Vista, Hilton, Royal Plaza, Buena Vista Palace Hotel & Spa, and Holiday Inn (which has reopened after an extensive refurbishment)—though inside Walt Disney World boundaries, are neither owned nor operated by Disney. However, a few have been here since the park opened in 1971 or soon thereafter (sometimes under different names), accommodating Mickey enthusiasts from the beginning. The hotels are not themed, but the three largest (the Hilton, Buena Vista Palace, and Wyndham) do have meals hosted by Disney characters.

Often referred to as the Downtown Disney Resort Area Hotels, they line the mile-long Hotel Plaza Boulevard. The Hilton, Buena Vista Palace, and Wyndham are across the street from the Marketplace, with its shops, restaurants, and nightlife. The other four properties are a 10- to 25-minute stroll away. They are also close to Crossroads at Lake Buena Vista shopping center, home to inexpensive eateries and a 24-hour grocery. The privileges of staying in one of these hotels include:

• Car rental desk on the premises (at press time, at all but the Royal Plaza).

• Free bus service to the four theme parks, with limited service to Downtown Disney, Typhoon Lagoon, and Blizzard Beach. The buses, which are not part of the Disney transportation network, make two trips every hour; be sure to allow extra time for bus travel. One bus serves the Hilton, Doubletree, and Royal Plaza; another serves the other hotels (it takes at least ten minutes to stop at all resorts on the loop). Note that buses load and unload in the middle of the parking lot at some parks.

• Flexibility to book tickets for both on- and, in most cases, off-WDW-property attractions.

• Preferred access to Disney golf courses.

• A "Passport to Savings" coupon book with exclusive discounts and specials on dining, shopping, and entertainment.

• Reservations for Disney dinner shows and theme park restaurants.

Note that guests staying in the resorts on Hotel Plaza Boulevard do have to pay for parking at Disney parks and other Walt Disney World attractions, and they cannot charge purchases made at Disney World shops and restaurants with a resort ID.

To book a room, call the individual hotel's toll-free number or WDW Central Reservations at 407-W-DISNEY (934-7639). The resorts on Hotel Plaza Blvd. are included in several Walt Disney Travel Company packages. Internet users can get information via *www.downtowndisneyhotels.com*.

All of the hotels offer nonsmoking rooms and accommodations for travelers with disabilities. To get to the hotels from the airport, take Exit 68 off I-4.

BEST WESTERN LAKE BUENA VISTA RESORT: This mostly leisure-oriented, 18-story hotel is surrounded by pines and has an entry lined with oaks draped in Spanish moss. Each of the 325 spacious, smoke-free rooms and suites has either one king-size bed and a queen sofa bed or two queen-size beds, as well as a balcony. Rooms also come with complimentary Wi-Fi, voice mail, coffeemaker, safe, hair dryer, and iron with board. Baths have one sink and plenty of counter space. Small refrigerators rent for $10 a day.

Each of the four suites occupies a corner of the 18th floor and features a wet bar, two phones, two TVs, a refrigerator, whirlpool tub, and an impressive glassed-in porch with skylights and a ceiling fan. Rooms on the seventh floor and higher offer fine views of the other resorts on Hotel Plaza Boulevard. There is an Enterprise car rental desk in the lobby.

The hotel also has a fitness center, business center, a game room, a heated pool, small kiddie pool, shop, and guest laundry facilities. Other amenities include room service and complimentary Wi-Fi throughout the resort.

The hotel's lobby and restaurant area features Trader's Island Grill and the Parakeet Café for breakfast, dinner, and snacks. The Flamingo Cove offers poolside or inside seating and serves lunch, dinner, cocktails, and snacks. For a quick pizza fix, try Pizza Hut Express.

Rates for this hotel range from about $99 to $239 for rooms; about $299 to $399 for suites. Parking is free, with optional valet parking for a fee. Best Western Lake Buena Vista Resort, 2000 Hotel Plaza Blvd., Lake Buena Vista, FL 32830; 407-828-2424 or 800-348-3765; *www.lakebuenavistaresorthotel.com.*

DOUBLETREE GUEST SUITES: This 229-unit property has a stellar staff, homey atmosphere, low-slung facade reminiscent of WDW's Contemporary hotel, bright colors and whimsical patterns throughout. In the lobby, a child's check-in desk adjoins the one for grown-ups. Kids get a bag of goodies, and everyone gets a chocolate chip cookie. The only all-suite hotel in the Downtown Disney area, it has roomy (625 square feet) units, each with a living room and sleeper sofa, dressing area, and separate bedroom. The one-bedroom suites sleep up to six; there are five two-bedroom suites. Most of the bedrooms have two double beds; a few king beds are available.

The renovated decor features cheerful blues and oranges offset by contrasting neutrals. Room amenities include two TVs, pay-per-view movies, refrigerator, coffeemaker, microwave oven, hair dryer, high-speed Internet access (for a fee), a desk, and safe.

Recreational facilities include a heated pool, kiddie pool, and a whirlpool in a landscaped area, plus a fitness room, two lighted tennis

courts, jogging trail, and small playground. Evergreen, a full-service restaurant with a pool bar, offers a breakfast buffet, lunch, and dinner as well as snacks and sandwiches throughout the day. Cocktails and wine are also available. A market/deli provides snack items and groceries, including more of those famous chocolate chip cookies (though you'll have to pay for these!). There is a Budget Rental Car desk by the lobby.

Rates range from $99 to $399. Parking charges apply. Doubletree Guest Suites, 2305 Hotel Plaza Blvd., Lake Buena Vista, FL 32830; 407-934-1000 or 800-222-8733; *www.doubletreeguestsuites.com.*

PHOTO BY JILL SAFRO

WYNDHAM LAKE BUENA VISTA RESORT:

The Wyndham sports a spiffy new look thanks to a $25 million top to bottom renovation. The transformation is obvious upon stepping into the cheerful Bermuda-themed lobby. The 626 refurbished rooms are in a 19-story tower and two wings framing two large courtyards. Most rooms have two double beds, though 77 king-bed rooms are available. There are 7 spacious suites. All accommodations include a refrigerator, coffeemaker, Wi-Fi (for a fee), flat-screen TV, plush bedding, safe, hair dryer, iron, and daily newspaper (by request). Guests receive a discount at many shops and restaurants at nearby Downtown Disney.

Extensive recreational facilities—the hotel's major appeal—include an exercise room, two lighted tennis courts, and a basketball court. The impressive Oasis Aquatic Playground features a heated pool with zero-depth entry, interactive features such as water cannons, and a relaxing hot tub with

a lovely view of the lake. Special, kids-only activities are scheduled throughout the day. There's a health club, arcade, and business center, too.

Lake View Restaurant (on the mezzanine level) serves breakfast and dinner. Breakfast is hosted by Disney characters on Tuesday, Thursday, and Saturday. Sundial (in the lobby), open 24 hours, has snacks and light fare. For cocktails, there's Horizons Bar (next to Lake View), the Eclipse lobby bar, and Oasis pool bar.

A lobby shop sells sundries and Disney-themed souvenirs. Room rates range from $79 to $159 year-round; suites range from $150 to $350. There is an additional resort fee that includes parking, Wi-Fi, and other amenities. Wyndham Lake Buena Vista Resort, 1850 Hotel Plaza Blvd., Lake Buena Vista, FL 32830; 407-828-4444 or 800-624-4109; *www.wyndhamlakebuenavista.com.*

HILTON: This hotel gets high marks for its 23 well-groomed acres, laid-back ambience, pool area, and upscale shops. The 814 rooms, all of which recently underwent extensive refurbishment, have mini-bars, voice mail, safes, and high-speed Internet access.

Among the resort's restaurants and lounges, Andiamo Italian Bistro & Grille offers American and Italian fare, while Benihana Steakhouse and Sushi serves Japanese favorites and entertainment (both eateries serve dinner only); Covington Mill serves breakfast and lunch (with Disney characters attending Sunday breakfast); Rum Largo Poolside Cafe serves burgers, sandwiches, salads, and tropical drinks alfresco; Mainstreet Market, open 24 hours, is part deli, part country store (serving Starbucks coffee). For light meals, snacks, or cocktails, drop by John T's

PHOTO BY JILL SAFRO

lounge; specialty coffees and ice cream are served at Mugs. There is an Avis car rental on the premises.

Recreational facilities include a tropical whirlpool, two heated swimming pools, a kiddie pool, fitness room, and large game room. Rates range from $99 to $299; suites are $149 to $1,500. Parking charges apply for self-parking and valet. Hilton in the Walt Disney World Resort, 1751 Hotel Plaza Blvd., Lake Buena Vista, FL 32830; 407-827-4000 or 800-782-4414; *www.hiltonorlandoresort.com.*

Note: This is the *only* hotel on Hotel Plaza Boulevard to offer Extra Magic Hours. For details about this program (which, on select days, lets guests enter a theme park an hour before it officially opens or stay up to three hours after it closes), ask at the front desk.

HOLIDAY INN IN THE WALT DISNEY WORLD RESORT: This family-friendly hotel has reopened following a $35 million renovation. All 323 rooms are nonsmoking and have either one king or two queen beds. Some are available with views of nearby Downtown Disney. Guestrooms are decorated in earth tones and include a flat-screen TV with DirecTV, coffeemaker, mini fridge, safe, and hair dryer. Bathrooms have granite countertops. Free high-speed Wi-Fi is available in all rooms, as well as the business center.

The Palm Breezes Restaurant, located in the atrium, serves three meals a day (kids through age 12 eat free). Palm Breezes has a "grab and go" section, a bar, and provides room service.

There is a zero-depth-entry heated pool, a whirlpool, arcade, and 24-hour fitness center.

Double room rates range from $99 to $149. Holiday Inn in the Walt Disney World Resort; 1805 Hotel Plaza Blvd., Lake Buena Vista, FL 32830; 407-828-8888 or 888-465-4329; *www. hiorlando.com.*

HOTEL ROYAL PLAZA: Soft hues of white, tan, and pale green permeate this property. The 394 guest units, including 23 suites, are divided between a 17-story main tower, with a glass-enclosed elevator scaling the facade, and two-story lanai wings offering traditional rooms with gated patios or small balconies.

Guestrooms are furnished with either a king-size bed or two double beds, and include a desk, dresser, safe, coffeemaker, ceiling fan, high-speed Internet (wired and wireless), and sitting area with a sleeper sofa. All baths have granite countertops and hair dryers, and some have oversized Roman tubs with separate showers; Premier Tower Rooms and Executive Suites have whirlpool tubs.

Facilities include a heated pool, a whirlpool, fitness room (for guests ages 16 and older), separate game rooms for adults and kids, and four lighted tennis courts. There is also a business center and a Disney merchandise shop.

The Giraffe Café offers all meals, including an ample breakfast buffet; Sips pool bar offers "grab and go" items; the Marketplace is open until 11 P.M. Rates range from $79 to $169 for up to five in a room; suites, $129 to $459.

Hotel Royal Plaza, 1905 Hotel Plaza Blvd., Lake Buena Vista, FL 32830; 407-828-2828 or 800-248-7890; *www.royalplaza.com.*

BUENA VISTA PALACE HOTEL & SPA: The tallest hotel in the Downtown Disney area and the largest of the resorts on Hotel Plaza Boulevard (it's actually at the intersection of Hotel Plaza Boulevard and Buena Vista Drive) is a cluster of towers set on 27 acres beside Lake Buena Vista. Each of the newly renovated 1,014 rooms has a ceiling fan, two phones (one cordless; both with voice mail and speakerphone), high-speed Internet access (wired and wireless), two queen beds or one king, a coffeemaker, 32-inch flat-panel TV, and weekday newspaper in the lobby. Most rooms have a balcony or patio. In addition, there are one- and two-bedroom suites and two-story penthouses with microwaves. Twin/queen sofa beds are in suites and rooms with king beds. All guestrooms have a safe and refrigerator.

The resort's 10,000-square-foot spa features myriad treatments and services, a full-service salon, fitness center, and a private lap pool. Recreation Island accommodates two swimming pools, a kiddie pool, whirlpool, lighted tennis court, sand volleyball court, and children's playground and arcade.

PHOTO BY JILL SAFRO

Shades of Green

Shades of Green is a recreational retreat for active and retired military personnel and their families, members of the reserves and the National Guard, and U.S. Department of Defense employees. This 586-room resort is near the Grand Floridian but is not linked with the monorail system.

The resort features two tennis courts, two pools, a small health club, restaurant, bar and lounge, gift shop, arcade, laundry facilities, and free transportation around WDW.

Room rates are based on military or civilian grade. Select multi-day tickets are offered at a discount. The property's three golf courses—the Palm, the Magnolia, and Oak Trail—are open to all WDW guests (see *Sports* for details). All other activities are for hotel guests and their families only.

Magical Express service is not available to guests at this resort. The number for Shades of Green is 407-824-3400; *www.shadesofgreen.org.*

The hotel also provides room service, and it has boutiques and a guest laundry room. Dining spots include the lakeside Watercress Cafe, which serves breakfast and lunch only (Disney characters are in attendance Sunday mornings); the Watercress Mini Market, open from 6 A.M. to midnight for baked goods and sandwiches; and the Outback Restaurant (not part of the chain) for seafood and steak. For light meals and cocktails, try the Lobby Lounge, the Kook Sports Bar, or the Castaway Grill and Shipwreck Bar.

Rates for rooms are generally $99 and up per night (no charge for kids under 18); suites, which sleep up to eight, are $149 and up. Rollaways cost $20 per night; cribs are free. There is an Alamo car rental desk here, too. Buena Vista Palace Hotel & Spa, 1900 Buena Vista Dr., Lake Buena Vista, FL 32830; *www.buenavistapalace.com;* 407-827-2727 or 866-397-6516.

Magic Kingdom

The Magic Kingdom is the most enchanting part of the World. Few who visit it are disappointed, and even the most blasé travelers manage a smile. The sight of the soaring spires of Cinderella Castle, the gleaming woodwork of the Main Street shops, and the crescendo of music that follows the parades never fail to have an effect. Even when the crowds are large and the weather is hot, a visitor who has toured this wonderland dozens of times can still look around and think how satisfying this place is for the spirit.

What makes the Magic Kingdom timeless is its combination of the classic and the futuristic. Both childhood favorites and space-age creatures have a home here. Every "land" has a theme, carried through from the costumes worn by the hosts and hostesses and the food served in the restaurants to the merchandise sold in the shops, and even the design of the trash cans. Thousands of details contribute to the overall effect, and recognizing these touches makes any visit more enjoyable.

But the delight most guests experience upon first glimpse of the Magic Kingdom can disappear when disorientation sets in. There are so many bends to every pathway, so many sights and sounds clamoring for attention, it's too easy to wander aimlessly and miss the best the Magic Kingdom has to offer. So we earnestly suggest that you study this chapter before your visit.

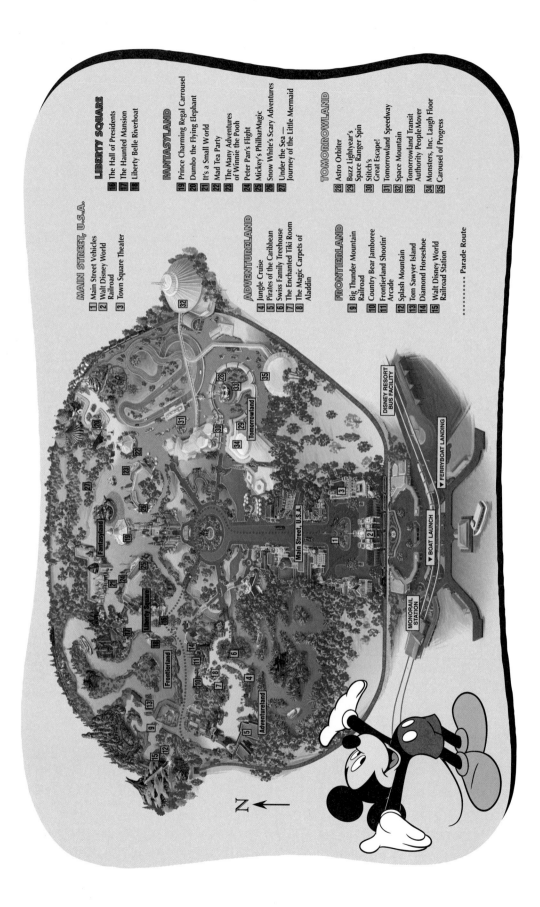

MAIN STREET, U.S.A.

1 Main Street Vehicles
2 Walt Disney World Railroad
3 Town Square Theater

LIBERTY SQUARE

16 The Hall of Presidents
17 The Haunted Mansion
18 Liberty Belle Riverboat

FANTASYLAND

19 Prince Charming Regal Carrousel
20 Dumbo the Flying Elephant
21 It's a Small World
22 Mad Tea Party
23 The Many Adventures of Winnie the Pooh
24 Peter Pan's Flight
25 Mickey's PhilharMagic
26 Snow White's Scary Adventures
27 Under the Sea — Journey of the Little Mermaid

ADVENTURELAND

4 Jungle Cruise
5 Pirates of the Caribbean
6 Swiss Family Treehouse
7 The Enchanted Tiki Room
8 The Magic Carpets of Aladdin

FRONTIERLAND

9 Big Thunder Mountain Railroad
10 Country Bear Jamboree
11 Frontierland Shootin' Arcade
12 Splash Mountain
13 Tom Sawyer Island
14 Diamond Horseshoe
15 Walt Disney World Railroad Station

TOMORROWLAND

28 Astro Orbiter
29 Buzz Lightyear's Space Ranger Spin
30 Stitch's Great Escape!
31 Tomorrowland Speedway
32 Space Mountain
33 Tomorrowland Transit Authority PeopleMover
34 Monsters, Inc. Laugh Floor
35 Carousel of Progress

·········· Parade Route

Getting Oriented

When you visit Walt Disney World's original theme park, it's vital to know the lay of the "lands." The Magic Kingdom has six lands—Main Street, U.S.A.; Adventureland; Frontierland; Liberty Square; Fantasyland; and Tomorrowland (Mickey's Toontown Fair has left town). Main Street begins at Town Square, located just inside the park gates, and runs directly to Cinderella Castle. The area in front of the castle is known as the Central Plaza or the Hub. Bridges over the waterways here serve as passages to each of the lands.

As you enter the park, the first bridge on your left goes to Adventureland; the next, to Liberty Square and Frontierland. On your right, the first bridge heads to Tomorrowland; the second, to Fantasyland. The end points of the pathways leading to the lands are linked by a street that is roughly circular, so that the layout of the Magic Kingdom resembles a wheel. All attractions, restaurants, and shops are found along the wheel's rim and spokes.

Guidemaps and Times Guides are available at the turnstiles, at City Hall in Town Square, and at many shops. Be sure to pick them up as soon as possible. You'll find them to be valuable navigational and scheduling resources.

HOW TO GET THERE

Take Exit 64B off I-4. Continue about four miles to the Auto Plaza and park; walk or take a tram to the main entrance complex, known as the Transportation and Ticket Center (TTC). Choose a seven-minute ferry ride or a slightly shorter trip by monorail for the last leg of an anticipation-filled journey.

By WDW Transportation: From the Grand Floridian and Polynesian: monorail or boat. From the Contemporary: monorail or walkway. (It is about a 10- to 15-minute stroll.) From Epcot: monorail to the Transportation and Ticket Center (TTC), then transfer to the Magic Kingdom monorail or ferry. From Disney's Hollywood Studios, Animal Kingdom, and the resorts on Hotel Plaza Boulevard: buses to the TTC, then transfer to ferry or monorail. From Fort Wilderness: boat or bus. From Disney's Wilderness Lodge: boat or bus. From Downtown Disney: bus to any Disney resort and transfer to the Magic Kingdom bus (or monorail). From all other Walt Disney World resorts: buses.

PARKING

All-day parking at the Magic Kingdom is $14 for day visitors (free to Walt Disney World resort guests with a valid resort ID or an annual pass). Simply bear left after passing through the Auto Plaza; attendants will direct you into one of a dozen lots, all named after Disney characters. Minnie, Sleepy, and Dopey are within walking distance of the TTC; other lots are served by trams.

Note the section and aisle in which you park. The parking ticket allows for re-entry to the parking area throughout the day.

HOURS

The Magic Kingdom is generally open from 9 A.M. to 8 P.M. However, during busy seasons, it's open later. It's best to reach the park entrance about a half hour before the opening time. To avoid the morning crush, consider postponing your visit until 1 P.M. or later.

Note that on select days, the Magic Kingdom opens early or stays open late for WDW resort guests only (this is known as Extra Magic Hours). For details and current schedules, visit *www.disneyworld.com* or call 407-824-4321. The park tends to be more crowded on such days, so consider starting here and "hopping" elsewhere later in the day.

GETTING AROUND

Walt Disney World Railroad steam trains make a 20-minute loop of the park, stopping to pick up and drop off passengers at stations on Main Street and Frontierland. (It's an efficient way to travel when parades are being run or there's a lot of foot traffic.) Horseless carriages, a fire engine, and horse-drawn trolleys take turns offering one-way trips down Main Street.

Park Primer

BABY FACILITIES

The best place in the Magic Kingdom to take care of little ones' needs is the Baby Care Center. This cheery site, equipped with changing tables and facilities for nursing mothers, is located next to the Crystal Palace restaurant. Disposable diapers are for sale at many Magic Kingdom shops (they're kept behind the counter, just ask). All park restrooms are equipped with changing facilities.

CAMERA NEEDS

The Camera Center in the Town Square Theater proffers memory cards and disposable cameras, plus film and batteries. Film is sold in many Magic Kingdom shops, but cannot be developed in the park.

DISABILITY INFORMATION

Most Magic Kingdom shops and restaurants, and many attractions, are accessible to guests using wheelchairs. Additional services are available for guests with visual or hearing disabilities. The *Guidemap for Guests with Disabilities* provides an overview of all services available, including transportation, parking, and attraction access. For more information, see the "Travelers with Disabilities" section of the *Getting Ready to Go* chapter.

FERRY VERSUS MONORAIL

For guests arriving by car or bus, it's necessary to decide whether to travel to the Magic Kingdom by ferry or monorail. The monorail makes the trip from the Transportation and Ticket Center (TTC) in about five minutes, while the ferry takes about seven. During busy seasons, the ferry will often get you there faster (long lines can form at the monorail, and most people don't make the short walk to the ferry landing). Vacationers who use wheel-chairs should note that while the monorail platforms are accessible, the ramp leading to the boarding area is a bit on the steep side.

FIRST AID

A registered nurse tends to minor medical problems at the First Aid Center, located near the Crystal Palace restaurant.

INFORMATION

City Hall, just inside the park entrance, serves as the Magic Kingdom's information headquarters. Guest Relations representatives can answer questions. Guidemaps and Times Guides, updated weekly (including details about entertainment, as well as character greeting times and locations), are available here, and all kinds of arrangements can be made, including reservations for restaurants. Should you have problems with your ticket or a question about the number of unused days remaining on a ticket, City Hall is the place to go.

LOCKERS

Attended lockers are located just inside the park entrance, all the way to the right. Lockers are also available at the Transportation and Ticket Center (TTC). Cost is $7–$9 per day, (plus a $5 refundable deposit) for unlimited use. If you "hop" to another park on the same day, you don't have to pay to get another locker. Simply present your receipt to the attendant and you're all set.

LOST & FOUND

On the day of your visit, report lost articles at City Hall or at the TTC. Recovered items can also be claimed at these locations. After your visit, call 407-824-4245.

HOT TIP!

Certain attractions keep shorter hours than the Magic Kingdom itself (e.g., The Hall of Presidents and Tom Sawyer Island). To make sure you catch all your favorites, check a Times Guide when you enter the park.

LOST CHILDREN

Report lost children at City Hall or the Baby Care Center, and alert the nearest Disney employee to the problem.

MONEY MATTERS

The Magic Kingdom has five Automated Teller Machines (ATMs): near the locker rental site just inside the entrance; inside City Hall on Main Street, U.S.A.; near the Frontier Shootin' Arcade; near Pinocchio Village Haus; and at the Tomorrowland Light & Power Co. arcade (next to Space Mountain). Most foreign currency can be exchanged at City Hall.

Credit cards (American Express, Visa, MasterCard, JCB, Discover Card, Diner's Club, and the Disney Visa card) are accepted as payment for admission, merchandise, and meals at all full-service restaurants and fast-food locations. Traveler's checks, Disney gift cards, and Walt Disney World resort ID cards are also accepted in most places. Some food and souvenir carts accept cash only.

Disney Dollars are available at City Hall (as well as all Disney Stores) in $1, $5, and $10 denominations. They are accepted for dining and merchandise throughout Walt Disney World and can be exchanged at any time for U.S. currency.

PACKAGE PICKUP

Individual shops can arrange for purchases to be transported to the Package Pickup at the Main Street Chamber of Commerce, next to City Hall, for pickup between noon and park closing time (at least three hours after purchase). Packages may be sent to Disney resorts, too. The delivery service is free.

SAME-DAY RE-ENTRY

Be sure to retain your ticket if you plan to return later the same day. A hand stamp is no longer required for re-entry.

SECURITY CHECK

Guests entering Disney theme parks are subject to a security check. Backpacks, parcels, purses, etc., will be searched by Disney security personnel before guests are permitted to pass through the turnstiles.

STROLLERS & WHEELCHAIRS

Wheelchair Rental, located just inside the turnstiles, all the way to the right, offers wheelchairs (some oversized) and Electric Convenience Vehicles (ECVs). Strollers are

available under the Main Street Train Station. The cost for strollers and wheelchairs is $15 per day ($13 per day with a multi-day rental); double strollers cost $31 per day ($27 a day with a multi-day rental); $50 per day for ECVs, with a $20 refundable deposit. Quantities are limited. Hold on to your receipt; it can be used on the same day to get a replacement stroller or wheelchair at any of the theme parks. Multi-day rentals, called Length of Stay tickets, save you two dollars off the daily price. Keep your receipt handy.

Note that during busy times, the park may offer "stroller express" service. Guests pre-pay for a stroller before passing through the turnstiles and bypass the line once inside.

To prevent your stroller from getting lost in a sea of stroller clones, consider personalizing it with an item such as a ribbon, a balloon, or better, yet—your name.

TIP BOARDS

Located at the end of Main Street, U.S.A., closest to Cinderella Castle, the Tip Board is an excellent source of information on waiting times for attractions, as well as showtimes and other entertainment information. The board is often overseen by a park-savvy employee, ready and willing to answer guest questions.

Admission Prices

ONE-DAY BASE TICKET
(Restricted to use only in the Magic Kingdom. **Prices do not include sales tax and are likely to change in 2012.**)
Adult $85
Child* $79
*3 through 9 years of age; children under 3 free

Main Street, U.S.A.

Most of the structures along the thoroughfare are given over to shops, and each one is different. Some emporiums are big and bustling, others are relatively quiet and orderly; some are spacious and airy, others are cozy and dark. Inside and out, maintenance and housekeeping are superb.

> **HOT TIP!**
>
> Plan to do your shopping in the early afternoon, rather than at day's end when the Main Street shops are normally jammed.

White-suited sanitation workers patrol the street to pick up litter and quickly shovel up any evidence of the horses that pull the trolley cars from Town Square to the Hub. As in the rest of the Magic Kingdom, the pavement here is washed down every night with hoses. There's one crew of maintenance workers whose sole job is to change the little white lights around the roofs; another crew devotes itself to keeping the woodwork painted. As soon as these people have worked their way as far as the Hub, they start all over again at Town Square. The greenish, horse-shaped, cast-iron hitching posts are repainted 20 times a year on average—and totally scraped down each time.

Stepping onto Main Street, U.S.A., is like jumping through a time portal. Welcome to turn-of-the-twentieth-century America! Horse-drawn trolleys are the transportation of choice, peppy patriotic music underscores the bustle of merry, moving masses, and the tantalizing aroma of fresh-baked cookies constantly perfumes the air.

A rose-colored retrospective? Maybe. But this is Disney's version of a small-town Main Street—and the charm of this nostalgic land is lost on no one. Anchored by an old-fashioned train station at one end and a fairy-tale castle at the other, Main Street, U.S.A., whisks you from reality to fantasy in a few short blocks.

All of the addresses here feature just-dried coats of paint, curlicued gingerbread moldings, and pretty details. Add to that the baskets of hanging plants and genuine-looking gaslights, and Main Street, U.S.A., becomes a true showplace—both in the bright light of high noon and after nightfall, when the tiny lights edging all of the rooflines are flicked on.

The street represents an ideal American town. Although such a town never really existed, many claim to have served as the inspiration for it. Chances are Walt Disney got the idea from Marceline, Missouri, the tiny rural town that was his boyhood home.

The "attractions" along Main Street, U.S.A., are relatively minor compared to the really big deals such as Tomorrowland's Space Mountain, Frontierland's Splash Mountain, or The Haunted Mansion in Liberty Square. But each and every shop has its own quota of merchandise that is meant as much for show as for sale. It's almost as entertaining to watch the cooks stir up gooey batches of fudge or peanut brittle at the Main Street Confectionery as it is to actually savor a sample. The shop windows, particularly at the Emporium, are also worth a look.

Once you start to meander along Main Street, be sure to notice the names on the second-story windows. Above the Uptown Jewelers store (near the Confectionery) is that of Walt's nephew, Roy E. Disney. And you'll see Walt's name above the ice-cream parlor. Other names are those of people connected with The Walt Disney Company.

Note: Attractions in Main Street, U.S.A., are described in the order in which they are encountered upon entering the park.

WALT DISNEY WORLD RAILROAD: The best introduction to the Magic Kingdom, the 1½-mile journey on this rail line is as much a must for the first-time visitor as it is for railroad buffs. It offers an excellent orientation as it passes by most of the park's major lands.

The 1928 steam engine happens to be exactly the same age as Mickey Mouse. Walt Disney himself was a railroad aficionado. During the early years of television, viewers watched films of him circling his own backyard in a one-eighth-scale train, the *Lilly Belle* (named for his wife).

The Walt Disney World Railroad also has a *Lilly Belle* among its quartet of locomotives. The others are named *Roy O. Disney*, *Walter E. Disney*, and *Roger E. Broggie* (a Disney Imagineer who shared Walt Disney's enthusiasm for antique trains). All of them were built in the U.S. around the turn of the century and later taken to Mexico to haul freight and passengers in the Yucatán, where Disney scouts found them in 1969. The United Railways of Yucatán was using them to carry sugarcane. Brought north once again, they were completely overhauled, and even the smallest of parts were reworked or replaced.

The train circles the park in 20 minutes, making stops in Frontierland and Main Street, U.S.A. Trains arrive in each station every 4 to 10 minutes. The line is usually shorter in Frontierland, but there's rarely a long wait at either station. The train is the most efficient way to reach the exit when parades take over Main Street, U.S.A.

PHOTO BY JILL SAFRO

HOT TIP!
Guests staying at the Contemporary resort can walk to and from the Magic Kingdom's front gate. The trip takes about 10 to 15 minutes. It's handy when there's a long line for the monorail.

Note: The Walt Disney World Railroad does not run during fireworks presentations.

MAIN STREET VEHICLES: A number of these can be seen traveling up and down Main Street—horseless carriages and jitneys patterned after turn-of-the-century vehicles (but fitted with Jeep transmissions and special mufflers that make a putt-putt-putting sound); a spiffy scarlet fire engine; and a troop of trolleys drawn by Belgians and Percherons, two strong breeds of horse that once pulled plows in Europe. These animals—weighing in at about a ton each and shod with plastic (easier on their hooves)—pull the trolley the length of Main Street about two dozen times during each of their working days. Between shifts, they can be seen resting inside Main Street's Car Barn. Feel free to stop by and say hello. At day's end, they go home to their barn at Fort Wilderness (where you can also visit them). The horses are sometimes hosed down next to the Main Street firehouse. Youngsters love to watch.

TOWN SQUARE THEATER: **FP** Themed as a Victorian-era theater, this is an ideal spot to meet and mingle with Mickey, Minnie, and favorite Disney princesses. Of course, this being a *magic* kingdom, Mickey has a few tricks up his sleeve. Yep, in addition to all his other skills, the Mouse is a master magician. Who knew? Note that this is strictly a "backstage" experience, as Mickey's magic show is still in the rehearsal stage.

The wait here can be long—get a Fastpass if you can. There are two separate lines to meet Mickey and Minnie and the princesses, but one Fastpass will get you into both rooms.

HOT TIP!
Mondays and Saturdays tend to be the most crowded days at the Magic Kingdom.

MAGIC KINGDOM

Adventureland

Adventureland seems to have even more atmosphere than the other lands. That may be a result of its neat separation from the rest of the Magic Kingdom by the bridge over Main Street on one end and by a gallery-like structure (where it merges with Frontierland) on the other, or, possibly, it's because of the abundance of landscaping.

The centrally located attraction, The Magic Carpets of Aladdin, sets the tone for this corner of the Kingdom. Still surrounded by tropical splendor, the area has the look and feel of a bustling marketplace—the likes of which one might stumble upon in Agrabah. The shops here offer imports from around the globe.

As guests stroll away from Main Street, U.S.A., they just may hear the sound of beating drums, the squawks of parrots, and the regular boom of a cannon. Paces quicken. And the wonders soon to be encountered do not disappoint.

SWISS FAMILY TREEHOUSE: "Everything we need is right at our fingertips," said the father in Disney's 1960 rendition of the classic story *Swiss Family Robinson*. He was describing the treehouse that he and his kids built for the family after their ship was wrecked in a storm. When given a chance—several adventures later—to leave the island, all but one son decided to stay on. That decision is not hard to understand after a tour of the Magic Kingdom's version of the Robinsons' banyan-tree home. This is everybody's idea of the perfect treehouse, with its many levels and comforts—patchwork quilts, lovely mahogany furniture, candles stuck in abalone shells, even running water in every room. (The system is rather ingenious.)

The Spanish moss draping the branches is real; the tree itself—unofficially christened *Disneyodendron eximus*, a genus that is translated roughly as "out-of-the-ordinary Disney tree"—was constructed entirely by the props department. Some statistics: The roots, which are made of concrete, poke 42 feet into the ground, and about 300,000 lifelike polyethylene leaves "grow" on the tree's 1,400 individual branches.

JUNGLE CRUISE: **FP** Inspired in part by the 1955 documentary film *The African Lion*, this ten-minute adventure is one of the crowning achievements of Magic Kingdom landscape artists for the way it takes guests through

> ### HOT TIP!
> During non-peak seasons, Jungle Cruise may open one hour after the rest of the Magic Kingdom opens for the day.

surroundings as diverse as a Southeast Asian jungle, the Nile Valley, and an Amazon rainforest. Along the way, passengers encounter zebras, giraffes, lions, headhunters, and more (all of the Audio-Animatronics variety); they also see elephants bathing and tour a temple—while listening to an amusing, though corny, spiel delivered by the skipper. (Bet you didn't know that Schweitzer Falls was named after the famous doctor Albert . . . Falls.)

This adventure, which is best enjoyed by daylight, is one of the park's slower-moving attractions, and tends to be quite crowded from late morning until late afternoon.

MAGIC KINGDOM

THE ENCHANTED TIKI ROOM: The Tiki Room is back under its original management! That's right, Iago is out and José, Michael, Pierre, and Fritz have once again taken center stage—as they did when the attraction first opened in 1963. Cherished for its historical significance (the Tiki Birds starred in the first Audio-Animatronics attraction ever), the Tiki show has evolved a bit over the years.

The show features the aforementioned fine-feathered friends, plus some 200 birds, flowers, and tiki statues singing up a tropical storm. Let's all sing like the birdies sing!

THE MAGIC CARPETS OF ALADDIN: Welcome to Agrabah! Adventureland's high-flying attraction is conveniently situated in the center of the action. It features not one, but 16 carpets that soar through the air in a fashion similar to those airborne elephants over in Fantasyland. Each flying carpet accommodates four guests at a time. Depending on where you sit, you'll have control of the carpet's movement (the vertical controls are in the front; side-to-side are in the back). Be prepared to dodge the occasional stream of liquid, courtesy of an expectorating camel.

BIRNBAUM'S BEST **PIRATES OF THE CARIBBEAN:** Quite simply, this is one of the very best of the Magic Kingdom's classic adventures. The beloved ten-minute cruise is a Disneyland original, added to Walt Disney World's Magic Kingdom (in slightly revised form) due to popular demand. Here, guests board a small boat and set sail for a series of scenes showing a pirate raid on a Caribbean island town, dodging cannon fire and weathering one small, though legitimate, watery dip along the way. There are singing marauders, plastered pigs, and wily wenches; the observant may note a couple of new rapscallion residents. Yep, that beloved scallywag Captain Jack Sparrow has dropped anchor here, as has his nefarious nemesis Captain Barbossa.

While it's by no means the most politically correct attraction on-property (far from it, actually), the rendition of "Yo Ho, Yo Ho, a Pirate's Life for Me"—the catchy theme song—makes what is actually a rather brutal scenario into something that comes across as good fun.

And, yes, this is the attraction that inspired the *Pirates of the Caribbean* movies—which, in turn, inspired the attraction!

Frontierland

With the Rivers of America lapping at its borders and Big Thunder Mountain rising up in the rear, this re-creation of the American Frontier encompasses the area from the Mississippi River to the Southwest, from the 1770s to the 1880s. In these parts, shops, restaurants, and attractions have unpainted barn siding or stone or clapboard walls, and there are several wooden sidewalks of the sort Marshal Matt Dillon used to stride along. The Walt Disney World Railroad makes a stop here.

FRONTIERLAND SHOOTIN' ARCADE: This modest arcade is set in an 1850s town in the Southwest Territory. Positions overlook Boothill, a town complete with bank, jail, hotel, and cemetery.

Genuine Hawkins .54-caliber buffalo rifles have been refitted, and when the infrared beam strikes any of the targets, an interesting result is triggered. Struck tombstones rise, sink, spin, or change their epitaphs; hit a cloud and a ghost rider gallops across the sky; a bull's-eye on a grave digger's shovel causes a skull to pop out of the grave. It is possible to have fun here, but this arcade is in dire need of an upgrade.

There is an additional charge to play here (usually about 50 cents).

COUNTRY BEAR JAMBOREE: The Country Bears may never make it to the Grand Ole Opry, but they don't seem to mind. Disney's brood of banjo-strummin' bruins has been playing to packed houses in Grizzly Hall for more than a quarter century. Judging by all the toe tappin' and hand clappin' that accompany each performance, the show remains a countrified crowd-pleaser. As for the few folks who aren't charmed by the backwoods ballads and down-home humor, well, they just have to grin and *bear* it.

As guests are settling into their seats (all of which provide a decent view), Buff, Max, and Melvin are beginning to grumble. Despite their status as permanent fixtures in the theater, the mounted animal heads would rather not "hang around all day" waiting for the show to get going. The 17-minute revue opens with a rousing ditty by the Five Bear Rugs. The wheels set in motion, the remaining songs come fast and furious. Together, they capture the spirit of a genre that has a tendency to celebrate and lampoon itself simultaneously.

For example, Bunny, Bubbles, and Beulah bemoan "All the Guys That Turn Me On Turn Me Down;" Henry, the easy-going emcee who sports a coonskin cap (still attached to the 'coon), belts out "The Ballad of Davy Crockett;" and Big Al, the oversize tone-deaf fan favorite, woefully croons "Blood on the Saddle," much to the delight of the giggle-prone audience.

Timing Tip: This attraction opens at 10 A.M. each day, even when the rest of the park opens earlier in the morning.

TOM SAWYER ISLAND: This patch of land in the middle of the Rivers of America has hills to scramble up; a working windmill, Harper's Mill, with an owl in the rafters and a perpetually creaky waterwheel; and a few pitch-black caves. To reach the island, guests take a raft across the river. (It's the only way to get there and back.)

Paths wind this way and that, and it's easy to get disoriented. Keep an eye out for mounted maps scattered about the island.

There are two bridges here—a suspension bridge and a barrel bridge, which floats atop some lashed-together wooden barrels. When one person bounces, everybody lurches—and all but the most chickenhearted laugh. Both of the bridges are easy to miss, so be sure to keep your eyes peeled.

Across the suspension bridge is Fort Langhorn. Poke around and you'll discover a twisting, dark, and occasionally scary escape tunnel. Walk along the pathway on the banks of the Rivers of America and you'll find your way back to the bridges.

The whole island seems as rugged as backwoods Missouri and, probably as a result, it actually feels a lot more remote than it is—enough to be able to provide some welcome respite from the bustle.

One particularly pleasant way to relax here is at a waterside table. It's sometimes possible to buy a snack—and you are always welcome to bring your own. Restrooms are beside the main raft landing and inside Fort Langhorn.

Timing Tip: This attraction closes at dusk.

BIRNBAUM'S
★BEST★ **SPLASH MOUNTAIN:** FP On the day this attraction made its official 1992 Walt Disney World debut, *everyone* got soaked—thanks in part to a particularly potent Florida rain cloud. But the rain wasn't entirely responsible for the sea of soggy Magic Kingdom guests. The five-story drop into an aqueous briar patch was. And a steady stream of thrill seekers has been taking the plunge ever since.

In this guaranteed smile-inducer, guests enjoy a waterborne journey through brightly colored swamps and bayous, and down waterfalls, and are finally hurtled from the peak of the mountain to a briar-laced pond five stories below.

> ## HOT TIP!
> If you'd like to get soaked on Splash Mountain, sit on the right side of the log.

Splash Mountain is based on the animated sequences in Walt Disney's 1946 film *Song of the South*. The scenery entertains as the story line follows Br'er Rabbit as he tries to reach his "laughin' place." It's tough for a first-time rider to take in all the details, since the tension of waiting for the big drop is all-consuming.

It is a bit terrifying at the top, but once back on the ground, it seems most riders can't wait for another trip—even though they may get drenched. (Water-wary guests are often seen wearing rain ponchos on this attraction. On the other hand, if you *want* to get wet, try to sit up front or on the right; seats in the back receive a smaller splash.)

By the second or third time around, it's possible to relax a bit, enjoy the interior scenes, and take in the spectacular views of the Magic Kingdom from the top of the mountain. At this point, you may even manage to keep your eyes open for the duration of the final fall—or at least part of it.

Splash Mountain's designers not only borrowed characters and color-saturated settings from *Song of the South*, but also used quite a bit of the film's Academy Award-winning music in this attraction. As a matter of fact, the song in Splash Mountain's final scene, "Zip-a-Dee-Doo-Dah," has become something of a Disney anthem over the years.

Note: You must be at least 40 inches tall to ride Splash Mountain. (There is a small play area nearby to keep little ones occupied while older kids ride.) If you'd like to absorb as little precipitation as possible, sit on the left side of the log.

BIRNBAUM'S ★BEST★ **BIG THUNDER MOUNTAIN RAILROAD: FP** It's certainly not hard to spot Big Thunder, the lone red rock formation this side of the Mississippi. Even newcomers to the Magic Kingdom will be able to distinguish the landmark from its famed counterparts—Splash and Space mountains—because it's the only one that actually looks like a real mountain range. The designers took Utah's Monument Valley as inspiration, and the resemblance is quite remarkable.

According to Disney legend, the 2.5-acre mountain is chock-full of gold. Unfortunately for the residents of Tumbleweed, the local mining town, a flood has ruined any chance of uncovering the remaining gold. Before the prospectors find drier land, they are having one last party at the saloon to celebrate their riches. Even though in danger of washing away, they don't seem too worried, and guests who decide to take a trip on the Big Thunder Mountain Railroad have nothing to worry about either.

As passengers board the 15-row train, they are advised to "hang onto your hats and glasses 'cause this here's the wildest ride in the wilderness." Do heed the warning, but don't despair. The ride, though thrilling, is relatively tame, so relax and enjoy the sights. Note that passengers seated nearest the caboose experience more turbulence than those seated closer to the front.

A bleating billy goat atop a peak, a family of possums hanging overhead, and a dark cavern full of bats, not to mention chickens, donkeys, and washed-up miners, can be spotted along the way. Be sure to keep an eye out for the not-yet-sunken saloon—it's easy to miss the first time around.

A continuous string of curves and dips around Big Thunder's pinnacles and caverns is sure to please thrill seekers of all ages, but the adrenaline surge is caused by more than just the speed of the trip. The added sound of a rickety track, a steam whistle that blows right before the train accelerates into a curve, and an unexpected earthquake all compound the passengers' anticipation, making this attraction one of the Magic Kingdom's most popular.

Note: You must be at least 40 inches tall and immune to motion sickness to experience the Big Thunder Mountain Railroad attraction.

Timing Tip: Plan to visit early in the morning, during a parade, or just before closing time. Of course, you can always plan ahead and get a Fastpass. If you will be visiting during a parade, consider taking the Walt Disney World Railroad to the Frontierland station. The train circumvents much of the parade congestion.

Liberty Square

The transition between Frontierland on one side and Fantasyland on the other is so smooth that it's hard to say just when you arrive at Liberty Square, yet ultimately, there's no mistaking the location. The small buildings are clapboard or brick and topped with weather vanes; the decorative moldings are Federal or Georgian in style; the glass is sometimes wavy; and there are flower boxes in shop windows. There's a bounty of shops, plus two of the park's most famous attractions—The Haunted Mansion and The Hall of Presidents—and the Liberty Tree Tavern, one of the few table-service restaurants in the Magic Kingdom.

THE HALL OF PRESIDENTS: The Hall of Presidents attraction made its debut with the park, way back in 1971. Though revered for its status as a classic Magic Kingdom attraction, it was starting to lose some of its luster. It was time for a change. And change it did. The revamped and revitalized show boasts cutting-edge technology and a new storyline—not to mention a new president. (Barack Obama, the most advanced and life-like Audio-Animatronics figure to date, is the seventh Chief of State to be added to the attraction since it opened.)

The 25-minute celebration of U.S. leaders begins with a stirring, original film. It covers the country's origins, the framing of the Constitution, and national triumphs and struggles from the Civil War (which leads Abraham Lincoln to deliver the Gettysburg Address) to the present day. Throughout, it focuses on the role of U.S. presidents in the shaping of American history and applauds the ordinary people who rose to the nation's highest office and led us through extraordinary circumstances.

Following the film, the curtain rises and all 44 U.S. presidents are represented. (The observant may note that there are only 43 Audio-Animatronics figures on the stage. No, the Disney Imagineers did not misplace a president! Grover Cleveland served two non-consecutive terms, so he is the 22nd and 24th president of the United States.) After all the Commanders in Chief are introduced, both George Washington and Barack Obama deliver rousing, patriotic speeches (and, yes, that's really Mr. Obama's voice).

Displays in the pre-show area give guests a chance to gaze upon bits of Americana such as painted eggs from a White House Easter egg hunt and dresses from former first ladies (exhibit items will change from time to time).

LIBERTY BELLE RIVERBOAT: Based in Liberty Square and built in dry dock at Walt Disney World, this is a genuine steamboat. Its boiler turns water into steam, which is then piped to the engine, which drives the paddle

wheel that propels the boat. It is not the real article in one respect, however: It moves through the nine-foot-deep Rivers of America on an underwater rail.

The pleasant ride, with narration by an actor playing Mark Twain, is a good way to beat the heat on steamy afternoons. En route, a variety of props create a sort of Wild West effect: moose, deer, a burning cabin, and the like. The tour is completed within 17 minutes. Note that this attraction usually opens an hour or so *after* the park itself and shuts down *before* other park attractions do.

BIRNBAUM'S ★BEST★ — THE HAUNTED MANSION:

This eerie, eight-minute experience is among the Magic Kingdom's most enjoyable. However, guests who expect to be scared silly when they enter the big old house, modeled after those built in New York's Hudson River Valley in the 18th century, will be just a tad unfulfilled. This haunted house steers clear of anything too terrifying, and a good-spirited voice-over keeps the mood light. Still, some of the scenes, as well as the darkness, may be too much for some tykes.

Once you're inside the portrait hall, entered after passing through the front doors, it's amusing to speculate: Is the ceiling moving up, or is the floor dropping? It's also where you will meet your "Ghost Host" and learn how he met his untimely demise.

The spooky journey through the mansion takes place in a "Doom Buggy." The attraction is full of tricks and treats for the eyes; just when you think you've seen it all, there's something new: staircases to nowhere, bats' eyes on the wallpaper, a suit of armor that comes alive, a terrified cemetery watchman and his mangy mutt, and the image of a creepy lady in a floating crystal ball.

One of the biggest jobs of the maintenance crews here is not cleaning up, but keeping things dirty. The mansion is littered with some 200 trunks, chairs, dress forms, harps, rugs, and assorted knickknacks and requires a lot of dust. Cobwebs are bought in liquid form and strung up by a secret process.

When waiting to enter, take time to enjoy the new interactive queue area. And on the way out, take a moment to pay your respects at the pet cemetery. Mr. Toad, we hardly knew you. Sniff, sniff.

Fantasyland

Walt Disney called this a "timeless land of enchantment," and his successors termed it "the happiest land of all"—and it is, for some. It is the home of a number of rides that are particularly well liked by children. *Fantasyland is undergoing a major metamorphosis and parts of it will be closed or under construction throughout 2012.*

CINDERELLA CASTLE: Just as Mickey stands for all the merriment in Walt Disney World, this storybook castle represents the hopes and dreams of childhood—a time in life when anything is possible.

At a height of about 190 feet, Cinderella Castle is nearly twice the height of Disneyland's Sleeping Beauty Castle. For inspiration, Disney Imagineers looked to the palaces of Charles Perrault's France, still showplaces of Europe. Their design took the form of a romanticized composite of such courts as Fontainbleu, Versailles, and famed chateaux of the Loire Valley. Of course, they also turned to the original designs for the fairy-tale castle in Disney's 1950 classic, *Cinderella*.

Unlike real European castles, this one is made of steel and fiberglass; in lieu of dungeons, it has service tunnels. Its upper reaches contain security rooms; there's even a special Cinderella Castle Suite. It was created to fulfill guests' dreams during The Year of a Million Dreams celebration. (Future plans for this spectacular space were undetermined at press time. Though we will happily

volunteer to move in!) From any vantage point, Cinderella Castle looks as if it came straight from the land of make-believe.

Mosaic Murals: The elaborate murals beneath the castle's archway rank among the true wonders of the World. They tell the story of the little cinder girl and one of childhood's happiest happily-ever-afters, using a million bits of glass in some 500 different colors, plus real silver and 14-karat gold.

Cinderella Wishing Well: This pleasant alcove, nestled along a path to Tomorrowland, is a nice spot from which to gaze at the castle. Any coins tossed into the water are donated to children's charities. Don't forget to make a wish as you part with your penny.

PRINCE CHARMING REGAL CARROUSEL: Not everything in the Magic Kingdom is a Disney version of the real article. This carrousel, discovered at the now-defunct Olympic Park in Maplewood, New Jersey, was built back in 1917. That was the end of the golden century of carrousel building, which began around 1825. During the Disney refurbishing, many of the original horses were replaced with horses made of fiberglass.

FAIRYTALE GARDEN: This special spot is tucked beside Cinderella Castle. Several times a day, Rapunzel and Flynn Rider (from *Tangled*) stop by to mingle with guests. Check a Times Guide for appearance schedule. *This may change in 2012.*

BIRNBAUM'S ★BEST★ MICKEY'S PHILHARMAGIC: Mickey Mouse and a panoply of his pals (including Donald, Simba, and Ariel) strut their musical stuff in this 3-D production.

The show is an ambitious amalgam of music, special effects, and animated film. Of course, this being Fantasyland, the film is by no means ordinary. It's crisp, colorful, and to the delight of many a goggle-wearing guest, three-dimensional. The experience unfolds on a 150-foot-wide canvas. Special effects and surprises take place off-screen, too. Overall, the experience is intended to engage guests of any age.

As with many attractions, there are moments of darkness. If you're unsure as to whether your child might find this (or any attraction) unsettling, express your concern to an attendant. They'll help you make the right decision.

PETER PAN'S FLIGHT: 🅵🅿 "Come on, everybody, here we go!" So says Peter Pan at the start of this nonstop flight to Never Land. The three-minute adventure, which takes you soaring in a pirate ship, fancifully retells the story of Peter Pan—a boy with a knack for flying and an immunity to maturity. The effects in this classic Fantasyland attraction are simple, but enchanting.

The journey starts in the Darling family nursery—which siblings Wendy, Michael, and John quickly abandon to follow Peter Pan on a trip to his homeland. As in Disney's animated feature, one of the most beautiful scenes—and one that makes this attraction a treat for grown-ups as well as smaller folk—is the sight of nighttime London, dark blue and speckled with twinkling lights. Keep your eyes peeled for Big Ben and Tower Bridge.

By the time you spot your first mermaid, you're deep in the heart of Never Land. Alas, something is terribly wrong—Captain Hook and his buccaneer buddies have taken the Darling kids captive. It's all really a trap for Peter (Hook is still peeved at Pan for serving his hand to a hungry crocodile). Does everyone live happily ever after? We'll *never* tell.

Timing Tip: The slow-moving lines for this popular attraction can be somewhat daunting. Take advantage of the Fastpass option. Or plan to arrive close to when the park opens, late in the evening, or during any of the parades throughout the day.

IT'S A SMALL WORLD: *Hola! Guten Tag! Hello!* No matter what language you speak, what you look like, or where you live, you still have a lot in common with folks the world over (including an especially high tolerance for a singsong melody that repeatedly reminds us that it's a small world, after all). That's the message driving this ten-minute boat ride around the world.

Originally created for New York's 1964–65 World's Fair, the attraction is an oldie-but-

goodie (and is quite popular with young children). The ride moves at slightly swifter than snail's pace, drifting past hundreds of colorfully costumed dolls from around the world—all of whom know all the words to the ride's infectious theme song.

PHOTO BY JILL SAFRO

A showcase of diversity, the attraction is a simple celebration of human similarities. It's also a relaxing alternative to many of the park's higher-tech, longer-line attractions. (This attraction underwent a massive refurbishment in 2005 and has been surging in popularity ever since.)

DUMBO THE FLYING ELEPHANT: This is purely and simply a kiddie ride, though children of all ages have admitted to loving it. A beloved symbol of Fantasyland, the ride is moving from its original location and doubling in size—but rest assured, the Dumbo experience will remain the same. Consider stopping here first thing in the morning, or during a parade, when the line—which is often prohibitively long—thins a bit. Inspired by the 1941 film classic *Dumbo*, the ride lasts a memorable two minutes. Incidentally, the rodent in the center of the circle of flying elephants is Dumbo's faithful sidekick, Timothy Mouse.

MAD TEA PARTY: The theme of this two-minute ride—in a group of oversize pastel-colored teacups that whirl and spin wildly—was inspired by a scene in the Disney Studios' 1951 movie production of Lewis Carroll's novel *Alice in Wonderland*. During the sequence in question, the Mad Hatter hosts a tea party for his un-birthday.

Unlike many rides in Fantasyland, this is not just for younger kids; the 5-to-20-something crowd seems to like it best. Keep in mind that when the cups stop spinning, your head may continue to do so. Skip this ride if you suffer from motion sickness or if you've recently

---

HOT TIP!
Don't plan on visiting Mickey's Toontown Fair—it has moved out of the Magic Kingdom. Toodles, Toontown!

enjoyed a snack. Don't miss the woozy mouse that pops out of the teapot at the center of the platform—he ignored our advice.

BIRNBAUM'S ★BEST★ THE MANY ADVENTURES OF WINNIE THE POOH: FP
Perhaps as a tribute to the mischievous Mr. Toad, the host of the attraction previously housed here, everyone's favorite honey-lovin' cub treats Magic Kingdom guests to a wild and whimsical 3½-minute tour of his home turf.

The attraction features a most unlikely form of transportation: honey pots! They whisk (and bounce) guests through the pages of a giant storybook and into the Hundred Acre Wood, where the weather's most blustery. The wind is really ruffling the feathers of one of the locals. It seems Owl's treehouse has been shaken loose and just may topple to the ground—and onto the honey pots below. Similar sight gags abound, from a bubble-blowing Heffalump (hey, this is Fantasyland) to a treacherous flood that threatens to sweep Tigger, Piglet, and the rest of the gang away. When Pooh saves the day, it's time to celebrate—and everyone is invited to the party.

Note that, like other Fantasyland attractions, some parts of this one take place in the dark. Some children may find it a bit unsettling. That said, little ones dig Pooh's new, interactive queue area. While waiting to ride or for others to do so, youngsters can bang on giant vegetable "drums," play tug-of-war with a gopher, and scrawl their names in a flowing wall of honey.

SNOW WHITE'S SCARY ADVENTURES: At press time, this attraction, which made its debut along with the Magic Kingdom Park in 1971, was getting ready to retire. If you have a chance to take one last spin, by all means go for it. But keep in mind that the twisting, turning journey has a tendency to scare timid tots.

Once the witch moves out of these parts, expect Disney princesses to take over. The Princess Fairytale Hall will invite guests of all ages to visit their favorite regals in a festive new locale. Remember those cameras and autograph books! To learn more about Princess Fairytale Hall and other Fantasyland additions, visit *www.disneyworld.com.*

Fantasyland Expansion

Big doin's in Fantasyland—it's undergoing the biggest expansion in Magic Kingdom history! What do we have to look forward to? Among other happy additions, there will be a brand-new attraction featuring everyone's favorite little mermaid (Under the Sea—Journey of the Little Mermaid), several new neighborhoods inhabited by Disney royalty, and even Beast's Castle (with the Be Our Guest Restaurant offering quick-service meals by day and table-service dinner by night). Of course, Cinderella Castle will still be here, as well as most of Fantasyland's treasured attractions.

One such attraction, Dumbo The Flying Elephant, is doubling in size and relocating to a new area known as Storybook Circus (which takes over the real estate previously occupied by Mickey's Toontown Fair). Dumbo's neighbor, a zippy, kid-friendly roller coaster called The Great Goofini, will be a re-themed version of the Barnstormer.

When Snow White's Scary Adventures moves out of town, Disney princesses will move in. They will greet Magic Kingdom guests throughout the day in the new Princess Fairytale Hall. And a new thrill ride known as The Seven Dwarfs Mine Train will take guests on a rollicking, musical trip into the mine "where a million diamonds shine!"

The first phase of Fantasyland's growth spurt, which includes Under the Sea—Journey of the Little Mermaid, is expected to open in late 2012. The rest of the pixie dust should be settled in 2013.

Tomorrowland

The original Tomorrowland attempted a serious look at the future. But as Disney planners discovered, it isn't easy to portray a future that persists in becoming the present. So the old Tomorrowland has given way to a friendlier, space-age town whose neighborhood atmosphere is more in keeping with the other lands in the Magic Kingdom. This is the future that never was, the fantasy world imagined by the science-fiction writers and moviemakers of the 1920s and '30s. It's a land of sky-piercing beacons and glistening metal, where shiny robots do the work, whisper-quiet cars glide along an elevated highway, and even time travel is possible.

Note: Tomorrowland attractions are described in the order in which they are encountered upon entering the land from the Hub and heading (counterclockwise) away from Cinderella Castle.

STITCH'S GREAT ESCAPE!: Like its predecessor, the ExtraTERRORestrial Alien Encounter, this attraction features the adventures of a renegade alien. In this case, however, said extraterrestrial is more of a menace than a threat—not so much scary as ill-mannered and mischievous. The 20-minute show is a prequel to *Lilo & Stitch*, but one need not be

HOT TIP!

Parents take note: This attraction is much less scary than The ExtraTERRORestrial Alien Encounter. Still, there are moments of darkness, and Stitch's madcap shenanigans may be daunting to little ones.

familiar with the drooling, intergalactic imp to follow the attraction's story line.

The action begins with a short pre-show, followed by the crowd spilling into a circular theater-type room. All chairs face center, where there's a mysterious tube. (Sit up straight when the shoulder harness is lowered—this will enhance the effects and make for a less restraining experience.)

What's all the fuss about? Bad-boy Stitch, aka Experiment 626, is being moved to a prison processing center and you have been recruited to keep an eye on him. Up to the task? Chances are you're not: The little blue rascal manages to escape every time. And when he does, chaos ensues. This attraction tends to be best appreciated by younger park-goers and Stitch groupies.

Note: Some youngsters may be frightened by dark moments and loud noises. Also, shoulder restraints may spook claustrophobes. You must be at least 40 inches tall to enter.

BIRNBAUM'S ★BEST★ BUZZ LIGHTYEAR'S SPACE RANGER SPIN: **FP** The Evil Emperor Zurg is up to no good. As soon as he swipes enough batteries to power his ultimate weapon of destruction—KERPLOOEY!—it's curtains for the toy universe as we know it. It's up to that Space Ranger extraordinaire Buzz Lightyear and his Junior Space Rangers (that means you) to save the day.

So goes the story line of Tomorrowland's video-game-inspired spin through toyland. The adventure is experienced from a toy's point of view. Guests begin their 4½-minute tour of duty as Space Rangers at Star Command Action Center. This is where Buzz gives his team a briefing on the mission that lies ahead. Then it's off to the Launch Bay to board the ride vehicles. The ships feature dual laser cannons, glowing lights, and a piloting joystick.

Once Junior Space Rangers blast off, they find themselves surrounded by Zurg's robots, who are mercilessly ripping batteries from toys. As Rangers fire at targets, beams of light fill the air. For every target hit, you will be rewarded with sight gags, sound effects, and points. The points, which are tallied automatically, are accumulated throughout the journey. Although the vehicles follow a rigid "flight" path (they're on a track), the joystick allows riders to maneuver the ships, arcing from side to side or spinning in circles while taking aim at your surroundings.

When the star cruiser arrives at Zurg's spaceship, it's showdown time. Will good prevail over evil? Or has time run out for the toy universe? And will you score enough points to be a Galactic Hero? Most people improve their scores with a little practice.

MONSTERS, INC. LAUGH FLOOR: That Mike Wazowski is one enterprising eyeball. It seems the fuzzy fellow from *Monsters, Inc.* has opened something of a comedy club. Why? Well, it seems his hometown is experiencing a bit of an energy crisis. Mike's plan is to tap into a decidedly alternative (not to mention free) fuel source to provide power for Monstropolis . . . laughter. But where can he gather enough giggles to fuel a whole city? In a 400-seat theater in Tomorrowland, that's where. To accomplish his goal, Monster of Ceremonies Mike has recruited a couple of cornball comedians. Their job is to make you laugh yourself silly. And they are not too proud to resort to slapstick while doing so. Guests are encouraged to text their favorite joke while waiting in the queue. (Standard text messaging rates apply.)

PHOTO BY JILL SAFRO

TOMORROWLAND TRANSIT AUTHORITY PEOPLEMOVER: Boarded near Astro Orbiter, these trains (known to Disney purists as the WEDway) move at a speed of about seven miles per hour along almost a mile of track, beside or through most of the attractions in Tomorrowland. They are operated by a linear induction motor that has no moving parts, uses little power, and emits no pollution.

The peaceful, breezy excursion through Tomorrowland takes about ten minutes. There's rarely a wait to board. It's one of our favorites. However, moments of darkness (as the train passes through Space Mountain), may be unsettling for little ones.

ASTRO ORBITER: Here, passengers fly around for two minutes in machine-age rockets designed to look more like oversize Buck

and disc brakes, but unlike most cars, they run along a track. Yet, even expert drivers have trouble keeping them going in a straight line. (Don't panic when you notice the lack of a brake pedal—when you take your foot off the gas, the car comes to a quick, if not screeching, halt.) The one-lap tour of Tomorrowland takes about five minutes.

Note: You must be at least 54 inches tall to drive the car by yourself. Guests must be at least 32 inches tall to ride shotgun. Babies younger than 12 months may not ride.

Rogers toys than 21st-century space shuttles. Riders are surrounded by vibrantly colored, whirling planets as they get an astronaut's-eye view of Tomorrowland.

BIRNBAUM'S ★BEST★ SPACE MOUNTAIN: FP This attraction, which blasted onto the Magic Kingdom scene in 1975 (and was completely refurbished in 2009), is a can't miss crowd-pleaser for throngs of thrill seekers. Rising to a height of more than 180 feet, this gleaming steel-and-concrete cone houses an attraction that most people call a roller coaster. The ride takes place in an outer-space-like darkness that gets inkier and scarier as the journey progresses. The rockets that roar through this blackness attain a maximum speed of just over 28 miles per hour—but somehow it feels much faster.

The Space Mountain experience is wild enough to send glasses, purses, wallets, and even an occasional set of false teeth plummeting to the bottom of the track, so be sure to find a safe place for your possessions before the ride starts. It's also turbulent enough to upset the stomachs of those so unwise as to ride it immediately after eating. (Those who chicken out at the last minute have access to an exit.)

Note: Guests who are under 44 inches are not permitted to ride, and you must be in good health and free from heart conditions, motion sickness, back or neck problems, or other physical limitations to ride. Expectant mothers should skip the trip. Children under age 7 must be accompanied by an adult.

TOMORROWLAND SPEEDWAY: Little cars that burn up the tracks at this attraction provide quite a bit of the background noise in Tomorrowland. Kids especially enjoy the not-so-speedy, herky-jerky driving experience.

The vehicles have rack-and-pinion steering

WALT DISNEY'S CAROUSEL OF PROGRESS: First seen at New York's 1964–65 World's Fair and moved here in 1975, this 20-minute experience showcases the evolution of the American family and how life changed—and ostensibly progressed—with the advent of electricity. The hook here is that as a scene ends, the audience moves to the next one—not unlike being on a carousel (hence the name of the attraction). This is a great place to escape the crowds and heat, not to mention take a much-needed load off weary feet.

Shopping

No one travels to the Magic Kingdom just to shop. But as many a visitor has learned, shopping is one of the most enjoyable pastimes here.

The Magic Kingdom's boutiques and stores stock much more than just Disneyana. Along with the more predictable items in Main Street shops, it's possible to find cookbooks and stoneware dishes, pirate hats and toy frontier rifles, 14-karat gold charms and filigreed costume jewelry. In Adventureland, shops boast many items imported from the exotic regions the area represents. Throughout the park, stores generally have merchandise that complements the themes of the various lands.

HOT TIP!

Your WDW shopping spree doesn't have to end when your vacation does. Simply log onto *www.DisneyParks.com/store* and you'll have access to some souvenir items previously available only at WDW.

In some shops, you can watch people at work—a candy maker pouring peanut brittle in the Main Street Confectionery, a glassblower crafting wares in Main Street's Crystal Arts, etc.

We recommend shopping in the early afternoon, rather than at the end of the day, when the shops are more crowded. However, keep in mind that Main Street shops do stay open about a half hour after park closing, in case you need any last-minute gifts on the way out.

Main Street

THE ART OF DISNEY: Nestled inside the Main Street Cinema, the shop showcases Disney animation art, including production cels, hand-painted limited-edition cels, character figurines, fine-art serigraphs, lithographs, Disney Parks "vinylmation" collectibles, and more. And, yes, you can still catch classic Mickey cartoons here, too! An artist may even be on hand to enhance a watch or character sketch on-site.

THE CHAPEAU: This Town Square shop is the place to buy Mouse ears and have them monogrammed, and to shop for straw hats, baseball caps, and assorted other headgear. It's also possible to "build your own ear hat." Just select a base hat and mix and match ears, patches, and other personalized items.

CRYSTAL ARTS: Cut-glass bowls, vases, glasses, and plates glitter in the mirror-backed cases of this crystal-chandeliered emporium. An engraver or a glassblower is almost always at work. There's a fireplace, too. Stop here to watch craftspeople mold shields and carve metal. They are quite impressive.

DISNEY CLOTHIERS: This shop offers clothing, including shirts and sleepwear, all of which incorporate Disney characters. Bags, jewelry, and accessories round out the selection.

MAGIC KINGDOM

Where to Eat in the Magic Kingdom

A complete listing of all eateries— full-service restaurants, fast-food emporiums, and snack shops— can be found in the *Good Meals, Great Times* chapter. See the Magic Kingdom section, beginning on page 232.

EMPORIUM: Framed by a two-story-high portico, the Magic Kingdom's largest gift shop (which has expanded, taking over the space formerly occupied by the Center Street flower garden and the Harmony Barber Shop) stocks stuffed animals and toys, sundries, film, T-shirts, and more.

The cash registers always seem to be busy, especially toward the end of the afternoon and before park closing. Nearby lockers make for convenient storage of purchases.

Don't forget to peer into the windows, which usually feature elaborate displays ranging from seasonal themes to character tableaux from the latest Disney movie.

HARMONY BARBER SHOP: Situated next door to the Main Street Car Barn, the quaint, old-fashioned setting for this working shop (complete with occasional appearances by a harmonizing quartet) merits a peek even if you have no need for a trim. It's open from 9 A.M. to 4:30 P.M. daily. This is a popular spot for a child's first haircut.

MAIN STREET ATHLETIC CLUB: Sports-related gifts and apparel are the hallmarks of this shop. The merchandise features images of Disney characters pursuing their favorite sports. The shop also stocks golf shirts with a small Mickey embroidered on the pocket.

Let It Rain

The show doesn't stop just because of a storm. Instead, shops throughout the Magic Kingdom sell plastic Mickey ponchos and umbrellas to outfit guests who have left their own rain gear back home, at their hotel, or in the car.

MAIN STREET CHAMBER OF COMMERCE: This is the place to go if you have any Magic Kingdom purchases "sent to the front of the park" (aka Package Pickup). Allow at least three hours for the package to get here. It's near City Hall.

MAIN STREET CONFECTIONERY: Tasty chocolates are sold in this old-fashioned pink-and-white paradise. A delight at any time of day, but especially when the cooks in the shop's glass-walled kitchen are pouring peanut brittle onto a table to cool. Then the candy sends up clouds of aroma that you could swear were being fanned out onto the street. The peanut brittle is for sale in small bags, along with jelly beans, marshmallow crispy treats, and dozens of other confections that will satisfy any sweet tooth. The caramel-coated apples are especially scrumptious.

NEWSSTAND: No newspapers are sold in the Magic Kingdom—even at its newsstand, which is near the park entrance. (It's to the left, just inside the turnstiles.) The stand sells character merchandise and souvenirs.

THE SHADOW BOX: Watching Rubio Artist Co. silhouette cutters snip black paper into the likenesses of children is one of Main Street's more fascinating diversions. The Shadow Box is at the corner of Main and Center streets.

TOWN SQUARE THEATER: This is the spot for memory cards, film, batteries, collectible pins, photo albums, disposable cameras, and picture frames.

UPTOWN JEWELERS: Designed to resemble a turn-of-the-century collectibles shop, this spiffy store specializes in jewelry and other gift items, including an extensive selection of pins. One counter stocks souvenir charms in 14-karat gold and sterling silver; among them Tinker Bell, Cinderella Castle, and the Walt Disney World logo (a globe with mouse ears). There's also a selection of Disney character figurines. Clocks and watches in all shapes and sizes are available here, including Mickey Mouse watches in a variety of configurations.

WHEELCHAIR AND ECV RENTAL: Inside the turnstiles on the right as you enter the Magic Kingdom, this rental concession offers a limited number of wheelchairs and Electric

Disney's PhotoPass

As you wander the theme parks, chances are Disney cast members will attempt to snap your picture (with permission, of course). After mugging for the camera, you'll get a card called a PhotoPass. It'll link all such photos together for viewing on the Internet. You can ogle and e-mail the low-res images for free for up to 30 days after they are taken. High-quality prints of various sizes are for sale. Visit *www.disneyphotopass.com* to purchase or peruse. Each theme park has a spot for free photo-viewing. Check a park guidemap for locations. We were skeptical about this at first, but really is a convenient way to get quality shots of your whole party. Say cheese!

Convenience Vehicles (ECVs). They are available on a first-come, first-served basis. (Hold onto your receipt—it'll get you a replacement wheelchair or ECV should yours mysteriously disappear during the day.) Keep in mind that wheelchairs and ECVs rented here cannot be taken outside the park itself.

Adventureland

AGRABAH BAZAAR: Clothing with a safari theme is featured at this shop. In addition, look for souvenirs of the *Aladdin*, *Jungle Book*, and *Winnie the Pooh* ilk—many with a safari theme.

BWANA BOB'S: Stop here for tropical jewelry, leis, bags, pins, sunglasses, and more.

ISLAND SUPPLY: This small tropical surf shop features a surprisingly large selection of surfing attire and accessories.

THE PIRATES LEAGUE: More than just a crew of plank-walkers, this group of savvy pirates transforms guests into one of their own —in exchange for booty, of course! Once you're swashbuckled up, they'll snap your photo in the "secret" treasure room. Call 407-

WDW-CREW (939-2739) for pricing or to make a reservation. You'll find the Pirates League in the Plaza del sol Caribe Bazaar by the Pirates of the Caribbean.

PLAZA DEL SOL CARIBE BAZAAR: Ahoy there, mateys! A swashbuckler's delight, the joint adjoining the Pirates of the Caribbean sells stuff celebrating both the attraction and the feature films of the same name. It also stocks nautical gifts and other pirate booty, including Jolly Roger flags, rings, dolls, sailing-ship models, ships in a bottle, and eye patches. If that's not enough treasure for you, check out the candy and snacks, straw hats (including colorful sombreros), and piñatas. The *piece de résistance* for pirate fans? Pirate makeovers! This is one of our favorite shops.

ZANZIBAR TRADING COMPANY: Across from Adventureland's famed Egg Roll Wagon, this corner shop stocks jungle collectibles, including hand-crafted wood items imported from Kenya: giraffes, letter openers, and rain sticks. Also found here are straw and woven items, baskets, and drums.

Frontierland

BIG AL'S: Named for the most popular (and least talented) member of the Country Bears, this riverfront shop is known for its selection of headwear, including Davy Crockett caps.

BRIAR PATCH: Toys and cuddly character items, plus Magic Kingdom logo merchandise, are featured wares at this shop, located near the Splash Mountain exit. There's also a pair of rocking chairs for those who need to take a load off.

FRONTIER TRADING POST: This is the place to shop for collector pins and the associated accoutrements. Since it's got the largest selection of pins in the park, they might want to rename this the Pin Trading Post.

PRAIRIE OUTPOST & SUPPLY: Stop by this turn-of-the-twentieth-century general store for candy, coffee, and cookies.

Liberty Square

HERITAGE HOUSE: Early American reproductions predominate the stock of this store next to The Hall of Presidents. Parchment copies of famous American documents are popular with youngsters. Collectors are tempted to snap up Americana items from books to clothing. Tucked into a corner is a family name history and coat of arms area. Campaign buttons, flags, T-shirts, and Statue of Liberty items are available.

LIBERTY SQUARE PORTRAIT GALLERY: In the midst of Liberty Square, guests may have their portraits drawn in this open-air studio.

MADAME LEOTA'S CART: This shop gives guests on their way to The Haunted Mansion a taste of things to come, with monster masks and ghoulish goodies. There are items featuring scenes and characters from the classic attraction, too. It's also the place to pick up an invisible pooch. FYI: Madame Leota is the spirit featured in the crystal ball inside The Haunted Mansion.

YANKEE TRADER: This quaint little building near The Haunted Mansion is filled with housewares, snow globes, picture frames, and blankets. Weary soles, er, souls enjoy the rocking chairs on the porch.

YE OLDE CHRISTMAS SHOPPE: A wide variety of festive and decorative Christmas items, including tree-top dolls, angel figurines, and souvenir ornaments—Disney-themed and traditional—is available year-round.

Fantasyland

BIBBIDI BOBBIDI BOUTIQUE: Housed inside Cinderella Castle, this shop offers young guests the opportunity to be transformed into "little princesses" and princely "cool dudes." Magical makeovers are available from 8 A.M. to 7 P.M. Prices vary. Magic Kingdom admission is required to enter this location. (There is an additional Bibbidi Bobbidi Boutique inside the World of Disney shop at Downtown Disney. While there is no admission fee, there is a charge for services at both locations.) For pricing information or to book a reservation, call 407-WDW-STYLE (939-7895). Reservations are strongly recommended.

CASTLE COUTURE: Can't get enough Disney fairy merchandise? Stop here for toys, costumes, dolls, and kids' clothing, plus personalized beaded jewelry. It goes without saying that Cinderella is well represented at this spot (as are her fairy friends). The shop offers a vast array of princess dresses and accessories. Bibbidi Bobbidi Boutique guests can get their photos snapped here, too.

HUNDRED ACRE GOODS: Located at the exit of The Many Adventures of Winnie the Pooh, this shop has wares featuring the folks from the Hundred Acre Wood. Among the items the Pooh bear proffers are cuddly toys, hats, shirts, board games, and honey (of course).

SIR MICKEY'S: Expect to find all sorts of Disney-themed clothing and souvenir items in this shop with a theme based on *The Brave Little Tailor*—the cartoon in which Mickey defeats a giant to win the hand of Princess Minnie. (It was one of the most elaborate and expensive Mickey Mouse cartoons ever made.) Mouse ears may be monogrammed here, too.

Tomorrowland

MERCHANT OF VENUS: The place for anything and everything Stitch, from plush toys to games to clothing.

MICKEY'S STAR TRADERS: This is one of the better places to go in the Magic Kingdom for Disney-themed items: plush toys, towels, hats, shirts, dishes, candy, etc. Film, sunglasses, and sun-care products are also available. The Tomorrowland Transit Authority passes through here, too.

Entertainment

In this most magical corner of the World, a tempting slate of live performances ranks among the more serendipitous discoveries. The Magic Kingdom's entertainment mix includes dazzling high-tech shows and old-fashioned numbers alike. To keep apprised of the offerings on any given day, stop at City Hall upon arrival at the park to pick up a current guidemap and Times Guide.

While specifics are subject to change, the following listing is a good indication of the Magic Kingdom's repertoire. As always, we advise calling 407-824-4321 to confirm specifics and schedules.

CAPTAIN JACK SPARROW'S PIRATE TUTORIAL: So you wanna be a pirate? Who doesn't these days?! It just so happens, Captain Jack and his mate Mack are looking for new recruits near the Pirates of the Caribbean in Adventureland. They'd like to test your pirate skills (swordplay, menacing looks, etc.) and decide whether you're worthy of the Pirate's Oath and the title of honorary buccaneer.

CASEY'S CORNER PIANO: A peppy pianist tickles the ivories of a snow-white upright daily just outside Casey's Corner restaurant on Main Street.

DAPPER DANS: You just might encounter a barbershop quartet while strolling down Main Street. Conspicuously clad in straw hats and striped vests, the ever-so-jovial Dapper Dans tap-dance and let one-liners fly during their short, four-part-harmony performances.

DREAM ALONG WITH MICKEY: There's a dream-inspired party being thrown in front of Cinderella Castle—and just about everyone is invited. Mickey, Minnie, Donald, and oodles of other Disney characters join the festivities as their dreams of adventure and "happily ever after" come to life through music and dance. That is, until evil party crasher Maleficent shows up to wreak a little havoc. Her goal? To turn everyone's happy dreams into nightmares. Collectively, however, party guests prove that believing in your dreams is more powerful than Maleficent's sorcery. The 20-minute show is presented several times a day.

BIRNBAUM'S ★BEST★ FIREWORKS: "Wishes," a dynamite, pyrotechnic extravaganza, is presented most nights when the Magic Kingdom stays open after dark. Narrated by Jiminy Cricket, this is one of the biggest, boldest, and truly eye-popping fireworks shows ever presented in the park. Showtimes vary—check a park Times Guide for specifics. Wishes is ideally viewed from Main Street, U.S.A., but can be seen from many vantage points. It is presented rain or shine.

FLAG RETREAT: At about 5 P.M. each day (check a current Times Guide), patriotic music fills the air as a color guard marches to Town Square, in Main Street, U.S.A., and takes down the American flag that flies from the flagpole. On special occasions, a band plays live music.

FAIRYTALE GARDEN: Rapunzel is free from her tower and, along with Flynn Rider, greets guests in this nook beside Cinderella Castle each day. Check a Times Guide for specifics.

CELEBRATE A DREAM COME TRUE PARADE: Meant to evoke happy memories and spark inspiration, this processional winds its way down Main Street once a day. As it does, gymnasts, trampoline performers, and aerial artists dazzle guests, as do dozens of familiar Disney characters.

The parade, which lasts about 20 minutes, brings dream themes to life through music. It is usually presented each afternoon. Check a Times Guide for current details and showtimes. *This parade may change in 2012.*

Holiday Happenings

It's a rare holiday that passes quietly in the Magic Kingdom. During certain holidays, such as Christmas, New Year's Eve, and the Fourth of July, this Kingdom usually breaks curfew, staying open extra late and stepping up its nighttime entertainment. On these occasions, special performances of the SpectroMagic parade and the fireworks are often in store. Of course, entertainment plans are subject to change, so it's important to call 407-934-7639 for information and performance schedules.

EASTER: Easter is a delightful, if a bit crowded, time to visit the Magic Kingdom. Mr. and Mrs. Easter Bunny have been known to appear in the park to help guests celebrate the occasion.

FOURTH OF JULY: The busiest day of the summer—and with good reason: There's a double-size fireworks extravaganza whose explosions light up the skies not only above Cinderella Castle, but also over Seven Seas Lagoon. It's a thrilling display.

HALLOWEEN: This most spooky of holidays is celebrated on select nights from September through October (though not actually on Halloween itself) with a special-ticket event: Mickey's Not-So-Scary Halloween Party. The park closes a bit early on nights when the party takes place. (Guests bearing tickets to the party can stay in the park.) Expect characters in costume, creepy music and fog effects, and trick-or-treating throughout the park. It's a hoot! Mickey's Boo-to-You Halloween Parade takes place, as does a special edition of the fireworks show. Visit *www. disneyworld. com*, or call 407-824-4321 to order tickets to the party.

CHRISTMAS: A towering Christmas tree goes up on Main Street, and the Magic Kingdom is decked out as only Disney can do it. (Cinderella Castle is draped in 250,000 sparkling lights!) On select nights in November and December, the Magic Kingdom hosts a special-admission celebration known as Mickey's Very Merry Christmas Party.

The festivities, complete with hot chocolate, cookies, and snow flurries on Main Street,

Where to Find the Characters

Mickey and his pals make appearances throughout the day. Alice and her Wonderland friends may be found near the Mad Tea Party. Pooh and Tigger frequent Fantasyland. Woody, Jessie, and Bullseye have been known to appear in Frontierland. Ariel and Goofy have been spotted at Adventureland. Character meals at Crystal Palace and Cinderella's Royal Table offer guests a chance to meet Disney princesses and pals from the Hundred Acre Wood. Mickey, Minnie, and Disney princesses greet guests all day long at Main Street Theater Hall. And a variety of characters greet guests in Town Square at park opening time. Check a Times Guide for updated information.

include a running (or two) of Mickey's Once Upon a Christmastime Parade and holiday shows, plus a special Wishes fireworks show. Disney characters are on hand, too.

The Christmas party is a very popular (and enjoyable) event. Purchase tickets way ahead of time. And don't forget to wear red and green. (Some folks even wear hats and scarves.)

NEW YEAR'S EVE: It has always been true that on December 31 the throngs here are body to body. Expect a dazzling, super-size fireworks display and oodles of happy holiday decorations. There's plenty of nip in the air as the evening goes on, so dress accordingly.

The Main Street Electrical Parade

BIRNBAUM'S ★BEST Whether you are experiencing the Main Street Electrical Parade for the first time or for the first time in 20 years, we guarantee you'll be back for more. This enchanting classic, which made its Walt Disney World debut in 1977, is back after a lengthy hiatus. Cue applause!

A mesmerizing mix of shimmering lights (nearly half a million of them) and merry music, the parade features 23 illuminated floats (some of the originals have been retired and a few new floats have been added) plus 80 performers. As visually stunning as this processional is, it's the infectious score that makes it a truly unforgettable show. The "electro-syntho-magnetic" musical sound of Baroque Hoedown brings a smile to all faces, young and old.

The parade follows the Magic Kingdom's traditional parade route (heading from Main Street, U.S.A., to Frontierland and vice

PHOTO BY JILL SAFRO

MAGIC KINGDOM

versa). There are excellent viewing locations throughout the route, with many along the curbs of Main Street. It gets quite crowded there, so you must plan to claim your foot of curb about 45 to 90 minutes ahead of time (particularly for the earlier running).

The parade is presented during peak seasons and select evenings throughout the year.

Timing Tip: When the parade runs twice a night, the earlier presentation is always more crowded than the later one. So, if your party hasn't run out of steam, stick around for the late show. You'll be glad you did.

Note: Some performances may be canceled due to inclement weather.

PHOTO BY JILL SAFRO

Hot Tips

- Start the day by picking up a Fastpass assignment for your favorite attraction.

- For the best fireworks view, stand on Main Street between Town Square and Casey's Corner. (If you stand too close to the castle, some of the show may be blocked.)

- If there are two performances of the evening parade, the later one tends to draw smaller crowds.

- If you're driving to the park, start out very early. Most people arrive between 9:30 A.M. and 11:30 A.M., and the roads and parking lots are jammed. Plan to be at the gates to the Magic Kingdom before they open, and then be at the end of Main Street when the rest of the park opens.

- Table-service restaurants are in high demand in this park. Book yours as early as possible. And don't forget to confirm.

- Dying to meet Mickey Mouse? Head for the Town Square Theater on Main Street (near the train station). He, Minnie, and Disney princesses greet visitors there all day.

- You can usually get in line for an attraction right up until the minute the park closes.

- Avoid the mealtime rush hours by eating early or late: Before 11:30 A.M. or after 2 P.M., and before 5 P.M. or after 8 P.M.

- At busy times, take in these less-packed attractions: Walt Disney World Railroad, Liberty Belle Riverboat, Hall of Presidents, and Tomorrowland Transit Authority.

- Check the Tip Board for information on the wait times for popular attractions.

- Break up your day. Consider heading back to your hotel (if it's not too far) for some swimming. Be sure to hold onto your admission pass, stroller and/or wheelchair receipt(s), and your parking stub, so that you can re-enter the Magic Kingdom.

- If your party decides to split up, set a meeting place and time. Avoid meeting in front of Cinderella Castle, since this area can become quite congested.

- If an attraction has two lines, the one on the left usually will be shorter.

- For a full-service meal, be sure to make reservations in advance by calling 407-WDW-DINE (939-3463).

- There are picnic facilities at the Transportation and Ticket Center (TTC).

- Park guests have the right to chicken out at any time while waiting in line. In other words, should you or a member of your party have second thoughts about soaring on Space Mountain, visiting with the grinning ghosts of the Haunted Mansion, or another attraction, simply inform an attendant and you'll be discreetly whisked out a special exit.

- If you've rented a stroller, consider returning it just before the night's fireworks presentation. That way, after the show, you'll be able to make a beeline for your bed rather than stand in a line to return your stroller.

- Merchandise found in shops at Walt Disney World is also available through mail order. Call 407-363-6200 for info.

- Travel light. The fewer bags you have, the faster you'll pass through security.

- Allow extra time to get through the turnstiles on the way into the park—security and the "ticket tag" system can make for big delays—especially during peak times and on Extra Magic Hours days.

Epcot

Imagine a place whose entertainment inventory includes both a rich sampling of world cultures and a fun, enlightening journey to the technological frontier. You now have an inkling of the eye-opening and mind-broadening potential of Epcot—a place that's evolved most imaginatively in each of the 30 years it's been open.

Walt Disney suggested the idea back in 1966: "Epcot will be an experimental prototype community of tomorrow that will take its cue from the new ideas and technologies that are emerging from the creative center of American industry." It would never be completed, he said, but would "always be introducing and testing and demonstrating new materials and systems." On October 1, 1982, Walt Disney's dream became a reality. Test Track puts guests on the thrilling inside track of the fast and perilous world of automobile testing. Soarin' delivers the breathtaking sensation of flight. And favorites like The Seas with Nemo & Friends and Imagination! continue to ignite the creative forces within us all.

The park consists of two areas of exploration: Future World and World Showcase. The former examines ideas in science and technology in ways that make them seem not only comprehensible but downright irresistible. The latter celebrates the diversity of the world's peoples, portraying a stunning array of nations, with extraordinary devotion to detail.

Think of Epcot as Disney's playground for the curious and the thoughtful. The experiences it delivers—all of them wonders of the real world— continue to amaze, educate, inspire, and (of course) entertain.

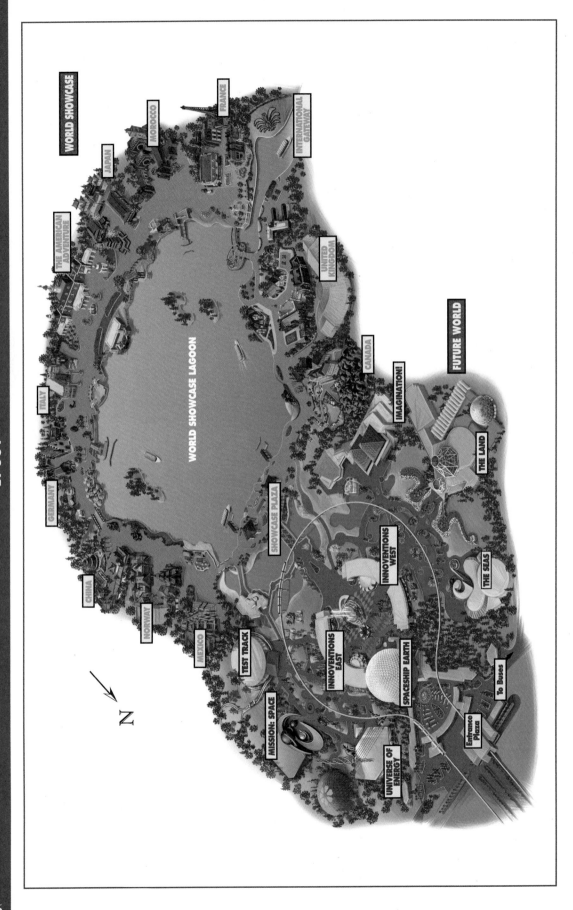

WORLD SHOWCASE

MOROCCO

FRANCE

JAPAN

INTERNATIONAL GATEWAY

THE AMERICAN ADVENTURE

UNITED KINGDOM

ITALY

CANADA

FUTURE WORLD

IMAGINATION!

GERMANY

THE LAND

WORLD SHOWCASE LAGOON

THE SEAS

CHINA

SHOWCASE PLAZA

INNOVENTIONS WEST

NORWAY

INNOVENTIONS EAST

MEXICO

TEST TRACK

SPACESHIP EARTH

To Buses

MISSION: SPACE

UNIVERSE OF ENERGY

Entrance Plaza

N

Getting Oriented

Triple the Magic Kingdom park and you have an idea of the size of Epcot. As for layout, the park is shaped something like a giant hourglass. The pavilions of Future World fill the northern bulb, while the international potpourri called World Showcase occupies the southern bulb. Future World is anchored on the north by the imposing silver "geosphere," dubbed Spaceship Earth.

As you pass through Epcot's main Entrance Plaza, Spaceship Earth looms straight ahead. Pathways curve around the 180-foot-tall geosphere, winding up at Innoventions Plaza. Here, in addition to a show fountain, you'll see signs for Innoventions, whose two buildings cradle the east and west sides of the plaza. Beyond this central area, there are two roughly symmetrical north-south avenues; these are dotted with the seven pavilions that form the outer perimeter of Future World. Mission: SPACE, Test Track, and Universe of Energy flank Spaceship Earth on the east, while Imagination!, The Land, and The Seas with Nemo & Friends lie to the west.

In World Showcase, the international pavilions are arranged around the edge of sparkling World Showcase Lagoon, with The American Adventure directly south of Spaceship Earth on the lake's southernmost shore. A walkway from Future World leads to World Showcase Promenade, a 1.2-mile thoroughfare that wraps around the lagoon, winding past each World Showcase pavilion in the process.

HOW TO GET THERE

Take Exit 67 off I-4. Continue along to the Epcot Auto Plaza; if you park in a distant lot, take a tram to the park's main entrance.

By WDW Transportation: From the Grand Floridian, Contemporary, and Polynesian: hotel monorail to the Transportation and Ticket Center (TTC), then switch to the TTC-Epcot monorail. From the Magic Kingdom: express monorail to the TTC, then switch to the TTC-Epcot monorail. From Downtown Disney: bus to any resort, then transfer to an Epcot bus or boat. From Disney's Hollywood Studios, Animal Kingdom, all other Walt Disney World resorts, and the resorts on Hotel Plaza Boulevard: buses.

Note: A second Epcot park entrance, called International Gateway, provides entry directly to World Showcase. It may be reached via walkways and the *FriendShip* water launches from Disney's Hollywood Studios, plus the Swan, Dolphin, Yacht and Beach Club, and Board-Walk resorts. The boat deposits guests between the France and United Kingdom pavilions. It is possible to purchase theme park admission here, at Epcot's "back door."

PARKING

All-day parking at Epcot is $14 for day visitors (free to Disney resort guests with a resort ID, as well as annual passholders). Attendants will direct you to park in one of several lots named for steps in the creative process, such as Discover and Imagine. Trams circulate regularly, providing transportation between the distant lots and the main entrance. Be sure to note the section and aisle in which you park. Parking tickets allow for re-entry to the area (and the other theme parks) throughout the day.

HOURS

Future World is usually open from about 9 A.M. to 9 P.M. (though some attractions may close at 7 P.M.). World Showcase hours are about 11 A.M. to 9 P.M. During certain holiday periods and the summer months, hours are extended. It's best to arrive a bit before the posted opening time, particularly during these busy seasons. On select days, the park opens one hour early or stays open three hours late for Disney resort guests only. Call 407-824-4321 for schedules, or visit *www.disneyworld.com*.

GETTING AROUND

Water taxis, called *FriendShip* launches, ferry guests across the World Showcase Lagoon. Docks are located near Mexico, Canada, Germany, and Morocco. (The only other way to traverse the vast area is on foot.)

Admission Prices

ONE-DAY BASE TICKET
(Restricted to use in Epcot. **Prices do not include sales tax and are likely to change in 2012.**)
Adult $85
Child* $79
*3 through 9 years of age; children under 3 free

Park Primer

EPCOT

BABY FACILITIES

There are changing tables and facilities for nursing mothers at the Baby Care Center in the Odyssey Center, between Test Track and Mexico. Disposable diapers are kept behind the counter at many Epcot shops; just ask.

CAMERA NEEDS

The Camera Center in Entrance Plaza and World Traveler at International Gateway stock memory cards, film, batteries, and disposable cameras, as well as frames, photo albums, and other accessories.

DISABILITY INFORMATION

Nearly all attractions, shops, and restaurants are accessible to guests using wheelchairs. Parking for guests with disabilities is available. Additional services are available for guests with visual and hearing disabilities. The complimentary *Guidemap for Guests with Disabilities* is available at Guest Relations. It provides a detailed overview of all services. For more information, turn to the *Getting Ready to Go* chapter of this book.

FIRST AID

Minor medical problems can be handled at the First Aid Center, in the Odyssey Center, between Test Track and Mexico. Keep in mind that many guests could avoid a trip to First Aid simply by staying well hydrated. If you have an emergency, notify an employee and call 911.

INFORMATION

Guest Relations, which has one location to the right of the main entrance plaza and another next to Spaceship Earth, is equipped with guidemaps, Times Guides, and a helpful staff.

LOCKERS

Lockers are found immediately west of Spaceship Earth. Cost is $7–$9, plus a $5 refundable deposit for unlimited use all day.

LOST & FOUND

Lost and Found is located at Guest Relations in Innoventions East. To inquire about lost items after your visit, call 407-824-4245. If you find an item, present it to a cast member (aka park employee).

LOST CHILDREN

Alert an employee and report lost children at Guest Relations or the Baby Care Center.

MONEY MATTERS

There are ATMs at the main entrance, on the path between Future World and World Showcase, and at The American Adventure. Some foreign currency may be exchanged at Guest Relations. Credit cards (American Express, JCB, Discover, Diner's Club, Visa, MasterCard, the Disney Visa card), traveler's checks, Disney Dollars, Disney gift cards, and WDW resort IDs (backed with a credit card) are accepted for admission and merchandise, as well as meals at most Epcot restaurants.

PACKAGE PICKUP

Epcot shops can arrange for most purchases to be transported (for free) to the Gift Stop in Entrance Plaza or International Gateway in World Showcase for later pickup.

SAME-DAY RE-ENTRY

Be sure to retain your ticket if you plan to return later the same day. A hand stamp is no longer required.

SECURITY CHECK

Guests entering Disney theme parks will be subject to a security check. Backpacks, parcels, purses, etc., will be searched by security personnel before guests are permitted to enter.

STROLLERS & WHEELCHAIRS

Strollers, wheelchairs, and Electric Convenience Vehicles (ECVs) may be rented from venues at both park entrances. Wheelchairs are also available at the Gift Stop. Cost is $15 for single strollers, $31 for double strollers, and $15 for wheelchairs. A Length-of-Stay rental yields a $2-per-day discount. It's $50 a day for an ECV, plus a $20 refundable deposit. Quantities are limited. ECVs tend to sell out early. Keep your rental receipt; it can be used that same day to get a replacement at Epcot or another theme park.

TIP BOARDS

Check a digital board in Innoventions Plaza, near The Land, or by Mission: SPACE to learn current waiting times for popular attractions.

Future World

A mere listing of the basic themes covered by the pavilions at Future World—agriculture, communications, car safety, the ocean, the land, energy, imagination, and space—tends to sound a tad academic. But when these serious topics are presented with a special flair, they become part of an experience that ranks among Disney's most entertaining.

Some of these subjects are explored in the course of lively and unusual "adventures," involving a whole arsenal of motion pictures, special effects, and Audio-Animatronics figures so lifelike that it is hard to remain unmoved. The basic elements are also appealing in their own right, from the palm-tree-dotted Entrance Plaza to the dramatic fountain just past Spaceship Earth, the many-faceted "geosphere" that has become the universal symbol of Epcot.

The park is so vast that it's hard to know what to do first. Many guests simply stop at Spaceship Earth on their way into Future World. As a result, they end up spending more time waiting in line than they need to. A wise alternative is to save Spaceship Earth for later in the day (when the lines inevitably thin out), and head for Soarin', the "less intense, non-spinning" Mission: SPACE, The Seas with Nemo & Friends, and Test Track (if motion sickness isn't an issue for you) as soon as the park opens (the lines tend to stay long

throughout the day). Take in as many Future World attractions as time allows, making sure to see the ImageWorks playground in the Imagination! pavilion, and save World Showcase for the evening hours. This strategy works well for families. (Refer to page 33 for a detailed version of this plan of attack.)

Another alternative—one that requires quite a bit of extra walking, but can help skirt a long line or two—is to explore Future World until World Showcase opens at 11 A.M. Then, in the afternoon, when many guests have shifted over to World Showcase, return to the Future World area. Innoventions is not only an interesting spot to pass the busy hours after lunch, but also a cool refuge when high temperatures prevail outdoors. And although queues can be found during peak seasons at Soarin', Mission: SPACE, Test Track, Imagination!, The Seas with Nemo & Friends, and Living with the Land throughout most of the late morning and afternoon, the period from late afternoon until park closing is usually less hectic. But don't forget to make it back to World Showcase in time to see the nighttime spectacular, IllumiNations—Reflections of Earth.

Left a Legacy?

Epcot has invited guests to "Leave a Legacy" near its front gate since its big Millennium Celebration. And? More than 550,000 have done so! They left their mark, in the form of a one-inch-square tile affixed on massive stone walls. While the program has officially come to a close, the cluster of monoliths continues to stand near the base of Spaceship Earth.

To locate a tile, inquire at the Leave a Legacy locating station inside the Camera Center by Spaceship Earth.

Spaceship Earth

As it looms impressively just above the Earth, this great, faceted silver structure looks a little bit like a spaceship ready to blast off. It appears large from a distance, and it seems even more immense when viewed from directly underneath. It's no surprise that some visitors simply stop beneath it and gawk.

The recently "refreshed" show inside, which explores the continuing quest by human beings to create the future, remains one of Epcot's compelling—if slower moving— attractions. It's an intriguing, narrated journey through time. It's also got a new interactive element that's a real hoot.

A common misconception about Spaceship Earth is that it is a geodesic dome. Not so. It is a geosphere. A geodesic dome is only half a sphere, while Spaceship Earth is almost completely round. Affectionately known to many simply as "the Ball," Spaceship Earth is indeed a sight to behold.

Noted science-fiction writer Ray Bradbury, together with consultants from the Smithsonian Institution, the Los Angeles area's

prestigious Huntington Library, the University of Southern California, and (among others) the University of Chicago, collaborated with Disney in developing this memorable 14-minute journey. It begins in an inky-black time tunnel, complete with a musty smell that suggests the dust of ages, and continues through history from the days of Cro-Magnon man (30,000 or 40,000 years ago) to the future.

Every scene is executed in exquisite detail. The symbols on the wall of that Egyptian temple really are hieroglyphics, and the content of the letter being dictated by the pharaoh was excerpted from a missive actually received by an agent of a ruler of the period.

Epcot veterans will notice two cool new scenes: a 1970s mainframe computer room and a garage scene depicting the creation of the personal computer.

All of these sights are enough to keep heads turning as the "time machines" wend their way upward. The most dazzling scene is saved for the ride's finale, when the audience is placed in the heart of a communications revolution amid interactive global networks that tie all the peoples of the world together.

The post-show area—Project Tomorrow— features five interactive areas, all emphasizing technology and its influence on daily life. Themes include medicine, power, and accident avoidance. You can also take a peek at a photo of yourself (surreptitiously snapped while you were experiencing the Spaceship Earth attraction). Expect to spend up to an hour in this high-tech playground.

Innoventions

Creativity abounds at Innoventions as guests celebrate the ingenuity and wonders of modern life. This imaginative zone is filled with interactive, hands-on exhibits. A highlight for daredevils is the Sum of All Thrills—an exhibit that explains the importance of science and math in roller coaster design. Oh, yeah—it also lets guests design and *ride* their own coaster! This experience is one of the most popular additions to Epcot in recent years.

Another stop here presents a new twist on the old adage "a penny saved is a penny earned." The Great Piggy Bank Adventure challenges guests of all ages to learn the importance of sound financial planning. Over at Where's the Fire?, guests learn about fire safety and get their photo snapped at a 30-foot pumper truck. Little ones love it.

> **HOT TIP!**
> The line for Spaceship Earth is usually quite long during the early morning hours and relatively short in the late afternoon and evening.

One of Walt Disney's dreams for Epcot was for the exhibits to change periodically. And indeed they do. Innoventions covers two buildings, referred to as East and West. The area between the pavilions is filled with color, light, spinning mobiles, and sidewalks glistening with fiber-optic lighting effects.

Above all, count on spending time exploring the exhibit areas (at least an hour). There's so much to see and do that curiosity will often get the better of any schedule here.

MOUSE GEAR: This enormous shop continues to offer a seemingly infinite and top-notch selection of Disney merchandise. Mouse Gear stocks character memorabilia, key chains, T-shirts, hats, books, candy, mugs, photo albums, jewelry, towels, footwear, Figment (the popular purple dragon from Epcot's Imagination! pavilion) toys, and much more—making this the best source for character merchandise in Epcot. There are also items related to the park itself, along with Disney-themed apparel and children's clothing. It is one of the best shops at Disney, and it stays open at least a half hour longer than the park does. It's a nice place to browse as the crowds exit the park after IllumiNations.

THE ART OF DISNEY: This is Epcot's spot for a unique assortment of Disney collectibles. The store showcases a wide variety of Disney animation art, including production cels, hand-painted limited-edition cels, small and oversize character figurines, fine-art serigraphs, postcards, and lithographs.

The Seas with Nemo & Friends

Welcome to one of the largest facilities ever dedicated to humanity's relationship with the ocean. It was designed by Disney Imagineers, in cooperation with distinguished oceanographic experts and scientists.

Though it enjoys the distinction of being one of Future World's original pavilions, what used to be known as The Living Seas is as fresh as ever—thanks to a little clownfish called Nemo and some of his fishy friends.

Once inside, guests can find the animated critters' real-life counterparts, including clownfish, blue tangs, sharks, and puffer fish.

The pavilion also features a Nemo-themed ride, an interactive encounter with an animated turtle, and an engaging post-show area. Little ones enjoy frolicking in Bruce's Shark World—a hands-on play area that celebrates the ocean's toothiest residents. From there, take a look at a simulated Caribbean coral reef environment. For the record, the crowning jewel of the pavilion is the simple-but-spectacular Turtle Talk with Crush.

BIRNBAUM'S
★BEST★

TURTLE TALK WITH CRUSH: If ever there was an attraction that left guests smiling and asking "How do they do that?!"—this is it. The concept is simple enough—a 10-minute, animated show featuring the surfer-dude sea turtle from *Finding Nemo*. The amazing part?

PHOTO BY JILL SAFRO

Under the Sea

Three behind-the-scenes tours offer guests a closer look at life in The Seas with Nemo & Friends underwater environs: DiveQuest gives certified scuba divers the opportunity to explore one of the world's largest aquariums. Epcot Seas Aqua Tour lets guests snorkel The Seas. And Dolphins in Depth offers guests the chance to learn about dolphin behavior as they closely observe researchers and trainers interacting with dolphins. Reservations for any tour can be made by calling 407-WDW-TOUR (939-8687). For more information on all of these programs, turn to page 218 of the *Everything Else in the World* chapter.

PHOTO BY JILL SAFRO

The cartoon critter interacts with the audience. In doing so, he imparts turtle-y wisdom, answers questions, and cracks more than a few jokes. You have to see it to believe it. To do that, you'll have to wait in line—it's extremely popular with guests of all ages. It's totally awesome, dude.

THE SEAS WITH NEMO & FRIENDS ATTRACTION: Imagineered in the style of classic family attractions, this undersea adventure is fun for everyone. In it, guests climb aboard a "clam-mobile" and enter a colorful coral reef. It seems Nemo has wandered off again and his teacher, Mr. Ray, needs help finding him. So keep your eyes peeled! There's a bit of suspense involved—including moments of darkness and a jellyfish encounter—but rest assured, it all ends happily.

CARIBBEAN CORAL REEF: The man-made reef exists in an enormous tank that holds about six million gallons of water and more than 60 species of sea life. Among the 2,000 or so inhabitants are turtles, angelfish, sharks, dolphins, and diamond rays. It's worth it to stop by as the park opens—that's usually when breakfast is served to the fish.

Guests sometimes get to see scuba divers testing and demonstrating diving gear and underwater monitoring equipment as they carry on training experiments with dolphins.

The Land

Occupying six acres, this enormous skylighted pavilion examines the nature of one of everybody's favorite topics—food. It also gives guests a chance to soar above the clouds in a celebration of flight. A film, *The Circle of Life*, uses characters from *The Lion King* to deliver

an entertaining yet inspirational message about humanity and the environment. A boat ride explores farming in the past and future. Narration gives visitors the chance to learn about the experimental agricultural techniques practiced in the pavilion.

Timing Tip: Soarin' is a wildly popular attraction. So much so that Fastpass assignments may be all gone before noon. It's best to visit first thing in the morning and get a Fastpass while the gettin's good!

LIVING WITH THE LAND: FP The 13½-minute boat ride through the rainforest and greenhouses in this pavilion opens with a dramatic storm scene. Guests sail through tropical rainforests, prairie grain fields, and a family farm. As the boat passes through each realistic setting, recorded narration offers commentary on humanity's ongoing struggle to cultivate and live in harmony with the land. Note the details that make each setting so convincing, such as sand blowing over the desert and light flickering from the television in the farmhouse window.

In the next segment, guests enter a plant research laboratory and solarium. Here, our planet's major food crops are being grown in research projects, along with rare new crops that may someday help meet Earth's ever-growing dietary needs.

Also of interest are the experiments being conducted to explore the practice of farming fish, and a desert farm area, where plants get nutrients through a drip irrigation system that delivers just the right amount of water—important in a dry climate.

As unreal as they appear, all the plants on view in the experimental greenhouses are living. In contrast, those in the biomes (the ecological communities viewed from the boat ride) were made in Disney studios out of lightweight plastic that simulates the cellulose found in real trees. The trunks and branches were molded from live specimens; the sycamore in the farmhouse's front yard, for example, duplicates one that stands outside a Burbank, California, car wash. Thousands of polyethylene leaves were snapped on.

BIRNBAUM'S ★BEST★ **SOARIN':** FP Up, up, and away! On this high-flying Epcot attraction (it's one of the most popular attractions at Walt Disney World), you'll be suspended in a hang glider 45 feet in the air, above a giant IMAX projection dome,

and treated to an aerial tour of some of the most awe-inspiring landscapes the state of California has to offer.

With the wind in your hair and your legs dangling in the breeze, the multi-passenger hang glider feels so convincingly real that you may even be tempted to pull up your feet for fear of tripping over a treetop as you dip down toward the ground. During the rather peaceful journey, flyers glide toward the Upper Yosemite Falls of Yosemite Valley, past an active naval aircraft carrier in San Diego Bay, by San Francisco's Golden Gate Bridge, and then down over the vast desert of Death Valley and the lush wine country of

Club Cool

Future World's Club Cool (formerly known as Ice Station Cool) is a great place to beat the heat. Located near Innoventions, it is Coca-Cola's International Tasting Station. Here, you can sample eight different soft drinks from around the world, some tastier than others.

After you've quenched your thirst, courtesy of the Coca-Cola Company, you may have a desire to do some shopping. Not coincidentally, there's plenty of Coke merchandise to choose from (at this point, you will have to open your wallet if you'd like a souvenir).

At press time, Club Cool was open for business during Future World's regular operating hours.

Napa Valley. In all, the airborne trip takes about five minutes and employs synchronized wind currents, scent machines, and a moving musical score set to a film that wraps 180 degrees around you, making this a thoroughly enveloping experience.

Note: You must be 40 inches tall and free of back problems, heart conditions, motion sickness, and other physical limitations to ride. It's calmer than traditional "thrill" rides, but the sensation of flight is quite realistic. If you're afraid of heights, sit this one out.

THE CIRCLE OF LIFE: This 20-minute film uses animation and live action to illustrate some of the dangers to our environment, as well as potential solutions. Presented as a fable featuring *The Lion King* favorites Simba, Timon, and Pumbaa, the film takes an optimistic approach to a serious subject. It is shown in the Harvest Theater, just inside the entrance to The Land. Soon after the film begins, Simba's startled by the exuberant shout of "Timber!" and is drenched by the splash of a fallen tree in the water. The culprits are none other than his friends Timon and Pumbaa, who are clearing the savanna for the development of the Hakuna Matata Lakeside Village. Simba seizes the opportunity to tell them a tale about creatures who sometimes forget that everything is connected in the circle of life: humans.

Simba demonstrates to Timon and Pumbaa the consequences of progress, as his lessons

Mad about the Mouse?

Can't get enough of all things Disney? Then D23 is the place to be. It's the official community for Disney fans. To join, you'll need unebbing enthusiasm for the House that Walt built and $35 (Silver-level annual dues). Membership nets access to special events, an official membership card and certificate, a collectible gift (plus the chance to purchase exclusive merchandise), and more. Gold level ($75) includes a subscription to the D23 magazine. For details or to join the club, visit *www.disney.com/D23*. FYI: Walt Disney founded what would become the Disney Studios in 1923. Hence, the name D23.

are driven home by visual evidence of humans' mistreatment of the air, water, and land. (Timon: "And everybody was *okay* with this?") The effect is a mix of entertainment and a message about responsibility.

Imagination!

The oddly shaped pyramids that house the Imagination! pavilion are striking to behold. They certainly set the stage for the engaging experiences inside, some of which are among the most whimsical at Epcot. The undisputed crown jewel here is a 3-D movie called

PHOTO BY JILL SAFRO

Character Connection

Where do Disney characters hang out when they aren't marching in parades or dancing in stage shows? The Epcot Character Spot! This brilliantly hued, Zip-a-Dee-Doo-Dah zone is *the* place to go to meet Disney faves such as Mickey and Minnie Mouse, Chip 'n' Dale, Pluto, and Goofy. The gang's here all day long, but it's best to arrive early in the morning—as the line gets downright beastly in the afternoon. The entrance to the Character Spot is next to Fountain View Ice Cream (near Innoventions West). Check a Times Guide for the character appearance schedule during your visit to Epcot.

Captain EO. Guests are also invited behind the scenes of the Imagination Institute in a slow-moving attraction known as Journey Into Imagination with Figment.

Another pavilion highlight is the pair of quirky fountains outside—the Jellyfish Fountains, which spurt streams of water that spread out at the top, looking for an instant like their namesake sea creature, and the Leap Frog Fountains, which send out smooth streams of water that arc from one garden plot to another in the most astonishing fashion. Kids just can't get enough of them.

CAPTAIN EO: 🅵🅿 The newest show in town is actually a blast from the past—a classic musical spectacular known as *Captain EO*, starring Michael Jackson. Back by popular demand, this crowd-pleasing film originally ran from 1986 through 1994 in this very theater.

Produced by George Lucas and directed by legendary Hollywood helmsman Francis Ford Coppola, EO is a thrilling, musical, space-fantasy adventure. Better yet, it's in 3-D!

It's fun for all ages, but some youngsters may be frightened when EO and his crew encounter a dark planet and its villainous Supreme Leader. Of course, good prevails when the gang magically—and musically—transforms the darkness into a happy and colorful world.

In addition to the King of Pop, the 17-minute *Captain EO* film features a cast of mythical space critters such as Hooter (a little green elephant-like fellow who sneezes musical notes), Fuzzball (an orange-haired monkey with butterfly wings), the golden-haired, two-headed Geex, and many more.

Note: *Captain EO* has returned for a limited engagement and is presented in the theater formerly occupied by Honey, I Shrunk the Audience (which is expected to return at a future date).

Timing Tip: This attraction tends to be less crowded very early or later in the day.

JOURNEY INTO IMAGINATION WITH FIGMENT: He's back! Figment, the tiny purple dragon with the orange wings and yellow eyes, is on hand to guide guests on an imaginative quest. The goal? To figure out, once and for all, the best way to capture your imagination.

The journey takes place at Imagination Institute, where guests are invited to tour the institute's various labs, such as the Sight Lab, the Sound Lab, and the Smell Lab. All in all, it's a tame experience, save for the occasional blast of air or flashing lights.

Nostalgia buffs, take note: The classic song "One Little Spark," which made its debut with the original incarnation of this attraction, underscores the show once more.

IMAGEWORKS LABS: It's a rare Image-Works visitor who doesn't experience at least some of the emotion felt by the little kid who

HOT TIP!
At press time, new activities were in the works for ImageWorks Labs. Be sure to stop by in 2012 to check them out!

cried when her parents tried to tear her away. That's not surprising, because the area is filled with activities that give every visitor the chance to have some fun while stretching the imagination. Plan to spend up to an hour exploring these entertaining labs.

IMAGEWORKS SHOP: This spot at the exit to the ImageWorks Labs offers merchandise themed to the Imagination! pavilion (including the ever-popular Figment). It also provides a service whereby your image can be captured by computer and reproduced onto items such as ornaments and crystal cubes. You can even have your mug slapped onto a poster, or a variety of other accessories. Film, disposable cameras, and other photographic essentials are available, too.

Test Track 🄵🄿

BIRNBAUM'S ★BEST★ Fasten your safety belt! This industrial-looking pavilion puts guests through the frenetic motions of automobile testing. As vehicles progress along the track, they whiz down straightaways, hug hairpin turns, and face near-collisions—and not always in ideal road conditions. En route, riders learn how tests are performed in real facilities (called proving grounds) and discover why certain procedures are crucial to car safety.

Before developing the attraction, Disney Imagineers toured GM proving grounds around the country. The result: From the steely facade to the rows of authentic testing equipment inside, Test Track bears more than a passing resemblance to the real thing.

> ## HOT TIP!
> If you don't mind splitting up your party, head for the "single rider" line at Test Track. It generally moves faster than the standby line.

The experience begins with a pre-show walking tour of the plant that reveals the incredible amount of component testing performed before automakers commit to production. Guests witness automotive testing vignettes, with everything from human interface (our courageous, crash-prone counterparts) to tires, brakes, air bags, and even seats being put through their paces.

The computer-controlled, six-seater vehicles are equipped with video and audio, but no steering wheels or brake pedals. The roads bear the familiar lines and signage of the real world, adding to the attraction's realism.

The five-minute ride begins with an uphill acceleration test. Then the suspension gets a workout, as vehicles descend over a bumpy surface that puts the wheels at odds with one another. During environmental testing, riders feel the heat and get the shivers as vehicles pass first through a radiant heat chamber, then a cold chamber. Roadside robots pitch in by spraying the fenders and door panels with water to test for corrosion.

The ride takes a dramatic turn during the road-handling segment. Vehicles course along a winding road, complete with mountain scenery, and into a darkened tunnel. Passengers hear a horn blast, see the high beams of a tractor trailer, and swerve to avoid the truck. As they emerge, there is a crash; guests round a corner to witness a barrier crash test. Their own vehicles then accelerate toward the barrier.

A long straightaway feeds into a series of banked turns and another straight shot that sends vehicles rocketing around the pavilion at top speed (up to 65 miles per hour).

Note: Kids under 7 must be accompanied by an adult; guests under 40 inches cannot ride; passengers must be free of back problems, heart conditions, motion sickness, and other physical limitations. Pregnant women are advised to sit this one out.

Mission: SPACE FP

Think you've got "the right stuff"? Well, this is your chance to prove it. Epcot's out-of-this-world attraction has a bold mission—to give you a chance to feel the excitement and extreme intensity of space travel without ever leaving the planet.

There are actually two ways to travel to Mars at this attraction: the "highly intense" way (aka Orange Team) and the "less intense" experience (Green Team). The original Mission: SPACE attraction provides a galaxy of thrills for many brave and sturdy theme park guests. The adventure begins with a white-knuckle blast-off of a spacecraft (which has snug seating for four) on an important mission to Mars. The sustained G-force during the launch is intended to be most realistic. Once en route, expect a rather strange, spectacular sensation. It's not quite weightlessness, but according to astronauts who've felt the real thing, it's pretty darn close. (So much so that it also tends to duplicate the not-so-spectacular sensation of space sickness. In fact, Mission: SPACE has the dubious distinction of being the first attraction in theme park history to be equipped with motion-sickness bags.)

Throughout the journey, you're expected to work with your fellow crew members (assuming the roles of navigator, captain, engineer, and pilot) to accomplish the mission. For the "highly intense" version, we recommend ignoring this call to duty and keeping your eyes glued to the screen. This will allow you to sit back and enjoy the ride and decidedly downsize the dizziness factor.

HOT TIP!

Epcot is bigger than it seems, so allow lots of time to get from place to place. (It can take a half hour to walk from Spaceship Earth to The American Adventure in World Showcase.) Keep this in mind if you have restaurant reservations or hope to snag a nice fireworks viewing location on the World Showcase promenade.

The original attraction can wreak havoc on the equilibrium. To cut the chances of losing your lunch, keep your eyes open at all times and fixed on the screen in front of you. You may be tempted to tilt your head or shut your eyes. Don't. (We promise you will arrive on Mars whether you fulfill your astronaut duty or not.)

Bottom line? Most guests who don't get queasy on the "highly intense" version tend to rave about Mission: SPACE. For us, well, we're proud to admit we choose the alternative, gentler version of this ride. It's intended for those who would rather not take the risk. The experience is a bit different on "Mission: SPACE-lite," but it gives everyone a chance to ride without turning green. The effects may be toned down, but they are quite extraordinary. We enjoy the "less intense," non-spinning mission to Mars.

All guests must be at least 44 inches tall and free of back and heart problems, motion sickness, and other physical limitations. Pregnant women should skip the trip, as should anyone with claustrophobic tendencies. In fact, if you have any health issues whatsoever, sit this out. And don't eat before riding!

EPCOT

Universe of Energy

In the mood for a chuckle? Set a course for this attraction. You'll get a few giggles and learn something to boot.

Although it's easy to spot this pavilion's mirrored pyramid, the facade does not provide any clue at all to the 45 minutes of surprises in store. One of the most technologically complex experiences at Epcot, a show called Ellen's Energy Adventure consists of several movies and a ride-through segment. None of these is exactly what Epcot guests might expect.

The show begins with a film (featuring a few familiar faces). In it, Ellen DeGeneres is watching *Jeopardy!* One of the contestants is Ellen's annoying college roommate, Judy.

Ellen plays along but keeps striking out, particularly in the ENERGY category. As she watches, her neighbor Bill Nye, the Science Guy, pops in and is aghast at Ellen's ignorance. Shortly thereafter, Ellen dozes off.

Ellen dreams she is a contestant on the show, competing against Albert Einstein and her former friend Judy. This time, all of the questions are about energy. As Einstein ponders and Ellen fumbles, Judy is racking up points. Ellen, who has a negative score ("this nightmare game is a lot harder than the home version"), decides to freeze her dream and ask Bill Nye, the Science Guy, for some help.

The second segment leads guests into a theater, where Bill vows to educate Ellen about the importance of energy. He persuades her to travel back in time to see where some of our energy sources came from. Suddenly (but very slowly), the whole seating area rotates, then breaks up into six sections that inch forward. The vehicles embark with Ellen upon an odyssey through the primeval world. Gigantic prehistoric trees crowd the forest. Apatosauruses wallow in the lagoon out front. A lofty allosaurus battles with an armored stegosaurus, and an elasmosaurus bursts out of a tide pool with frightening suddenness—all under the watchful gaze of winged pteranodons. (This zone may spook toddlers.)

Did You Know?
There are two acres of solar panels on the rooftop of Future World's Universe of Energy pavilion. Together, they generate 15 percent of the energy it takes to power the attraction housed inside. (It's enough energy to run six average homes.)

Next, guests move out of the forest and view a montage of pictures capturing the history of civilization, from cave dwellers to the present. The issue of alternative-energy sources is raised, and the message is that there is no save-all source, but rather there are many possibilities with promise.

The attraction winds up with Ellen returning to the game show of her dreams. This time, she's beating her friend Judy, who is not at all happy about how much Ellen has learned during the commercial break. To win, she must name the one energy source that will never be depleted. (We won't reveal the answer, but we got it right!)

Almost as intriguing as the attraction is the technology behind it. The vehicles weigh about 30,000 pounds when fully loaded with passengers, yet are guided along the floor by a wire that is only *one-eighth inch thick.*

PHOTO BY JILL SAFRO

World Showcase

PHOTO BY JILL SAFRO

Noble sentiments about humanity and the fellowship of nations, which have motivated so many World's Fairs in the past, also inhabit World Showcase. But make no mistake about it: This area of Epcot is unlike any previous international exposition.

The group of pavilions that encircles World Showcase Lagoon (a body of water that is the size of several football fields, with a perimeter of about 1.2 miles) demonstrates Disney conceptions about participating countries in remarkably realistic, consistently entertaining styles. You won't find the real Germany here —rather, the country's essence, much as a traveler returning from a visit might remember what he or she saw.

Shops, restaurants, and attractions are housed in a group of structures that is an artful pastiche of all the elements that give that nation's countryside and towns their distinctive flavor. Although occasional liberties have been taken when scale and proportion required them, careful research governed the design of every nook and cranny.

Equally impressive is the cuisine. With no fewer than 13 upscale eateries to choose from, it's no wonder some guests here do nothing but nosh. (That is especially true during Epcot's popular Food and Wine Festival, a time when dozens more nations contribute to an already fortified international menu. See page 10 for additional information.)

In the shops, many of the wares represent the country in whose pavilion they are sold. Craftspeople are occasionally on hand to demonstrate their arts. Thanks to special cultural-exchange programs and recruiting efforts, many World Showcase staffers hail from the countries the pavilions represent.

A diverse lineup of entertainment ensures that all visitors experience more than a little culture, foreign or otherwise. The entertainment is as authentic as the Disney casting directors can make it, with native performers commonly featured and new festivities always in the works.

> ## HOT TIP!
> World Showcase pavilions may open at 11 A.M. or later. However, guests may use the International Gateway entrance as much as a half hour prior to Future World's official opening time.

Kim Possible World Showcase Adventure

Calling all secret agent wannabes! How would you like to help save the world from super-villains? Here's your chance. The interactive game is based on the Disney Channel show *Kim Possible*. Of course, one need not be familiar with the show to get a kick out of the Epcot version. Once guests borrow a "Kimmunicator" from a recruitment station (near Innoventions or on the bridge to World Showcase), you are ready to start the scavenger hunt.

If you and your team follow instructions and find the clues, you will complete your very important mission: to save the world! There is no extra charge to play this game, but guests do have to return the Kimmunicators after they declare "mission accomplished."

Pavilions are described in the order in which they would be encountered while moving counterclockwise around the World Showcase Lagoon after crossing the bridge from Future World.

Canada

Celebrating the many beauties of the U.S.A.'s neighbor to the north, the area devoted to the Western Hemisphere's largest nation is complete with its own mountain, waterfall, rushing stream, rocky canyon, mine, and splendid garden massed with colorful flowers. There's even a totem pole, a trading post, and an elaborate, mansard-roofed hotel similar to ones built by Canadian railroad companies as they pushed west around the turn of the 20th century. All

PHOTO BY JILL SAFRO

this is imaginatively arranged somewhat like a split-level house, with the section representing French Canada on top, and another devoted to the mountains alongside it and below. From a distance, the Hôtel du Canada, the main building here, looks like little more than a bump on the landscape—as does Epcot's single Canadian Rocky Mountain. But up close they both seem to tower as high as the real thing.

The gardens were inspired by the Butchart Gardens, in Victoria, British Columbia, a famous park created on the site of a limestone quarry. The hotel is modeled, in part, after Ottawa's Victorian-style Château Laurier. Entertainment is provided by a troupe of Celtic rock musicians, called Off-Kilter. They perform on a stage facing the promenade.

O CANADA!: Step into the Circle-Vision 360 film, *O Canada*, and find yourself surrounded by the breathtaking sights and sounds of America's neighbor to the north. Of course, you won't be alone—Canadian actor Martin Short stars as your guide, taking guests through prairies, plains, snowfields, rivers, rocky mountainsides, and beyond. Humor and hockey are included. The motion picture provides a you-are-there feeling that makes all of this spectacular scenery still more memorable. Note that there are no seats in this theater.

NORTHWEST MERCANTILE: Found to the left upon entering the pavilion's plaza, this spot features NHL T-shirts (Canadian teams, of course), plush toys (moose, owls, otters, etc.), and candy, plus other Canada-themed collectibles. Skeins of rope, tin scoops, lanterns, and antique ice skates hanging from the long beams overhead set the mood, together with the structure itself.

EPCOT

150

United Kingdom

In the space of only a few hundred feet, visitors to this pavilion stroll from an elegant London square to the edge of a canal in the rural countryside—via a bustling urban English street framed by buildings that constitute a veritable rhapsody of historic architectural styles. But one scene leads to the next so smoothly that nothing ever seems amiss. Here again, note the attention to detail: the half-timbered High Street structure that leans a bit, and the hand-painted "smoke" stains that make the chimneys look as if they have been there for centuries. When a thatched roof is required, it's right where it should be—though the roof may be made of plastic broom bristles because fire regulations prohibit the real thing. Off to the side is a pair of scarlet phone booths identical to those that used to be found around the U.K. And there are eight architectural styles characteristic of the streetscapes, from English Tudor to Georgian and Victorian.

There is no major attraction in this pavilion; instead, it features half a dozen shops and a pub that serves a selection of beers and ales that would be the toast of any "local" in London itself. There's lots of entertainment, including a group of comedians called the World Showcase Players, who, when not engaged in general clowning on the World Showcase Promenade, coax audience members into participating in their farcical playlets.

In the pub, a pianist has been known to play late into the evening. A live band known as British Revolution plays classic rock favorites in the garden courtyard. They're a true crowd-pleaser. (Entertainment is subject to change.)

THE CROWN & CREST: This shop looks like a backdrop for a child's fantasy of the days of King Arthur, with its high rafters decked out with bright banners, a vast fireplace (and crossed swords above), and wrought-iron chandelier. Souvenirs featuring the Union Jack flag and the Rose & Crown Pub (the U.K. pavilion's popular watering hole) are the stock-in-trade at this emporium adjoining the Sportsman Shoppe. Name histories and family crests are also available, as are swords, shields, and knights in shining armor.

HOT TIP!

A great place to watch IllumiNations is from the Rose & Crown Pub in the United Kingdom pavilion. Try to snag a lagoonside table—whether within the pub's boundaries or in the self-serve sitting area nearby—about 30 minutes before the show is set to begin. (Note that on nights when the wind is blowing directly toward the Rose & Crown, it might be better to grab a bite and watch the show from Mexico's Cantina, on the other side of the lagoon.)

SPORTSMAN SHOPPE: Head here for clothing and accessories centered on uniquely British locales and sports. You can expect to find a large selection of football (soccer) team gear. Don't miss the tartan map on the wall opposite The Crown & Crest; it identifies plaids from Glen Burn and Gordon to Langtree and St. Lawrence. Outside, the shop resembles a stone manor built during the last half of the 16th century.

THE TEA CADDY: Fitted out with heavy wooden beams and a broad fireplace to resemble the Stratford-upon-Avon cottage of William Shakespeare's wife, Anne Hathaway, this shop stocks English teas, both loose and in bags, in a wide variety of flavors. Other items include teapots, china, biscuits, and assorted candies.

PHOTO BY JILL SAFRO

THE TOY SOLDIER: This shop presents a nice selection of rock-'n'-roll-themed items, highlighting well-known British bands, as well as merchandise featuring the gang from the Hundred Acre Wood: Pooh, Piglet, Eeyore, and Tigger, too. Also found here? Toy swords and shields, books, and candy.

THE QUEEN'S TABLE: This shop (opposite the Sportsman Shoppe) may be one of the loveliest in Epcot. That is particularly true of the store's elegant Adams Room, embellished with elaborate moldings and a crystal chandelier. The setting is a lovely background for the handbags, perfumes, soaps, and other fragrant items that are available.

Don't neglect to inspect small, serene Britannia Square outside the shop farthest from the promenade. But for its small size and the Florida climate, it feels like London itself.

THE MAGIC OF WALES: This small store specializes in souvenirs from Wales.

International Gateway

Informally known as Epcot's back door, the International Gateway is located between the United Kingdom and France pavilions. There's a ticket window just outside the turnstiles (Yes, it's possible to enter and exit the park here.) You'll also find:

FRIENDSHIP LANDING: Disney's water taxis, known as *FriendShip* boats, ferry guests to the Yacht and Beach Club, BoardWalk, and the Swan and Dolphin resorts, and finally to Disney's Hollywood Studios (which is the last stop before the boat returns to the resorts and back to Epcot). The dock is located outside the International Gateway turnstiles.

Where to Eat in Epcot

A complete listing of all eateries—full-service restaurants, fast-food emporiums, and snack shops—can be found in the *Good Meals, Great Times* chapter. See the Epcot section, beginning on page 237.

STROLLER AND WHEELCHAIR RENTAL:
Strollers and wheelchairs are available for rent at this location. Remember to keep your rental receipt; it can be used on the same day in the Magic Kingdom, Disney's Hollywood Studios, Animal Kingdom, or again in Epcot, should you leave and return later on. It is also possible to get a replacement stroller here.

WORLD TRAVELER: Candy, soft drinks, books, kitchen items, convenience items, strollers (for purchase), and a package pickup depot are located at this spot near the United Kingdom pavilion. Disney fashions, home items, character merchandise, and Epcot souvenirs are also for sale here.

France

The buildings here have mansard roofs and casement windows so Gallic in appearance that you may expect to see a Bohemian poet looking down from above. A canal-like offshoot of the lagoon seems like the Seine itself; the footbridge that spans it recalls the old Pont des Arts. There's a kiosk like those that punctuate the streets of Paris and a bakery whose heavenly rich aromas announce its presence long before it's visible.

Shops sell perfumes and other items. Their roofs are of real copper or slate, and the cabinetry is finely crafted. Galerie des Halles—the iron-and-glass-ceilinged market that Paris once counted as one of its most beloved institutions—lives again. But perhaps most special of all are the people. Hosts and hostesses who hail from Paris and the French provinces answer questions in French-accented English. Keep an eye out for Serveur Amusant, the comedic waiter who does one heck of a balancing act.

Some interesting background notes: The dusty rose-colored, lace-trimmed costumes that the hostesses wear were inspired by the dresses in *Le Bar aux Folies-Bergère* by the Impressionist painter Edouard Manet, and the main entrance to the pavilion recalls the architecture of Paris, most of which was built during the *Belle Epoque* ("beautiful age"), the last decades of the 19th century.

Don't miss the garden on the opposite side of this pavilion. It is one of the most peaceful spots in World Showcase.

BIRNBAUM'S ★**BEST**★ **IMPRESSIONS DE FRANCE:** Shown in the Palais du Cinéma, a little theater that's not unlike the one at Fontainebleau, this enchanting 18-minute film takes viewers on a trip through France.

The film shows off a beautiful tree-dotted estate, fields and vineyards at harvest time, a flower market and a pastry shop, a glacier, and a harbor full of squawking gulls. Viewers visit the Eiffel Tower; Versailles and its gilt Hall of Mirrors (just outside Paris); Mont Saint Michel; the French Alps; and Cannes, the star-studded resort city on the Mediterranean coast. All this is even more appealing thanks to a superb sound track, consisting almost entirely of the music of French-classical composers.

The exceptionally wide screen adds yet another dimension. This is not a Circle-Vision 360 film like the movies shown at China and Canada. The France film used only five cameras, and it is shown on five large projection surfaces—200 degrees around. It's a beautiful film, one of the park's best. We recommend stopping for a French pastry break after the show.

PLUME ET PALETTE: One of the loveliest shops in World Showcase, this Art Nouveau-inspired location is home to the Givenchy Shop—the only location in the world that carries the complete line of Givenchy fragrances, skincare products, and cosmetics.

LA SIGNATURE: Another beautiful spot, this boutique features a selection of Guerlain cosmetics and fragrances.

L'ESPRIT DE PROVENCE: This little shop stocks a selection of textiles, ceramics, and kitchen accessories from the Provence region of Southern France.

LES VINS DE FRANCE: Selections in this wine shop range from the inexpensive to the pricey, from *vin ordinaire* going for several dollars to upward of $99 for a rare vintage.

Wine tastings are held here to sample the offerings (note that a charge is levied for each taste). Other wares include books about wine, bottle openers and toppers, aprons, candy, kitchenware, and soaps.

HOT TIP!
Don't try to fit all of the World Showcase movies into one day, especially if you are traveling with kids.

SOUVENIRS DE FRANCE: Everything from Eiffel Tower statues to CDs with music by French composers is offered at this location near the exit of the cinema. Mugs, tote bags, T-shirts, berets, flags, and picture frames are among the offerings available. The area is based on Paris's now-demolished Les Halles, the city's old fruit and vegetable market. This space has indoor tables that are perfect for enjoying treats from the nearby bakery.

Morocco

Nine tons of tile were handmade, hand cut, and shipped to Epcot to create this World Showcase pavilion. To capture the unique quality of this North African nation's architecture, Moroccan artisans came to Epcot to practice the mosaic art that has been a part of their homeland for thousands of years. Koutoubia Minaret, a detailed replica of the famous prayer tower in Marrakesh, stands guard at the entrance. A courtyard with a

fountain at the center leads to the medina (Old City). Between the traditional alleyways and the more modern sections are the pointed arches and swirling patterns of the Bab Boujeloud gate, a replica of the one that stands in the city of Fez. An ancient working waterwheel irrigates the gardens, and the motifs repeated throughout the buildings include carved plaster and wood, tile, and brass. Mo'Rockin takes over the courtyard, with musicians playing lively Western music with an Arabic twist. (Entertainment varies.)

THE BRASS BAZAAR: Interspersed among the decorative brass plates in this store are ceramic pitchers, planters, pots, ornate bottles of rosewater, serving sets, soapstone carvings, wooden collectibles, books, framed prints, baskets, tiles, couscous, hummus, and tabbouleh mixes, and other Moroccan selections.

THE ART OF HENNA: In the market for a temporary henna body decoration? Look no

PHOTO BY JILL SAFRO

farther than this cozy corner of the Morocco pavilion. Henna "tattoos" are available—for a fee—in various sizes and designs between 1 P.M. and 9 P.M. daily (hours may vary).

CASABLANCA CARPETS: In addition to handmade carpets, this store features an intriguing and eclectic selection of merchandise. Look for lamps, fez hats, jewelry, books, and much more.

MARKETPLACE IN THE MEDINA: Hand-woven baskets, sheepskin wallets and bags, assorted straw hats, drums, sandals, postcards, scarves, and small carpets are among the available wares.

SOUK AL MAGREB: This small waterside enclave located on the World Showcase promenade spills over with crafted brass work. Moroccan baskets and leather goods also abound. In addition to henna tattoos (provided by a resident tattoo artist for a fee), one can also pick up toy camels, hats, and shirts.

TANGIER TRADERS: This is the place to shop if you're in the market for a fez, woven belts, leather sandals and purses, and other traditional Moroccan clothing and accessories.

Japan

Serenity rules in Japan. Except, of course, when the pavilion resounds with traditional music performed by a drum-playing duo or group.

The landscaping, designed in accordance with traditional symbolic and aesthetic values, contributes to the pavilion's peaceful mood. Rocks, which in Japan represent the enduring nature of the Earth, were brought from North Carolina and Georgia (since boulders are scarce in the Sunshine State). Water, symbolizing the sea (which the Japanese consider a life source), is abundant; the Japan pavilion garden has a stream and pools inhabited by *koi* (fish). Evergreen trees, which in Japan are symbols of eternal life, are here in force.

Disney horticulturists created this very Japanese landscape using few plants native to that country because the climate there is so

different from that of Florida. Among the few trees here native to Japan are the *sago*, near the courtyard entrance to the Yakitori House; the two Japanese maple trees, identifiable by their small leaves, not far away (near the first stairway from the promenade on the left side of the courtyard as you face it); and the prickly monkey-puzzle trees, near the walkway to the promenade, on The American Adventure side of the pagoda. Needle-sharp thorns make the latter the only species of tree that monkeys cannot climb.

The pagoda was modeled after an eighth-century structure located in the Horyuji Temple, in Nara, Japan. The striking *torii* gate on the shore of World Showcase Lagoon derives from the design of the one at the Itsukushima shrine in Hiroshima Bay.

BIJUTSU-KAN GALLERY: Housing a changing cultural display, this small museum has offered, among other exhibitions, the Kitahara Collection of Tin Toys, featuring toys produced from 1880–1970. Recently, the exhibit "Spirited Beasts—From Ancient Stories to Anime Stars" was featured here.

MITSUKOSHI MERCHANDISE STORE: There are kimonos, T-shirts bearing Japanese characters, traditional headdresses, and a selection of bowls and vases meant for flower arranging for sale at this spacious store set up by Mitsukoshi—a four-century-old retail firm.

Did You Know?

The five stories of the Japanese pagoda symbolize earth, water, fire, wind, and sky.

The shop features a selection of kimonos, as well as chopsticks, bonsai, jewelry, china, paper fans, and origami products. There is also a bounty of snacks, candies, and teas. The pleasant atmosphere and wide variety of merchandise make this establishment a most rewarding experience for both the casual browser and the serious shopper. The building's design was inspired by the Gosho Imperial Palace, which was constructed in Kyoto in 794 A.D.

The American Adventure

BIRNBAUM'S ★BEST When it came to creating The American Adventure, the centerpiece of World Showcase, Disney Imagineers were given relatively free rein. So the 110,000 bricks of the imposing Colonial-style structure that houses a spectacular show, fast-food restaurant, and souvenir shop are the real thing—patiently crafted *by hand* from soft Georgia clay.

The show inside stands out because of its wonderfully evocative settings, its detailed sets, and the 35 superb Audio-Animatronics players, some of the most lifelike ever created by the Disney organization. A stellar a cappella vocal group called Voices of Liberty periodically serenades guests in the building's foyer. By all means, catch a performance.

THE AMERICAN ADVENTURE SHOW: One of the most ambitious Epcot attractions, this 26-minute presentation celebrates the American spirit from the nation's earliest years right up to the present. Beginning with the arrival of the pilgrims at Plymouth Rock and their hard first winter on the western shore of the Atlantic, the Audio-Animatronics narrators—an amazingly lifelike Ben Franklin and a convincing, cigar-puffing Mark Twain—recall key people and events in American history: the Boston Tea Party, George Washington and the grueling winter at Valley Forge, the influential abolitionist Frederick Douglass, the celebrated 19th-century Nez Perce chief Joseph, and many more. The Philadelphia Centennial Exposition is remembered, along with women's rights campaigner Susan B. Anthony, telephone inventor Alexander Graham Bell, and the steel giant and philanthropist Andrew Carnegie. Naturalist John Muir converses onstage with Teddy Roosevelt. Charles Lindbergh, Rosie the Riveter, Jackie Robinson, and Walt Disney are represented. So are John Wayne, Lucille Ball, Margaret Mead, John F. Kennedy, Martin Luther King, Jr., and Billie Jean King.

The idea is to recall episodes in history, both negative and positive, that contributed to the

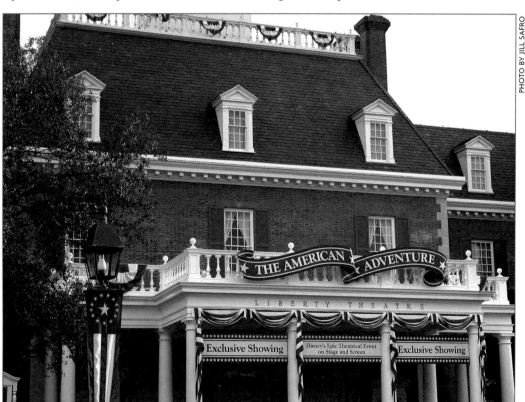

growth of the spirit of America, by engendering either "a new burst of creativity" (in the designers' words) "or a better understanding of ourselves as partners in the American experience." It was updated in 2008 and is rather compelling.

For information about how each of the many featured historical figures spoke during his or her lifetime, researchers contacted historians and cultural institutions—the Philadelphia Historical Commission, the State Historical Society of Missouri, the Department of the Navy's Ships Historical Branch, and others. When recordings were not available, educated guesses were made: Alexander Graham Bell's voice was created on the basis of contemporary comments about his voice's clarity, expressiveness, and crisp articulation, combined with the fact that his father taught elocution.

A highlight of the show is the majestic music played throughout by the Philadelphia Symphony Orchestra.

Seats toward the front of the house give the best view of the Audio-Animatronics figures. If you have some extra time before the show, be sure to read the inspirational quotes that line the walls—Jane Addams, Charles Lindbergh, Herman Melville, and Ayn Rand are among the prominent Americans who are quoted.

AMERICAN HERITAGE GALLERY: Located inside the American Adventure pavilion, the addition of this art gallery brought Epcot's grand total to six. Its current exhibition, is called "National Treasures." Among the interesting items to gaze upon? Thomas Edison's phonograph, Mark Twain's pen (and pocket knife), and a chair that once belonged to George Washington.

HERITAGE MANOR GIFTS: Visit this shop to find Americana in all of its red-white-and-blue glory. Gifts include patriotic clothing, flags, and books about U.S. history.

THE AMERICA GARDENS THEATRE: An ever-changing slate of live entertainment is presented throughout the year in this lakeside amphitheater in front of the American Adventure pavilion. Showtimes are also posted on the promenade and in the park Times Guide.

Be sure to note the pruning of the western sycamores overhead: The old-fashioned pollarding method used, which involves trimming the treetops flat and allowing the lower branches to interlock, produces a thick canopy. The flower beds are planted appropriately with red, white, and blue blossoms.

Italy

The arches and cutout motifs that adorn the World Showcase reproduction of the Doge's Palace in Venice are just the more obvious examples of the attention to detail lavished on the individual structures in this relatively small pavilion. The angel perched atop the scaled-down campanile was sculpted on the model of the original, right down to the curls on the back of its head. It was then covered with real gold leaf, despite the fact that it was destined to be set almost 100 feet in the air.

The other statues in the complex, including the sea god Neptune presiding over the fountain in the rear of the piazza, are similarly exact. And the pavilion even has an island like Venice's own, its seawall appropriately stained with age, plus moorings that look like barber poles, with several distinctively Venetian gondolas tied to them. St. Mark the Evangelist is also remembered, together with the lion that is the saint's companion and Venice's guardian. These can be seen atop the two massive columns that flank the small arched footbridge that connects the island to the mainland. The only deviation from Venetian reality is the alteration of the site of the Doge's Palace in reference to the real St. Mark's Square.

The quaint pavilion is equally interesting from a horticultural point of view. The island boasts kumquat trees, citrus plants typical of the Mediterranean, and a couple of olive trees that can be seen on both sidewalls of the Enoteca Castello and La Bottega Italiana. Originally located in a Sacramento, California, grove, the olive trees arrived in Florida via flatbed truck a bit slimmer than when they started out. (Arizona border inspectors decreed that the trees be trimmed to the ten-foot width required by state law; therefore, the ancient olives were shorn en route. The hardy trees survived, leaving only their scars to remind visitors of the ordeal; the darker bark is what remains of the original, while the lighter areas are new growth.) The tall, narrow trees that stand like dark columns are Italian cypresses, which are extremely common in their native country.

ENOTECA CASTELLO: This shop on the edge of the piazza features a selection of red and white Italian wines. Items such as chocolate, espresso, cookbooks, and decorative bottle toppers are also on hand.

IL BEL CRISTALLO: There is an abundance of sports-themed apparel and accessories, plus purses, wallets, and bags inside this shop (just off the promenade on the Germany side of the piazza). Other featured wares include scarves, ties, fragrances, and jewelry. This shop also boasts an assortment of exquisite, handcrafted Venetian masks (which range in price from about $30 to $500).

LA BOTTEGA ITALIANA: This shop sells a mix of decorative ceramics and glassware.

Germany

There are no villages in Germany quite like this one. Inspired by various towns in the Rhine region, Bavaria, and the German north, it boasts structures reminiscent of those found in urban enclaves as diverse as Frankfurt, Freiburg, and Rothenburg. There are stair-stepped rooflines and towers, balconies and arcaded walkways, and so much overall charm that the scene seems to come straight out of a fairy tale. The beer hall to the rear is almost as lively as the one at Munich's famed Oktoberfest, especially late in the evening. The shops, which offer a range of merchandise from wine and sweets to ceramics and cuckoo clocks, toys, and books—and even art—are so tempting that it's hard to leave the area empty-handed.

The elements that constitute the Germany pavilion are described here as they would be encountered while walking counterclockwise around the cobblestone-paved central plaza, which is known as the St. Georgsplatz, after the statue at its center. St. George, the patron saint of soldiers, is depicted with a dragon that legend says he slew during a pilgrimage to the Middle East.

Try to time your World Showcase peregrinations to take you to Germany on the hour, when the handsome, specially designed glockenspiel at the plaza's rear can be heard chiming in a melody composed specifically for the pavilion.

DAS KAUFHAUS: This two-story structure, whose exterior is patterned after a merchants' hall known as the Kaufhaus (located in the German town of Freiburg im Breisgau), stocks athletic apparel and footwear. Film and sundries are also available.

DER TEDDYBAR: Located adjacent to Volkskunst, this is a toy shop with a bit of flare. It's home to one of Walt Disney World's best selections of toys, including an assortment of stuffed keepsakes. Duffy the Disney Bear is among the plush items sold here.

KARAMELL KÜCHE: This caramel kitchen tempts with housemade sweet treats made from buttery caramel. Many items are made fresh in an on-stage kitchen. Favorites include fresh strawberries hand-dipped in chocolate and drizzled with gooey caramel, caramel-filled chocolate chip cookies, crunchy apples enveloped in caramel, chocolate or vanilla cupcakes topped with rich vanilla icing with a

dab of caramel on top, packaged Werther's candies, and much more. Don't come here on an empty stomach—you could go bankrupt! It took over the space formerly occupied by Glas und Porzellan in late 2010.

KUNSTARBEIT IN KRISTALL: This shop to the left of the Biergarten features Austrian and crystal jewelry, tall beer mugs, wineglasses in traditional German tints of green and amber, and crystal decanters. Guests may have glassware etched on the spot.

STEIN HAUS: The "house" is really a tiny shop that sells German steins and collectibles.

VOLKSKUNST: Small and appealing, this establishment is filled with a burgher's bounty of German timepieces, plus a smattering of other items made by hand in the rural corners of the nation. As for cuckoo clocks, some are small and unobtrusive, while others are so immense that they'd look appropriate only in some cathedral-ceilinged hunting lodge. This is also one place to pick up a traditional German beer stein, wine accessories, bells, books, crafts, and music.

WEINKELLER: The Germany pavilion's wine shop, situated between the cookie shop and the crystal shop toward the rear of St. Georgsplatz, offers about 50 varieties of German wine. Wine tastings are held here daily (for a fee).

The selection includes not only those vintages meant for everyday consumption, but also fine estate wines. These are white (with a few exceptions), because white wine constitutes the bulk of Germany's vinicultural output. (Only 20 percent of German bottlings are red.) The setting itself is quite attractive—low-ceilinged and cozy, and full of cabinets embellished with carvings of vines and bunches of grapes.

DIE WEIHNACHTS ECKE: A shop like this can set a visitor's mind to thoughts of Christmas—even on the hottest dog days of summer. Ornaments, decorations, and gifts manufactured by various German companies line the shelves of this store.

One item of note is the pickle ornament. Pickle ornaments are considered a special Christmas tree decoration by many families in Germany. Historically, it is always the last ornament hung on the tree, with a parent hiding it among the other ornaments. Kids gleefully search for it—and the one who finds it gets a special little present from St. Nicholas, left for the most observant child.

China

Dominated by the Disney equivalent of Beijing's Temple of Heaven and announced by a pair of banners that proclaim good wishes to passersby (the Chinese characters translate to: "May good fortune follow you on your path through life" and "May virtue be your neighbor"), this pavilion conveys a level of serenity that offers an appealing contrast to the hearty merriment of the bordering Germany and the gaiety of nearby Mexico. Part of this quiet environment is the by-product of the soothing, traditional Chinese music. Live flute music is performed in the courtyard. The gardens also make a major contribution. They are full of rose-bushes native to China, and there is a century-old mulberry tree (to the left of the main

PHOTO BY JILL SAFRO

walkway into the pavilion), with a pome-granate tree and a wiggly-looking Florida native known as a water oak nearby.

The number of stones in the floor of the pavilion's main structure is not random; the center stone is surrounded by nine stones because nine is considered a lucky number in China. Around the edge of the outer room rise 12 columns—because 12 is the number of months in the year and the number of years in a full cycle of the Chinese calendar. Be sure to stand on the round stone in the center: Every whisper is amplified.

A spacious emporium is devoted to Chinese wares, and two restaurants add to the overall atmosphere. However, all this is secondary to the motion picture shown inside the Temple of Heaven—a Circle-Vision 360 film that is one of the most diverting World Showcase attractions. Keep in mind that this is a standing-room-only experience.

REFLECTIONS OF CHINA: This cinematic presentation shows the beauties of a land that few Epcot visitors have seen firsthand—and does it so vividly that it's possible to see the film twice and still not fully absorb all the wonderful sights.

The film replaces "Wonders of China," the Circle-Vision 360 movie that played at Epcot's China pavilion since 1982. Just as with the original, filmmakers used nine cameras to capture cultural and scenic images that wrap completely around viewers. The tour includes stops in

Village Traders

Located between the Germany and China pavilions, this open-air shop sports a selection of gift items from Africa, India, and Australia. Browse through such souvenirs as wind chimes, handbags, hats, and, of course, T-shirts.

Hong Kong, Macau, Beijing, and Shanghai.

The film includes footage of many landmarks, such as the 2,400-year-old Great Wall and Tiananmen Square, as well as some newer cultural developments. Overall, it showcases the majesty of this ancient country and highlights some of the more dramatic changes that have taken place over the past 20 or so years. Note that the theater has no seats.

HOUSE OF WHISPERING WILLOWS: When exiting, pass by the House of Whispering Willows, an exhibit of ancient Chinese art and artifacts. Changed about every six months, it invariably includes fine pieces from well-known collections.

YONG FENG SHANGDIAN: This vast Chinese emporium, located off the narrow, charming Street of Good Fortune, offers a huge assortment of merchandise—silk robes, prints, porcelain items, tea sets, and more. Trinkets, moderately priced items, and expensive antiques are available. The calligraphy on the curtains wishes passersby good fortune, long life, prosperity, and happiness.

Norway

Set between Mexico and China is Norway, a pavilion added to the World Showcase mix in 1988. Built in conjunction with many Norwegian companies, the pavilion celebrates the rich history, folklore, and culture of one of the Western world's oldest countries.

The cobblestone town square is an architectural showcase of the styles of such Norwegian towns as Bergen, Alesund, and Oslo. There's also a Norwegian castle fashioned after Akershus, a 14th-century fortress still standing in Oslo's harbor; the castle here houses the Akershus restaurant. Few can resist walking into the bakery for a taste of its treats. In a show of modernity, a statue of Norway's living legend, marathoner Grete Waitz, stands behind the bakery. Shops stock handicrafts and folk items: hand-knit woolens, wood carvings, and glass and metal artwork.

For a free guided tour of the pavilion in addition to a crash course in Norwegian culture and architecture, stop by the Norway Tourism desk.

MAELSTROM: 🎫 Visitors tour Norway by boat—16-passenger, dragon-headed longboats inspired by those Eric the Red and other Vikings used a thousand years ago. The five-minute voyage begins in a 10th-century Viking village, where a ship is being readied to head out to sea. Seafarers then find themselves in a mythical Norwegian forest, populated by trolls who cause the boats to plummet backward, through a maelstrom, to the grandeur of the Geiranger fjord, where the vessel nearly spills over a waterfall. After a plunge through a rocky passage, the boats wind up in the stormy North Sea. As the boats pass the legs of an oil rig, the storm calms and a coastal village appears on the horizon. Note that this attraction features an appearance by a three-headed troll and has some moments of darkness that tend to frighten tots.

Survivors disembark and enter a movie theater, where the journey continues on-screen for five more minutes. If you wish to skip the flick, walk straight through the theater to exit before the movie begins.

STAVE CHURCH GALLERY: Inside the wooden stave church, there is a small exhibit that explores Viking and Norwegian culture. It's interesting (and sad) to note that only 30 stave churches remain in Norway today.

THE PUFFIN'S ROOST: Norwegian gifts, sweaters, activewear, fragrances, jewelry, candy, toys, and trolls are the wares for sale here.

PHOTO BY JILL SAFRO

PHOTO BY MIKE CARROLL

Mexico

The tangle of tropical vegetation surrounding the great pyramid that encloses this pavilion and the Mexican restaurant at the lagoon's edge on the promenade provides only the barest suggestion of the charming area inside.

Dominated by a re-creation of a quaint plaza at dusk, the pyramid's interior is rimmed by balconied, tile-roofed, colonial-style structures. Crowding a pretty fountain area is a quartet of stands selling Mexican handicrafts, and to the left is a shop stocked with other handsome wares. The Mariachi Cobre band keeps things lively—as does the tequila bar. To the rear, the San Angel Inn serves authentic Mexican fare. Behind it, the pavilion's main show features a whirlwind tour of the country.

Take a look at the cultural exhibit inside the pyramid entrance on the way in. Note that the building itself was inspired by Meso-American structures dating from the third century A.D.

GRAN FIESTA TOUR STARRING THE THREE CABALLEROS: Big news! The Three Caballeros (that would be Donald Duck, José, and Panchito) are reuniting for a big show in Mexico City! Unfortunately, the ever-mischievous Donald has gone missing in Mexico—and guests join Panchito and José in the quest to find him. In doing so, you will be treated to a whirlwind (if slow-moving) boat tour of the country. The cheery montage of film, props, and Audio-Animatronics figures is reminiscent of It's a Small World, though on a smaller scale.

LA PRINCESSA DE CRISTAL: Presented by Arribas Brothers and located next to the entrance to the Gran Fiesta Tour Starring the

Three Caballeros attraction, this alcove offers crystal tiaras, character figurines, rings, bracelets, necklaces, and glass slippers. If you're lucky, you'll get to watch glass blown by an in-house artisan.

PLAZA DE LOS AMIGOS: Even if you're not in a buying mood, make a point of stopping by to take a look at this bustling marketplace. Brightly colored paper flowers, sombreros, malachite, baskets, mariachi music (available on CD), and pottery make this *mercado* (market) at the plaza's center as bright and almost as lively as one in Mexico itself. The brilliantly hued papier-mâché piñatas that figure strongly in the scenery here are quite popular. Authentic pre-Columbian figures are on display. Also available for purchase are spices, salsa, liquors (emphasis on tequila), cocktail accessories, candy, and musical instruments.

EL RANCHITO DEL NORTE: Located on the lagoon side of World Showcase Promenade, this spot features gifts and souvenirs.

Showcase Plaza

DISNEY TRADERS: Merchandise combining the charm of classic Disney characters and World Showcase themes is the primary stock-in-trade. Sundries are also sold. This is also the park's "Duffy Central." Stop here for all things related to Duffy the Disney Bear.

PORT OF ENTRY: A children's shop carrying infants' and kids' clothing, girls' character dresses, plush dolls, and toys.

PHOTO BY JILL SAFRO

Entertainment

Epcot presents an intriguing array of live performances each day, making it very important to consult a park Times Guide when you arrive. For updates, call 407-824-4321.

AMERICA GARDENS THEATRE: The lagoonside venue at The American Adventure pavilion hosts an ever-changing program of live entertainment. Check a Times Guide.

ILLUMINATIONS—REFLECTIONS OF EARTH: This nighttime spectacular presents the entire history of our planet in 13 minutes—from its creation to the present and a look toward the future. A dazzling mix of lasers, fireworks, fountains, and music, this show is a highlight of any Epcot visit.

The extravaganza, visible from anywhere on the World Showcase promenade, takes place nightly at closing time. There are excellent viewing locations all around the World Showcase Lagoon. Note that additional viewing areas have been added to the stretch between the Germany and China pavilions.

KIDCOT FUN STOPS: There is an activity area in each of the countries of World Showcase. These spots invite kids to play games and make colorful cut-outs of Duffy the Disney Bear.

WORLD SHOWCASE PERFORMERS: It's all but impossible to complete a circuit of World Showcase without catching performances en route. Keep an eye on the schedule and be sure to take in entertainment at each pavilion, often performed by natives of the country represented. Among the possibilities: worldly comedians, a Mexican mariachi band, an American a cappella group and Fife & Drum corps, Moroccan belly dancers, a Canadian rock band, and more.

Holiday Happenings

During certain holidays, such as Easter Week, the Fourth of July, Thanksgiving, Christmas week, and New Year's Eve, Epcot usually stays open extra late and presents additional entertainment for the occasion. Call 407-824-4321, or visit *www.disneyworld.com* for schedules and details.

CHRISTMAS: Epcot celebrates this holiday with a gigantic tree and its hugely popular candlelight choral processional.

The Candlelight Processional, a stirring presentation of traditional holiday songs, features a reading of the Christmas story by a celebrity narrator. This is a very popular event—and one of our favorites. See page 11 of the *Getting Ready To Go* chapter for details.

Hot Tips

- On your way into the park, pick up a free guidemap and a Times Guide. Consult the entertainment schedule first thing.

- Lines throughout Epcot are longest at mid-day and shortest in the early evening.

- During peak seasons, preferred reservation times at Epcot's table-service restaurants book quickly—make reservations as far in advance as possible. However, some tables may be available on a first-come, first-served basis (with a bit of a wait). Arrive a few minutes ahead of your reservation time.

- Most World Showcase restaurants seat guests until park closing. To make advance plans, call 407-WDW-DINE (939-3463).

- Check the Tip Boards in Innoventions Plaza and on both sides of Future World for wait times at the most popular attractions, and adjust your plans accordingly. And use Fastpass whenever possible.

- Interactive fountain areas at Epcot provide guests of all ages with an opportunity to cool off. Be sure to pack swimsuits (and water-proof diapers) for little ones who'll undoubt-edly spend time splashing in the water.

- If you plan to play at ImageWorks, the inter-active play area inside Imagination, take along the e-mail address of a friend. It may come in handy.

- Allow plenty of time to explore the hands-on exhibits at Innoventions East and West, and ImageWorks in the Imagination pavilion.

- When it comes to park-hopping, Epcot is an ideal park to hop to. It's usually open late.

- *FriendShip* water taxis are unlikely to trans-port you across World Showcase Lagoon any faster than a brisk walk, but they are a peaceful, foot-friendly way to make the half-mile-plus journey.

Where to Find the Characters

Epcot Character Spot is a fantastic place to meet classic Disney characters. (It's located in Innoventions West in Future World.) Characters such as Mickey Mouse, Chip, and Dale host dinner at the Garden Grill restau-rant in The Land pavilion in Future World. Disney princesses invite you to join them for a meal at Norway's Akershus Royal Banquet Hall. Snow White mingles at the Germany pavilion. Belle, Beast, Aladdin, Mulan, Duffy, and others have been known to greet guests at World Showcase. Check a park Times Guide for schedules and greeting locations.

Disney's Hollywood Studios

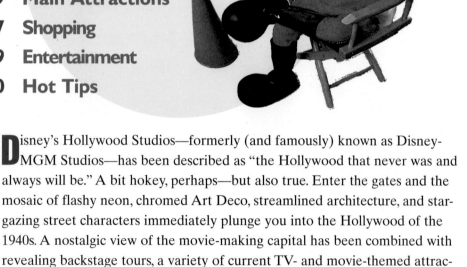

Disney's Hollywood Studios—formerly (and famously) known as Disney-MGM Studios—has been described as "the Hollywood that never was and always will be." A bit hokey, perhaps—but also true. Enter the gates and the mosaic of flashy neon, chromed Art Deco, streamlined architecture, and star-gazing street characters immediately plunge you into the Hollywood of the 1940s. A nostalgic view of the movie-making capital has been combined with revealing backstage tours, a variety of current TV- and movie-themed attractions, and a delightful selection of eateries to create this Walt Disney World enclave. Throw in a character-laden parade, and the result is an entertainment wallop worthy of a rave review.

The Studios' water tower, known to punsters (for obvious reasons) as the "Earful Tower," is reminiscent of the structures looming over Hollywood studios of the Golden Age. Here, however, it gets that special Disney touch—it's capped by a Mouseketeer-style hat. In true Hollywood style, this established star has been somewhat upstaged by the most unlikely of attention grabbers: a towering Sorcerer Mickey hat, stationed at the far end of Hollywood Boulevard.

Since opening in 1989, the park continues to expand and evolve. Its eclectic lineup of classic attractions is joined by such thrillers as an enhanced (and scarier) Tower of Terror, the rollicking Rock 'n' Roller Coaster, a dynamic vehicle stunt show, and an explosive struggle between good and evil in Fantasmic! Each adds a whole new dimension to the Hollywood term *action*.

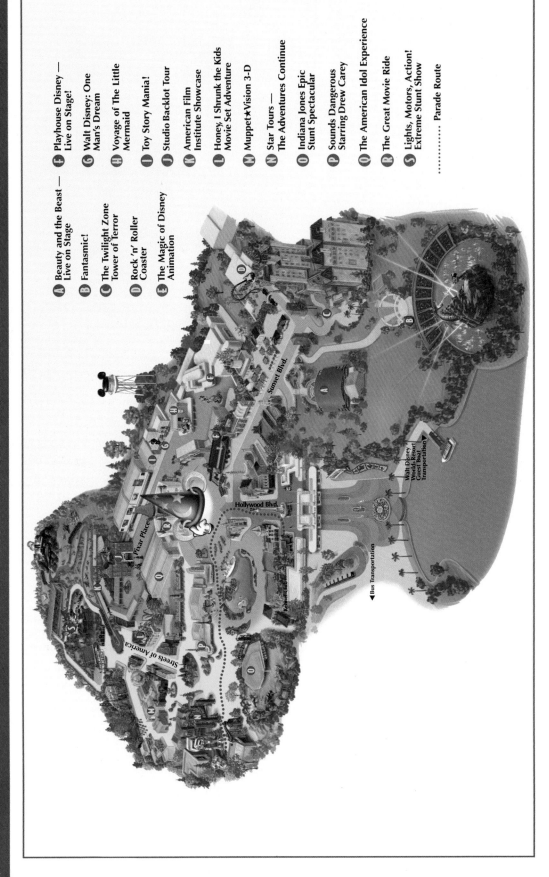

A Beauty and the Beast — Live on Stage

B Fantasmic!

C The Twilight Zone Tower of Terror

D Rock 'n' Roller Coaster

E The Magic of Disney Animation

F Playhouse Disney — Live on Stage!

G Walt Disney: One Man's Dream

H Voyage of The Little Mermaid

I Toy Story Mania!

J Studio Backlot Tour

K American Film Institute Showcase

L Honey, I Shrunk the Kids Movie Set Adventure

M Muppet★Vision 3-D

N Star Tours — The Adventures Continue

O Indiana Jones Epic Stunt Spectacular

P Sounds Dangerous Starring Drew Carey

Q The American Idol Experience

R The Great Movie Ride

S Lights, Motors, Action! Extreme Stunt Show

∙∙∙∙∙∙∙∙∙∙ Parade Route

Getting Oriented

Disney's Hollywood Studios, though festive, has a sprawling layout with no distinctive shape or main thoroughfare. As such, the Studios can be a bit of a challenge to navigate. Be sure to study a guidemap as you enter.

The park entrance is at Hollywood Boulevard. This shop-lined avenue leads straight to Hollywood Plaza, address of the Studios' Chinese Theater, a replica of Grauman's Theatre that doubles as the site of The Great Movie Ride (it's hidden behind the giant Sorcerer Mickey hat). Walking along Hollywood Boulevard, toward the plaza, you will come to Hollywood Junction. Here, a wide, palm-fringed street known as Sunset Boulevard branches off to the right.

Stroll down Sunset Boulevard and you'll come across The Hollywood Hills amphitheater, home of Fantasmic! and Rock 'n' Roller Coaster. At the street's far end is The Hollywood Tower Hotel, home of The Twilight Zone™ Tower of Terror. The strip is also graced with shops, the Sunset Ranch Market, and the Theater of the Stars amphitheater, where Beauty and the Beast—Live on Stage is performed daily.

Stand in Hollywood Plaza, facing the Sorcerer Hat, and you'll notice an archway just off to your right. This leads to Animation Courtyard. Pixar Place, the area on the street veering off to the left of Animation Courtyard, leads to Toy Story Mania! and the Studio Backlot Tour. If you turn left off Hollywood Boulevard and go past Echo Lake, you're on course for such attractions as Sounds Dangerous Starring Drew Carey, Indiana Jones Epic Stunt Spectacular, and Star Tours—The Adventures Continue. Just beyond Star Tours there is another entertainment zone, near the Streets of America (in the backlot area). The biggies to see here: Muppet*Vision 3-D, Lights, Motors, Action!—Extreme Stunt Show, and the Honey, I Shrunk the Kids Movie Set Adventure.

HOW TO GET THERE

Take Exit 64B off I-4. Continue about half a mile to reach the parking area. Take a tram to the park entrance.

By WDW Transportation: From the Swan, Dolphin, Yacht and Beach Club, and BoardWalk: boat or walkway. From Fort Wilderness: bus from the Outpost stop. From the Magic Kingdom: ferry or monorail to the TTC, then bus to the Studios. From Epcot, Animal Kingdom, all other Walt Disney World resorts and the resorts on Hotel Plaza Boulevard: bus. From Downtown Disney: bus to any WDW resort and transfer to a Studios bus or boat.

PARKING

All-day parking at the Studios is $14 for day visitors (free to WDW resort guests and annual passholders). Trams circulate regularly, providing transportation from the parking area to the park entrance. Be sure to note the section and the aisle in which you park. The parking ticket you receive allows for re-entry to the parking area throughout the day.

HOURS

Disney's Hollywood Studios is usually open from 9 A.M. until about one hour after sunset. During certain holiday periods and summer months, hours are extended. It's best to arrive about 20 minutes before the posted opening time—guests are often let in early. Depending on the season, some stage shows do not open until late in the morning.

Admission Prices

ONE-DAY BASE TICKET (Restricted to use only in Disney's Hollywood Studios. **Prices do not include sales tax and are likely to rise in 2012.**)
Adult $85
Child* $79
*3 through 9 years of age; children under 3 free

Park Primer

DISNEY'S HOLLYWOOD STUDIOS

BABY FACILITIES

Changing tables and facilities for nursing mothers can be found at the Baby Care Center at Guest Relations near the park entrance.

CAMERA NEEDS

The Darkroom on Hollywood Boulevard stocks memory cards, batteries, and disposable cameras. Film is sold in several Studios shops, but is no longer processed on-site.

DISABILITY INFORMATION

Most Walt Disney World attractions, restaurants, shops, and shows are accessible to guests using wheelchairs. Additional services are available for guests with visual or hearing disabilities. For a detailed overview of the services offered, including transportation, parking, attraction access, and more, pick up a free copy of the *Guidemap for Guests with Disabilities* at Guest Relations. For more information, refer to the *Getting Ready to Go* chapter of this book.

FIRST AID

Minor medical problems can be handled at the First Aid Center, located next to Guest Relations at the park entrance.

INFORMATION

Guest Relations, located just inside the park entrance, has free guidemaps, Times Guides, and an ever-resourceful staff. To make same-day dining arrangements for certain Studios eateries, head over to the booth at the junction of Hollywood and Sunset boulevards.

LOCKERS

Lockers, found by Oscar's Super Service, near the park entrance, cost $9 per day for large lockers, $7 a day for small ones (plus a $5 refundable deposit) for unlimited use. They may be rented from the Crossroads of the World kiosk, directly across from Oscar's classic pickup truck. Your receipt entitles you to a locker at any other theme park on the same day (not including the deposit).

LOST CHILDREN

Report lost children at Guest Relations and alert a Disney employee to the problem.

LOST & FOUND

Located at Guest Relations, near the park entrance. To report lost items after your visit, call 407-824-4245.

MONEY MATTERS

There is an ATM just outside the park entrance, near Keystone Clothiers, by Min and Bill's Dockside Diner, and inside the Pizza Planet Arcade. In addition to cash, credit cards (American Express, Visa, Discover, JCB, Diner's Club, Disney Visa, and MasterCard), traveler's checks, Disney gift cards, and WDW resort IDs are accepted for admission, merchandise, and meals at all restaurants. Some snack carts and souvenir stands are cash only.

PACKAGE PICKUP

Shops can arrange for purchases to be transported to Package Pickup, next to Oscar's Super Service (by the park entrance), where they can be picked up later. The service is free.

SAME-DAY RE-ENTRY

Be sure to retain your ticket if you plan to return later the same day. A hand-stamp is no longer required for re-entry.

SECURITY CHECK

Guests entering Disney theme parks will be subject to a security check. Bags will be searched by Disney security personnel before guests are permitted to enter the park.

STROLLERS & WHEELCHAIRS

Strollers, wheelchairs, and Electric Convenience Vehicles (ECVs) may be rented from Oscar's Super Service, inside the park entrance on the right. Cost for strollers and wheelchairs is $15. A double stroller costs $31. A Length of Stay rental ticket saves wheelchair and stroller renters $2 a day. Cost for ECVs is $50, plus a $20 refundable deposit. Keep the receipt —it can be used on the same day for a replacement at any theme park. Quantities are limited.

TIP BOARDS

Check the Tip Boards at the junction of Hollywood and Sunset boulevards and on the Streets of America to learn the waiting times for the most popular attractions in the park.

The Main Attractions

Disney's Hollywood Studios has a brand of attractions altogether unique. Some offer guests behind-the-scenes looks at the creative and technical processes that generate television, movies, and animation. Others go so far as to allow guests to gain a bit of showbiz experience along with the insight. Still others present popular characters and stories in new forms—from stage shows to thrill rides.

Many shows and attractions are presented at scheduled times, or keep shorter hours than the park itself—consult a Times Guide or the park's Tip Board for starting times.

The Twilight Zone™ Tower of Terror FP

BIRNBAUM'S ★BEST The Hollywood Tower Hotel is the creepy home of a spectacular thrill ride. On the facade of the 199-foot-tall building hangs a sparking electric sign. As the legend goes, lightning struck the building on Halloween night in 1939. An entire guest wing disappeared, along with an elevator carrying five people.

The line for the ride runs through the lobby, where dusty furniture, cobwebs, and old newspapers add to the eerie atmosphere. As guests enter the library, they see a TV brought to life by a bolt of lightning. Rod Serling invites them to enter The Twilight Zone.

Guests are led toward the boiler room to enter the ride elevator. (This is your chance to change your mind about riding—ask an attendant to point you toward the "chicken exit.") Once you take a seat in the elevator, the doors close and the room begins its ascent. At the first stop, the doors open and guests peek down a corridor. Among the effects is a ghostly visit by the hotel guests who vanished. The doors close and you continue the trip skyward.

At the next stop, you enter another dimension, a combination of sights and sounds reminiscent of *The Twilight Zone* TV series. In fact, Disney Imagineers watched each of the 156 original *Twilight Zone* episodes at least twice for inspiration. This part of the ride is a disorienting experience, in part because the elevator moves horizontally.

What happens next depends upon the whim of Disney Imagineers, who have programmed the ride so that the drop sequence is chillingly random. At the top (about 157 feet up), passengers can look out at the Studios below. Once the doors shut, you plummet 13 stories. The drop lasts about two seconds, but it seems a whole lot longer.

Just when you think it's over, the elevator launches skyward, barely stopping before it plunges again. And again. As you exit, Rod Serling claims this is the kind of thing "they don't tell you about in any guidebook." It's been our privilege to prove him wrong.

From the time you are seated, the trip takes about five minutes. Note that you must be at least 40 inches tall to ride. It is not recommended for pregnant women, people with heart conditions, or with back or neck problems. Though thrilling (and scary), the drops are surprisingly smooth. Still, if you'd rather not experience the sensation of being a human yo-yo, sit this one out.

Rock 'n' Roller Coaster Starring Aerosmith FP

BIRNBAUM'S ★BEST The fastest roller coaster in Walt Disney World history is guaranteed to rock your world. Rock 'n' Roller Coaster is ideally suited for those who consider the Tower of Terror a little on the tame side.

The indoor attraction reaches a speed of nearly 60 miles per hour—in 2.8 seconds flat. Other twists include two loops and a corkscrew—marking the first time Disney has turned guests upside down on American soil.

> ## HOT TIP!
> You'll need to stop at a locker (near the park entrance) before riding Rock 'n' Roller Coaster—there's no place to store loose articles in the ride vehicles.

The ride's premise is this: The rock band Aerosmith has invited you to a backstage party. The only thing standing between you and the big bash is a classically chaotic Los Angeles freeway.

To get to the party on time, you'll have to zip through the nighttime L.A. streets in a stretch limo. The ride vehicles (designed to resemble limousines) are equipped with a high-tech sound system (five speakers per seat make for a mega-decibel ride), and the remainder of the journey features rockin' synchronized sound—adding a very dramatic

dimension to the roller coaster experience most daredevils have come to expect.

You must be free of back, neck, and heart problems to experience this topsy-turvy tour. Expectant mothers should sit this one out. Guests must be at least 48 inches tall to ride.

Beauty and the Beast— Live on Stage

BIRNBAUM'S ★BEST Here's the show that inspired the Broadway musical. Several times each day, Belle, Gaston, Mrs. Potts, and the rest of the cast of the Disney film *Beauty and the Beast* come to life at the 1,500-seat Theater of the Stars, near the Tower of Terror, on Sunset Boulevard.

PHOTO BY JILL SAFRO

The 30-minute show is as entertaining as they come. The staging's just right and the music's simply addictive as it traces the classic tale—from Belle's dissatisfaction with her life in a small French town to the climactic battle between the staff of the Beast's castle and Gaston and the townspeople. Lumiere and friends perform the song "Be Our Guest" with a delightful display of dancing flatware. Check a park Times Guide for performance schedule.

The Magic of Disney Animation

This attraction gives guests an insider look at the creative process behind Disney's many animated blockbusters.

The majority of the action takes place in a theater. Here, you'll be greeted by a jovial, knowledgeable host and treated to a whimsical explanation of how Disney animators bring characters to life. This segment of the tour is co-hosted by Mushu, the wisecracking little dragon from the film *Mulan*. After breezing past desks once used by animators, you'll be invited to take part in a group animation lesson. The capacity for this part of the tour is smaller than the rest, so you may have to wait a bit to get in. If you don't want to stick around, there's an area where you can lend your voice to an animated character in a movie clip, stations where you can paint characters using a computer, and a personality test to see which Disney character you are most like.

There's a little treat at the end of the tour: Copies of some of the Academy Awards won by the Disney animation team are on display, along with drawings from famous films. Note that the working animation facility has been shuttered, so there are no actual animators to spy on anymore.

Before moving on, spend some time browsing at the Animation Gallery, where Disney animation cels, exclusive limited-edition reproductions, books, figurines, and many other collectibles are for sale.

Voyage of The Little Mermaid FP

One of Disney's Hollywood Studios' most popular attractions, this is a 17-minute live musical production, adapted from the Disney animated classic. The show is presented in a theater with an underwater feel. In it, many of the film's beloved animated characters, such as Flounder and Sebastian, are brought to life by puppeteers. The show opens with a lively rendition of "Under the Sea," then animated clips from the movie are shown as performers join the puppets onstage.

Ariel is the star and performs songs from the film. Prince Eric makes an appearance,

and an enormous Ursula glides across the stage to steal Ariel's voice. Of course, as in the movie, the happy ending prevails. The story line is a little bit disjointed, hopping from scene to scene, and some of the signature songs are missing. However, most viewers are familiar with the film, so this choppiness doesn't detract much from the show.

There are many special effects, including cascading water, lasers, and a lightning storm that may be a bit frightening for very young children. Note that many of the effects are best enjoyed from the middle to the rear of the theater. Keep in mind that, although this is a Fastpass attraction, performances are still presented at scheduled times throughout the day. Current showtimes are always listed on the Times Guide (available at many locations throughout the park).

Disney Junior— Live on Stage!

Fans of Playhouse Disney—Live on Stage (the show that used to play here) should enjoy this new production. It brings back three audience favorites— *Mickey Mouse Clubhouse*, *Handy Manny*, and *Little Einsteins*—and introduces elements of *Jake and the Neverland Pirates* (Disney Junior's new series). Jake and Skully (a pirate parrot) lead little ones in interactive, pirate-y adventures. Very young guests tend to be the most enthusiastic members of the audience.

The performance space holds large crowds (of mostly tiny people) at a time. There are just a handful of seats, but there's plenty of room to sprawl out on the carpeted floor. This show is presented at Playhouse Disney in the Animation Courtyard area of the theme park. The park Times Guide lists performance times.

Toy Story Mania! FP

BIRNBAUM'S ★BEST★ This engaging experience—it opened in 2008—is an energetic, interactive toy box tour with a twist: Guests wear 3-D glasses as they take aim at animated targets with toy cannons. The adventure is about as high-tech as they come, yet rooted in classic midway games of skill. As points are scored, expect effusive encouragement from a colorful cast of cheerleaders—*Toy Story*'s Woody, Buzz, Hamm, Rex, Trixie, and, of course, the Green Army Men.

Fans of the Magic Kingdom's Buzz Lightyear's Space Ranger Spin will no doubt delight in this adventure, which takes the experience of the interactive attraction into a whole new dimension. As far as skill level goes, there's something for everyone—from beginners to seasoned gamers alike.

Note: This is a wildly popular attraction with guests of all ages. Get there as early in the morning as possible and try to snag a Fastpass.

Studio Backlot Tour

Guests go backstage to see and experience some little-known aspects of TV and movie production on a tour of sets and prop stations. The 30-minute tour runs throughout the day.

The first stop is a large, outdoor special-effects area. This zone features a water tank, and teaches guests how special effects-laden waterborne scenes can be created on a set.

Guests then board the trams and travel to the backlot. Trips begin with a look at the vast wardrobe department. More than 100 designers create costumes for Disney's movie, TV, and other entertainment projects—and with 2.5 million garments for its workers, Disney World has the planet's largest working

wardrobe. Famous costumes are on display.

The tram then passes through the camera, props, and lighting departments. A look into the scene shop reveals carpenters at work on sets that will later be finished on the soundstages.

Where in Central Florida can you find an active oil field in the middle of a dry, rocky, barren desert canyon prone to flash floods? In Catastrophe Canyon! As the guide will tell you, crews are filming a movie in which a backstage tram gets stuck in the canyon during a flash flood. But supposedly it's safe to go in because they're not filming today.

In a series of special effects, a rainstorm begins. Then there's an explosion, complete with flames that are so hot even riders on the right side of the tram feel them, followed by a flash flood that is so convincing, it forces everyone to lean the other way. The road underneath the tram shifts and dips, lending even more reality to the adventure.

PHOTO BY JILL SAFRO

From Catastrophe Canyon, the tram rides by the Streets of America, where reproduced building facades line urban streets. Though the brickwork looks authentic, these backless facades are constructed mostly of fiberglass and Styrofoam. The skyscrapers, including the Empire State Building and the Chrysler Building, are actually painted flats. Forced perspective (the same technique that makes Cinderella Castle appear taller than it is) makes the four-story Empire State Building appear as if it were the actual 102-story structure. After the tour, if crews are not filming, guests may explore the Streets of America area on foot.

> ## HOT TIP!
> Guests on the left side of the tram may get wet at Catastrophe Canyon, while those on the right stay dry. Choose accordingly.

(It is possible to visit the area without experiencing the backlot tour.) The tram may also pass near the Lights, Motors, Action!—Extreme Stunt Show theater.

Lights, Motors, Action! Extreme Stunt Show

When it comes to action, this attraction takes the phrase "cut to the chase" quite seriously. Here, tires squeal and flames burst as cars hurtle over trucks and Jet Skis rocket from a canal. The overall guest experience is twofold: On the one hand, it is a thrilling display of seemingly death-defying feats; and on the other, it's an inside, backstage peek at how the movie magic happens.

Taking place in a huge theater beyond the Streets of America (on a site once occupied by Residential Street), the show is presented several times a day. Check a Times Guide for showtimes and arrive early (at least 15 minutes). This lavish show was originally presented at Disneyland Paris, where it is known as Moteurs . . . Action! Parts may be too loud or intense for some small children (for example, a stuntperson is set on fire).

American Film Institute Showcase

Though it is the final stop on the Backlot Tour, it is possible to visit this treasure chest of Hollywood memorabilia without taking the tour itself. Costumes, props, and set pieces used in recent, as well as classic, movies and television programs are on display in this ever-changing exhibit.

Although showcased items will be different when you visit, displays here have included

HOT TIP!
Don't miss the special tribute to the man who started it all: Walt Disney himself. The exhibit, entitled Walt Disney: One Man's Dream, is housed in a theater near the Pixar Place area of the park.

Barbara Stanwyck's costume from *Sorry, Wrong Number*, the police car from *Dick Tracy*, an Academy Award won by the film *My Fair Lady*, concept artwork from *Toy Story*, and live-action sets and stop-motion puppets from *James and the Giant Peach*.

The Great Movie Ride

Housed in a full-scale reproduction of historic Grauman's Chinese Theatre, this 19-minute attraction captivates guests' imaginations from the get-go. The queue area winds through a lobby and into the heart of filmmaking, where movie scenes are shown on a large screen.

The guided tour begins in an area reminiscent of the hills of Hollywood (which, as the famous, now abbreviated, sign indicates, was once known as Hollywoodland) in its heyday. As a ride vehicle whisks guests under a vibrant marquee, they are transported to the celluloid world of yesteryear. About 60 dancing mannequins atop a cake greet guests in a replay of the "By a Waterfall" scene from the

Busby Berkeley musical *Footlight Parade*.

Gene Kelly's memorable performance from *Singin' in the Rain* is the next scene, in which rain seems to drench the soundstage but does not dampen the spirits of the Audio-Animatronics representation of Mr. Kelly. (Gene Kelly personally inspected his likeness.) Then Mary Poppins and Bert the chimney sweep entertain (Julie Andrews and Dick Van Dyke, respectively), as Mary floats from above via her magical umbrella and Bert sings "Chim Chim Cher-ee" from a rooftop.

From the world of musical entertainment, guests segue to adventure. James Cagney recreates his role from *Public Enemy* as the ride proceeds along Gangster Alley. A mob shoot-out begins and puts guests in the midst of an ambush. An alternate route leads to a Western town, where John Wayne can be seen on horseback eyeing some would-be bank robbers. When the thieves blow up the safe and flames pour from the building, heat can be felt from the trams.

As the ride vehicle glides into the spaceship from *Alien*, Officer Ripley guards the corridor while a slimy monster threatens riders from overhead. (Note that this and other scenes may upset young children.)

The legendary farewell from *Casablanca* is also depicted, complete with a lifelike Rick and Ilsa. (Ingrid Bergman's daughter Isabella Rossellini once brought her kids here to "see Grandma.") Guests are moved from the airfield to the swirling winds of Munchkinland, where a house has just fallen on the Wicked Witch of the East. Her sister, as portrayed by

Margaret Hamilton, appears in a burst of smoke. This Audio-Animatronics figure is impressively realistic (and scary). But happy endings prevail, and guests follow Dorothy and company along the Yellow Brick Road to the Emerald City of Oz. As the ride draws to a close, guests view a montage of memorable moments from classic films.

Timing Tip: If the queue extends outside the building, you're in for a long wait. It takes about 25 minutes to reach the ride vehicles once you've entered the theater.

Sounds Dangerous Starring Drew Carey

As you streak around a hairpin curve, precariously positioned in the driver's seat of a speeding car, you may want to check the security of your safety belt. Don't bother. There are no seat belts. Why? As its name indicates, this attraction only *sounds* dangerous. The majority of the action takes place in your head, thanks to a personal headset and some remarkably convincing stereo sound effects.

PHOTO BY JILL SAFRO

This 3-D audio adventure occurs inside a television soundstage. Audience members (that's you) are on hand to watch a new show being filmed. The program follows a detective (played by Drew Carey) as he attempts to solve cases in the real world. Drew sports a tiny camera on his tie, so the audience can see and hear all the action.

Initially, all goes according to plan. Drew infiltrates a warehouse owned by the United Snowglobe Company. He suspects they are smuggling something, though he can't put his finger on exactly what the contraband is. (Nor does he catch on after brushing past a box labeled SMUGGLED DIAMONDS, KEEP CLEAR.)

As Drew breaks into a suspect's office, he pulls the camera out of his tie tack, to give the audience a closer look at his lock-picking prowess. The unexpected appearance of a security guard sends a wave of panic over our hero, and he quickly hides the camera . . . in his mouth. Snap, crackle, blackout—the camera's video feed shorts out. Fortunately, the audio is unaffected, so it's on with the show!

From here on in, it's all about 3-D sound. Drew's mad pursuit takes audience members everywhere from a room full of buzzing honeybees to a barbershop for a quick trim. The case is finally resolved at the circus, but not before a close encounter with a prancing pachyderm.

The show, which runs continuously, lasts about 12 minutes. It may be a bit unsettling for kids under the age of 7. *This attraction operates seasonally and may not be open during your visit to the Studios.*

The American Idol Experience

BIRNBAUM'S ★BEST★ Inspired by TV's *American Idol*, this interactive attraction invites park guests to sing their hearts out in an über realistic re-creation of the hit show. TV's famous judges may not be here, but Disney's judges are quite discerning. What's at stake (besides honor)? A chance to try out for the real *American Idol*—without having to wait in line. No kidding!

The show opens with an energetic host entertaining the (huge) audience and, eventually, teaching those seated the do's and don'ts of sitting in the theater. *Don't* boo the contestants. *Do* boo the judges—but only if they really deserve it (and at least one of them will!). *Do* vote for your favorite singer via the handy voting pad on your armrest.

Three contestants will attempt to dazzle you with their musical prowess. By show's end, the audience will have selected a favorite for that show. The last performance of the day pits all the day's favorites against each other in a final sing-off. The last one standing receives a special pass for any real American Idol audition across the country. It's the ultimate Fastpass. The preliminary shows run about 25 minutes, while the final show of the day lasts about 45 minutes. Check a Times Guide for the schedule.

Guests ages 14 and older may perform. If you would like a shot at stardom, arrive as the park opens for the day, head to the attraction, and request a pass for a performance time (passes are limited). For more information, visit *www.disneyworld.com/idol*.

Indiana Jones™ Epic Stunt Spectacular

Earthquakes, fiery explosions, and assorted other dramatic events give guests some insight into the science of movie stunts and special effects at this 2,000-seat amphitheater. Stunt people re-create scenes from Indiana Jones films to demonstrate the skill required to keep audiences on the edge of their seats. Show director Glenn Randall, who served as stunt coordinator of such films as *Raiders of the Lost Ark*, *E.T.*, and *Jewel of the Nile*, calls the show "big visual excitement." But the 30-minute show isn't all flying leaps. Guests also see how the elaborate stunts are pulled off—safely—while the crew and an assistant director explain what goes on both in front of and behind the camera.

In one segment, a scene from *Raiders of the Lost Ark* is staged. A 12-foot-tall rolling ball chases a Harrison Ford look-alike out of the temple. The steam and flames are so intense that the audience can feel the heat. The crew then dismantles the set, revealing the remarkable lightness of movie props, as assistants roll the ball uphill for the next show.

In a scene at a busy "Cairo" street market, "extras" chosen from the audience play the famous scene in which Indiana Jones pulls a gun while others are fighting with swords. The explosive action continues and leads to a desert finale in which the hero and his sweetheart make a death-defying escape.

There are moments during this show when audience members might wonder if something has actually gone wrong. But by revealing tricks of the trade, the directors and stars show that what appears to be dangerous is actually a safe, controlled bit of movie magic.

Star Tours—The Adventures Continue FP

BIRNBAUM'S ★BEST★ Inspired by George Lucas's blockbuster series of *Star Wars* films, this beloved attraction—which originally opened in 1989—just got even better! A new version of the experience touched down in 2011, complete with a new storyline and eye-popping technology. The 3-D experience offers guests the opportunity to ride on

StarSpeeders, the exact same type of flight simulator used by military and commercial airlines to train pilots.

The action takes place in the time period between the two sets of *Star Wars* trilogies. A galaxy of trouble awaits Jedi wannabes, but fear not—the Force will be with you.

This is a turbulent trip—seat belts are definitely required. Passengers must be free of back problems, heart conditions, motion sickness, and other physical limitations to ride. Guests under 40 inches tall and kids younger than 3 may not ride. Pregnant women should skip this one.

Muppet★Vision 3-D

BIRNBAUM'S ★BEST One of the most entertaining attractions at the Studios, this 3-D movie is quite remarkable. As with so many other Disney theme park attractions, much of the appeal is in the details. A funny 12-minute pre-show gives clues about what's to come. Once inside the theater, many will notice that it looks just like the one from Jim Henson's classic TV series *The Muppet Show*. Even the two curmudgeonly fellows, Statler and Waldorf, are sitting in the balcony, bantering with each other and offering their typically critical commentary on the show.

The production comes directly from Muppet Labs, presided over by Dr. Bunsen Honeydew —and his long-suffering assistant, Beaker— and introduces a new character, Waldo, the "Spirit of 3-D." Among the highlights is Miss Piggy's solo, which Bean Bunny turns into quite a fiasco. Sam Eagle's grand finale leads to trouble as a veritable war breaks out, culminating with a cannon blast to the screen from the rear balcony, courtesy of everyone's favorite Swedish Chef.

The 3-D effects, spectacular as they may be, are only part of the show: There are appearances by live Muppet characters, fireworks, and lots of funny details built into the walls of the huge theater. Including the pre-show, expect to spend about 29 minutes with Kermit and company. Shows run continuously throughout the day.

Honey, I Shrunk the Kids Movie Set Adventure

The set for the backyard scenes of the classic Disney movie has been re-created as an oversize, soft-surface playground. Enter it and experience the world from an ant's perspective.

Blades of grass soar 30 feet high, paper clips are as tall as trees, and Lego toys are practically big enough to live in. There are caves to explore and many climbing opportunities (tremendous tree stumps and sprawling spiderwebs are among the better ones). Kids love to crawl into the discarded film canister and slide out along an oversize piece of film.

A leaky hose also provides entertainment as it squirts in a slightly different location each time. The props make everyone look and feel as though they were, indeed, shrunk by *Honey, I Shrunk the Kids'* Professor Wayne Szalinski. It holds the greatest appeal for younger guests.

Shopping

Hollywood Boulevard

CELEBRITY 5 & 10: Modeled after a 1940s Woolworth's, this large shop carries housewares such as candles, aprons, bath items, and Mickey ice-cube trays, plus items that can be personalized—including Mouse ears.

COVER STORY: A small area located just through The Darkroom, this is the place to pick up your picture if you've had it taken by any of the park photographers.

CROSSROADS OF THE WORLD: In the middle of the entrance plaza, Mickey Mouse keeps watch from atop this Hollywood Blvd. landmark. The kiosk deals mostly in pins, but has some souvenirs and sundries. This is also the place to stop if you'd like to rent a locker.

THE DARKROOM: The Art Deco facade of this shop allows guests to peer through an aperture-like window. Cameras (including the disposable kind), film, and camera accessories are sold here.

KEYSTONE CLOTHIERS: Women's and men's fashions and accessories are Keystone Clothier's specialties of the house.

L.A. CINEMA STORAGE: A great source for kids' clothing and toys for infants, toddlers, and small children. Many items, such as watches and candy, feature classic Disney characters.

MICKEY'S OF HOLLYWOOD: The place to find character shirts, hats, plush toys, watches, socks, bags, books, and sunglasses, plus items emblazoned with the Studios park logo.

MOVIELAND MEMORABILIA: This kiosk, located just to the left of the Studios' main entrance, stocks stuffed toys, hats, sunglasses, film, key chains, and other souvenirs.

SID CAHUENGA'S ONE-OF-A-KIND: Autographed photos of past and present matinee idols and sports stars, old movie magazines and posters, and assorted Hollywood memorabilia, such as lunch boxes, mugs, magnets, and books have been among the many celebrity-oriented collectibles with which Sid's been willing to part—for a price.

Sunset Boulevard

LEGENDS OF HOLLYWOOD: Modeled after the Academy Theater, which was built in Inglewood, California, in 1939, this store offers Disney-themed items for the home, including plates, glasses, mugs, towels, and more.

MOUSE ABOUT TOWN: The best source for sportswear featuring the famed mouse subtly embroidered onto apparel. Expect to find hats, ties, shirts, jackets, pajamas, and more.

ONCE UPON A TIME: This shop's exterior replicates the Carthay Circle Theatre in Hollywood, where *Snow White and the Seven Dwarfs* premiered in 1937. The store specializes in apparel and accessories with Disney touches.

OSCAR'S SUPER SERVICE: In addition to renting strollers and wheelchairs, Oscar stocks diapers, strollers (to buy), snacks, sundries, soft drinks, and souvenirs.

PLANET HOLLYWOOD SUPERSTORE: This shop sells items branded with the P.H. logo.

ROCK AROUND THE SHOP: Survive the Rock 'n' Roller Coaster and earn the right to shop here. Expect to find music-related items, such as drumsticks and CDs.

SPECIAL FX MAKE-UP: Wanna get your face painted like a cat, puppy, princess, superhero or something equally festive? Head here. Most paint-jobs cost about $15.

SUNSET CLUB COUTURE: A sophisticated selection of mostly Mickey watches includes limited-edition pieces and pocket watches.

SUNSET RANCH: This open-air shop carries Disney character hats, totes, and apparel, plus sunscreen, film, and sundries.

SWEET SPELLS: This shop, which is within the Beverly Sunset building, has a super selection of candy, cookies, and other ooey, gooey snack items. The caramel apples are to die for.

TOWER GIFTS: Inside the Hollywood Tower Hotel, near the ride exit, this spot specializes in Hollywood Tower Hotel merchandise.

VILLAINS IN VOGUE: All villains, all the time. Look for souvenirs featuring your favorite Disney bad boys and girls—with an emphasis on characters from Tim Burton's *The Nightmare Before Christmas*.

Beyond the Boulevards

AMERICAN FILM INSTITUTE SHOWCASE: Looking for items featuring the likes of Marilyn Monroe, Abbott and Costello, or Lucille Ball? Head here. There is also a supply of Three Stooges stuff. Nyuk, nyuk, nyuk.

ANIMATION GALLERY: Don't overlook this pleasant shop in the Animation Building, where limited-edition figurines, Disney animation cels, books, statues, Vinylmation figurines, and other collectibles ensure great browsing, even if buying isn't on your mind.

THE DISNEY STUDIO STORE: Expect to find T-shirts, hats, and accessories inspired by Disney films at this Animation Courtyard shop.

IN CHARACTER: In front of the Voyage of The Little Mermaid, this costume shop has everything a child needs to dress like a Disney princess—plus dolls, pillows, and plush toys.

INDIANA JONES ADVENTURE OUTPOST: Next to the Indiana Jones attraction, you'll discover adventure clothing, as well as memorabilia emblazoned with the Indy insignia.

STAGE 1 COMPANY STORE: Situated near the exit of Muppet*Vision 3-D, guests can find toys, shirts, and other merchandise with the likenesses of Kermit the Frog, Miss Piggy, Fozzie Bear, and other Muppet characters, as well as items featuring Mickey and pals.

SUPERSTAR SHOP: Located near the American Idol Experience exit, this shop stocks hats, shirts, toys, and other souvenirs.

TATOOINE TRADERS: This shop near the exit of the Star Tours attraction offers intergalactic souvenirs tied to the family of *Star Wars* films, as well as Star Tours itself.

THE WRITER'S STOP: This nook next to Sci-Fi Dine-In Theater has coffee, souvenirs, and reading material—plus fresh-baked cookies.

Where to Eat at the Studios

A complete listing of eateries at the Studios—full-service restaurants, fast-food emporiums, and snack shops—can be found in the *Good Meals, Great Times* chapter. See the Disney's Hollywood Studios section, beginning on page 244.

Entertainment

In these parts, it's always showtime. The following list is a good indication of the Studios' stage presence. As always, we advise that you check a park Times Guide for specifics.

PIXAR PALS COUNTDOWN TO FUN!: This afternoon processional features characters from films such as *The Incredibles*, *A Bug's Life*, *Ratatouille*, *Monsters, Inc.*, *Up*, and *Toy Story*. It takes place daily.

DISNEY CHANNEL ROCKS!: The big Sorcerer's Hat on Hollywood Boulevard is the backdrop for this interactive dance party. The concert-style show celebrates Disney Channel hits, including *High School Musical*, *Camp Rock*, *StarStruck*, and more. It's presented daily.

JEDI TRAINING ACADEMY: *Star Wars* fans and Jedi-wannabes can learn the ways of the Force right here in Disney World. A Jedi Master is on hand to teach guests do's and don'ts of using a light saber, as well as help them fend off an unexpected march of Stormtroopers. Expect a special appearance by one notable Dark Lord who'll attempt to lure you to the dark side. "Younglings" ages 4 through 12 are invited to participate.

STREETMOSPHERE CHARACTERS: This troupe of performers infuses Hollywood Boulevard with old-time, Tinseltown ambience. Would-be starlets searching for their big break, fans seeking guests' autographs, and gossip columnists chasing leads entertain daily.

Holiday Happenings

The park usually stays open extra late to mark holidays such as New Year's Eve, the Fourth of July, and Christmas. During these times, lots of special entertainment is often in store. Call 407-824-4321 for up-to-the-minute schedules.

CHRISTMAS: The Osborne Family Spectacle of Dancing Lights is the Studios' twinkling homage to the season. The display featuring millions of lights is a perennial favorite. It's presented on the Streets of America. For updates, visit *www.disneyworld.com*.

Trip the Light Fantasmic!

BIRNBAUM'S ★BEST Fantasmic!, a lavish musical production, plays on select nights at The Hollywood Hills Amphitheater on Sunset Boulevard. A dramatic mix of fireworks, fountains, lasers, and Disney characters, it invites guests to take a peek into the dream world of Mickey Mouse.

Though similar to its Disneyland counterpart, half of this 26-minute production is original. The action follows Mickey through a series of dreams. In the first dream, he appears on a mountain, shoots fireworks from his fingertips, and conducts an orchestra of colorful fountains. (Guests seated up front get spritzed.) Soon Mickey is plagued by nightmares as Disney villains take over his dreams. (This has been known to scare small children.) In the end, the Mouse and his pals prevail (of course!).

Seating begins about 90 minutes before showtime—though some guests line up even earlier. Check a Times Guide for the schedule.

We recommend sitting toward the back—the view is good and it's easier to get out after the show. There is standing room, too.

After the finale, plan to sit for a bit. It can take 20 minutes for the crowd to exit the theater.

Timing Tip: Since it is not presented every night, check a Times Guide to see if the show will be performed during your visit to the park. On nights when it is presented twice, see the last show. Afterward, as the masses exit the park, take some time to browse the shops that keep their doors open after hours.

Hot Tips

- Some attractions keep shorter hours than the park itself. Check a Times Guide when you arrive. It lists current hours and schedules.

- Check the Studios' Tip Board often to get an idea of showtimes and crowds.

- Visit Rock 'n' Roller Coaster, Tower of Terror, Voyage of The Little Mermaid, and Toy Story Mania! early in the day, before crowds build up.

- Snag a spot along Hollywood Boulevard about 20 to 30 minutes before the Pixar Pals parade.

- Tower of Terror is a popular attraction with long lines. Use Fastpass whenever possible. And never ride immediately after a meal.

- The line for The Great Movie Ride is generally the longest early in the morning and immediately following the daily parade.

- For a full-service meal, make restaurant reservations when you arrive, at either Hollywood Junction or these eateries: 50's Prime Time Cafe, Mama Melrose's Ristorante Italiano, Hollywood Brown Derby, Sci-Fi Dine-In Theater, or Hollywood & Vine. For reservations, call 407-WDW-DINE (939-3463) up to 180 days ahead of your preferred dining date.

- The shops on Hollywood Boulevard are open a half hour past park closing.

- Park hoppers take note: There is a water taxi link between Disney's Hollywood Studios and Epcot. The boat docks to the left as you exit the Studios. You may also reach Epcot, as well as all other parks, by bus. Ambitious athletes may choose to walk. (It'll take you about 15 to 25 minutes to make the trip on foot.)

- Fantasmic! is no longer presented on a nightly basis. Call 407-939-7639 or check a Times Guide to see if it will be offered during your visit to Disney's Hollywood Studios.

- Many attractions and shows stop admitting guests prior to the park's closing time (and some don't open until a few hours after the park does). Check a Times Guide for schedules. Attractions that you may enter up until the very last minute include Rock 'n' Roller Coaster, The Twilight Zone™ Tower of Terror, The Great Movie Ride, Muppet*Vision 3-D, and Star Tours—The Adventures Continue.

- If you choose to skip Fantasmic!, plan to exit the park before the show ends. This way, you'll avoid the inevitable bottleneck at the exit. If you're watching the show, consider making your exit before the big finale.

- Toy Story Mania! is a tremendously popular attraction. If you hope to experience it without sacrificing 60 to 120 minutes waiting in the stand-by line, get a Fastpass as close to park opening time as possible. Good luck!

Where to Find the Characters

You'll find Disney Channel characters in Animation Courtyard. Woody, Jessie, Bullseye, and other *Toy Story* friends may be spotted on Pixar Place. Lots-O'-Huggin' Bear has been spotted near Animation Courtyard. *Cars* and *Monsters, Inc.* characters greet guests on the Streets of America. Mickey mingles with park-goers in several locations, including Animation Courtyard. He often appears at the park entrance when the park opens, too. Chip, Dale, and Donald Duck have been known to join him. Characters have been known to mingle with guests in the area in front of the big sorcerer's hat, too.

Disney's Animal Kingdom

With a mix of lush landscapes, thrilling attractions, and close encounters with exotic animals, this is clearly a theme park raised to a different level of excitement. Here, guests do more than just watch the action—they live it. They become paleontologists, explorers, and students of nature. And if, by doing so, they leave with nothing more than a great big smile, Disney will have accomplished one of its major goals. But many guests come away with a little bit more: a renewed sense of respect for our planet and for the life forms we share it with (not to mention a few boffo souvenirs).

The attractions at Disney's Animal Kingdom are meant to engage, entertain, and inspire. They immerse guests in a tropical landscape and introduce them to creatures from the past and present—as well as a few that exist only in our collective imagination.

The park, which is accredited by the American Association of Zoos and Aquariums, is home to more than 1,500 animals representing 300 different species. Most of the creatures are of the animate variety, as opposed to the Audio-Animatronics kind. Despite that, you won't see many beasts behind bars here. Instead, you'll go on safari and see a menagerie of wild critters living in spacious habitats, with remarkably few separations visible to the naked eye.

The following pages will help you get the most out of your visit to Disney's Animal Kingdom. It is, after all, a jungle out there.

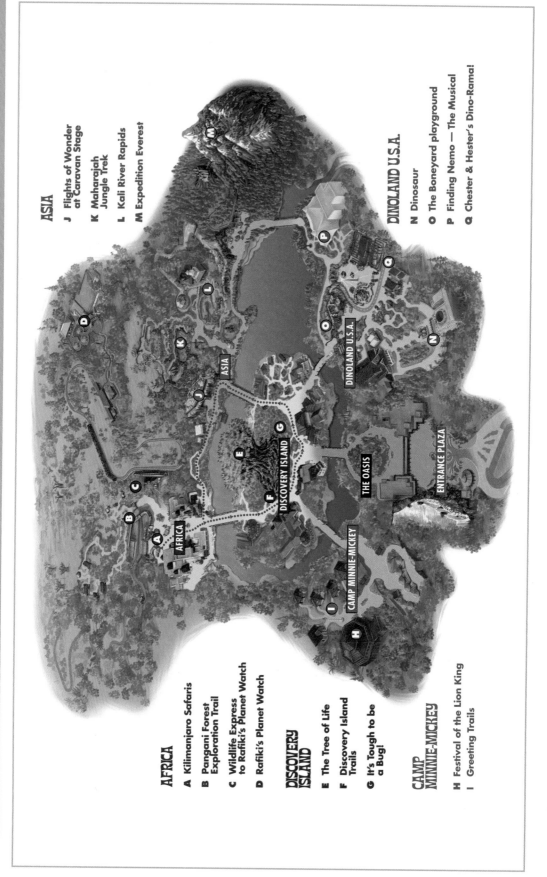

ASIA

J Flights of Wonder at Caravan Stage
K Maharajah Jungle Trek
L Kali River Rapids
M Expedition Everest

DINOLAND U.S.A.

N Dinosaur
O The Boneyard playground
P Finding Nemo — The Musical
Q Chester & Hester's Dino-Rama!

AFRICA

A Kilimanjaro Safaris
B Pangani Forest Exploration Trail
C Wildlife Express to Rafiki's Planet Watch
D Rafiki's Planet Watch

DISCOVERY ISLAND

E The Tree of Life
F Discovery Island Trails
G It's Tough to be a Bug!

CAMP MINNIE-MICKEY

H Festival of the Lion King
I Greeting Trails

Getting Oriented

Though Disney's Animal Kingdom encompasses about five times the area of its Magic counterpart, one need not be in training for the Olympics to tackle it. (Most of the land is reserved for non-homo-sapien critters.) By all estimates, pedestrians rack up about the same mileage in one day here as they do in a day at Epcot.

The park's layout is relatively simple: a series of sections, or "lands," connected to a central hub. In this case, the hub is Discovery Island (formerly known as Safari Village), an island surrounded by a river, and home to the Tree of Life, the park's icon. A set of bridges connect Discovery Island with other lands: the Oasis, DinoLand U.S.A., Asia, Africa, and Camp Minnie-Mickey.

As you pass through Animal Kingdom's entrance plaza, you approach the Oasis. Feel free to meander at a leisurely pace, absorbing the soothing ambience of a thick, elaborate jungle, or you can proceed more quickly and plan to revisit this relaxing region later on. Each of several pathways deposits you at the foot of a bridge leading to Discovery Island. As you emerge from the Oasis, you'll see the awe-inspiring Tree of Life, a 14-story Disney-made tree, looming ahead. The tree, which stands near the middle of the island, is surrounded by Discovery Island Trails. Off to the southwest is the character-laden land known as Camp Minnie-Mickey.

To the southeast lies DinoLand U.S.A., home of countless prehistoric animals, a fossil dig, a high-spirited stage show called Finding Nemo—The Musical, and an attraction that's sure to induce a mammoth adrenaline surge: Dinosaur. Behind Discovery Island and to the northwest is Africa, where guests may go on an African safari, explore a nature trail, and take the Wildlife Express train to Rafiki's Planet Watch, the park's research and education center.

Asia is northeast of Discovery Island. Here, guests come face to face with the Yeti, aka Abominable Snowman, on the Expedition Everest thrill ride, encounter real tigers on the exotic Maharajah Jungle Trek, and take a daring journey through the rainforest on a raft at the splashy Kali River Rapids.

HOW TO GET THERE

Take Exit 65 off I-4. Then follow the signs to Disney's Animal Kingdom. Trams run between the parking lot and the main entrance.

By WDW Transportation: From all Walt Disney World resorts: buses. From Downtown Disney: bus to any resort or the TTC, then transfer to an Animal Kingdom bus. From the Magic Kingdom: ferry or monorail to the TTC, then bus to Animal Kingdom. From Epcot, Disney's Hollywood Studios, and the resorts on Hotel Plaza Boulevard: buses.

PARKING

All-day parking at Animal Kingdom is $14 for day visitors (free to Walt Disney World resort guests with presentation of resort ID or Annual Pass). Trams circulate regularly, providing transportation from the parking area to the park entrance. Be sure to note the section and aisle in which you park. Also, be aware that the parking ticket allows for re-entry to the parking area throughout the day.

HOURS

Although hours are subject to change, the gates are generally open daily from about 9 A.M. until about an hour after dusk. During certain holiday periods and the summer months, hours may change. It's best to arrive up to a half hour before the official opening time. For current schedules, call 407-824-4321 or visit *www.disneyworld.com*.

Admission Prices

ONE-DAY BASE TICKET
(Restricted to use only in Disney's Animal Kingdom. **Prices do not include sales tax and are likely to change in 2012.**)
Adult $85
Child* $79
*3 through 9 years of age; children under 3 free

Park Primer

BABY FACILITIES

Changing tables and facilities for nursing mothers can be found at the Baby Care Center on Discovery Island, near Creature Comforts. It's also possible to purchase certain necessities, such as formula and diapers, at this facility.

CAMERA NEEDS

Camera supplies and disposable cameras can be purchased at Garden Gate Gifts, Disney Outfitters, Duka La Filimu, Mombasa Marketplace, and Chester and Hester's Dinosaur Treasures. Note that film processing is no longer available.

DISABILITY INFORMATION

Nearly all of the Animal Kingdom attractions, shops, and restaurants are accessible to guests using wheelchairs. Additional services are available for guests with visual or hearing disabilities. The *Guidemap for Guests with Disabilities* provides a detailed overview of the services available, including transportation, parking, and attraction access. (For more information, refer to page 51 of this book.)

FIRST AID

Minor medical problems can be handled at the First Aid Center, located on Discovery Island on the northwest side of the Tree of Life, near Creature Comforts.

INFORMATION

Guest Relations, located just inside the park entrance, is equipped with guidemaps, Times Guides, and a helpful staff. Free guidemaps are also available in many shops.

LOCKERS

Lockers are located just inside the main entrance area, near Guest Relations. Cost is $9 for large lockers, $7 for small ones (plus a $5 refundable deposit) for unlimited use all day.

LOST & FOUND

The department is located at Guest Relations, just inside the park entrance. To report lost items after your visit, call 407-824-4245. We recommend affixing contact information onto valuables. That'll make them easier to track.

LOST CHILDREN

Report lost children at the park's Baby Care Center, near Creature Comforts on Discovery Island, or alert the closest Disney employee to the matter.

MONEY MATTERS

There is an ATM at the park entrance and another in DinoLand. Currency exchange is done at Guest Relations. Disney Dollars, in $1, $5, and $10 denominations, are also available at Guest Relations. In addition to cash, credit cards (Disney Visa, American Express, Diner's Club, Discover Card, JCB, MasterCard, and Visa), Disney gift cards, traveler's checks, and Disney resort IDs are accepted for admission and merchandise, and meals at most restaurants.

PACKAGE PICKUP

Shops can arrange for purchases to be sent to Garden Gate Gifts for later pickup or directly to a WDW resort (packages should be ready for pickup about three hours after purchase). The service is free.

SAME-DAY RE-ENTRY

Be sure to retain your ticket if you plan to return later the same day. It is no longer necessary to have your hand stamped.

SECURITY CHECK

Guests entering Disney theme parks may be subject to a security check. Expect backpacks, parcels, purses, etc., to be searched.

STROLLERS & WHEELCHAIRS

Strollers, wheelchairs, and Electric Convenience Vehicles (ECVs) may be rented at Garden Gate Gifts. The cost is $15 for strollers and $12 for wheelchairs (double strollers cost $31 a day). Length of Stay rentals yield a $2-per-day discount. It's $50 for ECVs, plus a $20 refundable deposit. Quantities are limited (and they run out early in the day). Keep your receipt; it may be used the same day to get a replacement here or at the other theme parks.

TIP BOARD

There is a Tip Board on Discovery Island. Check it to learn the current wait times for popular park attractions.

The Oasis

Traditionally, one has to travel across a long, sunbaked stretch of desert in order to experience the soothing atmosphere of a tropical oasis. With that in mind, think of the Animal Kingdom parking lot as a concrete version of the Sahara. Once you've trekked across it, your journey takes you through the park's front gate and entrance plaza. What's that up ahead? Could it be a towering African tree? Here in Central Florida? It must be a mirage.

But, no. Within seconds you arrive at the Oasis, a thriving tropical garden filled with waterfalls, running streams, and lush vegetation. The transition is by no means a subtle one. Guests are immediately enveloped in a world of nature. The peaceful setting is most idyllic.

Though not a full-fledged "land" per se, this small jungle simply oozes atmosphere. It is thick and elaborate, and comes complete with critters. (Some are more difficult to spot than others. When searching for the naturally camouflaged creatures, remember to look up occasionally.) As park visitors walk along the pathways, they may catch glimpses of different kinds of animals, from deer and iguanas to anteaters and birds. As in the rest of the

Animal Kingdom, there is the illusion that guests are walking among the wildlife.

The Oasis is at once an exciting and calming experience. It sets the stage for what's to come. Guests have several options once they've entered the Oasis. They can continue on a northerly path, making tracks toward the Tree of Life and across a bridge to Discovery Island. They can proceed at a more snail-friendly pace, keeping a tally of the various life forms that slither by. Or they can simply take time to stop and smell the flowers.

> **"I have learned from the animal world. And what everyone will learn who studies it is a renewed sense of kinship with the Earth and all of its inhabitants."**
>
> **— Walt Disney**

Timing Tip: Making a trip through the Oasis is the only way to get in (and out of) Animal Kingdom. Some paths can become congested during the hours closest to opening and closing times. To beat the crowds, use a path to the left when you enter and exit the park.

Discovery Island

Once you've passed through the Oasis, you will come to a bridge spanning a peaceful river. The bridge leads to Discovery Island, an area at the center of Animal Kingdom and the hub from which all other realms of the park may be reached.

Discovery Island is defined by the brilliant colors, tropical surroundings, and equatorial architecture of Africa and the South Pacific. The facades of the buildings are all carved and painted based on the art of nations from around the world. Don't fail to notice all the bright, whimsical folk-art images representing various members of the animal kingdom.

This island is the shopping and dining center of Animal Kingdom. Many of the park's fast-food restaurants can be found here, including Pizzafari and Flame Tree Barbecue.

HOT TIP!

Take a minute to study a guidemap as you enter Animal Kingdom. It will give you a sense of the layout. The park Times Guide provides information about showtimes for Festival of the Lion King, Finding Nemo— The Musical, and other attractions.

By far the most striking element on Discovery Island is the Tree of Life. It is on the map, but chances are you'll have no trouble finding it. Rising from the middle of the island and as tall as a 14-story building, the Tree of Life is hard to miss.

The Tree of Life

The Tree of Life is the dramatic 145-foot icon of Disney's Animal Kingdom. The imposing tree, with its swaying limbs and gnarled trunk, looks an awful lot like the real thing—from a distance. Up close, it's apparent that this is a most unusual bit of greenery. Covered with more than 325 animal images, it is a swirling tapestry of carved figures, painstakingly assembled by a team of artisans. The tree, though inorganic, stands as a symbol of the connected nature of life on Earth. We think Joyce Kilmer would have approved.

DISCOVERY ISLAND TRAILS: Walkways that snake around the Tree of Life allow guests to get a close-up view of the trunk and even play a game of "spot the animals." (The spiraling animal images go all the way to the top of the tree. You'll need binoculars if you hope to see them all.) Scattered about the tree's base is a variety of animal habitats. Animals can be seen in a very open, somewhat traditional park-like setting, with lush grass, trees, and other vegetation. Among the creatures you may recognize are kangaroos, deer, porcupines, tortoises, flamingos, otters, and exotic birds. Others to which you may be introduced for the very first time as you

HOT TIP!

Children under age 5 may have enjoyed the film *A Bug's Life*, but few of them fancy It's Tough to be a Bug! As a matter of fact, it terrifies many of them.

meander through the exhibits include ring-tailed lemurs (not quite monkeys' uncles, more like cousins). The trails are accessible from several points around the tree.

BIRNBAUM'S **★BEST** **IT'S TOUGH TO BE A BUG!:** Inside the trunk of the Tree of Life is a 430-seat auditorium featuring an eight-minute, animated 3-D film augmented by some surprising "4-D" effects. The stars of the show are the world's most abundant inhabitants—insects. They creep, crawl, and demonstrate why, someday, they just might inherit the Earth. It's a bug's-eye view of the trials and tribulations of their multi-legged world.

As guests enter The Tree of Life Repertory Theater, the orchestra can be heard warming

Did You Know?

The napkins found throughout Walt Disney World might look dirty even before you use them. Fear not. Their sandy color is a natural one—no bleach was used to make them. It's a much more environment-friendly approach to cleaning up all those sticky faces and fingers.

up amid the sounds of chirping crickets. When Flik, the emcee (and star of *A Bug's Life*), makes his first appearance, he dubs audience members honorary bugs and instructs them to don their bug eyes (3-D glasses). Then the mild-mannered ant introduces some of his not-so-mild-mannered cronies, including a Chilean tarantula, dung beetles, and "the silent but deadly member of the bug world"—the stink bug. What follows is a manic, often humorous, revue.

Note: The combination of intense special effects and frequent darkness tends to frighten toddlers and young children. In addition, anyone leery of spiders, roaches, and their ilk is advised to skip the performance, or risk being seriously bugged.

Africa

The largest section of Animal Kingdom, Africa is bigger than the Magic Kingdom all by itself. This 110-acre, truer-than-life replica of an African savanna is packed with pachyderms, giraffes, hippos, and other wild beasts. All guests enter Africa through Harambe, a village based on a modern East African coastal town. It is the dining and shopping center of Animal Kingdom's Africa.

The instant you walk across the bridge to Harambe, you are transported to Africa. Everything here is authentic, from the architecture to the landscaping to the merchandise in the marketplace. The result was achieved after Disney Imagineers made countless trips to the continent. After seven years of observing, filming, and photographing the real thing, they re-created it here in North America.

The animals that live here, however, are not re-creations. They are quite real, most varied, and extremely abundant. In fact, this chunk of land puts the *animal* in Animal Kingdom.

Kilimanjaro Safaris FP

BIRNBAUM'S ★BEST★ The Kilimanjaro Safaris have something for everyone: lovely landscapes, majestic, free-roaming animals, and a thrilling adventure. It is everything you may expect from an actual trip to Africa, and (hopefully) more.

The 18-minute safari begins with a brief introduction from a guide who does double duty as your driver. Once you climb aboard the ride vehicle, look at the plates above the seat in front of you. They will help you identify the animals you see. And have those cameras ready.

As the vehicle travels along dirt roads, you'll spot free-roaming wild animals: zebras, gazelles, hippos, elephants, warthogs, rhinos, lions, and more. Some animals wander near your vehicle, and others cross its path. (Relax. Only the harmless critters will approach. Others, such as lions and cheetahs, only *appear* to invade your safe, personal space.)

HOT TIP!

There's no need to stampede toward the Kilimanjaro Safaris ride first thing in the morning—the animals are out and active throughout the day. That said, if you do ride early, consider coming back later in the day. The beauty of this attraction is that you tend to see something new each time.

The majesty of the Serengeti may lull you into a state of serenity, but it's merely the calm before the storm. You'll soon be jostled and jolted as the vehicle crosses pothole-filled terrain and rickety bridges—one of which puts you close to a horde of sunbathing crocodiles.

The safari experience takes a dramatic turn when a band of renegade ivory poachers is discovered hunting for elephants. Your guide chases the outlaws and takes you along for the ride. If you're prone to motion sickness, back trouble, or have other physical limitations, you may want to sit this one out. The ride is a rather bumpy one.

Pangani Forest Exploration Trail

This self-guided walking trail winds past communities of gorillas and other rare African animals. Access it at the end of the Kilimanjaro Safaris or by the entrance in Harambe.

The first major stop on the trail, the name of which translates to "place of enchantment" in Swahili, is the Research Station. The station contains exhibits, including naked mole rats. Just outside are a free-flight aviary and an aquarium teeming with fish. Not far away is the hippo exhibit, which provides close-up views of hippopotamuses both in and out of water.

Farther along the trail there is a scenic overlook point, where you can get an unobstructed view of the African savanna. This is also known as the "Timon" exhibit, featuring a family of perky meerkats. Afterward, you may catch an up-close glimpse (through a glass wall) of a cavorting gorilla or two.

As you come to the end of the suspension bridge, you'll find yourself in a beautiful green valley. Congratulations! You've finally reached the gorilla area—an experience well worth the wait. (Note that you may have to wait a little bit longer for that first gorilla sighting. Our evolutionary cousins have been known to play hide-and-seek in the lush vegetation.)

Rafiki's Planet Watch

On the east side of the village of Harambe is the Harambe Train Station. That's where you board the Wildlife Express and experience a behind-the-scenes look at a Disney park while en route to Rafiki's Planet Watch.

As part of the 5½-minute trip, you'll glide past the buildings where elephants, rhinos, and giraffes sleep at night. A guide narrates throughout the trip. All guests disembark at the Rafiki's Planet Watch station. (You must reboard the train to return to Harambe.)

While Animal Kingdom's stories often carry a conservation theme, this part really brings the message home. This area is the park's conservation headquarters. It's also a veterinary lab, as well as the research and education hub.

"Much of the world's wildlife is in imminent danger," says Judson Green, former chairman of Walt Disney Attractions. "Disney is working to save endangered animals, but we also hope to motivate our guests to support wildlife programs that are in urgent need of support." After spending some time at Rafiki's Planet Watch, visitors just might have the motivation they need. Exhibits are geared to spark curiosity and awe about wildlife and conservation efforts around the world. Here are a few highlights:

Habitat Habit!: An outdoor discovery trail that yields glimpses of cotton-top tamarins, and helpful hints on how to share our world with all members of the animal kingdom.

Affection Section: An animal encounter area with critters to see and touch. Most of the animals are exotic breeds of familiar petting-zoo types: goats, sheep, pigs, etc. However, this is still an enjoyable experience for young guests. Be sure to stop at the hand-washing station before leaving this area. And don't forget the soap!

Conservation Station: The center of Disney's effort to promote wildlife conservation awareness. Inside, you'll find:

Animal Cams: Guest-operated video cameras that observe gorillas, hippos, bats, and other critters throughout Animal Kingdom as they go about their daily business.

Animal Health & Care: A tour of veterinary labs and research facilities.

Eco Heroes: A set of touch-sensitive video kiosks that allow guests to interact with famous biologists and conservationists.

EcoWeb: A computer link to conservation organizations around the world.

Rafiki's Planet Watch Video: An interactive video, hosted by Rafiki, that gives guests information about endangered animals.

Song of the Rainforest: A thoroughly entertaining "3-D" audio show that surrounds guests with sounds of the rainforest.

Rafiki's Planet Watch is about a five-minute walk from the train depot. In addition to its educational appeal, this is also one of the best places to cool off at Animal Kingdom.

On the far side of a Himalayan-style bridge, beyond an ancient temple, lies the tranquil village of Anandapur (Sanskrit for "place of delight"). The buildings' design was inspired by structures in Thailand, Indonesia, and other Asian countries known for their rich architectural history.

A product of Disney Imagineering, the village epitomizes the complex, enduring relationship between the animals and ecosystems of the Asian continent. The tiny village borders an elaborate re-creation of a Southeast Asian rainforest. As such, Disney's Asia is an ideal location for trekking through the lush jungle, shooting the rapids on a raging river, and gazing upon the multi-hued inhabitants of this treasured terrain.

Kali River Rapids FP

BIRNBAUM'S ★BEST★ Before guests board rafts at Kali (pronounced KAH-lee) River Rapids, a wise voice admonishes that "the river is like life itself, full of mysterious twists and turns." What the voice doesn't say is that this particular river is also full of splashing water and a blazing inferno. This may be business as usual for some daring souls, but for most of us, these elements make for one dramatic, drenching adventure.

All guests begin the journey in the offices of Kali River Rapids Expeditions, a river rafting company. A slide show offers information on the sometimes unscrupulous business of logging—how it has ravaged the rainforest and deprived animals of their habitats. However,

thanks to ecotourism (among other things), there is hope. Peaceful voyages give people a new appreciation and sense of responsibility for this endangered land.

A 12-seater raft whisks "ecotourists" up a watery ramp and through an arching tunnel of bamboo. It proceeds onward, through a hazy mist and past remnants of an ancient shrine. As the raft moves along curves of the river, guests enjoy views of undisturbed rainforest.

The tranquility is shattered by a startling sight. A huge chunk of forest has been gutted by loggers. On both sides of the river, the forest has vanished. As guests absorb the image, they are besieged by more disturbing sights and sounds. Straight ahead, the river is choked with a tangled arch of burning logs— and the raft is headed straight for it. Suddenly, the rainforest isn't the only thing endangered.

Kali River Rapids is an especially soggy experience. It is the rare guest who leaves the ride without a thorough soaking. Should you wish to repel as much precipitation as possible, pack a plastic poncho.

Note: This is a bumpy adventure. In order to experience it, you must be at least 38 inches tall. It is not recommended for pregnant women, guests with heart conditions, people with back or neck problems, or anyone who wishes to stay dry.

Maharajah Jungle Trek

BIRNBAUM'S ★BEST★ Welcome to the jungle! The Maharajah Jungle Trek is a self-guided walking tour of a tropical paradise, complete with roaming tigers and dense greenery. Throughout the expedition, trekkers encounter a deluge of flora and fauna typically found in the rainforests of Southeast Asia. Tapirs, Komodo dragons, and a conglomeration of colorful birds call this corner of Animal Kingdom home. Majestic

ruins, strategically separated from would-be prey. Deer and antelope graze and frolic nearby, blissfully oblivious of their fearsome neighbors' proximity.

Approximately midway through the thicket stands a rustic, tin-roofed assembly hall. Step inside to witness the breathtaking sight of giant fruit bats showing off their six-foot wingspans. As you look through the windows, thinking that the crystal-clear glass was cleaned by a super-diligent window washer, think again. There is no glass in some of the windows—and, therefore, *nothing* separating you from the giant creatures fluttering about

on the other side. What keeps the big bats from getting up close and personal with guests? They're a lot less interested in humans than humans are in them. (Can't say that we blame them.) Note that some viewing areas are adorned with wire or glass—for guests who are more comfortable with a bat buffer.

Flights of Wonder

A 1,000-seat, open-air theater, the Caravan Stage features performances by actors wearing nothing but feathers and the occasional crown. Members of more than 20 different bird species have starring roles in Flights of Wonder, a high-flying celebration of the winged wonders of the world. Hawks, owls, falcons, and even chickens have been known to awe spectators as they swoop, soar, and strut their stuff in each 20-minute performance. Some demonstrate how they hunt. Others display their grape-grabbing or money-grubbing talents. Check a park Times Guide for the schedule.
This show has morphed quite a bit from its original incarnation. It's a hoot!

Expedition Everest FP

BIRNBAUM'S ★BEST★ Walt Disney World's mountain range is a bit more intense these days, as the world's tallest mountain—Everest—has risen from the peaceful village of Serka Zong in Animal Kingdom's Asia. Like its sister peaks, Space, Splash, and Big Thunder, this E-ticket precipice promises to deliver "coaster thrills, spills, and chills." Does it deliver on that promise? Boy, does it ever.

> **HOT TIP!**
> Fastpass assignments for Expedition Everest tend to be gone soon after the park opens. Get yours as early as possible.

The attraction features an old tea train chugging and churning as it climbs up and around snowcapped peaks. Suddenly, the track comes to an end in a gnarled mess of twisted metal. Lurching forward and backward, the train hurtles through caverns and icy canyons before depositing guests in the presence of the legendary Yeti (aka the Abominable Snowman)—who's not too happy that you've scaled the mountain he so fiercely protects.

Feeling up to the challenge of a dramatic, high-speed train ride? If you are free of heart, back, and neck problems, are not pregnant, have no fear of heights (or Abominable snowpeople), and are at least 44 inches tall, go for it. As always, never eat right before experiencing a ride as topsy-turvy as this one.

FP = Fastpass attraction (see page 25)

DinoLand U.S.A.

If the look and feel of DinoLand U.S.A. seems familiar, there's a reason: It was designed to capture the flavor of roadside America. It is a mixture of culture and kitsch—the likes of which you might stumble upon during a cross-country road trip. Here, you may ride a flying Triceratop, jump into gigantic footprints, and browse through a typically tacky roadside souvenir stand, where you can pick up some dinosaur mementos for the folks back home.

This corner of Animal Kingdom comes complete with its own dramatic entrance: a 50-foot skeleton of a brachiosaurus. As guests stroll beneath the bones, they find themselves smack in the middle of a paleontological dig. Here, guests of all ages (especially little ones) have the chance to play paleontologist as they dig through a fossil-packed pocket of dino discovery.

Did You Know?

Many of the benches in Disney's Animal Kingdom are made of recycled plastic milk jugs. It takes 1,350 jugs to make a single bench!

The dinosaurs that dwell here, though often quite animated, are all of the inanimate variety. But do keep your eyes peeled for the prehistoric life forms that actually *live* in this land. That is, for real creatures that exist in the here and now, but whose ancestors kept company with the likes of the carnotaurus and its cousins from the Cretaceous era.

The Boneyard

The Boneyard gives guests—especially the very young ones—an opportunity to dig for fossils in a discovery-oriented playground. They will excavate the ancient bones of a mammoth in this re-creation of a paleontological dig (think huge sandbox). They will also unearth clues that may help them solve the mystery of how and when the creature met its untimely demise.

For serious "boneheads" who just aren't satisfied with simple digging, there are plenty of other bone-related activities here. You can bang out a primitive tune on a bony xylophone (it's located near the car; to make a sound, simply press on a rib), zip down prehistoric slides, and work your way through a fossil-filled maze. While exploring, watch your step: If you accidentally wander into a giant dinosaur footprint, you'll be greeted with an ominous roar.

While in DinoLand, be sure to check out the OldenGate Bridge. It's a gateway structure made from a dinosaur skeleton. The bridge links one end of The Boneyard with the other. This is a good place to take young kids while other members of your party ride Dinosaur.

Chester & Hester's Dino-Rama!

A colorful land-within-a-land, Chester and Hester's is an area ideally suited for roadside carnival fans. Located just beyond The Boneyard playground, this wild-and-woolly zone features old-fashioned midway games and two rides: Primeval Whirl and TriceraTop Spin.

PRIMEVAL WHIRL: 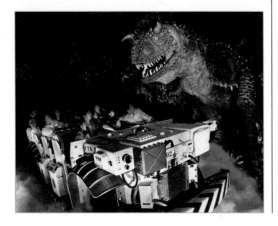FP A small roller coaster (with spinning cars) that seems to have been plucked from a traveling fair, this ride has a familiar feel to it. By all means, give it a whirl—it's a truly wild ride. You must be at least 48 inches tall to spin. Skip it if you are pregnant or susceptible to motion sickness.

TRICERATOP SPIN: The ride is apt to please fans of the Magic Kingdom's Dumbo the Flying Elephant and the Magic Carpets of Aladdin. Guests ride in one of the 16 flying dinos, each of which resembles an oversize tin toy. It's tame when compared to its Dinosaur attraction neighbor, but worth checking out—especially for young dinosaur groupies.

Dinosaur FP

BIRNBAUM'S ★BEST★ This dizzying adventure begins with guests being strapped into vehicles and catapulted back in time to complete a dangerous, albeit noble, mission: to rescue the last iguanodon—a 16-foot plant-eating dinosaur that you may remember from the Disney film *Dinosaur*—and bring him back to the present. The iguanodon, which lived more than 65 million years ago (during the Cretaceous period), just might hold the answer to the mysterious disappearance of his dino brethren.

Throughout the frenetic quest to locate the elusive iguanodon, you cling to an out-of-control vehicle while dodging blazing meteors and a mix of friendly and ferocious dinosaurs. Soon you encounter the carnotaurus—a fearsome, carnivorous dinosaur. The carnotaurus, which has horns like a bull and a face like a toad, is a remarkably unsightly specimen.

All of the dinosaurs are especially fierce-looking and move as though they were alive. Even their nostrils move as they "breathe."

This 3½-minute attraction offers more than a thrill a minute. You rocket through time, are practically pelted by meteors, and narrowly escape becoming a dino dinner as the carnotaurus suddenly turns the tables and chases after *you*.

Guests reach the attraction through the Dino Institute, a museum-like building deep in the heart of DinoLand. Here, you'll be treated to a pre-show by Bill Nye, the Science Guy (audio only), and see a dinosaur skeleton, and an assortment of fossils and other artifacts.

This is an extremely rough (and dark) attraction. You must be at least 40 inches tall to experience it. It is not recommended for pregnant women, or people with heart conditions, or back or neck problems. Small kids will certainly be frightened.

Finding Nemo— The Musical

BIRNBAUM'S ★BEST★ DinoLand is just about as far off Broadway as one could be. Yet, this show's got the ingredients of a Broadway smash: beloved characters (e.g., Marlin, the overprotective clownfish dad; Nemo, his curious son; and Dory, the endearing royal blue tang with the short-term memory loss); original songs by a Tony-winning composer (Robert Lopez); and dancers, acrobats, and the theatrical puppetry of Michael Curry (who designed the richly detailed puppets seen in the Broadway version of Disney's *The Lion King*). You can catch this 30-minute performance at the enclosed and air-conditioned Theater in the Wild. Check a Times Guide for showtimes—and get there early.

Camp Minnie-Mickey

What would a theme park be without a gregarious cast of handshaking characters? You will find the patented Disney character experience in all of its animated glory in Camp Minnie-Mickey. Set deep in a dense forest, this land is really a summer camp frequented by Mickey Mouse and all of his pals.

To find the characters, guests follow one of four short trails. Each one leads to an open-air hut, occupied by the likes of Mickey Mouse, Minnie Mouse, Donald Duck, Daisy Duck, or Goofy. Different characters make appearances at these pavilions throughout the day.

Camp Minnie-Mickey is also the home of one of Walt Disney World's most popular shows—Festival of the Lion King. Check a Times Guide for schedules.

Get Involved

When it comes to conservation efforts, the folks at the Walt Disney Company want you to do as they say—and as they do: The Disney Worldwide Conservation Fund helps nonprofit groups protect and study endangered and threatened animals and habitats. Among those groups are the Dian Fossey Gorilla Fund, Conservation International, the Wildlife Conservation Society, and Jane Goodall Institute. And guests who "Add a Dollar" while making purchases at Animal Kingdom shops and restaurants help, too.

Of course, as a trip to Animal Kingdom makes clear, there are many ways to help our planet's wild inhabitants. Stop by Rafiki's Planet Watch during your visit. There, you can get information about conservation efforts in your neck of the woods. Don't leave your enthusiasm behind when you leave the park!

Festival of the Lion King

BIRNBAUM'S ★BEST★ In addition to rustling up grubs in Camp Minnie-Mickey, the talented cast of *The Lion King* performs a 30-minute stage show in the Lion King Theater (which is now completely enclosed and thoroughly air-conditioned).

Presented in the round, this lavish revue is as bright and boisterous as they come. The dramatic opening features a parade of performers in colorful animal costumes. What follows is an intriguing, energetic interpretation of the film, including songs, dances, and acrobatics. With the exception of Timon, who plays himself, lead characters are portrayed by humans draped in bold African costumes.

Songs include Scar's nasty version of "Be Prepared," as well as "Can You Feel the Love Tonight?," "The Circle of Life," and a rousing rendition of "The Lion Sleeps Tonight."

Timing Tip: Although this enclosed theater accommodates nearly 1,400 guests at a time, we recommend arriving at least 30 minutes before the performance time. Take our word for it: It's worth the wait.

Greeting Trails

Tucked within Camp Minnie-Mickey (across from Festival of the Lion King) are several short trails. At the end of each one, you'll find very special furry friends: Disney characters! Mickey, Minnie, and their pals greet guests throughout the day. Don't forget to bring cameras and autograph books.

Shopping

Entrance Area

GARDEN GATE GIFTS: Stop here for souvenirs, snacks, sundries, and camera supplies. ECVs may be rented here. (Wheelchairs and strollers are available at a nearby counter.) This is also the park's package pick-up and PhotoPass viewing location.

OUTPOST: A small shop, located just outside the park's entrance, Outpost offers character merchandise, snacks, and more.

Discovery Island

BEASTLY BAZAAR: This spot sells items for the table and the tummy. There's a selection of accoutrements for the kitchen, plus gift items. Hungry guests can pick up a snack or light lunch at the bazaar's "grab and go" section. (There's no dining area in the shop.)

CREATURE COMFORTS: This shop offers items for kids—toys, clothes, costumes, hats, and more.

DISNEY OUTFITTERS: Nature-themed gifts and apparel are the stock-in-trade here. There's an abundance of clothing (for the whole family). Organic T-shirts and other eco-friendly items are available. Make a point of checking out the authentic carved animal totem poles in the center room—they are most impressive.

ISLAND MERCANTILE: This sprawling shop is themed as a shipping company that celebrates working animals—camels, elephants, beavers, and others. Here, you'll find character merchandise, clothing, candy, and Disney paraphernalia. Note that this shop stays open about a half hour after Animal Kingdom closes for the day.

Africa

DUKA LA FILIMU: Situated near the entrance to Kilimanjaro Safaris, this is an ideal place to load up on film for your trip.

MOMBASA MARKETPLACE AND ZIWANI TRADERS: An African marketplace and trading company, these connected shops feature animal toys, safari clothing, T-shirts, books, wine, and Africa-themed gifts such as pottery, masks, and musical instruments.

OUT OF THE WILD: Located just outside the exit of Rafiki's Planet Watch, this open-air shop stocks a variety of souvenirs, including shirts, hats, notebooks, and toys.

Asia

BHAKTAPUR MARKET: A small shop with a big Asian influence, Bhaktapur sells summer shoes, bags, robes, shirts, teapots and teas, toy dragons and plush animals, chopsticks, and items with a Yak & Yeti theme.

MANDALA GIFTS: Just a stone's throw from Royal Anandapur Tea Company, this spot offers wind chimes, jewelry, hats, and a selection of souvenirs featuring the Animal Kingdom park logo.

SERKA ZONG BAZAAR: Located at the exit of Expedition Everest (it can be accessed from the outside for those who skip the ride), this bustling bazaar sells souvenirs with a Yeti theme, plus a slew of shirts, hats, books, frames, etc., that celebrate the Expedition Everest attraction.

DinoLand U.S.A.

CHESTER & HESTER'S DINOSAUR TREASURES: Themed as an American roadside souvenir stand, this shop pays homage to all reptiles and prehistoric animals. Its focus is reflected in an assortment of wacky items strewn about the shop.

Entertainment

AFRICAN ENTERTAINMENT: Sounds of Africa often fill the air as bands serenade guests passing through Harambe. Entertainers perform around the park throughout the day.

ANIMAL ENCOUNTERS: Enjoy up-close encounters with some of the smaller members of the animal kingdom as they wander the park with their human keepers.

MICKEY'S JAMMIN' JUNGLE PARADE: Animal Kingdom celebrates the wonders of the natural world in this peppy parade. It features familiar Disney characters—including Mickey Mouse, Minnie Mouse, Goofy, Donald Duck, and Rafiki—cruising in jazzy jalopies. Stilt-walkers and puppets put in appearances, too. Check a Times Guide for the parade schedule.

Hot Tips

- Arrive at the park 20 minutes before park opening time. Animal Kingdom often kicks off the day with "The Adventure Begins"—a character-laden musical celebration. It's a very Disney way to start the day.

- Island Mercantile on Discovery Island stays open a half hour after the park closes.

- Most of Animal Kingdom's attractions take place outdoors. Don't become overheated! Make a point of slipping into an air-conditioned shop or restaurant from time to time to cool off.

- Narrow, winding paths, grooved pavement, and hilly terrain make this the most challenging Disney theme park in which to navigate a wheelchair.

- Check the Animal Kingdom Tip Board often to get an idea of showtimes and crowds.

- The line for Kilimanjaro Safaris tends to dwindle a bit by midday. See it then (the experience is enjoyable at any time of day).

- Get a Fastpass for Expedition Everest first thing in the morning—they are often gone before lunchtime.

- Rainforest Cafe generally keeps longer hours than the park does.

- When the weather gets steamy, keep a reusable water bottle with you at all times.

- If you plan to park hop, Animal Kingdom is a good park at which to begin the day.

Where to Eat in Animal Kingdom

A complete listing of eateries at Disney's Animal Kingdom—table-service restaurants, fast-food spots, and snack stands—can be found in the *Good Meals, Great Times* chapter. See the Animal Kingdom section, beginning on page 247.

Everything Else in the World

While the total turf of the World encompasses about 40 square miles, the theme parks cover a mere fraction of the property. Much of the remaining Walt Disney World terrain is crammed with irresistible activities of a variety and quality seldom found anywhere else.

There's superb golf and tennis, beaches for sunbathing, lakes for motorboating, fishing, and sailing, canoes to rent and winding streams to paddle along, bicycles for hire, campfire sites, horseback riding, race-car driving, nature trails, and picnic grounds. The recreation options continue with Typhoon Lagoon, a lushly landscaped, state-of-the-art water park complete with surfing lagoon; and Blizzard Beach, a thrilling, watery wonderland that translates the hallmarks of a ski resort to the realm of swimming.

A quartet of lavish spas provides guests with ample opportunity to pamper themselves silly. Intriguing "backstage" programs invite the curious to slip behind the scenes and learn about the workings of Walt Disney World. Add to all that, Downtown Disney—a dining, shopping, and amusement district encompassing Pleasure Island, an evolving mix of dining and shopping spots; the Marketplace, a colorful assortment of shops and restaurants; and the West Side, a cluster of themed eateries, shops, and entertainment experiences. It seems this really is a World without end.

Downtown Disney

Sprinkled across 120 waterfront acres are the shops, lounges, restaurants, and entertainment sites that collectively make up Downtown Disney. Like the downtown area of any thriving metropolis, Disney's Downtown consists of several distinct neighborhoods. In this case, they are known as the Marketplace, Pleasure Island, and the West Side. Unlike a typical downtown, however, the Disney depiction dispenses with the downside. You won't see litter on the streets, unsightly storefronts, or weary workers rushing home at five o'clock. What you *will* see is a series of spirited spots designed solely for your dining, shopping, and partying pleasure.

Judging by the throngs that descend upon this place, Downtown Disney is *the* place to be when you're not in the parks. That said, it can get a tad congested—especially on the roads leading here. However you're traveling, allow plenty of extra time to get to and from this fun zone. Note that all sections are connected by walking paths. For information, visit *www.disneyworld.com* or call 407-939-2648.

Downtown Disney Essentials

GUEST RELATIONS: Between Team Mickey Athletic Club and Ghirardelli Soda Fountain & Chocolate Shop in the Marketplace, and near DisneyQuest on the West Side, these information centers are also the places to go for help making reservations, Lost and Found, tickets, and more. Note that stroller and wheelchair rentals are available at DisneyQuest and at a location between Tren-D and Once Upon a Toy. There is an ATM near Tren-D in the Marketplace and another by Wetzel's Pretzels on the West Side.

HOW TO GET THERE: Downtown Disney is accessible from exits 67 and 68 off I-4.

By WDW Transportation: From Old Key West, Port Orleans French Quarter and Riverside, and Saratoga Springs: boats or buses. From all other WDW resorts: bus. There is no direct transportation from Disney theme parks to Downtown Disney. The Marketplace is within walking distance of several resorts on Hotel Plaza Blvd. For more information, turn to *Transportation & Accommodations*.

By Taxi: Yellow cabs service the Downtown Disney area. The cost to most WDW resorts is usually $8 to $22.

Note: Stick with authorized taxis such as Checker Cabs and avoid independent drivers. Their fees aren't regulated and are often outrageous. And pay attention to the route the driver takes to be sure it is direct.

West Side

Pleasure Island

Marketplace

Located on the shores of Lake Buena Vista, the Marketplace is a relaxing setting for shopping, dining, and much more. The waterside enclave is sprinkled with gardens featuring whimsical topiaries. Kids are fond of the Downtown Disney Marketplace Carousel (nestled between Pooh Corner and Earl of Sandwich). And adults may enjoy a drink at Cap'n Jack's Margarita Bar.

While many guests opt to eat in a restaurant, others grab a bite from the Earl of Sandwich and sit at waterfront tables. (Refer to *Good Meals, Great Times* for restaurant information.) Afterward, some gravitate toward the marina for boating or fishing. (Turn to the *Sports* chapter for details.)

Shopping

The descriptions below suggest the types of wares each store offers. Most shops in the Downtown Disney Marketplace are usually open daily from about 9:30 A.M. to 11 P.M.

ARRIBAS BROS.: This shop sells handcrafted items from Spanish artisans and designers. Large, cut-glass bowls and vases are available, along with mugs, sculptures, and other wares, all of which can be engraved.

THE ART OF DISNEY: Disney animation cels, porcelain figures, ceramics, posters, and other collectibles are available at this engaging gallery.

BASIN: Products designed to clean you up and calm you down are the stock-in-trade at this soothing establishment. Candles, soaps, and bath crystals are some of the wares on hand. A sampling area allows shoppers to try before they buy. The bath bombs are the best!

DESIGN A TEE: This shop is T-shirt central. Aspiring fashion designer? Simply step up to a kiosk and design away!

DISNEY'S DAYS OF CHRISTMAS: Here is the best place to deck the halls Disney style—it's the largest Christmas shop on Disney property. In addition to character items, the shop boasts a large assortment of handcrafted ornaments. Other items to look for: Christmas cards, candles, Santa hats with mouse ears, and books. Many items can be personalized.

DISNEY'S PIN TRADERS: This shop boasts a tremendous assortment of collector pins and various pin-collecting accessories. In fact, this is Walt Disney World's most elaborate pin-trading center.

GOOFY'S CANDY COMPANY: One-stop shopping to satisfy sugary cravings, this shop has a sumptuous selection of chocolates, a dipping kitchen, and much more. It also hosts birthday parties. Call 407-WDW-BDAY (939-2329) for information or to book a Princess- or Goofy-themed birthday party.

LEGO IMAGINATION CENTER: World of Disney's neighbor, this newly renovated emporium is a showcase for larger-than-life Lego models. It also invites guests to flaunt their creativity in an interactive outdoor play area. A new computer hub lets guests design

Marketplace

Lego structures and play games. The store sells a vast selection of Lego products.

LITTLE MISSMATCHED: The problem of mis-matched sock syndrome has finally been solved: *Nothing* here matches! In addition to socks (which are actually sold in packs of three), the store sells colorful pajamas, pencil pouches, backpacks, and other miscellany.

MARKETPLACE FUN FINDS: Stop here for Disney character merchandise at delightfully low prices.

MICKEY'S PANTRY: Stop here for Disney-themed glasses, mugs, cooking utensils, and small appliances, plus teas and coffees. Many of the designs are subtle, others not so much.

ONCE UPON A TOY: A sprawling toy box of a store, this site features interactive areas, colorful displays, and an outdoor play space. All the big brand names are represented, as are a few of the smaller ones.

TEAM MICKEY ATHLETIC CLUB: A cavernous store with a locker-room motif, this shop is the perfect setting for sports clothing, active-wear, and sports equipment. You'll find items with Disney characters in sporting poses emblazoned on them. It's also possible to customize bats, balls, gloves, batting helmets, and other baseball equipment.

TREN-D: The Mouse is quite a trend-setter. Need proof? Swing by this new boutique. It's bursting with quirky Disney merchandise, from organic lounge-wear to jeweled sunglasses and other trendy accessories.

WORLD OF DISNEY: A gigantic space stuffed with a huge selection of Disney merchandise, this is *the* place for one-stop shopping. Twelve colorful rooms provide the backdrop for the array of goods. Characters are available on everything from watches to luggage. (If you're an annual passholder, you may receive a discount when you present it at the register.)

Cinderella's Fairy Godmother has set up shop in the Princess Room. Her Bibbidi Bobbidi Boutique, which is run by "Fairy Godmothers in training," caters to royal-wannabes ages 3 and up. Here, kids can get their faces painted with glitter makeup, do their nails and hair, and even don tiaras. The boutique is open daily. Kids are transformed into princesses and princely "cool dudes." Reservations are encouraged; call 407-WDW-STYLE (939-7895).

There's a haven for pirate fans here, too. The Adventure Room invites young swashbucklers to sail the high seas, hoist the Jolly Roger, and fill treasure chests with buccaneer booty. They can make pirate hats, too.

Where to Eat at Downtown Disney

A complete listing of restaurants, bars, and snack spots can be found in the *Good Meals, Great Times* chapter. See the Downtown Disney restaurant listing, beginning on page 249. Most restaurants here are open from about 11:30 A.M. to midnight. Planet Hollywood serves until 1 A.M. West Side spots may serve as late as 2 A.M.

Pleasure Island

HOT TIP!
If you want to sip spirits of any kind, you'll have to prove you are at least 21 years old (the legal drinking age in Florida). To do so, present an official, government-issued photo ID. (A driver's license or passport will do the trick.) If you can't produce proper ID, you won't be allowed to imbibe. No exceptions.

A six-acre nighttime entertainment complex, Pleasure Island delivers a (growing) set of options that complement a day in the parks. In addition to a few lounges, there are several restaurants and shops here in the central area of Downtown Disney. *Note that Pleasure Island may get a new name in 2012.*

Restaurants & Lounges

RAGLAN ROAD: Straight from the Emerald Isle, this establishment captures the charm of an authentic Irish pub—not surprising, as all of the furnishings were designed and built in Ireland. Culinary temptations are courtesy of Kevin Dundon, one of Ireland's best-known chefs. The entertainment here is as free-flowing as the stout—expect a mix of traditional and contemporary music, storytelling, and dance. Guests of all ages are welcome here (as is the case with many traditional Irish pubs), but must be at least 21 years old to enjoy a pint or any other alcoholic beverage (valid, government-issued photo ID is necessary to show proof of age). Raglan Road, which is owned and operated by Great Irish Pubs Florida, is in the space previously occupied by the Pleasure Island Jazz Company. Live entertainment starts at 9 P.M. It comes in the form of an Irish band and dancer Monday through Saturday. On Sunday, live music starts at 8 P.M. *Sláinte!* (That's Gaelic for "Cheers!")

FUEGO BY SOSA CIGARS: Cigar aficionados, rejoice. There is one smoking bar in town and it boasts some 100 facings of hand-rolled, premium cigars. Fuego, a small, cozy-but-upscale lounge, invites guests to savor a smoke

(they've got everything from the legendary Fuente Fuente Opus X to the highly rated, house-branded Sosa cigars) and sip premium cocktails. Guests must be 18 to smoke, 21 to drink. You'll find it next to Raglan Road.

PARADISO 37—STREET FOODS OF THE AMERICAS: A festive, waterside eatery, Paradiso serves lunch and dinner selections from North, Central, and South America. In addition to signature frozen margaritas, an extensive tequila bar, and the "coldest beer in the world," the restaurant offers nightly entertainment. There is indoor and outdoor seating.

PORTOBELLO: There's plenty of seating at this modern yet rustic bar-within-a-restaurant (a classic Italian trattoria). A full selection of drinks is offered, but the big draw here is the wine list. An impressive variety of wines (from around the globe) may be ordered by the bottle, half bottle, or glass. There's an extensive reserve collection, too.

Shopping

CURL BY SAMMY DUVALL: You have to figure that anybody who spent not one but 17 years as a champion water-skier has to know quite a bit about trends in beach-wear and watersport equipment. See for yourself at this high-end surf shop. Inside, you'll find a selection of clothing and accessories, surf-boards, and skateboards. (Okay, skateboards may not be watersport-related, but they're still pretty cool.)

Cha Cha Cha, Changes

The patch of Walt Disney World known as Pleasure Island continues to undergo a massive metamorphosis. The most dramatic change? The dance clubs are no more. (However, guests who wish to exercise their happy feet may still do so at BoardWalk's Atlantic Dance—see page 205). What will guests discover here when the dust finally settles? Well, that's in the hands of the Disney Imagineers. At press time, we were told to expect, "an extraordinary mix of shopping and dining." To that end, the 6-acre area already boasts four bona fide dining destinations: Raglan Road, Portobello, Fulton's Crab House, and Paradiso 37—Street Foods of the Americas.

Will P.I. get a name change, too? Anything is possible! For updates on the progress at Pleasure Island, visit *www.disneyworld.com*.

ORLANDO HARLEY-DAVIDSON: No motorcycles for sale here (though any employee will happily tell you how to buy one), but the custom Harleys on display are definitely ogle-worthy. Hog fans can browse Harley-Davidson T-shirts, gifts, and other collectibles. Note that this shop may move locations in 2012.

Shopping at Crossroads

Originally conceived by the WDW folks, the Crossroads of Lake Buena Vista shopping center, near the resorts on Hotel Plaza Boulevard, is a convenient dining and shopping area. The center is anchored by a Gooding's supermarket, which is open 24 hours a day.

West Side

When Disney's shopping and entertainment district underwent its latest growth spurt, it did so in true American style: It went west. The West Side boasts a wide variety of restaurants, shops, movies, and clubs. Although it does not have an admission fee, some venues may charge a cover.

AMC DOWNTOWN DISNEY: The most popular multi-screen movie theater complex in Florida is also one of the largest. The many screens show a wide selection of current movie releases. The seats are roomy and comfortable—and some of the theaters offer seat-side food and beverage service (see page 249 for details). For current movie schedules, call 407-298-4488.

BONGOS CUBAN CAFE: Situated across from the AMC Theatres on the edge of Buena Vista Village Lake, Bongos echoes the style of clubs in Miami's South Beach. Created in part by Gloria Estefan, it features the flavors and rhythms of Cuba and other Latin American countries. The bold design is dramatic, yet whimsical. Guests dine and, if the mood strikes, even dance amid the colorful, tropical decor (and one remarkably oversized pineapple, which houses a multi-level cocktail lounge).

The food here moves to a Latin beat as well, with a slate of traditional and nouvelle Cuban dishes. There is entertainment on Friday and Saturday nights.

CIRQUE DU SOLEIL: The building that towers over all the others at Downtown Disney West Side is actually a tent—a circus tent. It's the home of a most extraordinary entertainment experience: Cirque du Soleil. This original show, titled La Nouba, is a Walt Disney World exclusive.

Known for their high energy and artistic performances, Cirque du Soleil shows feature a mix of acrobatics and modern dance combined with colorful costumes and dramatic original music. A cast of more than 60 international performers showcase their physical talents twice a day, five days a week (Tuesday through Saturday).

Tickets for the show may be purchased up to six months in advance. Call 407-939-7600, or visit *www.disneyworld.com* for information or to order tickets. If you have not already purchased tickets to La Nouba, consider stopping by the Cirque du Soleil box office at Downtown Disney West Side—some seats may be available at the last minute. Note that the show is quite popular.

DISNEYQUEST: This imaginative entertainment complex features high-tech activities that engage kids and grown-ups alike. Sometimes described as a self-contained, interactive theme park, the five floors under the DisneyQuest roof are packed with games—plus some blasts from the past.

Each floor features rides and games from the simple (classic video games such as Asteroids) to some of the more technologically advanced (e.g., Create's CyberSpace Mountain, in which guests not only design gravity-defying roller coasters but get to ride their creations in a simulator).

Expect to be engaged for two to three hours (or until sensory overload sets in). DisneyQuest is open daily from late morning till late evening. Admission covers most games. It's included with a Premium Annual Pass and the Water Park Fun & More add-on for a Magic Your Way base ticket. (If admission isn't included with your pass, pay at the entrance.)

Game on!

At press time it was announced that late 2012 would bring even more opportunities to play at Downtown Disney West Side. An entertainment complex dubbed Splitsville will feature bowling, billiards, and a whole lot more. In addition to games, Splitsville will serve (among other things) pizza, sushi, sliders, and a slew of desserts.

HOUSE OF BLUES: A combination restaurant-music hall with standing room for 2,000, House of Blues was inspired by one of America's most celebrated musical traditions. There is a lively dose of jazz and country, plus a little bit of R&B and some rock 'n' roll thrown into the music mix. The old-fashioned Southern cooking lures diners here—especially on Sunday mornings, when the chefs prepare an all-you-can-eat buffet feast, complemented by live gospel music. Tickets can be purchased through Ticketmaster (call 407-839-3900, or visit *www.ticketmaster.com*) or the House of Blues box office (407-934-2583).

The House of Blues restaurant features a mélange of Delta-inspired cuisine, including jambalaya, *étouffée*, and bread pudding.

WOLFGANG PUCK CAFE: There are three dining areas in this two-story restaurant—an express counter, a cafe, and a more formal dining room on the second floor—plus a sushi bar. All feature the celebrated chef's signature pizzas, rotisserie chicken, and other specialties.

Shopping

CANDY CAULDRON: Stop here for some homemade Southern-style sweets in an open candy kitchen. One of the biggest crowd pleasers here are the made to order specialty apples—fresh, crunchy apples slathered in the candy coating of your choice. Yum!

D STREET: This raw, industrial space show-cases a mix of Disney-inspired merchandise and Vinylmation collectibles. Also available are pop culture novelties, apparel, and more.

HOYPOLOI: The glass, ceramics, sculpture, jewelry, and other eclectic, decorative items on display here make this shop seem more like

an art gallery. It's worth a peek. Note that photography is not permitted in this shop.

MAGIC MASTERS: You won't believe your eyes when you enter this mysterious little space. There's not much merchandise on display. But there is a lengthy list of magical items, from crystal balls to linking handcuffs to a "wizard and book" (whatever that means). The cashier does double duty as the in-house magician. It's one of the more entertaining shops at Walt Disney World.

MAGNETRON: Your fridge will never be the same once you've paid a visit to this specialty magnet shop with its eclectic assortment of 50,000 magnets.

POP GALLERY: This gallery features artist-signed limited-edition sculptures and paintings, and high-end gift items. There's a champagne bar, too. Hence the "pop."

RIDEMAKERZ™: Build and customize a radio-controlled vehicle at this supercharged, inter-active store. Trick out real-world and concept cars: Ford Mustangs, Dodge Vipers, Chevy Corvettes, hot-rods, pick-up trucks, sports coupes, and much more. On-site "mechanics" can help you build your dream car. At press time, Ridemakerz was expected to move to a new location at the Marketplace.

SOSA FAMILY CIGARS: For grown-ups only, this shop specializes in premium cigars. Feel free to puff away here—the shop's a rare smoking zone.

SUNGLASS ICON: Looking to change your eyeglass image? Slip on shades that have been sported by the stars—or at least replicas of their shades.

BoardWalk

A stroll at Disney's BoardWalk is a journey back in time. Inspired by the Middle Atlantic seaside attractions of the early 1900s, BoardWalk recaptures the carefree atmosphere of that bygone era. The resort is surrounded by restaurants, clubs, and amusements similar to those enjoyed by beachgoers of yesteryear. It's bordered by a wood-planked walkway, which hugs the shore of Crescent Lake. By day, BoardWalk is a peaceful place to soak up sun, enjoy lunch, or simply walk the boards. After dark, the place turns into a twinkling center of nighttime activity—some of it elegant, some of it downright raucous.

Wyland Galleries, which features the world's foremost marine environmental art, is one of the more calming diversions. WildWood Landing challenges onlookers to test their luck and skill at a collection of classic carnival games. And strolling performers enchant passersby of all ages with magic shows, balloon tricks, or other antics.

BoardWalk is open to everyone. Although there is no admission price, individual venues may charge a cover. There is a $12 charge for valet parking (even for guests who are staying at a Disney resort). Self-parking is free. For restaurant information, refer to *Good Meals, Great Times*.

Clubs

ATLANTIC DANCE: This is a lovely atmosphere in which to dance the night away. A deejay cranks up tunes, tempting guests to twist and shout on the spacious dance floor. Request your favorite music videos and bust a move while they play on the big screen.

In addition to traditional cocktails, the club serves specialty drinks. Sample one in the "big room" or on the waterfront balcony.

Guests must be 21 or older, with a legal photo ID, to enter. There was no cover charge at press time, but that could change. Hours are generally 9 P.M. until 2 A.M., Tuesday through Saturday.

This club is known for reinventing itself: Specifics may be different during your visit.

ESPN CLUB: This club aims to please sports enthusiasts of all kinds, from the casual armchair quarterback to the most rabid fanatic. It includes a broadcasting facility, arcade, and table-service restaurant and bar.

More than 100 televisions broadcast live sports events, so guests always know the score. (Need to make a pit stop at a crucial moment of the game? Don't sweat it . . . there are even TVs in the bathrooms.)

As you enter the club, you're at The Sidelines area. You can catch a game on a TV above the "penalty box" bar or sit at a nearby table. Beer, wine, and soft drinks are available, as is the usual pub fare.

Sports Central, the main dining area, has a big screen showing—what else?—the big game. The kitchen is open until 11:30 P.M. for meals, 12:30 A.M. for appetizers.

JELLYROLLS: You might want to warm up your vocal cords before crossing the threshold. They don't call it a sing-along bar for nothing: Guests are expected to sing, clap, and join in the fun at this warehouse home of dueling pianos. You'll hear everything from Gershwin to *Grease*. The piano players take requests, so plan ahead. Write the request—a cocktail napkin will do—and slip it onto the piano. (Although it's not required, we recommend slipping a tip along, too. It will increase the odds of you hearing the request *and* help the musicians pay their rent.)

Jellyrolls is open from 7 P.M. until 2 A.M. nightly. There is usually a $10 cover charge to enter. (Note that the cover charge may vary.) To get in, you must be at least 21 years old and willing to prove it. It's often quite chilly in this venue (year-round). Bring a sweater.

Water Parks
Typhoon Lagoon

This watery playground was inspired by an imagined legend: A typhoon hit a tiny resort village many years ago, and the storm—plus an ensuing earthquake and volcanic eruption—left the village in ruins. The locals, however, were resourceful and rebuilt their town as this "wateropolis."

The centerpiece of Typhoon Lagoon is a huge watershed mountain known as Mount Mayday. Perched atop its peak is the *Miss Tilly*, a marooned shrimp boat originally from Safen Sound, Florida. *Miss Tilly*'s smokestack erupts every half hour, shooting a 50-foot flume of water into the air.

The surf lagoon is huge: Huge slides snake through caves, tamer ones offer twisting journeys, and tiny slides delight small kids. Guests under age 10 must be accompanied by an adult.

SURF POOL: The main swimming area contains nearly three million gallons of water, making it one of the world's largest wave pools. The Caribbean-blue lagoon is surrounded by a white-sand beach, and its main attraction is the waves that come crashing to the shore every 90 seconds. The less adventurous can loll about in two relatively calm tide pools, Whitecap Cove and Blustery Bay.

CASTAWAY CREEK: This 2,100-foot circular river that winds through the park offers a lazy, relaxing orientation to Typhoon Lagoon. Tubes may be borrowed for free and are the most enjoyable way to make the trip along the three-foot-deep waterway. The ride takes guests through a rainforest, where they are cooled by mists and spray; through caves and grottoes that provide welcome shade on hot summer days; and through an area where "broken" pipes from a water tower unleash showers on helpless passersby. There are exits along the way, where guests can hop out for a while and do something else. It takes 20 to 35 minutes to ride around the park without taking a break.

CRUSH 'N' GUSHER: This "water coaster" thrill ride is one of a kind. In it, daredevils are

PHOTO BY JILL SAFRO

whisked along a series of flumes and tossed and turned as they weave through an abandoned tropical fruit factory. There are three spillways to choose from: Banana Blaster, Coconut Crusher, and Pineapple Plunger.

GANGPLANK FALLS, KEELHAUL FALLS, AND MAYDAY FALLS: These white-water rides offer guests a variety of slippery trips, two of them in inner tubes. All of the slides course through caves and waterfalls, and past rockwork, making the scenery an attraction in itself. Gangplank Falls gives families a chance to ride together in a three- to five-passenger craft.

HUMUNGA KOWABUNGA: These three speed slides, reported to have been carved into the landscape by the historic earthquake, will send guests zooming through caverns at speeds of 30 miles per hour. The 214-foot slides each offer a 51-foot drop, and the view from the top is a little scary. But it's over before you know it, and once-wary guests hurry back for another try. Guests must be at least 4 feet tall, and free of back trouble, heart conditions, and other physical limitations to take the trip. Pregnant women are not permitted to ride.

KETCHAKIDDEE CREEK: Open only to those children 4 feet tall or under (and their adult guardians), this area has small rides for pint-size visitors. All children must be accompanied by an adult. There are slides, fountains, waterfalls, squirting whales and seals, a mini-rapids ride, an interactive tugboat, and a grotto with a veil of water that kids love to run through.

SHARK REEF: Guests borrow snorkel equipment for a swim through a coral reef, where they come face to face with sharks and fish. The reef is built around a sunken tanker. The sharks, by the way, leopard and bonnethead, are passive members of the species. Everyone must shower before entering. Guests must be older than age 5 to experience Shark Reef. Kids under 10 must be accompanied by an adult.

STORM SLIDES: The Jib Jammer, Rudder Buster, and Stern Burner body slides send guests off at about 20 miles per hour down winding fiberglass slides, in and out of rock formations and caves, and through waterfalls. It's a somewhat tamer ride than Humunga Kowabunga, but still offers a speedy descent. The slides run about 300 feet, and each offers a different view and experience.

SURFING: Surf clinics are offered on select mornings before the park opens. For information, call 407-WDW-SURF (939-7873).

Essentials

WHEN TO GO: Typhoon Lagoon gets very crowded early in the day. Hours vary seasonally, but the park is generally open from 10 A.M. to 5 P.M., with extended hours in the summer months. All of the pools are heated in the winter. Note that this park is usually closed for refurbishment during certain winter months. The park may also close due to bad weather. Call 407-824-4321 for updates.

HOW TO GET THERE: Bus service begins from all resorts approximately one hour before Typhoon Lagoon opens for the day. The buses stop at the water park and then at the Downtown Disney Marketplace before 10 A.M. After 10 A.M., resort buses stop at the Marketplace and then Typhoon Lagoon. Buses stop running from the water park about one hour after it closes. Parking is free.

LOCKER ROOMS: Restrooms with showers and lockers are located close to the entrance. Other restrooms are available farther into the park. Small lockers cost $8 (plus a $5 deposit) to rent for the day, while large lockers cost $10, plus a $5 deposit. Towels rent for $2; life jackets and tubes are available free of charge.

WHERE TO EAT: Both Typhoon Lagoon eateries offer similar fare and outdoor seating. Leaning Palms has burgers, pizza, salads, and snacks. Typhoon Tilly's serves chicken tenders, wraps, barbecued pork sandwiches, and ice cream. Let's Go Slurpin' sells frozen drinks and spirits. Guests may bring their own food to enjoy in designated picnic areas. Alcoholic beverages and glass containers may not be brought into the park. Coolers are allowed.

FIRST AID: A first-aid station capable of handling minor medical problems is located just to the left of Leaning Palms.

BEACH SHOP: Singapore Sal's, located near the park's main entrance, is set in a ramshackle building left a bit battered by the typhoon. Swimsuits, sunglasses, hats, towels, sunscreen, souvenirs, water shoes, and Typhoon Lagoon logo products are available.

Admission Prices

Prices do not include sales tax and are subject to change. **Note:** Admission is an option with a Magic Your Way ticket that includes a Water Park Fun & More add-on and is also included with a Premium Annual Pass.

	Adults	Children*
One-Day Ticket	$49	...... $41
Annual Pass	$100	...... $81

*3 through 9 years of age; children under 3 free

Blizzard Beach

A wintry, watery wonderland, Blizzard Beach is said to be the result of a freak storm that dropped a mountain of snow onto Walt Disney World, prompting the quick construction of Florida's first ski resort. When temperatures soared and the snow began to melt, designers prepared to close the resort. But when they spotted an alligator sliding down the slopes, they realized that they had created an exhilarating water adventure park. The slalom and bobsled runs became downhill waterslides. The ski jump is one of the world's tallest (120 feet) and fastest (60 miles per hour) free-fall speed slides.

The centerpiece of Blizzard Beach is the snowcapped Mount Gushmore and its Summit Plummet. Most of the more thrilling runs are found on the slopes of this mountain, which tops out at 90 feet. At the summit, swimmers have a choice of speed slides, flumes, a whitewater raft ride, and an inner-tube run. Guests may reach the top of Mount Gushmore via chairlift. The lift has a gondola for guests with disabilities. There are stairs, too.

This is the most action-packed Disney water park yet, with enough activities for the entire family to fill at least a day. Note that kids under 10 must be accompanied by an adult.

CROSS COUNTRY CREEK: This meandering 3,000-foot waterway circles the entire park. A slow current keeps visitors moving merrily along. Inner tubes, which are free, are the most pleasant way to travel. The ride includes a trip through a bone-chilling ice cave, where guests are splashed with the "melting ice" from overhead.

DOWNHILL DOUBLE DIPPER: Guests travel down these two parallel 230-foot-long racing slides at speeds of up to 25 miles per hour. The partially enclosed water runs feature ski-racing graphics, flags, and time clocks. You must be 48 inches tall to ride.

MELT-AWAY BAY: This one-acre pool at the base of Mount Gushmore is equipped with its own wave machine. There are no tsunamis here, however—just a pleasant, bobbing wave.

RUNOFF RAPIDS: On this inner-tube run, guests careen down three twisting, turning flumes in a single or double tube.

SKI PATROL TRAINING CAMP: An area designed specifically for preteens, Frozen Pipe Springs looks like an old pipe and drops sliders into eight feet of water. The Thin Ice Training Course tests agility as kids try to walk along broken "icebergs" without falling into the water. Snow Falls's "wide" slides allow a parent and child to ride together. At the Ski Patrol Shelter, guests grab onto a T-bar for an airborne trip. At any point in the ride they can drop into the water below. Ski patrol participants also experience Cool Runners, where riders can count on hurtling and whirling over lots of moguls on twin inner-tube slides. No bunny slopes for these brave daredevils.

SLUSH GUSHER: This relatively tame, double-humped waterslide offers a brisk journey through a snow-banked mountain gully. Topping out at 90 feet, Slush Gusher is the tallest slide of its kind. You'll find it on Mount Gushmore, next to Summit Plummet. Guests must be at least 4 feet tall to ride.

SNOW STORMERS: A trio of flumes descends from the top of the mountain. Guests race down on a switchback course that includes ski-type slalom gates.

SUMMIT PLUMMET: This thrilling ride begins 120 feet in the air on a platform 30 feet above the top of Mount Gushmore. Brave souls travel about 60 miles per hour down a 350-foot slide. You must be at least 4 feet tall to take the plunge.

TEAMBOAT SPRINGS: The longest family white-water raft ride in the world takes six-passenger rafts down a twisting, 1,400-foot series of rushing waterfalls.

HOT TIP!
Premium cabana-like spaces known as Polar Patios are available for daily rental. They include an attendant, refreshments, towels, and more. Each patio accommodates up to six guests and costs about $250 per day. Premium beach spaces are available, too. For details or to make a reservation, call 407-WDW-PLAY (939-7529).

TIKE'S PEAK: A kid-size variation of Blizzard Beach, this attraction features miniature versions of Mount Gushmore's slides and a snow-castle fountain play area. Adults must be accompanied by a child to enter this zone.

TOBOGGAN RACERS: An eight-lane water-slide sends guests racing over a number of dips. They lie on their stomachs on a mat and travel headfirst down the 250-foot route.

Essentials

WHEN TO GO: As a guest favorite, Blizzard Beach tends to get very crowded early in the day. Hours vary seasonally, but the park is generally open from 10 A.M. to 5 P.M., with extended hours in summer. On select "peak" days, Blizzard Beach may offer an Extra Magic Hour to guests staying in a WDW-owned-and-operated resort and at the Hilton on Hotel Plaza Boulevard. All pools are heated in winter. The park is often closed for refurbishment during certain winter months. It may also close due to inclement weather. For schedules, call 407-WDW-PLAY (939-7529).

HOW TO GET THERE: Blizzard Beach is served by the buses that go to and from Animal Kingdom. There is service to and from Epcot and Disney's Hollywood Studios, as well. Parking is free.

LOCKER ROOMS: There are restrooms with showers near the main entrance. Other restrooms and dressing rooms are located around the park. Small lockers cost $8, plus a $5 deposit for the day, while large lockers cost $10, plus a $5 deposit. Towels rent for $2, and life jackets and tubes may be used for free.

WHERE TO EAT: Burgers, hot dogs, salads, and drinks are sold at Lottawatta Lodge in the main village area. Two snack stands with limited offerings are located in more remote areas: Avalunch and The Warming Hut. Polar Pub offers drink specialties and spirits. Those in need of a java fix can get one at Frosty the Joe Man Coffee Shack, while those looking for frozen lemonade or fresh fruit can find it at Frostbite Freddy's. There are picnic areas for those who pack their own food. Alcoholic beverages and glass containers may not be brought into the park. Coolers are allowed.

FIRST AID: Minor medical problems are handled at this station near the main entrance.

BEACH SHOP: The Beach Haus shop stocks bathing suits, T-shirts, shorts, sunglasses, hats, sunscreen, beach towels, and more.

Admission Prices

Prices do not include sales tax and are likely to change in 2012. **Note:** Admission is an option with a Magic Your Way ticket that includes a Water Park Fun & More add-on and is included with a Premium Annual Pass.

	Adults	Children*
One-Day Ticket	$49	$41
Annual Pass	$100	$81

*3 through 9 years of age; children under 3 free

Daredevil Disney

You've catapulted through the galaxy on Space Mountain, survived the role of crash dummy on Test Track, and become something of a human yo-yo on the Tower of Terror. Now what? Believe it or not, there are plenty of thrills awaiting you outside the theme park turnstiles. Some of them, such as the wedgie-inducing slides at the water parks, are well known. Others may be lower key, but they're definitely high octane. Here's a rundown of our favorite theme-park-alternative thrill rides.

BALLOONING: Going up! A colorful, tethered, helium balloon known as "Characters in Flight" began lifting guests 400 feet high in the sky in the spring of 2009. Moored to a landing at Downtown Disney West Side, the balloon can accommodate up to 30 guests at a time—treating all to sweeping panoramic views of Walt Disney World and beyond. It operates on a first-come, first-served basis Sunday through Thursday from 10:30 A.M. until 11 P.M. and from 10:30 A.M. until midnight on Friday and Saturday. Adults pay about $18 per flight, while kids (ages 3 through 9) pay about $12. Expect to be airborne for about six minutes. This attraction does not operate during inclement weather.

MOTORBOATING: If you've been to Walt Disney World before, you've no doubt seen folks tooling about in zippy little motorboats. But have you ever actually given one a try? It's an experience we highly recommend.

For starters, the watercraft known as Sea Raycers are indeed speedy. And it's an experience everyone can enjoy (though guests need to be at least 12 years old and at least 5 feet tall to drive). Expect to pay about $35 for a half hour. Be sure to wear a watch, as you're apt to lose track of time. For more info, turn to page 225.

PARASAILING: Even if you've never had the urge to be a human kite, consider giving this a whirl. After a simple lift-off from the back of a boat, you and your parachute gradually climb skyward. Before you know it, you're eye level with the roof of the Contemporary resort hotel. A few peaceful minutes later, the hotel and the nearby Magic Kingdom appear to have shrunk considerably. It's not unlike the illusion of flying over London in Peter Pan's Flight. Only this flight's no illusion: You're really 450 or so feet above it all. And don't worry about the landing. It's as smooth as the trip itself. The attendants simply reel you in for a soft touchdown on the back of the boat.

For information on prices and reservations, turn to page 225.

STOCK CAR RACING: Few people can say they've ridden shotgun in a race car, let alone driven one. And this is the real deal. Whether you do it as a driver or a passenger, the Richard Petty Driving Experience is guaranteed to deliver the adrenaline surge of a lifetime. The track is a bit off the beaten path (though it is close to the Magic Kingdom parking lot), so some Walt Disney World guests fail to notice it. Those who do tend to come back for more.

For the ride-along experience, you'll don a helmet and climb through the window into the passenger seat. Buckle up and . . . you're off! The big challenges here: (1) not obsessing over the speedometer (it may reach 145 mph) and (2) keeping your head straight (the force from the velocity tends to push noggins to the right).

The expert driver will take you inches from the wall and zip in and out of traffic. (Yes, there are other cars on the track at the same time.) If you're in the driver's seat, you'll have an expert driver to follow.

For details on pricing and reservations, turn to page 230.

SURFING: When the sun comes up, so does the surf at Disney's Typhoon Lagoon. On select days, guests can take part in a surf clinic taught by competitive surfers. Instructors control the height of the waves—and they give Mother Nature a run for her money.

If you've never hung ten before, know this: It ain't easy. But once you've managed to get up on a board, it's a blast.

For more information, call 407-939-7873.

WATERSKIING: Florida weather being what it is (hot!), waterskiing (as well as wakeboarding and tubing) never really goes out of season. It's a refreshing way to see the sights of Bay Lake—and a serious workout to boot. Sammy Duvall instructors are on hand to assist. For more information, see page 226.

Fort Wilderness

In a part of the state where campgrounds tend to look like dried pastures—barren and very hot—the Fort Wilderness Resort and Campground, located almost due east of the Contemporary resort, is an anomaly—a forested, 750-acre wonder of tall slash pines, white-flowering bay trees, and ancient cypresses hung with Spanish moss. Seminole Indians once hunted and fished here.

There are nearly 800 campsites arranged in several campground loops (including sites that are big-rig ready). There are more than 400 Wilderness Cabins (which fall into Disney's "moderate" resort category) available for rent, completely furnished and fitted with all the comforts of home. For more information, refer to our *Transportation & Accommodations* chapter.

Scattered throughout the campground loops are sporting facilities, including two tennis courts and many small playgrounds, basketball, tetherball, and volleyball courts. Fort Wilderness has riding stables (with rather mellow horses), two swimming pools, a marina full of boats, a canoe livery, a beach, bikes and golf carts for rent, and a nature trail. Some facilities are available to Fort Wilderness guests only; some are open to all.

There's a pony farm (which offers rides to young guests) and a barn that's home to the horses that pull the Magic Kingdom's Main Street trolleys. The barn houses a small museum that celebrates horses and the cherished role they've played in Disney history.

Two stores—the Settlement Trading Post and the Meadow Trading Post—stock campers' necessities, a limited supply of groceries, and souvenirs. And then there's Pioneer Hall, the home of the Hoop-Dee-Doo Musical Revue dinner show (described in the *Good Meals, Great Times* chapter). This rustic structure (made of white pine shipped from Montana) also houses a popular (and reasonably priced) buffet restaurant and a small lounge area. Mickey's Backyard Barbecue is offered here during busy times of the year.

ARCHERY: It takes a steady hand to hit the bullseye at the Fort Wilderness Archery Experience. After a brief training session led by a skilled guide, participants (ages 6 and up) get to shoot for that coveted bullseye. Cost is about $25. To book the Fort Wilderness Archery experience, call 407-WDW-PLAY (939-7529).

BEACHES AND SWIMMING: The beach on the shore of Bay Lake is a good spot for sunning or snoozing in a hammock. There are also two pools for campers' use. The Meadows Pool complex has a new slide and water play area. Note that the beaches and pools are open to Fort Wilderness guests only. Swimming and wading are not allowed at the beach (due to a naturally occurring bacteria found in many Florida lakes).

BIKE RENTALS: Bikes may be rented at the Bike Barn for trips along the bike paths and roadways of Fort Wilderness—or just for getting around. Bikes cost about $9 per half hour or $22 per day.

BLACKSMITH SHOP: The pleasant fellow who shoes the draft horses that pull trolleys in the Magic Kingdom park is on hand most mornings to answer questions and talk about his job; occasionally, guests may even watch him at work, fitting the big, friendly animals with the special polyurethane-covered, steel-cored horseshoes that are used to protect the animals' hooves. This shop is located at the Tri-Circle-D Ranch.

BOATING: Fort Wilderness is ribboned with tranquil canals that make for delightful canoe trips of one to three hours—or longer if you take fishing gear and elect to wet your line. Canoe rentals are available at the Bike Barn for about $8 per half hour or $12 per hour. For a trip around Bay Lake, zippy little Sea Raycer motorboats, Boston Whaler Montauks, and pontoon boats are available for rent at the marina, at the north end of the campground. (Refer to the *Sports* chapter for details.)

CAMPFIRE SING-A-LONG: Held nightly (weather permitting) near the Meadow Trading Post at the center of the campground, this evening program features Disney movies, a sing-along, and a marshmallow roast. Chip and Dale often put in an appearance. It's open to WDW resort guests only. There is no charge to attend, but marshmallows come with a small fee.

CARRIAGE RIDES: Guests may enjoy a relaxing and intimate carriage ride through the picturesque grounds of Fort Wilderness. The rate for each 25-minute ride is $45.

Small carriages can hold up to 2 adults and a small child. Larger carriages fit 4 adults, or 2 adults and up to 3 small kids. Reservations are a must. Rides are offered nightly. Call 407-WDW-PLAY (939-7529) for information or to make a reservation. Walk-up reservations are sometimes possible. (Ask the driver about buying tickets. If they're available, expect to pay with cash or a Disney Resort ID card. Credit cards are not accepted.) Rides may be canceled due to inclement weather. Cancellations must be made at least 24 hours ahead to avoid paying full price.

Note that guests are picked up in front of Crockett's Tavern at Pioneer Hall. Feel free to bring your own liquid refreshments.

ELECTRIC CART RENTALS: Available at Reception Outpost (about $49 for 24 hours) for sightseeing or transportation. Renters must be at least 18 years old and have a valid driver's license. Reservations are necessary; call 407-824-2742 for reservations and information.

FISHING EXCURSIONS ON BAY LAKE: Walt Disney World's restrictive fishing policy means plenty of angling action—largemouth bass weighing two to eight pounds, mainly—for those who sign up for fishing excursions.

The fee ranges from about $225 to $250 for up to five people for a two-hour excursion (one additional hour is about $100) and includes gear, a guide, and soft drinks; no license is required. The price varies based on time of day, with the early morning trips commanding the highest rate.

Note that all fishing is strictly catch-and-release. Call 407-WDW-BASS (939-2277) for exact times and to make reservations.

FISHING IN THE CANALS: In addition to largemouth bass, catfish and panfish can be caught here as well. Those without their own gear will find cane poles and lures for sale at the trading posts; equipment is also available for rent at the Bike Barn. No license is required. Fort Wilderness resort guests may toss their lines in right from the shore. All Walt Disney World fishing is strictly catch-and-release. For pricing and additional info, visit *www.disneyworldfishing.com*. Fort Wilderness is the only place on Walt Disney World property where canal fishing is allowed.

LAWN MOWER TREE: The remnants of a tree that mysteriously grew around a lawn mower is a Fort Wilderness point of interest worth seeking out. It's just off the path leading to the marina, across the way from the Meadow Trading Post.

PLAYGROUNDS, VOLLEYBALL, TETHER-BALL, AND BASKETBALL COURTS: These are scattered throughout the camping loops. There is no charge to use the courts.

ELECTRICAL WATER PAGEANT: Originally presented for the dedication of the Polynesian Luau dinner show in 1971, this cavalcade of lights is presented nightly on the waters of Bay Lake and the Seven Seas Lagoon. The simple pageant consists of two strings of seven barges, each carrying a 25-foot-tall screen of lights featuring King Neptune and creatures of

the sea. And it's all set to music. The show can be seen from the beach at Fort Wilderness, as well as from the Contemporary, Polynesian, and Grand Floridian resorts. (We've caught it while waiting for the monorail at the Magic Kingdom, too.) Ask for the schedule at your resort's lobby concierge desk.

PONY FARM: This enclave just behind Pioneer Hall is home to some friendly ponies. Pony rides, offered seasonally, are available between 10 A.M. and 5 P.M. for $5. (The pony-ride weight limit is 80 pounds.) The farm is a good place to visit before the Hoop-Dee-Doo Musical Revue.

TENNIS: Two tennis courts are available; play is on a first-come, first-served basis.

TRAIL RIDES: Guided horseback trips depart four times daily from the Trail Blaze Corral and take riders on a leisurely, meandering ride through the Florida wilderness, where it is not uncommon to see birds, deer, and even an occasional alligator. Galloping is not part of the experience, so you don't need riding know-how to sign up. Cost is about $46 per person. No children under age 9 are permitted to ride. There is a weight limit of 250 pounds. Reservations are necessary; call 407-WDW-PLAY (939-7529) up to 180 days in advance.

TRI-CIRCLE-D RANCH: This corner of Fort Wilderness is the place that the world champion Percherons and the draft horses that pull trolleys down Main Street in the Magic Kingdom call home. You may watch them chomping on their food and occasionally see young colts and fillies as well. The Tri-Circle-D insignia above the barn door—two small circles atop a large one with the letter *D* inside—is the WDW brand. The barn is also the site of a museum that pays tribute to horses and their role in Disney history.

WAGON RIDES: The wagon departs from Pioneer Hall at 7 P.M. and 9:30 P.M. and carries guests on a trip through wooded areas near Bay Lake. Each ride lasts about 45 minutes and concludes at Pioneer Hall. Purchase tickets from the wagon ride host: $8 for adults, $5 for children 3 through 9. Kids under 12 must be accompanied by an adult.

On nights when the Magic Kingdom offers a fireworks presentation, Fort Wilderness offers "fireworks wagon rides." These excursions are in addition to those regularly scheduled. Expect fireworks wagon rides to depart at 8:30 P.M. for a 9 P.M. fireworks show. The fireworks are viewed from a distance, but the experience is made special by plugging into the show's audio sound track.

Group wagon rides are available by calling 407-824-2734 (at least 24 hours in advance). The price is about $300 per hour.

WILDERNESS BACK TRAIL ADVENTURE:
A 2-hour "off-road" Segway tour of Fort Wilderness, this experience costs about $85 per person. For details, refer to page 220 or call 407-WDW-TOUR (939-8687).

Essentials

HOW TO GET THERE: From outside the World, take Magic Kingdom Exit 64B off I-4 onto U.S. 192, go through the Magic Kingdom Auto Plaza, and, bearing to your right, follow the Fort Wilderness signs. This is the most expeditious way to go, even for Walt Disney World resort guests.

By WDW Transportation: Buses or boats. Buses can get you just about anywhere, but allow yourself plenty of time—the system, while efficient, is time-consuming.

Boats are also available from Magic Kingdom marinas (about a 30-minute ride) and from the Contemporary and Wilderness Lodge resorts (about a 25-minute ride).

WHERE TO EAT: For a description of the Trail's End restaurant at Fort Wilderness, refer to the *Good Meals, Great Times* chapter.

The Settlement Trading Post, located not far from the beach at the north end of the campground, and the Meadow Trading Post, located near the center of Fort Wilderness, offer a limited supply of food staples. For serious grocery shopping, head to a nearby supermarket. Ask the lobby concierge for directions.

HOT TIP!
Festive, horse-drawn "sleigh rides" may be offered at Ft. Wilderness from Thanksgiving week through December. For details or reservations, call 407-WDW-PLAY.

WDW Spas

For many guests, a day at the theme parks is an exciting test of physical endurance—complete with sprinting (say, from Dumbo to Splash Mountain before that Fastpass time expires), weight lifting (toting tired toddlers), and long-distance hiking (covering more than a mile to reach the American Adventure pavilion from Epcot's front gate—and back again!). Fortunately, there are many ways to rest and rejuvenate weary bones, throbbing feet, and noise-addled noggins. Chief among them is a visit to a soothing spa (ahhhh). There are four such spots on Disney property, open to WDW resort guests and day visitors alike.

Spa Tips

- Reserve treatments far in advance and be sure to confirm all appointments.

- If you'll feel more comfortable with either a male or a female spa therapist, let your preferences be known when you make your reservation. The spas strive to accommodate such requests whenever possible.

- Plan to arrive a few minutes early. That'll give you time to change and relax.

- If you're scheduled for a body treatment, leave all clothes in a locker. Robes (and slippers) are provided.

- Don't forget to remove all jewelry before a treatment. (You can leave it in the safe in your resort room.)

- Bathing suits are optional for the separate men's and women's saunas and whirlpools.

- It's always a good idea to take a quick shower before a treatment—especially if you've been at the beach or running around theme parks beforehand.

- Drink plenty of water after your spa experience. It'll counter any dehydrating effects.

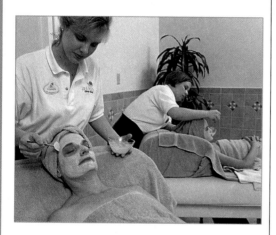

GRAND FLORIDIAN SPA: A short walk from the Grand Floridian Resort, this casual retreat is located right next to the tennis courts. Though hardly plush, the facility's saunas, steam rooms, whirlpools, and even the locker rooms promote pampering. Options include revitalizing aromatherapy baths, a deluxe facial, complete with hand and foot massage, and a cooling lavender body wrap, guaranteed to take the sting out of any sunburn. Other services include aromatherapy and massage (including Swedish, sports, reflexology, and one specially designed for expectant mothers). Manicures, pedicures, and other hand and foot treatments are also available. There is a lineup of kids' treatments, too.

Health club hours are generally from 6 A.M. to 9 P.M., but may vary. Treatment hours are usually 8 A.M. to 8 P.M. daily. Prices start at about $120 for a 50-minute massage and about $130 for a facial. Full- and half-day packages are available. For more information, call 407-824-2332 or visit *www.relaxedyet.com*.

Reservations for the spa are accepted up to one year in advance.

MANDARA SPA AT THE DOLPHIN: As exotic as it is peaceful, this retreat officially pampered its first visitors in 2006. Guests have been stepping up to swap their stress for smiles ever since.

Mandara, which has locations throughout the world, specializes in treatments that are meant to reflect the "beauty, spirit, and traditions of both Eastern and Western cultures." The spa menu showcases Balinese massage, a variation of Swedish massage. It incorporates stretching, "vigorous yet relaxing" movements, and elements of acupressure. Of course, that's just one of many services offered here— all of which emphasize physical wellness and spiritual well-being. Other treatments include the Mandara Four Hand massage, Elemis Aroma Stone Therapy, and Elemis Deep Tissue Muscle massage. The Elemis Visible

Brilliance Facial ($160) is perfect for those dark circles under the eyes while smoothing wrinkles. And the exotic Frangipani Body Nourish Wrap ($220, plus gratuity, for 75 minutes) includes 50 minutes of massage and incorporates a special oil from the rare and fragrant Balinese Frangipani flower.

In addition to Balinese-inspired architecture, two interior gardens provide retreats before guests begin the spa ritual. The goal here is to provide a place for guests to rejuvenate their minds as well as those aching "I can't believe I covered four theme parks in two days!" muscles. For more information, call 800-227-1500 or 407-934-4772, or visit *www.swandolphin.com.*

THE SPA AT DISNEY'S SARATOGA SPRINGS: Terra-cotta colored tiles and teal towels accent this spa's 10 treatment rooms. Signature services include the Adirondack and Mystical Forest massages. Also on tap: aromatherapy, reflexology, sports and Swedish massage and hydrotherapy, plus a variety of body wraps, and scrubs. Manicures, pedicures, and facials are also options. The locker rooms are equipped with a steam room, sauna, and whirlpool.

Located on the shore of Village Lake, the spa is in the Fitness Center at the Saratoga Springs resort. Spa hours are generally from 8 A.M. to 8 P.M. The fitness center is open 6 A.M. to 9 P.M. A 50-minute massage costs about $120, with facials going for about $130 (plus gratuity). Full- and half-day packages are available. For information, call 407-827-4455. Reservations are taken up to one year ahead.

THE SPA AT BUENA VISTA PALACE: A plush, peaceful place, this spa is as well equipped as they come. High-tech chairs with whirlpool foot baths make getting a pedicure a real event. And a cool-mud Theme Park Leg Relief Wrap can put the spring back in the step of even the most labored lower limbs. Landscaped, outdoor whirlpools, plus locker room saunas and steam rooms are there to aid the relaxation process.

Among the more than 75 soothing treatments from which to choose are aromatherapy and massage, including shiatsu, Swedish, deep-tissue, and reflexology. A variety of special facials (including one for sun-stressed skin), scrubs, and wraps are available. A salon offers the usual lineup of services.

The Spa at the Buena Vista Palace hotel is situated opposite the Downtown Disney Marketplace, on Buena Vista Drive. Hours are usually 8 A.M. to 8 P.M., but vary seasonally. A 25-minute massage costs about $70, and facials are about $70. Full- and half-day packages are available, as are custom packages. For information, call 407-827-3200. Reservations are recommended and are accepted up to one year in advance.

Internet Access at WDW

We'll resist the urge to chastise you for insisting on checking your e-mail while on vacation (since we're similarly obsessed) and instead happily report that all Walt Disney World resorts offer in-room, high-speed Internet access. Of course, you'll need to supply the laptop (a connection cable is provided)—and pay $9.95 for each 24-hour period that you choose to use the service.

For those guests who prefer not to be tethered to the wall while exploring the Net, do know that Wi-Fi (wireless fidelity) is a reality at several locations. You can use the service for $4.99 per hour or for $9.95 for 24 hours at a time. As it is not provided by the Walt Disney Company, it will not be billed to your room like most purchases made on Disney property. Instead, you'll pay via the Internet itself, using a credit card. Of course, your computer must be Wi-Fi ready. At press time, the following resorts had areas that offered wireless Internet service: BoardWalk, Contemporary, Coronado Springs, Grand Floridian, Yacht and Beach Club, and the Swan. Note that in-room, high-speed Internet service (with a connection cable) is also available at the Swan and Dolphin.

Finally, if you'd like to access the Internet but prefer not to lug your own computer, simply ask your lobby concierge to direct you to the nearest resort business center. There you can check your e-mail, peruse the news, manage your fantasy sports teams, and more. Fees vary—be sure to inquire before you start surfing.

Just For Kids

Walt Disney World may appeal to the kid in all of us, but some activities are meant for the actual young—not just the young at heart. With the exception of the Princess Tea Party, the following programs are specifically for guests who can't remember life before the Internet. (Grown-ups can relax while their kids are entertained.) The programs are popular and accommodate a limited number of guests—so book early (up to 180 days ahead): 407-WDW-PLAY (939-7529). Note that the adventures listed are not offered every day.

ALBATROSS TREASURE CRUISE: Thar be treasure in Crescent Lake! Kids are invited to follow clues and join in the hunt. The 2-hour quest takes young adventurers to several stops and includes a reading of the "The Legend of the Albatross." The ship weighs anchor at the Yacht Club marina on select mornings at about 9:30 A.M. Cost per child is about $34. It's open to potty-trained guests ages 4–12. Participants should wear socks and sneakers.

BAYOU PIRATE ADVENTURE: Young adventurers sporting bandanas board a pirate vessel at Port Orleans Riverside and learn all about Captain John Lafitte as they follow his map on a quest for booty. Cost per child is about $34. It's open to potty-trained guests ages 4–12 on select mornings. Participants should wear socks and sneakers.

ISLANDS OF THE CARIBBEAN PIRATE CRUISE: Young buccaneers board a battered pirate ship at Caribbean Beach resort and set sail with a seasoned scallywag at the helm. The captain tells tall tales and leads his crew through treacherous waters (okay, so they're not really treacherous) on a hunt for treasure. Cost per child is about $34. It's open to potty-trained guests ages 4–12. Participants should wear socks and sneakers.

MY DISNEY GIRL'S PERFECTLY PRINCESS TEA PARTY: Young regals (and their grown-up guardians) are encouraged to dress like their favorite princess for this festive tea party, offered daily from 10:30 A.M. to noon (except Tuesdays and Saturdays) in the Garden View Lounge at Walt Disney World's Grand Floridian resort. The tea party is hosted by Miss Rose Petal, a magical rose from Aurora's garden that has come to life to lead storytelling, sing-alongs, and a princess parade. Guests may take a break from sipping tea and eating cake to visit with Princess Aurora, aka Sleeping Beauty.

All guests between the ages of 4 and 12 receive a My Disney Girl doll, dressed as Princess Aurora, plus accessories. The cost for one adult and child (ages 4–12) is $250, including gratuity (tax is extra). Each additional child is $165 (plus tax), while an extra adult pays $85 (plus tax). Reservations are required and may be made up to 180 days ahead.

PIRATE ADVENTURE: Ahoy there, mateys! In this adventure, young pirates don red bandanas and hit the high seas in search of treasure. The ship shoves off at the Grand Floridian marina on select mornings. From there, it visits exotic ports of call (other resort marinas), where guests collect valuable treasures and enjoy a light snack. It's available to potty-trained kids ages 4–12 on select mornings. Cost per child is about $34. Reservations are required and are available up to 180 days ahead. Note that participants should wear socks and sneakers.

WONDERLAND TEA PARTY: Fans of Alice and her Wonderland friends will have a blast at this party presented at 1900 Park Fare at Disney's Grand Floridian resort. During the hour-long event, kids make and eat cupcakes. They'll also be treated to a story and have tea with the characters. The cost is about $40 per child, ages 4–12 (potty-trained). The tea party is offered Monday through Friday at 1:30 P.M. Reservations are required and are available 180 days in advance.

Specialty Cruises

At Walt Disney World, every evening ends with a bang—which comes in the form of elaborate pyrotechnic displays. Two such presentations, the Magic Kingdom's Wishes fireworks and Epcot's IllumiNations: Reflections of Earth, are seen by thousands of park-goers on a nightly basis. However, these dazzling displays are also enjoyed by a privileged few, far removed from the hubbub of the theme park crowds, yet close enough to marvel at the subtleties of each brilliant burst. These are the guests who chose to book a boat for a specialty cruise. This vintage vantage point is available to everyone, provided that the rates don't break the budget and that reservations are made in advance. Of course, there is the other extreme: a peaceful, moonlit cruise on the quiet waterways of the World. This option is also available to guests who book a specialty cruise.

Reservations are accepted up to 24 hours ahead; advance reservations, accepted up to 180 days ahead, are strongly recommended. While specifics may change, the following is an indication of what was available at press time.

Wild Africa Trek

A thrilling, 3-hour adventure, the Wild Africa Trek is not for the faint of heart or those with any trepidation about teetering on a rickety rope bridge a mere 10 feet above a congregation of crocodiles—who have been known to leap as much as 8 feet at a time!

The guided tour, which is offered daily at Disney's Animal Kingdom park, is a VIP safari adventure for groups of 12 or less. It includes hiking through jungle, near the edge of a cliff, and over the savanna—plus many up-close encounters of the animal kind.

Available to guests ages 8 and above, the rain-or-shine trek costs $189 per person and includes snacks and a Photopass CD. Park admission is required, but not included. This is an active experience—be sure to wear comfortable shoes and attire. Note that there are no "chicken exits" here. For details, visit *www.disneyworld.com*. To make a reservation, call 407-939-8687.

THE GRAND I: This striking 52-foot Sea Ray yacht escorts up to 18 guests at a time. A private tour of the Seven Seas Lagoon and Bay Lake culminates with a front-row seat for the Magic Kingdom's fireworks, when possible. (The vessel drops anchor in the vicinity of the park entrance, and has an audio feed that allows guests to hear the show's sound track.)

The *Grand I* departs from the Grand Floridian, but stops at the Polynesian, Contemporary, Wilderness Lodge, or Fort Wilderness on request. It costs about $480 per hour to rent, with the per-boatload fee covering up to 18 guests, plus a driver and a deckhand. A 180-minute rental runs about $720. Butler and private dining service is available. Call 407-824-2682 to reserve it.

PONTOON BOATS: More practical than luxurious, Disney's fleet of pontoon boats still deliver a crowd-pleasing cruise experience. The boats, which accommodate up to 10, take guests on tours of the Seven Seas Lagoon and Bay Lake, near the Magic Kingdom, as well as Crescent Lake, near Epcot's World Showcase. Those in the Magic Kingdom area are treated to VIP viewing of the Wishes fireworks show (as well as the audio), while Epcot-area cruisers take in IllumiNations: Reflections of Earth, when available. Larger pontoon boats carry the Wishes sound track—a special treat!

Pontoon cruises last about one hour. Magic Kingdom fireworks excursions (with audio) depart from the Grand Floridian, Polynesian, Contemporary, Wilderness Lodge, and Fort Wilderness marinas. IllumiNations cruises leave from the Yacht Club marina. The cost for cruises (which includes a driver) starts at about $225 to $275 per boatload (higher for fireworks cruises). Call 407-WDW-PLAY (939-7529) for details or to make reservations.

Tours and Programs

Here's your chance to experience Walt Disney World from the inside out. Adult guests may be required to carry a photo ID when attending backstage programs. Tours and prices (which include tax) are subject to change; for information or to make reservations, call 407-WDW-TOUR (939-8687) between 8 A.M. and 8 P.M. (daily) and have your credit card handy. Photography is not permitted while in "backstage" areas of Walt Disney World. **Note:** Tours marked with an asterisk (*) may be included with the Magic Your Way Premium Package, though restrictions may apply. Prices quoted do not include tax.

AROUND THE WORLD AT EPCOT* (daily; 7:45, 8:30, 9, and 9:30 A.M.): A 2-hour tour around the World Showcase Lagoon with a twist. Instead of using your feet, you'll take in the sights from a Segway Human Transporter (a personal transportation device). The minimum age is 16; the maximum weight is 250 pounds; minimum weight is 100 pounds. Minors must get a signature of a parent or guardian. Cost is about $99, plus park admission. Tours start at the Guest Relations lobby inside the main entrance. Guests should arrive 15 minutes early.

BACKSTAGE MAGIC (Monday through Friday; 9 A.M.): This is one of Walt Disney World's best programs. Highlighting the nearly 8-hour exploration of the Magic Kingdom, Disney's Hollywood Studios, and Epcot may be an underground tour of the Magic Kingdom's

Utilidors—Disney's tunnel system. Lunch is included, as are a few surprises. Cost is $224. Park admission is not required or included. This is a very popular tour—book in advance.

BACKSTAGE SAFARI* (Monday, Wednesday, Thursday, Friday; 8:30 A.M. and 1 P.M.): This 3-hour tour offers guests a look at conservation, animal care, behavioral studies, the Animal Nutrition Center and Veterinary Hospital, plus a special ride on Kilimanjaro Safaris. The cost is $72, plus theme park admission. Guests must be at least 16 years old to participate.

BEHIND THE SEEDS* (daily; every hour between 10:30 A.M. and 4:30 P.M.): An opportunity for guests of all ages to get a closer look at the four greenhouses and fish farm that are part of The Land pavilion at Epcot. During the encounter, guests will have close encounters with insects and plants. A guide shares knowledge of hydroponics growing systems and interesting crops from around the globe. You may have a chance to release some ladybugs or feed the fish. Expect to be on your feet for the full hour of this experience. Cost is $16 per adult, $12 per child (ages 3–9). This tour is best enjoyed by older kids. Reservations may be made in advance or at the tour desk on the lower level of The Land (near the entrance to Soarin').

DISNEY'S FAMILY MAGIC TOUR* (daily; 10 A.M.): Families and friends may join in this 2-hour "scavenger-hunt-style" quest to save the Magic Kingdom. Cost is $34 (it's available to everyone, but recommended for parties with children between the ages of 4 and 12). Magic Kingdom admission is required but is not included.

DIVEQUEST (Tuesday–Thursday; 4:30, 5:30, and 6:30 P.M.; Friday and Saturday; 4:30 and 5:30 P.M.): The highlight of the 2½-hour program is a 40-minute underwater adventure—complete with sharks, turtles, rays, and other fish—in The Seas with Nemo & Friends aquarium. Participants must present proof of current scuba certification. Cost

VIP Tour? Sure!

You may have seen them in the theme parks—those cheery folks in the plaid vests. They are VIP guides, leading guests on customized trips through Walt Disney World.

The point is to minimize the hassle-factor, while maximizing the overall magic component. Though participating in a VIP tour won't necessarily let you cut the line, it may yield some special seating for stage shows and parades. One tour guide can host up to 10 guests at a cost of about $175–$315 per hour. There is a 6-hour minimum. Parties larger than 10 will require a second guide. Make your needs known when you book the tour. Cancellations must be made at least 48 hours in advance to avoid a fee. Call 407-560-4033 for additional information or to make a reservation.

is about $175. Guests ages 10–12 are required to dive with a parent or guardian. Gear is provided. Park admission isn't required or included.

DOLPHINS IN DEPTH (Tuesday–Saturday; 9:45 A.M.): This 3-hour Epcot program (about 30 minutes takes place in the water) teaches guests about dolphin behavior as they interact with the animals and observe researchers and trainers working with them. Cost is about $194. Minimum age is 13. Guests 13–17 must be accompanied by a paying adult. Park admission is not required or included. Wet suits are provided; wear your own swimsuit.

EPCOT SEAS AQUA TOUR (Tuesday–Saturday; 12:30 P.M.): A 2½-hour program (about 30 minutes of which is in the water) that lets guests learn about and interact with

ocean life in The Seas with Nemo & Friends pavilion. First, guests watch a video about sea creatures, then they join them in their habitat using a Supplied-Air Snorkel system. Cost is about $140. Gear is included, as are refreshments, a T-shirt, and a group photo. Guests must wear a bathing suit. Ages 8 and up. Park admission is not required or included.

KEYS TO THE KINGDOM* (daily; 8:30, 9, and 9:30 A.M.): A 5-hour tour that offers an on-site orientation to the history and workings of Walt Disney World's original theme park, the Magic Kingdom. Guests visit an attraction (waiting in the regular attraction line) and take a peek at the Utilidors (the legendary tunnels underneath the park). Cost is about $70, plus theme park admission. Lunch is included. Ages 16 and up.

THE MAGIC BEHIND OUR STEAM TRAINS* (Monday–Saturday; 7:30 A.M.): A 3-hour tour that gives guests an inside look at the Walt Disney World Railroad. In addition to an exploration of Walt Disney's passion for steam trains, guests visit the backstage "roundhouse" where the steam trains are stored and join the opening crew as they prepare for the daily railroad operation in the Magic Kingdom.

Guests must be at least 10 to take the tour. Cost is about $49 per person. Theme park admission is required, but not included.

MICKEY'S MAGICAL MILESTONES* (Monday, Wednesday, Friday; 9 A.M.): A 2-hour celebration of the world's most successful mouse includes visits to Magic Kingdom attractions and locations that retrace his storied career. Tours cost $25 per person (plus park admission). Guests should arrive 15 minutes early and wear their most comfortable walking shoes (expect to cover quite a bit of territory). It's available to everyone, but best enjoyed by guests ages 10 and up.

SIMPLY SEGWAY EXPERIENCE* (daily; 11:30 A.M.): This is a beginner's Segway (Human Transporter) class for guests ages 16 and up. The class includes some training and indoor riding time (at no point will you take the Segway outdoors). The one-hour classroom experience provides guests with helmets and a thorough product overview. Cost is $35 per person. Epcot park admission is required, but not included. Keep in mind that it helps to be physically fit to best enjoy the Segway experience. Guests check in at the Guest Relations lobby, inside Epcot's main entrance.

THE UNDISCOVERED FUTURE WORLD*
(Monday, Wednesday, Friday; 9 A.M.): Walt Disney dreamed about making the world a better place. In this 4-hour tour, guests are taken back to the creation of Epcot and learn about Walt's lofty ambitions and his legacy.

Guests walk to Future World pavilions and learn how each area celebrates humanity's accomplishments and challenges. The goal is to share the vision behind the park.

Cost is $55 per person. Guests must be at least 16 years old to attend this walking program. Park admission is required, but not included.

WANYAMA SAFARI
(daily; 3:45 P.M.): A 3-hour experience that includes a private tour of the animal savannas surrounding Disney's Animal Kingdom Lodge. Following the tour, guests have dinner at Jiko restaurant. (A family-style, multicultural meal.) Guests must be at least 8 years old and staying at Animal Kingdom Lodge. Cost is about $182 per person. (Price includes tax and gratuity.) The Wanyama Safari may be booked up to 180 days in advance. Call 407-939-4755 for more information or to make a reservation.

WILD BY DESIGN*
(Monday, Wednesday–Friday; 8:30 A.M.): A 3-hour experience that invites guests to learn how art, architecture, historical artifacts, and storytelling were combined to create Disney's Animal Kingdom. The tour takes place in the park, not behind the scenes. As guests explore various lands, a guide offers insight into the complexities of caring for wild animals and their habitats.

A light continental breakfast is served at the tour's halfway point. Cost is about $60 per person. Theme park admission is required, but not included. Guests must be at least 14 years old to participate.

WILDERNESS BACK TRAIL ADVENTURE
(Tuesday through Saturday): A 2-hour experience, this adventure lets guests explore the Fort Wilderness area while aboard a Segway personal transporter. (It's a special model with "off-road" type tires.) The first hour is devoted to training (it's not as easy as it looks!), with the second spent exploring with an experienced, storytelling guide. Guests must be at least 16 and in good health. (You'll

be on your feet the whole time, and operating the Segway requires more muscle than one might expect.) Cost is about $90.

YULETIDE FANTASY
(seasonal): A festive 3½-hour experience, this program showcases the way Disney weaves stories and folklore into decorations found in the theme parks and resorts. It offers a unique perspective on how colors, textures, architecture, and illusions help Walt Disney World deck the halls for the holidays.

Cost is about $84 per person. Theme park admission is not included, nor is it required. Guests must be at least 16 years old to participate. All guests must present a photo ID.

Do-it-Yourself Disney Resort

No, you can't get Mickey Mouse or Stitch to call and wake you up after you check out, but you can re-create a bit of the Disney resort experience in your own home. A visit to the Web site *disneyresortcollection.com* allows guests to purchase the same beds, bedding, soaps, clocks, etc., that are used throughout Walt Disney World resorts. They even have Mickey Mouse lamps. The Disney Resort Collection can be accessed by telephone, too: 877-888-8287.

Sports

First-time visitors don't always realize that Disney provides a plethora of sporting opportunities. Within WDW's 40 or so square miles, there are more tennis courts than at most tennis resorts and more holes of championship-caliber golf than at most golf centers, plus so many other diversions—from fishing and biking to boating, swimming, parasailing, and horseback riding—that the quantity and variety are matched by few other vacation destinations.

So while the family golfers are pursuing a perfect swing on one of four first-rate, 18-hole courses, tennis buffs can be wearing themselves out on the courts, sailors can be sailing, water-skiers can be skimming back and forth across powerboat wakes, and anglers can be casting away in hopes of hooking a big bass. Those who prefer to spectate rather than participate can visit a virtual sports mecca at the ESPN Wide World of Sports complex, an enormous, state-of-the-art facility that hosts a staggering array of sporting events, both amateur and professional. And those who prefer the sedate can treat themselves to a soothing spa treatment.

Instruction, as well as guides, drivers, and assorted supervisors, makes every sport as much fun for beginners as for hard-core aficionados. Moreover, the ready accessibility of WDW sporting activities—via an excellent system of public transportation (see *Transportation & Accommodations*)—means that no family member need curtail playtime to chauffeur others around.

Note: *All prices are subject to change.*

WDW Golf

Most people don't immediately think of Walt Disney World when they contemplate a golf vacation. Yet, there are four superb 18-hole courses here: The Magnolia and the Palm are situated across from the Polynesian resort and extend nearly to the borders of the Magic Kingdom. A short drive away are the Lake Buena Vista and Osprey Ridge courses. The former's fairways are framed by Saratoga Springs Resort & Spa and Old Key West resort.

While the original Joe Lee-designed courses (the Palm, Magnolia, and Lake Buena Vista) won't set anyone's knees to knocking in terror from the regular tees, all three are demanding enough to have merited the status of a stop on the PGA Tour tournament trail.

Depending on the tee from which a golfer plays, Disney courses will prove challenging and/or fun, and all are constructed to be especially forgiving for the mid-handicap player.

PALM & MAGNOLIA: The wide-open, tree-dotted Magnolia measures 5,232 yards from the front tees, 6,642 from the middle, and a staggering 7,516 from the back. The Palm is tighter, with more wooded fairways and nine water hazards; it measures 5,311 yards from the front, 6,461 from the middle, and 7,010 from the back. Both courses have received a four-star ("outstanding") rating from *Golf Digest* magazine. The Magnolia and Palm share two driving ranges and putting greens.

Oak Trail: This nine-hole, 2,913-yard layout, a walking course tucked into a corner within the Magnolia, was designed for beginners and junior golfers, but it has some tough holes, including two par 5s.

OSPREY RIDGE: This par-72 course plays from Osprey Ridge Golf Club. The Tom Fazio-designed Osprey Ridge measures 5,402 yards from the front tees, 6,680 from the middle, and 7,101 from the back. It takes guests into

Missing Links

Walt Disney World golf veterans may find themselves scratching their heads while reading this section. Why? One of WDW's championship golf courses is missing! This is not an oversight on our part. In 2007, the Walt Disney Company announced plans to convert the Eagle Pines and Osprey Ridge courses into a "luxury resort and golf community." Said community will include, among other things, a luxury hotel (courtesy of Four Seasons) and an 18-hole championship golf course (Osprey Ridge). Plans were not finalized at press time, but the resort was expected to be completed soon. While the Osprey Ridge course is expected to remain open to guests throughout 2012, Eagle Pines has closed for good. For updates and additional information, go to *www.disneygolf.com*.

remote areas as it winds through wooded landscape near Fort Wilderness. Dramatic contouring puts some tees 20 to 25 feet above the basic grade. There is a driving range and a putting green, too.

LAKE BUENA VISTA COURSE: This Joe Lee design measures 5,194 yards from the front tees, 6,264 from the middle, and 6,749 from the rearmost markers. Among the shortest of the 18-hole, par-72 courses, it has a fair amount of water, and its tree-lined fairways are Disney's narrowest. The course is well suited for beginners but challenges experienced players. A driving range and putting green are available.

Essentials

WHEN TO GO: January through April is peak golfing season. To beat the crowds, play on a Monday or Tuesday, and tee off in the late afternoons. Summer discounts may apply. From May through late September, guests pay as little as $49 after 10 A.M. at Lake Buena Vista and Palm; and $59 at Magnolia after 10 A.M. After 3 P.M., the price drops to $39. Mid-morning and mid-afternoon discounts, as well as Florida resident specials, may be offered. Annual golf memberships are also a possibility.

RESERVATIONS: Call 407-WDW-GOLF (939-4653), or visit *www.disneygolf.com* to confirm rates and to secure tee times. From January through April, morning and early afternoon tee times should be reserved well in advance; starting times after 3 P.M. are often available at the last minute. Guests with confirmed reservations at a WDW-owned-and-operated resort, Swan, Dolphin, or at a resort on Hotel Plaza Boulevard may reserve 90 days ahead and save up to $20 per round. Others may book tee times 60 days ahead. Reservations must be made with a major credit card. Cancellations must be made at least 48 hours ahead to avoid paying in full.

FEES: At the 18-hole courses, greens fees (including a required cart) vary with the course and season. Rates range from about $99 to $169 for day visitors. Rates are generally discounted for guests staying at Disney-owned-and-operated resorts, as well as the resorts on Hotel Plaza Boulevard.

Mid-afternoon rates, known as "twilight rates," may yield steep discounts. Available throughout the year, twilight rates run about $39 to $94.

Cost for adults to play Oak Trail is $38 for 9 holes; juniors (17 and under) pay $20 for 9 holes. Prices include tax and are likely to rise in 2012.

INSTRUCTION: At the Walt Disney World Golf Studio at the Palm and Magnolia, private 45-minute lessons cost $75 for adults and $50 for juniors (up to age 17). Lessons are customized to all levels of experience. Video analysis may be used. Reservations are necessary and may be made up to 120 days in advance; call 407-WDW-GOLF (939-4653).

DRESS: Proper golf attire is required. Collared shirts or golf-style collarless shirts are necessary, and any shorts must be Bermuda length.

EQUIPMENT RENTAL: Equipment can be rented at all courses; club rentals start at about $55, plus tax. Photo ID is required for club rentals. Range balls (about $7 per basket) are among the items available. Guests staying at most Walt Disney World resorts receive complimentary club rental when they purchase a non-discounted round of golf at Disney's Palm, Magnolia, Lake Buena Vista, or Osprey Ridge courses. Also included are range balls and transportation to and from the WDW resort. (Swan and Dolphin are not included in transportation).

HOT TIP!
Single-rider adaptive golf carts and clubhouse accommodations are available for guests with disabilities at all Walt Disney World resort golf courses. Call 407-WDW-GOLF (939-4653) for information.

Tennis, Everyone

No one comes to Walt Disney World strictly for a tennis vacation; it just doesn't exude the country-club ambience of a tennis resort, where everyone is immersed in the game. But the facilities and instruction programs here are extensive enough that such holidays are possible. Certainly, playing a couple of sets of tennis on one of the World's resort courts is a good way to unwind after a morning in a park.

The Grand Floridian Resort and Spa is "center court" for Walt Disney World tennis. It boasts a pair of soft-surface clay courts and a full-service pro shop (stocking tons of tennis-related paraphernalia, but not clothing). Professional programs and clinics are available, as are private or group lessons, seasonal camps, and organized convention-style tournaments for groups. Experienced players may take part in the Play the Professional program. All WDW tennis activities are overseen by M.D. Tennis, Inc.

B.Y.O.R.

Though it may be possible to rent or borrow a tennis racquet at one of Disney's resort courts, we recommend bringing your own equipment. While you're at it, pack a can or two of tennis balls as well. (Even if you can buy these on property, they're likely to be cheaper if purchased in the real world.)

Saratoga Springs Resort & Spa also has two clay courts. All other Walt Disney World tennis is played on hard courts. Yacht and Beach Club share one court; Fort Wilderness, Saratoga Springs, Contemporary's Bay Lake Tower, Animal Kingdom's Kidani Village, and BoardWalk each have two; Old Key West has three; and the Swan and Dolphin share a four-court facility. Tennis courts may be used by guests staying at any Disney-owned-and-operated resort. There is a fee to play at the Grand Floridian. All other courts are free. For information or to make lesson reservations, call 407-621-1991.

Essentials

WHEN TO GO: Courts are often open from 8 A.M. to 7 P.M. daily (hours are seasonal; call ahead for exact times); courts at the Swan and Dolphin are open 24 hours; lighted courts are available at each of them. In February, March, April, June, and July, the courts may endure heavy use, but there is often a lull between noon and 3 P.M., and again from dinnertime until closing time. Weather-wise, January, October, and November are prime months for playing tennis.

Equipment rental is limited at Walt Disney World. Guests should bring their own tennis racquets and balls.

All courts are available on a first-come, first-served basis. During very busy periods, the length of time a single group of players can occupy a court is restricted to two hours on any morning, afternoon, or evening.

DRESS: Tennis whites are appropriate, but not required, for play on Disney's courts. Tennis shoes are a must.

Waters of the World

Boating

Walt Disney World is the home of the country's largest fleet of pleasure boats. Cruising on Bay Lake and the Seven Seas Lagoon can be excellent sport, and a variety of boats are available for rent at WDW resort marinas. Bay Lake excursions originate from the Contemporary, on the lake's western shore; Wilderness Lodge, on the south shore; and Fort Wilderness, which occupies the lake's southeastern shore. The Polynesian and Grand Floridian send boaters out from their marinas on the southern shore of Seven Seas Lagoon. The Caribbean Beach resort leases watercraft for use on its own 45-acre Barefoot Bay. The Yacht and Beach Club, BoardWalk, Swan, and Dolphin share a boating haven in 25-acre Crescent Lake. And marinas at Port Orleans, Old Key West, and the Downtown Disney Marketplace set guests up to cruise the waterways adjoining the 35-acre Village Lake. Guests at Coronado Springs may rent watercraft for use on the 15-acre Lago Dorado (this marina operates seasonally).

To rent, day visitors and resort guests alike must show a driver's license or a valid passport. Rental of certain craft may carry other requirements (described below). Note that no privately owned boats are permitted on any Walt Disney World waters. Also, all prices and times are subject to change.

BOSTON WHALER MONTAUK BOATS:

These 17-foot motorboats are a good choice for relaxing cruises. They accommodate up to six passengers, and may be rented for about $45 per half hour at the Downtown Disney Marketplace, Polynesian, Contemporary, Grand Floridian, Wilderness Lodge, Yacht and Beach Club, Old Key West, Port Orleans, Caribbean Beach, and Fort Wilderness marinas.

CANOEING: A long paddle down the Fort Wilderness canals is such a tranquil way to pass a misty morning that it's hard to remember that the bustle of the Magic Kingdom is not far away. Canoes may be rented at the Bike Barn at Fort Wilderness (about $8 per half hour, $12 per hour). Most excursions last 1–3 hours. Canoes may also be rented at the Caribbean Beach marina. Ocean Kayaks (open-top kayaks) may be rented at La Marina at Coronado Springs (seasonally), Fort Wilderness Bike Barn, and at the marina at Port Orleans Riverside (about $8 per half hour, $12 per hour).

MOTORBOATING: It seems there are always dozens of small boats zipping back and forth across Bay Lake, Seven Seas Lagoon, Lake Buena Vista, Crescent Lake, and Barefoot Bay. These are called Sea Raycers, and they're just as much fun as they look. The boats are so small that a rider feels every bit of speed, and they're quick enough so that a lot of watery terrain can be covered in a half-hour period (for about $35).

Sea Raycers can be rented year-round at the Grand Floridian, Polynesian, Wilderness Lodge, Contemporary, Yacht and Beach Club, Fort Wilderness, Caribbean Beach, Port Orleans Riverside, Old Key West, and Downtown Disney Marketplace marinas. At Coronado Springs, they are available on a seasonal basis. When the weather is warm, lines start to form at about 11 A.M. and hold steady until about 4 P.M. Guests must be at least 12 years old and 5 feet tall to rent Sea Raycer boats. Kids under the minimum age and height may ride as passengers, but they're not allowed to drive. We suggest that drivers wear a waterproof watch—it's amazing how the time flies!

PARASAILING: Excursions are offered at the Contemporary resort marina. Each 8- to 10-minute flight costs about $95 for one person to soar to 450 feet and $130 to rise to 600 feet, $170 for two to ride tandem at 450 feet and $195 for two to hit a height of 600 feet. Reservations must be made at least 24 hours in advance and may be made up to a year ahead; visit *www.sammyduvall.com*, or call 407-939-0754. Same-day walk-ups are accepted on a first-come, first-served basis. Guests younger than 18 must have an adult present.

PEDAL BOATS: These craft rent for about $7 per half hour or $11 per hour at the Caribbean Beach, Coronado Springs (seasonally), Old Key West, and Swan and Dolphin marinas. Watercraft are available to all guests at these locations. Hydro Bikes (boats resembling bicycles affixed to pontoons) may be rented at the Swan and Dolphin marina when it isn't too windy; single-bike units cost about $8 per half hour at each location; doubles, about $16 per half hour.

PERSONAL WATERCRAFT AND GUIDED EXCURSIONS: Three-seat personal Jet Ski-style watercraft are available for rent at Sammy Duvall's Watersports Center at the Contemporary resort. Hours to rent are 9 A.M. to 5 P.M. The cost is about $80 (plus tax) for a half hour, $135 (plus tax) for an hour for up to three passengers (of any age). The maximum weight total per vehicle is 400 pounds. Participants must be at least 16 years old to drive. Guests under age 18 must have an adult sign a waiver prior to the trip.

It's also possible to start the day with a guided excursion aboard a 3-seat personal watercraft. Departing daily at 9 A.M. from the Contemporary resort marina, a guide will call attention to points of interest on and around Bay Lake and the Seven Seas Lagoon. At the end of the tour, guests have time to ride on their own, under the guide's supervision. A maximum of four rental units operate during each excursion. Cost is about $135 (plus tax) for up to 3 people. For information or to make reservations, visit *www.sammyduvall.com*; 407-939-0754.

PONTOON BOATS: Motorized, canopied platforms on pontoons are perfect for families, inexperienced boaters, and visitors more interested in serenity than in thrills. Available at most resort marinas, the 21-foot craft hold up to ten adults and cost about $48 per half hour. Guests must be at least 18 years old to rent a pontoon boat.

SAILBOATS: The running room and usually reliable winds of Bay Lake and Seven Seas Lagoon make for good sailing, and the Polynesian marina rents a variety of craft so that guests might get a little wind in their sails on the 600-acre expanse. The Caribbean Beach resort rents sailboats from its marina, too. Various types of sailboats are available; models accommodate two to six people and rent for about $22 per hour.

WATERSKIING, WAKEBOARDING, AND TUBING: Ski boats with Sammy Duvall instructors and equipment are available at the Contemporary resort marina. Watercraft may be reserved here, too. Reservations must be made at least 24 hours in advance and may be made up to a year ahead of time. Same-day walk-ups are accepted on a first-come, first-served basis; call 407-939-0754, or visit *www.sammyduvall.com* for pricing and to make reservations.

Fishing

The 70,000 bass with which Bay Lake was stocked in the mid-1960s have grown and multiplied as a result of WDW's restrictive fishing policy. (It's strictly catch-and-release.) No angling is permitted on Bay Lake or the Seven Seas Lagoon, except on the guided fishing expeditions. Largemouth bass weighing two to eight pounds are the most common catch.

Fishing excursions are presented by BASS, the world's largest fishing organization. Guests who participate in a Walt Disney World excursion receive a one-year BASS membership, which includes 11 issues of *Bassmaster Magazine*, a membership pack with a membership card, decal, member handbook, eligibility to compete in national events, discounts, and other benefits.

Excursions depart from the marinas daily (call 407-WDW-BASS [939-2277], or visit *www.disneyworldfishing.com* for exact times and prices); five people can be accommodated on a trip. The trip lasts two or four hours and includes guide, gear, and refreshments (coffee and soft drinks). Guides will pick up guests at the Contemporary, Grand Floridian, Polynesian, Fort Wilderness, and Wilderness Lodge resort marinas.

Other trips depart from Downtown Disney Marketplace marina at 7 A.M., 10 A.M., and 1:30 P.M. for fishing on Lake Buena Vista and adjoining waterways. Guides will also pick up guests at Old Key West, Saratoga Springs, and Port Orleans Riverside and French Quarter. Two- and four-hour excursions accommodate up to five anglers and include guide, gear, and refreshments. Kids under 16 must be accompanied by an adult.

Anglers might also consider two-hour tours that depart from the Yacht and Beach Club at 7 A.M., 10 A.M., and 1:30 P.M. All trips accommodate up to five people. Two-hour trips depart the BoardWalk dock at 7 A.M., 10 A.M., and 1:30 P.M. daily. A guide, gear, and refreshments are included.

The Magic Kingdom resorts, Coronado Springs, and Caribbean Beach resorts offer two-hour excursions on Nitro bass boats that accommodate one or two guests. They depart from the resort marinas at 7 A.M., 10 A.M., and 1:30 P.M. daily. The $225 to $270 price includes equipment and a guide.

Reservations for all fishing excursions must be made at least 24 hours in advance and may be made up to 180 days ahead; call 407-WDW-BASS (939-2277).

Fishing on your own—again, strictly catch-and-release—is permitted in the canals at Fort Wilderness. Fort Wilderness guests may toss in lines from any campground canal shore. Fishing licenses are not required. Rods and reels, and cane poles are available for rent at the Fort Wilderness Bike Barn. Bait (in the form of worms) may be purchased.

Swimming

Between Bay Lake and Seven Seas Lagoon, Walt Disney World resort guests have five miles of powdery white-sand beach at their disposal. Although the beaches are strictly for sunbathing and sandcastle construction, swimmers may splash in one of the many pools that come in every shape and size imaginable. Typhoon Lagoon and Blizzard Beach (see *Everything Else in the World*) only add to the fun.

BEACHES: When Walt Disney World was under construction during the mid-1960s, Bay Lake had an 8-foot layer of muck on its bottom. The lake was drained and cleaned, and below the muck, engineers unearthed the pure, white sand that now edges Disney resort shorefronts, most notably at the Contemporary, Grand Floridian, Caribbean Beach, and Fort Wilderness. These four sections of beach, plus the ones at the Polynesian, Wilderness Lodge, Yacht and Beach Club, Coronado Springs, and Swan and Dolphin, make up WDW's sandy areas. They aren't walk-forever strands, but they are long enough that most people don't bother to go to the end. Note that Disney resort beaches are open only to those guests staying at the respective hotels.

POOLS: Walt Disney World resorts have at least one pool apiece. With the exception of the sister resorts (Yacht and Beach Club; Port Orleans French Quarter and Riverside;

All-Star Movies, All-Star Music, and All-Star Sports; and Swan and Dolphin), which share some of their recreational facilities, WDW hotel pools are open only to guests staying at those resorts. This policy was initiated to prevent overcrowding. Note that the pools are heated in winter. Resort guests may borrow life jackets at no cost for the length of their stay at Walt Disney World.

Featuring one pool apiece are the Animal Kingdom Lodge and Port Orleans French Quarter. The Grand Floridian, Contemporary, Polynesian, Fort Wilderness, Wilderness Lodge, and the All-Stars have two pools each. Art of Animation, BoardWalk, and Pop Century feature three pools; Coronado Springs, Old Key West, and Saratoga Springs have four swimming holes each; Port Orleans Riverside has six; and Caribbean Beach has seven. The Yacht and Beach Club resorts have between them three unguarded pools plus a small water park, called Stormalong Bay, that features slides, jets, and a sand-bottomed wading area. Saratoga Springs resort has four pools. The Swan and Dolphin share a lovely, themed grotto pool with a slide, one huge rectangular pool, and a third smaller pool. For descriptions of the themed pools at Walt Disney World resorts, consult the *Transportation & Accommodations* chapter.

There are no diving boards; swimmers in search of a big splash should head to Blizzard Beach or Typhoon Lagoon. Lifeguards are on duty during most daylight hours at the resorts' main pools. The resorts' secondary "quiet" pools are unguarded. In addition, each of the resorts on Hotel Plaza Boulevard has its own pool. Guests must be registered at the hotel to swim in its respective pool.

HOT TIP!
As signs posted along the beaches indicate, swimming is not permitted in any of Walt Disney World's lakes. It's Disney's way of protecting guests from overexposure to naturally occurring bacteria common to lakes in Florida.

ESPN Wide World of Sports Complex

Variety is the name of the game at the ESPN Wide World of Sports complex. The multi-million-dollar complex invites athletes and spectators alike to dive into more than 60 types of sporting experiences. It's a grand slam for die-hard sports fans.

The 220-acre facility—which recently teamed up with ESPN—hosts amateur and professional events in everything from archery to wrestling. The home of many Amateur Athletic Union (AAU) championship events is also the spring training site for Major League Baseball's Atlanta Braves.

Designed as a modern vision of old-time Floridian building styles, the architecture harks back to the days when sports facilities were extensions of their neighborhoods; to that end, there is even a town commons.

The complex includes a baseball stadium; a field house that accommodates basketball, wrestling, and volleyball; a track-and-field complex; tennis courts; and multipurpose fields fit for football, soccer, and more.

A general-admission ticket costs about $15 for adults and $10 for kids ages 3 through 9. Tickets may be purchased at the front gate and allow guests to watch all "nonpremium" events. Guests are only admitted on days when events are scheduled. Tickets to premium events, such as Atlanta Braves spring training games (beginning in late February or early March), may be purchased through Ticketmaster (800-745-3000; or *www.ticketmaster.com*) and include general admission to the complex.

Premium-event tickets may also be purchased at the Wide World of Sports complex box office on the day of an event, depending on availability. Prices vary from event to event. Note that in addition to traditional seats, the baseball stadium has lawn seating. If you purchase lawn tickets, bring something to sit on and get there as early as possible. Prime locations go fast!

Another Sports Complex crowd-pleaser is the interactive Playstation Pavilion, adjacent to the World Wide of Sports Cafe. The cost is $5 for 30 minutes of playtime (all ages).

Essentials

HOW TO GET THERE: Direct bus transportation is available at All-Star, Pop Century, and Caribbean Beach resorts. Other WDW resort guests must take a bus (plan to transfer at a park or Downtown Disney) to one of these resorts. Allow at least an hour for the commute (more if you're attending a premium event). Buses run Thursday through Monday from 5 P.M. until about 11 P.M. The resort buses will also run when events are taking place, starting one hour prior to complex opening time, until 11 P.M. or the time the complex closes (whichever is later). If you are driving, take Exit 65 off I-4 to Victory Way. The complex is between U.S. 192 and Osceola Parkway. Parking is free.

WHERE TO EAT: The big-ticket eatery here is ESPN Wide World of Sports Grill. *(This venue operates on event days and nightly Thursday through Monday 5 P.M. to 10 P.M.)*

There are more than 30 concessions for those seeking a somewhat lighter bite. They offer hot dogs, popcorn, soft drinks, and beer, as well as a few more substantial, yet just as portable, snacks. Note that food and drink may not be brought in from outside.

Touch Base

The Wide World of Sports complex recently teamed up with ESPN. Does that mean changes are a-brewin'? We're guessing yes! Get the scoop by calling 407-939-4263 or visiting *www.disneysports.com*.

More Sporting Fun

BIKING: Pedaling along the rustic pathways and lightly trafficked roads at Fort Wilderness can be a pleasant way to spend a couple of hours. Both areas are spread out, so bicycles are a practical way to get around. Bikes are available for rent year-round at Old Key West, Wilderness Lodge, Port Orleans, Caribbean Beach, BoardWalk, Yacht and Beach Club, and Saratoga Springs. They are available on a seasonal basis at Coronado Springs. The cost is about $10 an hour or $20 per day. Bikes with training wheels or baby seats are available. Helmets are mandatory for guests up to age 16 and may be borrowed for free.

JOGGING: Except from late fall to early spring, the weather is usually much too steamy in Central Florida for jogging. If you run very early in the morning in warm seasons, the heat is somewhat less daunting. The 1.4-mile promenade around the lake at the Caribbean Beach resort is ideal for jogging, as is the three-quarter-mile promenade that surrounds Crescent Lake (a waterway that's bordered by the Swan and Dolphin, Yacht and Beach Club, and Board-Walk resorts), and the nearly mile-long path circling Coronado Springs' Lago Dorado. Fort Wilderness and the Wilderness Lodge share a three-quarter-mile path with exercise stations.

Old Key West also has scenic routes. Courses are all about one mile in length.

MINIATURE GOLF: The Fantasia Gardens Miniature Golf complex, located near the Swan, Dolphin, and BoardWalk resorts, offers players two 18-hole courses themed to the Disney film *Fantasia*. The Fantasia Fairways course offers a difficult layout sure to tantalize serious golfers. It features traditional golf obstacles, such as water hazards, doglegs, and roughs. Don't be fooled by the small size of the course—the challenges are big. (The record for the par-61 course is 47.)

Fantasia Gardens, on the other hand, is all in fun, with clever things (a dancing hippo, xylophone stairs, brooms dumping buckets of water) at every hole. The degree of difficulty varies from hole to hole, but overall this is an easy course to conquer. There are several challenges out there, however. Hole 15, for example, is one of the trickier ones. Here, golfers aim through mini-geysers that randomly squirt water into the air.

Disney's Winter Summerland miniature golf course is a mere stone's throw from the Blizzard Beach water park. Designed as a vacation retreat for Santa and his elves, the two 18-hole courses boast a delightfully festive atmosphere, complete with Christmas carol sound tracks. The sandy-surface course is just a bit more of a challenge than its snowy-surface counterpart.

A round on any course costs about $13 for adults, $11 for kids ages 3 through 9. The second round is half price. Typical playing time is about an hour. Hours are generally 10 A.M. to 11 P.M., but vary seasonally. For information, call 407-WDW-PLAY (939-7529).

SPAS AND HEALTH CLUBS: While some of the fitness centers within Walt Disney World hotels are reserved for guests staying at the resort that houses them, several have open-door policies and are accessible to all WDW resort guests. Health clubs include the Contemporary's Olympiad Fitness Center, Sturdy Branches at Wilderness Lodge,

Zahanati at Animal Kingdom Lodge, La Vida at Coronado Springs, Saratoga Springs Spa & Fitness Center, Muscles & Bustles at Board-Walk, the Health Club at the Grand Floridian, Resort Fitness Center at Old Key West, Ship Shape at the Yacht and Beach Club, and the fitness center at the Swan. Registered guests may use their respective resort's facility for free. Guests not registered in a resort with a health club can use the facilities for a fee. The Contemporary Health Club has strength and cardio equipment and offers massage. Others have more extensive equipment. Ship Shape has a whirlpool and steam room. Muscles & Bustles has a steam room and massage services. La Vida has a tanning bed and massage.

In addition to fitness centers, spas are located at the Grand Floridian Spa & Health Club, the Saratoga Springs Resort & Spa, the Dolphin, and Buena Vista Palace. The Spa at Saratoga Springs has a modern facility with the best lineup of exercise machines on Disney property. There are special spa packages available at each of these resorts.

STOCK CAR RACING: The Richard Petty Driving Experience (RPDE) takes motorsports fans out of the grandstands and into a scene that most can only dream about: behind the wheel of a stock car. The RPDE, located at the Walt Disney World Speedway, near the Magic Kingdom guest parking lot, is a training ground for racer wannabes. It offers several different levels of actual driving experiences.

For the less "driven" daredevils, there is the Riding Experience, which sends guests zooming around the track at blazing speeds while still maintaining their passenger status. No reservations are required for the Riding Experience. Rides begin at 9 A.M. daily. The cost is about $116, plus tax.

The Rookie Experience includes instruction and eight high-speed (up to 145 miles per hour) laps around the one-mile oval track, as well as a warm-up and a cool-down lap. The three-hour program costs about $479, plus tax. Reservations are required.

The King's Experience is a total of 18 laps behind the wheel. Cost is about $904, plus tax. Reservations are required.

The Experience of a Lifetime is a 30-lap program completed over three sessions. Participants work on building speed and establishing a comfortable driving line. The cost is about $1,385, plus tax. Reservations are an absolute must.

The RPDE operates daily year-round. Shuttle transportation is provided from the Transportation and Ticket Center (TTC). Call 800-237-3889, or visit *www.1800bepetty.com* for information and to make reservations. To drive, guests must have a valid license and the ability to drive a stick shift. Prices are subject to change.

TRAIL RIDES: Guided horseback rides into pine woods and palmetto country set off from the front of Fort Wilderness four times daily. This trip is not meant for seasoned gallopers—you can't wander off on your own. The horses have been culled for gentleness, so trips are especially suitable for novices. Cost is about $46 per person for a 45-minute tour. Kids under the age of 9 are not allowed to ride, and there's a weight limit of 250 pounds. (Younger kids can saddle up on ponies at the Fort Wilderness Pony Farm.) Reservations are necessary and can be made up to 180 days ahead by calling 407-WDW-PLAY (939-7529).

VOLLEYBALL & BASKETBALL: Resort volleyball courts are reserved for Walt Disney World resort guests. The Grand Floridian, Yacht and Beach Club, Fort Wilderness, Swan and Dolphin, Coronado Springs, and Old Key West have volleyball courts. Contemporary, Fort Wilderness, Saratoga Springs, Animal Kingdom Lodge (Kidani Village), and Old Key West have basketball hoops.

Good Meals, Great Times

Although fast food is in great supply, it is hardly the entire Walt Disney World dining story. Epcot adds international flavors to the WDW menu. Tempting options at the other theme parks, BoardWalk, and Downtown Disney—not to mention new dining frontiers in the ever-growing brood of WDW resorts—make deciding where to eat a mouth-watering dilemma. Disney's ongoing effort to expand its culinary horizons has certainly been successful, producing prominent palate-pleasers such as California Grill and Artist Point, plus family favorites like Chef Mickey's and Cinderella's Royal Table.

Because there's such a large number and variety of eateries around the World, this chapter presents dining information in two formats. First, we've included an area-by-area rundown—a comprehensive section whose descriptions of food purveyors, including sample menu options, will prove most helpful when you get hungry in a particular part of the World. Second, we've compiled a collection of what we consider to be the best restaurants in a particular category. To select these standouts, we looked at the menu, theme, and overall enjoyability of each restaurant. And, of course, we sampled the food.

Finally, in the chapter's last section, we offer a guide to the varied lounges of the World, along with a briefing on Disney's reservations system and dinner show options—and assurance that great times are destined to follow.

The Restaurants of WDW
In the Magic Kingdom

The lion's share of eateries here in Walt Disney World's first theme park are fast-food spots. These establishments' colorful facades and costumed servers are natural extensions of the fantasy surrounding the park's six distinct "lands." The healthy variety of food available on the fly is a testament to Magic Kingdom visitors' typical preference for a quick bite with no need for firm plans. For those who prefer an all-out meal, the park's handful of table-service restaurants offer fine mealtime escapes.

First Things First

The letters at the end of each entry refer to the meals served there: breakfast (B), lunch (L), dinner (D), or snacks (S).
• When you see a not-so-hidden Mickey (🐭) at the end of an entry, it means that eatery was a Basic Disney Dining Plan* participant at press time (see page 19).
• Eateries in this chapter have been designated inexpensive (under $15), moderate ($15 to $36), expensive ($36 to $60), and very expensive ($60 and up). Prices are based on an adult-sized meal consisting of a beverage, entrée, and either one appetizer, side order, or dessert (not including tax and tip). These classifications are reflected by dollar symbols at the end of each entry (all symbols are defined by the key at the bottom of each page). Note that breakfast and lunch generally cost less.
• All Walt Disney World restaurants and fast-food spots (except some with outside seating or at the Swan and Dolphin resorts) are nonsmoking only. Some restaurants at BoardWalk and Downtown Disney may set aside outdoor sections for smokers.
• Reservations for table-service restaurants (and dinner shows) should be made 180 days in advance; call 407-WDW-DINE (939-3463) or visit www.disneyworld.com/dining/.
  We recommend calling 407-WDW-DINE to confirm all WDW restaurant information.
*Disney Dining Plan locations are subject to change without notice.

Adventureland
Fast Food & Snacks

ALOHA ISLE: This snack stand located near the Swiss Family Treehouse sells refreshing pineapple spears and juice, along with other tropical offerings, including pineapple floats and the especially popular frozen Dole Whip pineapple soft serve. It's a Magic Kingdom classic. **S** $ 🐭

TORTUGA TAVERN: The shady spot, located across from the Pirates of the Caribbean offers light Mexican fare. Expect selections such as a chicken, vegetable, or beef burrito (more of a wrap than a traditional burrito) and taco salad. Kids enjoy the pint-sized quesadilla made especially for junior diners. There is a toppings bar. **L D S** $-$$ 🐭

SUNSHINE TREE TERRACE: Offerings at this snack spot located near The Enchanted Tiki Room include floats with choice of soda, pineapple juice floats, milk shakes, soft serve ice cream cups or cones (chocolate, vanilla, or swirl), orange or raspberry-lemonade slush, chips, and cookies. Cappuccino, espresso, and soft drinks are also available. **S** $

Fantasyland
Table Service

CINDERELLA'S ROYAL TABLE: Good news: Cinderella is now in the house for breakfast, lunch, and dinner! She greets guests (and poses for photos) in the lobby for every meal. Disney princesses mingle with guests in the dining room throughout the day for Fairytale Dining at Cinderella's Royal Table.
  Hostesses at this festive establishment wear Renaissance-inspired garb and address guests as "my lady" or "my lord." The hall itself is high-ceilinged and as majestic as the old mead hall it is designed to represent. Its second-story setting offers a pleasantly peaceful view of Fantasyland. Decor tends to royal blues and

purples, with tapestry-backed chairs.

At lunch and dinner, guests of the princess dine on menu items such as herb-crusted pork, beef tenderloin, grilled pork chop, or braised cobia. The all-inclusive cost for breakfast is about $39 for adults and $26 for kids (ages 3 through 9); lunch is about $42 for adults, $27 for kids; dinner is about $49 for adults, $30 for kids. The price includes a photo package (all parties are invited to pose [as a group] with Cinderella in the lobby). Prices may be higher during peak times of year. Reservations are an absolute must. *A 180-day advance booking is recommended for all meals. Full payment is required at time of booking.*

Cancellations must be made at least 24 hours in advance to get a refund. Cinderella recommends that you arrive a few minutes early. This is an extremely difficult table to reserve—don't get little ones' hopes up until you actually book it. **B L D** **$$$** 🍴

Fast Food & Snacks

ENCHANTED GROVE: A small stand that's a good spot to cool off with a lemonade, lemonade slush, orange juice, or iced cappuccino. The Grove serves muffins, too. **S** **$** 🍴

PINOCCHIO VILLAGE HAUS: Located near It's a Small World (some tables offer a peek at the attraction via sizable picture windows), this is another one of those Magic Kingdom restaurants that seem a lot smaller from the outside than they really are, thanks to a labyrinthine arrangement of a half-dozen rooms decorated with antique cuckoo clocks, oak peasant chairs, and murals depicting characters from Pinocchio's story. The menu offers pizza, Mediterranean salads, Caesar salads, yogurt, fries, chocolate cake, and soft drinks. We like to make a meal of side dishes such as tomato basil soup and breadsticks with pizza sauce. Kids' selections include cheese pizza, mac & cheese, and PB&J sandwiches (which come with a choice of apple sauce, fries, or a cookie, and a soft drink). **L D S** **$-$$** 🍴

THE FRIAR'S NOOK: A walk-up window next to Mrs. Potts', this place sells hot dogs, fries, sandwiches, salads, freshly made potato chips (with toppings such as cheese, bacon, and chili), and snacks such as carrot cake, and apple and caramel dippers. **S** **$** 🍴

Frontierland
Fast Food & Snacks

GOLDEN OAK OUTPOST: In the mood for chicken? Head here. They've got chicken nuggets and fried chicken sandwiches. Also on the menu? Vegetarian flatbreads, fries, cookies, and soft drinks. **L D S** **$** 🍴

PECOS BILL CAFE: Sooner or later, almost every guest passing from Fantasyland into Frontierland—ambling along the banks of the river on their way to Splash Mountain—walks by Pecos Bill Cafe. Cheeseburgers, (excellent) made-to-order veggie burgers, pulled-pork sandwiches, chicken wraps, and salads (Caesar and taco) are the staples. If you'd rather not get fries, let them know when you place your order—you can swap them for apple slices. The excellent fixin's bar (which includes fresh lettuce and tomato, sautéed mushrooms and onions, and pickles) and ample seating make this spot one of the most popular fast-food restaurants in the Magic Kingdom—it's one of our favorites, too. Do take advantage of the express order stations. They'll no doubt save you time in line. **L D S** **$-$$** 🍴

STORYBOOK TREATS: Ice cream gets top billing here. There are soft-serve cones; hot fudge, strawberry shortcake, and brownie sundaes; and shakes and floats. **S** **$** 🍴

Liberty Square
Table Service

LIBERTY TREE TAVERN: At this pillared and porticoed eatery opposite the riverboat landing, the floors are wide oak planks, the wallpaper looks as if it might have come from

🍴 Disney Dining Plan participant at press time

Williamsburg, Virginia, the curtains hang from cloth loops, and the venetian blinds are made of wood. The rooms are chock-full of mementos that might have been found in the homes of Thomas Jefferson, George Washington, and Ben Franklin, and the window glass was made using 18th-century casting methods. Such charming environs make the food served therein seem almost secondary.

The à la carte lunch includes salmon cakes, pot roast, turkey, creamy New England clam chowder, sandwiches, and soups.

Dinner is an all-you-can-eat feast served family-style. *Note that the meal is no longer hosted by Disney characters.* Menu items have included salad, roast turkey breast, carved beef, ham, macaroni and cheese, mashed potatoes, garden vegetables, and stuffing. Dinner costs about $32 for adults and $16 for children ages 3 through 9. Note that some beverages cost extra. Reservations are recommended. **L D** $$–$$$ ♥

Fast Food & Snacks

COLUMBIA HARBOUR HOUSE: A fast-food fish house with a touch of class. Fried fish, fried chicken strips, clam chowder, soup of the day, yogurt, and assorted sandwiches (including tuna salad and a vegetarian option) and salads grace the menu. The food is usually quite good, and there are enough antiques and other knickknacks decking the halls to raise this establishment,

located near the Liberty Square entrance to Fantasyland, well above the ordinary. Model ships, harpoons, nautical instruments, lace tieback curtains, and low-beamed ceilings give the restaurant a homey air. The upstairs dining rooms are particularly charming (and often less crowded). **L D S** $–$$ ♥

SLEEPY HOLLOW: Ice cream cookie sandwiches, ice cream cups, cookies, funnel cakes, Mickey waffles (with various toppings), and other desserts—all made fresh—are the sweets for sale at this snack stand located in The Hall of Presidents' neighborhood, near the Liberty Square bridge. Velvety chicken and wild rice soup is usually on the menu, too. It's pleasant to eat and relax on the nearby brick patio. It has a lovely view of Cinderella Castle. **S** $ ♥

Main Street
Table Service

CRYSTAL PALACE: What's the big draw here? Winnie the Pooh and his pals are here three meals a day. One of the Magic Kingdom's cherished landmarks, this spot takes its architectural cues from a similar structure that once stood in New York, and from San Francisco's Conservatory of Flowers, which still graces that city's Golden Gate Park. The place is spacious, with tables scattered amid a Victorian-style indoor garden, complete with fresh flowers and hanging greenery. Tables in the front look out on flower beds, while those at the east

PHOTO BY JILL SAFRO

Healthier Options

Health-conscious folks need not abandon all restraint for want of suitable sustenance. Walt Disney World recently phased out added trans fats and partially hydrogenated oils from food served in parks and resorts. Most restaurants offer low-fat, low-cholesterol, low-salt, low-carb, and vegetarian entrées. Even fast-food stands feature healthier fare such as fresh salads, grilled chicken sandwiches, fresh fruit, and turkey burgers. The WDW trend toward healthier dining extends to kids' meals, too. They come with a beverage choice of low-fat milk, 100 percent fruit juice or water, and a side dish such as unsweetened applesauce, baby carrots, or fresh fruit.

end have views of a courtyard. The restaurant is located on a pathway at the end of Main Street, U.S.A.

Four topiaries—Winnie the Pooh, Tigger, Eeyore, and Piglet—greet guests at the entrance, a sign of the character presence here. None other than Winnie the Pooh himself and his friends from the Hundred Acre Wood circulate throughout meals.

Offerings vary according to season and available produce. The all-you-can-eat buffet features a full variety of traditional breakfast items every morning; a salad bar, deli bar, pasta dishes, chicken, and fish for lunch; and spit-roasted beef, chicken, pastas, fish, carved meats, and inventive sides for dinner. The evening salad bar, with its grilled vegetables, peel-and-eat shrimp, cold pasta salads, and variety of greens and grains, is first-rate. Kids love the ice cream sundae bar offered at lunch and dinner. Cost for breakfast is about $23 for adults and $13 for children ages 3 through 9; lunch is about $25 for adults and $14 for children; dinner is about $37 for adults and $18 for children. Prices may be higher during peak times of year. Reservations are recommended. **B L D** $$-$$$ 🎭

PLAZA RESTAURANT: This airy, many-windowed establishment, around the corner from the Plaza Ice Cream Parlor, is done up in mirrors with sinuous Art Nouveau frames. The menu offers chef's salads, burgers, and hot and cold sandwiches—plus ice cream, milk shakes, malts, floats, and the biggest sundaes in the Magic Kingdom. Reservations are recommended. **L D S** $$ 🎭

TONY'S TOWN SQUARE: The decor was inspired by Walt Disney's classic feature *Lady and the Tramp* (which can be viewed in the restaurant's waiting area). The terrazzo-style patio offers a fine view of Town Square (though tables there are in limited supply). The lunch menu offers Italian specialties, including *paninis* (sandwiches). Pizzas with selected toppings are good bets. Other staples include Caesar salad, sandwiches, and pasta.

At dinner, select from chicken parmigiana, steak, pork tenderloin, and spaghetti, along with daily specials. For dessert, tempting Italian sweets complement a cup of espresso or cappuccino. Reservations are recommended. **L D** $$$ 🎭

Fast Food & Snacks

CASEY'S CORNER: The small round tables at this old-fashioned red-and-white stop on the west side of Main Street (adjacent to Crystal Palace) spill out onto the sidewalk. Even if you're not a fan of our national pastime, this baseball-themed spot is perfect for ballpark favorites—hot dogs in jumbo sizes, corn dog nuggets, nachos, chili dogs, fries, brownies, soft drinks, and coffee. During daytime hours, a pianist plinks away on the restaurant's white upright. There's also a back room with bleacher seating. (Seats face a screen showing cartoons with a sporting theme.) **L D S** $ 🎭

MAIN STREET BAKERY: If the sight of this old-fashioned storefront doesn't lure you in, the aroma most certainly will. The Main Street Bakery is a pleasant place for a light breakfast, lunch, mid-morning coffee break (they have espresso and cappuccino drinks in addition to straight Nescafe), or mid-afternoon rest stop. Assorted pastries, cakes, and pies are the main temptations. Also offered are pre-made sandwiches, and fresh-baked cookies (chocolate chunk, oatmeal raisin, and sugar). Ice cream cookie sandwiches are "built to order." **B L S** **$** 🐭

PLAZA ICE CREAM PARLOR: Ice cream lovers converge on this corner of the park, which boasts the Magic Kingdom's largest variety of hand-scooped ice cream flavors. Floats and sundaes are served, too. **S** **$** 🐭

Tomorrowland
Fast Food & Snacks

AUNTIE GRAVITY'S GALACTIC GOODIES: This spot located across from the Tomorrowland Speedway (between Merchant of Venus and Mickey's Star Traders) offers refreshing smoothies, soft-serve ice cream, sundaes, floats, juice, and soft drinks. **S** **$** 🐭

COSMIC RAY'S STARLIGHT CAFE: The largest fast-food location in the Magic Kingdom is located directly across from the Tomorrowland Indy Speedway. Three menus are offered at separate sections along the lengthy counter. *Bay 1* serves rotisserie chicken, grilled chicken sandwiches, chicken nuggets, barbecue ribs, and salads; *Bay 2* has cheeseburgers, veggie burgers, and hot dogs; and *Bay 3* offers soups, salads, wraps, and barbecue pork sandwiches. Kosher selections are available.

An Audio-Animatronics lounge lizard known as Sunny Eclipse entertains with songs and jokes in the dining area. **L D S** **$–$$** 🐭

LUNCHING PAD AT ROCKETTOWER PLAZA: Located at the base of the Astro Orbiter in the center of Tomorrowland's concrete plaza, this window offers "gourmet" hot dogs, soda slushies, and soft drinks. **S** **$** 🐭

TOMORROWLAND TERRACE: This sleek spot on the edge of Tomorrowland was not operating at press time, but was scheduled to re-open in 2012. **L D S** **$** 🐭

PHOTO BY JILL SAFRO

Magic Kingdom Mealtime Tips

- The hours from 11:30 A.M. to 2 P.M., and again from about 5 P.M. to 7 P.M., are the mealtime rush hours in Magic Kingdom restaurants. Try to eat earlier or later whenever possible.
- When a fast-food restaurant has more than one service window, don't just amble into the nearest queue. Instead, inspect them all, because, occasionally, the one farthest from an entrance will be wait-free (or nearly so).
- Table-service restaurants offering full-scale meals are usually less crowded at lunch than they are at dinner.
- To avoid queues, eat lunch or dinner at a restaurant that offers reservations—Tony's Town Square, Crystal Palace, or the Plaza Restaurant on Main Street; Liberty Tree Tavern in Liberty Square; or Cinderella's Royal Table in the castle. Restaurant reservations may be made in advance by calling 407-WDW-DINE (939-3463). Check for same-day seating at the individual restaurant or City Hall (as early in the day as possible).
- Consider taking the monorail to the Contemporary, Polynesian, or Grand Floridian to have lunch or dinner in a resort restaurant, and then return to the Magic Kingdom after you eat. (Remember to keep your ticket handy for re-entry to the park.)

GOOD MEALS, GREAT TIMES

In Epcot

The various areas that make up Epcot offer a spectrum of eating options that extends from the usual burgers and fries to mouthwatering international specialties. Future World counts a please-all food court among its fast-food spots, plus two atmospheric table-service restaurants. World Showcase, on the other hand, is characterized by international flavors. Here, the cuisine of each country is served in settings that strive to transport visitors, if just for the duration of their meal. While the abundance of appealing table-service restaurants makes World Showcase a very popular dining destination, the promenade is also ringed with fast-food spots, most of which feature international fare. Reservations are an important part of the Epcot dining equation; call 407-WDW-DINE (939-3463) up to 180 days in advance. Character-hosted meals are offered, too. (For specifics on dining with Disney characters, see page 260–263.)

Future World
Table Service

CORAL REEF (The Seas with Nemo & Friends): Decorated in cool greens and blues to complement its surroundings, this restaurant offers diners a panoramic view of the coral reef through large windows. The windows are eight feet high and more than eight inches thick. The dining room has several tiers, so all guests get a decent view. The menu features fresh fish and shellfish—including seasonal catch, mahi mahi, shrimp, and salmon—prepared in a number of creative ways. Landlubber selections, such as New York strip steak and grilled chicken breast, are also available. The menu may vary seasonally. Reservations are recommended. **L D** **$$$** ♥

GARDEN GRILL (The Land): Sleek, wood-trimmed booths illuminated with brass lamps help to make this a festive eatery. The restaurant itself revolves (very slowly), moving past a mural of giant sunflowers and above scenes of the thunderstorm, sandstorm, prairie, and rainforest featured in the Living with the Land boat ride. The scenes were designed with diners in mind, and provide them with a peek into a farmhouse window that's out of viewing range of the waterborne passengers.

Chip and Dale (and friends) host the nightly character dinner. The menu features rotisserie meats and sustainable fish of the day. Cost is about $35 for adults, $17 for kids. (Prices may be higher during peak times of year.) Beverages and dessert are included. Meals are served family-style (communal platters for the table). There is a special "little gardeners" menu with kid-friendly selections. Note that lunch is no longer served here. Reservations are recommended. **D** **$$–$$$** ♥

Fast Food & Snacks

FOUNTAINVIEW ICE CREAM (Innoventions Plaza): Set beside that drama queen of a water fountain known as Fountain of Nations, this snack spot dispenses hand-scooped ice cream. Single or double scoops come in cups or waffle cones. Ice cream sundaes, floats, and sandwiches are offered, too. Flavors include vanilla, chocolate, strawberry, chocolate chip, chocolate chip cookie dough, dulce de leche, and no-sugar-added butter pecan. **S** **$** ♥

ELECTRIC UMBRELLA (Innoventions Plaza): This large establishment is a good bet when the weather is temperate enough to allow dining at the tables on the terrace outside—or when bound for the World Showcase with finicky eaters in tow. Offerings include Greek salad with chicken, meatball subs, mushroom and blue cheese burgers, fries, and soft drinks. Dessert options include fruit cups, strawberry cheesecake chocolate chip cookies, and no-sugar-added brownies. It's possible to get grapes or carrots instead of fries with some menu selections. **L D S** **$–$$** ♥

SUNSHINE SEASONS (The Land): One of the most interesting of the Future World dining options, this handful of diverse stands

PHOTO BY JILL SAFRO

is on the lower level of the Land pavilion. There is ample seating at tables beneath colorful hot-air balloons. Note that it can be extremely busy at mealtimes, and the dining area gets downright chaotic. Because of the wide variety of foods available here, this is one of the best places in Epcot for a family that can't agree on what to eat—there's bound to be something for everyone.

Sandwich Shop is home of the oak-grilled vegetable flatbread, Reuben panini, and more. The *Soup and Salad Shop*'s creative salads include roasted beet and goat cheese, and seared tuna with sesame rice wine dressing. Three different soups are made fresh daily. *The Grill Shop* features rotisserie chicken and rotisserie pork chop. Rotisserie beef and grilled salmon are also offered. *Wok Shop* serves Mongolian beef with jasmine rice, and noodle bowls such as Thai chili chicken. The *Bakery* offers fresh-made desserts. In addition to the house specialty—Soarin' Crème Brûlée—expect to find brownies, ice cream bars, and other sweet treats. There is also a "grab and go" area that stocks items such as sushi, fruit and cheese plates, salads, ice cream, and other snacks. **B L D S** $-$$ 🐭

World Showcase
Table Service

AKERSHUS ROYAL BANQUET HALL
(Norway): The Norwegian castle of Akershus dominates Oslo's harbor, and is the most impressive of all Norway's medieval fortresses. It is actually half fortress and half palace, and many of its grand halls continue to be used for elaborate state banquets. At Epcot's castle-like Akershus, guests are treated to authentic royal Norwegian cuisine. They also get to dine with royalty—as Disney princesses interact with guests during all meals every day of the week.

If you can't snag a reservation at Cinderella Castle, Akershus' Princess Storybook meals

are a good alternative. An all-inclusive price entitles hungry Epcot guests to enjoy dishes that don't often leave Scandinavia. Included in the family-style sampling of the Norwegian *koldbord* is smoked salmon and seafood, Norwegian cheese, and chilled salads. Norwegian-inspired entrées include seafood, beef, and poultry selections. A kids' menu is available. Dessert and soft drinks are included.

For breakfast, guests enjoy the all-you-can-eat fare (bacon, eggs, potatoes, and other traditional American breakfast selections are brought to your table), while Disney princesses wander about and mingle with guests. Belle, Jasmine, Snow White, Sleeping Beauty, and even Mary Poppins have made appearances. The character appearance schedule varies. Reservations are recommended. A deposit of $10 per person is required for all meals. Breakfast costs about $33 for adults (ages 10 and up) and $20 for kids (ages 3 through 9); lunch is about $35 (adults) and $21 (kids); dinner costs about $40 (adults) and $22 (kids). Prices may be higher during peak seasons. **B L D** $$-$$$ 🐭

BIERGARTEN (Germany): Located at the rear of the St. Georgsplatz in the Germany pavilion, this huge, tiered restaurant is an especially jolly stop on the Epcot world tour. This is partly because of the long tables that encourage a certain togetherness among guests. But equal credit for the *gemütlich* atmosphere must go to the restaurant's lively entertainment.

There are scheduled appearances by traditional Bavarian musicians—each clad in *lederhosen* or *dirndl*—who play accordions, cowbells, a musical saw, and a harp-like stringed instrument known as the "wooden laughter." The entertaining shows take place at scheduled times in the dining room. The schedule is usually posted at the door. Diners are usually invited to join the fun on the dance floor.

The food is hearty and presented as an all-you-can-eat buffet, featuring all sorts of sausages (bratwurst, *Debrizinger, Bauernwurst*), frankfurters, rotisserie chicken, *spaetzle*, assorted cold dishes, potato salad, cucumber salad, and many more German specialties. Because entertainment is intermittent, there's plenty of time to enjoy the pleasant setting. Reservations are highly recommended, particularly during peak seasons (book as early as possible). **L D** $$-$$$ 🐭

BISTRO DE PARIS (France): One flight above Chefs de France, this restaurant evokes the charm of early 20th-century Paris. A traditional bistro menu (created by the same renowned French chefs responsible for the fare at Chefs de France) features such tempting "préludes" as the escargot (snails) and mushroom cassolette; smoked salmon; and tuna tartare.

The entrée menu includes rack of lamb, duck breast, and Maine lobster risotto. There is a four-course tasting menu for $54 per person ($89 with wine-pairing). Be aware that this can be one of the most expensive World Showcase restaurants and there is no kids' menu. Reservations are recommended. **D** $$$$

CHEFS DE FRANCE (France): This charming restaurant has a bright, airy feel, with yellow and cream-colored walls drenched in natural light. It boasts a large glass-enclosed "outside" dining area with a conservatory motif. Behind the restaurant's well-appointed scenes, a team of internationally acclaimed chefs have prepared a tempting nouvelle menu. The menu features fresh ingredients readily available from Florida purveyors. In addition, the restaurant imports as many key ingredients from France as possible.

As you might expect, the fare here is delightfully French, but the foundation of the menu is nouvelle cuisine, which involves lighter sauces using less cream and butter than in some French cooking. Menu items include beef tenderloin, broiled salmon, and lamb. Soups and appetizers, such as onion soup and escargot, are all-day staples. Apple tarts and crème brûlée are dessert specialties of note. Reservations are recommended (book as early as possible). **L D** $$$-$$$$

LE CELLIER STEAKHOUSE (Canada): Boasting a new chef and a new status—Walt Disney World "signature" restaurant—Le Cellier is as popular as ever. Tucked away on the lowest level of the pavilion near Victoria Gardens, this low-ceilinged, lantern-lighted, stone-walled establishment looks a little like the ancient wine cellars for which it is named. It offers a menu of traditional Canadian foods, with hearty sandwiches and salads for lunch. In addition to its signature, succulent steaks, free-range chicken and fresh salmon are among the offerings for dinner. And the cheese soup remains a fan favorite. For menu updates, visit *www.disneyworld.com*. Reservations are recommended. **L D** $$-$$$

MARRAKESH (Morocco): The most savory part of the Morocco pavilion features classic and modern Moroccan cuisine. Waiters are dressed in traditional Moroccan costumes. Menu specialties include roast lamb, chicken brochette, beef shish kebab, and couscous (steamed semolina served with your choice of lamb, chicken, or vegetables). Sampler platters are also available. The tilework was done by Moroccan craftsmen. Belly dancers and musicians entertain diners at lunch and dinner. Reservations are recommended. **L D** $$$

MITSUKOSHI (Japan): A complex of dining and drinking spots, all run by the Japanese firm for which it is named, occupies the second level of the large structure on the west side of the Japan pavilion. There are two options:

The ***Teppan Edo*** eatery aspires to capture the spirit of authentic Japanese cuisine as demonstrated through the culinary feats of Teppan chefs. Reservations are recommended. **L D** $$-$$$

Let 'em Eat Cake!

What could possibly make celebrating a special occasion at Walt Disney World even more special? How about a custom-made, personalized cake? You can have one delivered to just about any table-service eatery on Disney property. Simply call the Cake Hotline (407-827-2253) at least 48 hours in advance to place an order.

If you miss the ordering deadline, don't despair—no one has to go cake-free at Disney World (perish the thought!). Spontaneous cake delivery is possible, provided you request one at the podium when you check in at a restaurant. At meal's end, you will receive a 6-inch non-personalized cake. It'll add about $21, plus tax (and a few more calories), to the total.

Tokyo Dining features sushi and tempura temptations. Reservations are recommended. **LD** $$–$$$ ♥

NINE DRAGONS (China): This stop on Epcot's varied international restaurant tour transports guests to modern China when in the palatial dining room. Meals are presented family-style and allow guests to sample provincial cuisines. A new menu includes starters such as lightly spiced cucumber salad, shrimp summer rolls, chicken dumplings, and a beef flatbread. Entrées offer everything from sweet-and-sour pork to Kung Pao chicken, vegetable stir-fry, five-spiced fish, and a peppery shrimp with spinach noodles. A selection of Chinese teas, beers, and wines is available. The dessert menu features red bean ice cream, ginger cake, and coconut rice pudding. Reservations are recommended. **LD** $$$ ♥

ROSE & CROWN PUB AND DINING ROOM (United Kingdom): The fare here never disappoints. Expect traditional pub fare—that is, exceptional fish and chips and meat pies, as well as hearty entrées such as bangers and mash (sausages with mashed potatoes), steak and fish, vegetarian shepherd's pie, and grilled pork loin. Appetizer-wise, we recommend the smoked Scottish salmon on a crisp potato cake with dill aioli (lunch only) and the Rose & Crown cheese plate. One of the side dishes that makes us happy? Mushy peas! (Sort of a lumpy-but-flavorful pea porridge.) For dessert, there's Scotch whiskey cake, sticky toffee pudding, coffee-flavored trifle, and chocolate torte with Guinness glaze. Bass Ale from England, and Harp lager and Guinness stout from Ireland, are on tap. (They're served cold, in the customary fashion, not at room temperature, as some British guests may prefer.)

The decor is pretty—mainly polished woods, etched glass, and brass accents. In fine weather,

PHOTO BY JILL SAFRO

it's pleasant to lunch under a canopy on the terrace outside and watch the *FriendShip* water taxis cruising across World Showcase Lagoon. On the little island just to the east, the wind ruffles the leaves of the Lombardy poplars, a species of tree that is found along roadsides all over Europe.

As for the pub's architecture, it incorporates three distinct styles. The wall facing the World Showcase promenade is reminiscent of urban establishments popular in Britain since the

Special Requests

All WDW table-service eateries that accept reservations strive to accommodate food allergies and intolerances such as gluten, wheat, shellfish, lactose, peanuts, etc., if requested at least 72 hours in advance. Kosher meals may be requested up to 24 hours in advance at most eateries. Note that 48-hours notice is needed for eateries at the Swan and Dolphin, Yak & Yeti restaurant, and Rainforest Cafe. (Kosher meals are not available at Garden View Afternoon Tea [Grand Floridian], and Epcot's Teppan Edo and Tokyo Dining.) Make your request when booking your table by calling 407-WDW-DINE (939-3463). Note that kosher requests require a credit card guarantee and must be canceled within 24 hours to avoid a penalty.

1890s, while that on the south side evokes London's 17th-century Cheshire Cheese pub, with its brick-walled flagstone terrace, slate roof, and half-timbered exterior. The canal facade, with its stone wall and clay-tile roof, reminds visitors of the charming pubs so common in the English countryside.

The pub section of the Rose & Crown serves such snacks as fresh fruit and cheese plates, and fish and chips—along with all the brews noted above and traditional British mixed drinks, such as shandies (Bass Ale and Sprite), and black and tans (Bass Ale and Guinness stout). The pub is quite popular, so it's often necessary to queue up at the door. Note that the pub section also spills out onto the World Showcase promenade—where the first-come, first-served waterside tables make for a nice spot to sip a drink and, possibly, enjoy some fish and chips from a nearby window. Reservations are not available in the pub areas, but recommended for the adjacent dining room. **L D S** $$$ 🍴

LA HACIENDA DE SAN ANGEL (Mexico): Open for dinner (starting at 4 P.M.), this festive newcomer sits on the shore of World Showcase Lagoon. The menu features starters such as *queso fundido* (warm cheese with poblano pepper and chorizo); a taco trio with rib eye, and traditional black bean soup. Entrées include a mixed grill for two; roasted shrimp in pepper garlic broth, and grilled red snapper with roasted corn and cactus leaves. For dessert, there's chocolate churros, sweet tamales, and fruit empanadas. **D** $$$ 🍴

SAN ANGEL INN (Mexico): The food at this establishment located to the rear of the plaza inside the Mexico pyramid (a corporate cousin of the famous Mexico City restaurant of the same name) may come as a surprise to most visitors. Although the tacos and tortillas and other specialties that usually fall under the broad umbrella of Mexican food are available, the menu also offers a wide variety of more subtly flavored fish, poultry, and meat dishes.

To start, there's *tostadas de jaiba* (fried corn tortillas and shredded crab meat with chipotle mayo, red onions, cilantro, and lime juice) or *sopa azteca* (yummy tortilla soup with avocado, cheese, and pepper). As entrées, the menu offers grilled rib eye with chipotle sauce, scallions, and avocado; *ensalada Mexicana* (greens with grilled chicken, tomatoes, avocado, turnip,

cheese, and cactus strips tossed in a tortilla shell); plus much more. The dinner menu is a bit more elaborate than at lunch. Mexican desserts are largely unfamiliar to many diners, with the possible exception of the custard known as *flan*, but are well worth trying. *Bebidas* (drinks) such as Dos Equis, Sol, and Tecate beer, and margaritas make good

accompaniments. Note that some of the dishes here have a bit of a kick. Oddly enough, this eatery does not offer hot sauce as a condiment. (Though you can buy it just outside the eatery, should you have a hankerin' for heat.) Reservations are recommended. **L D** $$$ 🍴

TUTTO ITALIA (Italy): There's an impressive menu at one of the most popular World Showcase destinations, and the addition of outdoor tables makes it one of the more appealing spots for an Epcot meal (though open doors can raise the temperature of the indoor dining room a bit too high). Traditional starters such as fried calamari, fresh mozzarella with tomatoes and basil, and Caesar salad can actually make a meal in and of themselves. Entrées extend toward fresh pastas—spaghetti, bucatini, tagliatelle, and lasagna. The menu includes fish, pork, and chicken. *Paninis* are offered at lunch. Reservations are recommended. **L D** $$$–$$$$ 🍴

HOT TIP!
Thanks, in part, to the Disney Dining Plan and "Epcot After 4" (an admission pass for locals), World Showcase tends to be exceptionally busy in the evening hours year-round. Reservations for table-service eateries are an absolute must.

VIA NAPOLI (Italy): It was a long time coming (roughly 30 years!), but Epcot's Italy *finally* has a pizza place. Tucked into the back of the pavilion, this welcome addition has a casual atmosphere and seating for 300 (in- and outdoors). In addition to Neapolitan-style pizza made in wood-burning ovens, specialties include pastas, salads, sandwiches, soft drinks, and Italian wine. Reservations are recommended for this eatery. **L D S** $$$ 🐭

Fast Food & Snacks

BOULANGERIE PATISSERIE (France): This bakery and pastry shop in the France pavilion is not hard to find: Just follow the wonderful aroma, then watch the crowds line up to consume the fresh baguettes, croissants, quiches, cheese plates, ham and cheese or turkey sandwiches, cheese tartines, éclairs, fruit tarts, and chocolate mousse. The treats are served under the management of the chefs who operate the popular Chefs de France restaurant not far away. Hint for those who hate to wait: This has become a favorite snack spot among Epcot veterans; your best bet is to stop here as soon as World Showcase opens or during the nightly presentation of IllumiNations. **S** $-$$ 🐭

LA CANTINA DE SAN ANGEL (Mexico): Located just outside the entrance to Mexico's pyramid, this newly refurbished eatery serves hearty chicken and beef tacos (on fresh corn tortillas); nachos topped with cheese, ground beef, black beans, jalapeños, tomatoes, and sour cream; cheese empanadas; handmade guacamole with corn tortilla chips; and *churros con cajeta* (churros with caramel) and *paletas* (fruit popsicles). Beer, frozen margaritas, and soft drinks (including Mexican apple soda) are available. Kids' picks include cheese empanadas and chicken tenders, both served with tortilla chips and fruit. **L D S** $-$$ 🐭

COOL POST (between Germany and China): This is a perfect spot for a refreshing cold drink (soft drinks and beer are served). Frozen beverages, and chocolate and vanilla soft-serve ice cream are also available. The ice cream comes in a waffle cone, as a sundae, or in a float. They have hot dogs, too. **S** $ 🐭

FIFE & DRUM TAVERN (The American Adventure): Located on the promenade, in front of the Liberty Inn, this small brick edifice proffers American favorites. Among the options: turkey legs, pretzels, popcorn, soft-serve ice cream, frozen lemonade, soft drinks, and Sam Adams beer. **L D S** $-$$

KRINGLA BAKERI OG KAFE (Norway): Tucked between the Norway pavilion's wooden church and a cluster of shops, this popular eating spot serves *kringlas*, sweet pretzels reserved for special occasions in Norway; cloudberry horns (flaky pastry filled with cream and tart cloudberries); and *smørbrøds*, sandwiches such as smoked salmon and scrambled eggs, roast beef, and chicken salad. You'll also find exceptionally good soups of the day, as well as tossed salads, berry tarts, strawberry cheesecake, Norwegian school bread, fruit cups, apple danish, rice pudding, and no-sugar-added chocolate mousse. Wine and Carlsburg beer are served. There is a shaded outdoor eating area directly under the grass-thatched roof. **L D S** $-$$ 🐭

LIBERTY INN (The American Adventure): To many visitors from other countries, American food means hot dogs, burgers, chicken nuggets, apple slices and fries—and these are the staples at the Liberty Inn, located to the left of The American Adventure show on the far side of the lagoon. Veggie burgers, salads, assorted sandwiches, iceberg wedge salads, veggie wraps, apple cobblers, and no-sugar-added brownies round out the selections. The veggie burgers are top notch. Liberty Inn is a good destination for kids and unadventurous eaters. There is a kosher option, too. **L D S** $-$$ 🐭

LOTUS BLOSSOM CAFE (China): Adjacent to Yong Feng Shangdian shopping gallery in the China pavilion, this fast-food counter recently underwent an extensive refurbishment. The menu offers orange chicken with steamed rice, beef noodle soup, vegetarian stir fry, shrimp fried rice, Mongolian barbecue beef sandwich, and sesame chicken salad, plus pot stickers, egg rolls, and kid-friendly selections. Unlike most traditional Chinese cooking, the food here is prepared on a flat grill, as opposed to stir-fried. There is a covered outdoor seating area nearby. **L D** $-$$ 🐭

REFRESHMENT PORT (Canada): Another good spot for a quick thirst quencher or a savory snack. Located on the World Showcase promenade, stop here for fries, chicken nuggets, and shakes. **S** $ 🐭

B breakfast **L** lunch **D** dinner **S** snacks $ *under $15* $$ *$15-$36* $$$ *$36-$60* $$$$ *$60 and up*

SOMMERFEST (Germany): Bratwurst sandwiches, frankfurters served on a roll with sauerkraut, soft pretzels, Black Forest cake, apple strudel with vanilla sauce, cheesecake, Schnapps, Jagermeister, and German beer and wine are offered at this covered spot located toward the rear of the pavilion; seating is nearby. (Did you know that *Spätburgunder* means pinot noir?) **L D S** $-$$ 🐭

TANGIERINE CAFE (Morocco): Named for the Moroccan city of Tangier, this casual spot serves lentil salad, hummus, and tabbouleh, as well as meatball platters, Mediterranean "sliders," rotisserie chicken, beef, and lamb presented as sandwiches (served on Moroccan bread), and combination platters (including one of the vegetarian variety). For dessert, there are pastries and baklava. Specialty coffees, frozen drinks, and beer are available, too. **L D S** $-$$ 🐭

YAKITORI HOUSE (Japan): Located in the gardens to the left of the plaza, the restaurant occupies a scaled-down version of the 16th-century Katsura Imperial Summer Palace in Kyoto; sliding screens, lanterns, and kimono-clad servers add to the authentic atmosphere.

Among the fare here is Japanese beef curry (spicy sauce with beef, onions, potatoes, and carrots, served over white rice). That, along with teriyaki chicken (it's basted with soy sauce and sesame oil as it broils), sushi (spicy tuna rolls, plus avocado, cucumber, and crab meat rolls), miso soup, and chicken ginger salad, typify the offerings here. The beverage selection includes sake, plum wine, green tea, beer, and soft drinks. A nearby garden serves as a peaceful respite for those who wish to take a break from the hustle and bustle of a busy Epcot day. And kids dig the koi pond—the fish are enormous! **L D S** $-$$ 🐭

YORKSHIRE COUNTY FISH SHOP (United Kingdom): Located next to the Rose & Crown Pub, this popular walk-up window serves delicious fish and chips, shortbread cookies, beer, and soft drinks. **L D S** $-$$ 🐭

Epcot Mealtime Tips

- The international restaurants of World Showcase offer some of the best dining on the property. Since many of them are very popular, it's a good idea to arrange advance reservations for all table-service restaurants by calling 407-WDW-DINE (939-3463) long before arriving. However, it's important to note that some tables may be available for same-day seating. To make arrangements, head to Guest Relations first thing in the morning or to the kiosk located by the Tip Board in Innoventions Plaza. Meals may also be booked at the individual restaurants.

- Don't dismiss the idea of an early seating if you can get it: A 5 P.M. dinner may not only be welcome, but may provide an opportunity to spend time enjoying the pleasant, more temperate evening hours at Epcot's World Showcase.

- Lunch provides guests with another chance to enjoy the most popular Epcot restaurants. It also has an additional appeal: With reservations for 1 P.M., it's possible to spend some of the busiest hours in the park consuming a pleasant meal while less fortunate visitors are waiting in some of the longest lines of the day.

- If you aren't able to secure reservations for a meal, don't despair. There are satisfying alternatives to a table-service restaurant. Japan has Yakitori House, good for sushi and skewered bits of barbecued chicken. Sample Mexican lunch specialties at La Cantina, on the banks of the lagoon. Be sure to try the smoked salmon sandwiches at Kringla Bakeri og Kafe in Norway, the fish and chips in the United Kingdom, or Germany's bratwurst sandwiches and soft pretzels. Those in need of a quick Chinese food fix should be pleased with the menu at Lotus Blossom Cafe.

- Cravings for conventional fast foods will be satisfied at the Electric Umbrella in Innoventions and at the Liberty Inn in the American Adventure. Sunshine Seasons, in the Land pavilion, offers a bit of everything. However, it can get extremely congested at mealtime rush hours.

- The most unadventurous eaters can still find something pleasing—even in the more exotic restaurants of World Showcase. If you're undecided, ask at Guest Relations to see a booklet describing the menus. Keep in mind that most restaurants have menus for kids.

The eateries at Disney's Hollywood Studios are a breed apart. Some feature decor that returns guests to a bygone era; others recapture memorable moments from the big or small screen. All reprise a beloved part of Hollywood's star-studded heritage. The Studios has five full-service restaurants, whose atmospheres and menus are so distinct they satisfy altogether different moods and whims. Reservations are available for these dining rooms; call 407-WDW-DINE (939-3463). A solid—and fairly diverse—ensemble of fast-food places hits the spot for eaters on the move.

Table Service

50'S PRIME TIME CAFE: The setting is straight out of your favorite classic sitcoms of the 1950s. Each of the plastic-laminate kitchen tables is set under a pull-down lamp, evoking a suburban kitchenette. Televisions around the room broadcast black-and-white clips from favorite fifties comedies (all related to food). Guests are waited on by "Mom" (and other family members) with considerable enthusiasm—they make recommendations and encourage everyone to keep their elbows off the table and clean their plates (*or no dessert!*). These elements alone make this special spot a perennial guest favorite.

Adding to the appeal is the menu, which is packed with "comfort foods." For openers, there's a choice of homemade chicken noodle soup or onion rings. Specialties of the house include meat loaf, served with mashed potatoes and vegetables; fried chicken; and old-fashioned pot roast. There are also Caesar salads and sandwiches. Milk shakes, ice cream sodas, and root beer floats are filling accompaniments. And when you've finished everything on your plate, "Mom" will ask if you'd like dessert. Standouts include s'mores—a graham cracker topped with chocolate and toasted marshmallows (you'll feel like you're at summer camp); sundaes; seasonal cobbler; and no-sugar-added cheesecake topped with whipped cream and strawberry sauce. Kids love this place. Grown-ups tend to enjoy the not-so-subtle reminders to eat their vegetables, too. A full bar is available. Reservations are recommended. **L D** $$–$$$ 🐭

HOLLYWOOD & VINE: The distinctive Art Deco facade ushers guests into a contemporary version of a 1950s diner—all stainless steel with pink accents. An elaborate 42-by-8-foot wall mural depicts notable Hollywood landmarks, including the Disney Studios, Columbia Ranch, and Warner Brothers (back when they were the only film studios in the San Fernando Valley). At the center of the mural is the Carthay Circle Theatre, where *Snow White and the Seven Dwarfs* premiered in 1937.

The buffet breakfast and lunch, known as Disney Junior Play 'N Dine, are character affairs featuring June and Leo from *Little Einsteins*, Special Agent Oso, and Handy Manny. The morning meal includes Mickey waffles, frittatas, fresh fruit, and house-made pastries. Lunch may offer items such as salmon with maple mustard glaze, multigrain pasta with plum tomatoes and mushrooms, and salads. Dinner, which is character-free, features carved meats, peel-and-eat shrimp, and mussels. Some soft drinks are included. Beer and wine are served at an extra cost.

The dinner buffet costs about $31 for adults and $16 for kids. (Prices may be higher during peak times of year.) Reservations are recommended. **B L D** $$–$$$ 🐭

HOLLYWOOD BROWN DERBY: The home of the famous Cobb salad is alive and well. This re-creation of the former Vine Street mainstay is quite faithful, right down to the caricatures (reproduced from the original Derby collection) that cover the walls. Arch gossip queen rivals Louella Parsons and Hedda Hopper (portrayed by convincing actresses) may still be spotted dining here, just as they did in the heyday of the real Brown

PHOTO BY JILL SAFRO

The restaurant is also notable for its hot and cold sandwiches. Selections include smoked turkey sandwiches, reubens, and flame-broiled hamburgers. A recent visit also presented the option of smoked baby back ribs, seared marinated tofu, and shrimp bowtie pasta. There's also a slate of tempting desserts, including peanut butter-chocolate cake, milk shakes, and ice cream sundaes. Reservations are recommended. *Note that some of the movie trailers feature monsters and may frighten little ones.* **LD** $$–$$$ 🐭

Derby. The place is decorated predominantly in teak and mahogany, and the elegant chandeliers and perimeter lamps (shaped like miniature derbies) are reminiscent of those in the original eatery.

The menu features the famed Cobb salad, created by owner Bob Cobb in the 1930s. It's a mixture of ever-so-finely chopped fresh salad greens, tomato, bacon, turkey, egg, blue cheese, and avocado, served with French dressing. Desserts are tempting—particularly the banana white chocolate toffee tower on a cocoa-almond cookie and the legendary grapefruit cake, a Brown Derby institution. The slightly formal atmosphere is not likely to enchant most kids. Reservations are recommended. **LD** $$$ 🐭

MAMA MELROSE'S RISTORANTE ITALIANO:

This quirky Italian restaurant (with a California twist) is located in a warehouse that has been converted into a dining room. Fabulous flatbreads are prepared in a wood-burning oven. The menu also features pasta, grilled tuna, and vegetarian options. Favorite dishes include sirloin steak, oak-grilled pork chop, and sautéed clams and pancetta tossed with spaghetti and white clam sauce. Reservations are recommended. **LD** $$–$$$ 🐭

SCI-FI DINE-IN THEATER:

This 250-seat eatery re-creates a 1950s drive-in theater. The tables are actually flashy, 1950s-era cars, complete with fins and whitewalls. Fiber-optic stars twinkle overhead in the "night sky," and real drive-in theater speakers are mounted beside each car. All the tables face a large screen, where a 45-minute compilation of the best (and worst) of science-fiction trailers and cartoons plays in a continuous loop.

Fast Food & Snacks

ABC COMMISSARY: This restaurant, located near the Chinese Theater, features chicken sandwiches, fried fish, Asian salad, chicken curry, and cheeseburgers. Desserts include chocolate mousse, and no-sugar-added strawberry parfait. There is ample seating, though diners are subjected to never-ending ads for ABC shows. **LDS** $ 🐭

BACKLOT EXPRESS: Designed to resemble the old crafts shops on studio backlots, this spot seems rather authentic. There's a paint shop, stunt hall, sculpture shop, and model shop. The paint shop has paint-speckled floors, chairs, and tables; the prop shop is decked out in car engines, bumpers, and fan belts. There is indoor and outdoor seating. Served here: cheeseburgers, hot dogs, salads, grilled turkey sandwiches, and vegetable *paninis*. For dessert, there's marble cheesecake and no-sugar-added strawberry parfait. **LDS** $ 🐭

DINOSAUR GERTIE'S ICE CREAM OF EXTINCTION: Soft-serve ice cream is Gertie's go-to treat—vanilla, chocolate, or swirl, served in a cup or cone. Also on the menu? Mickey-shaped ice cream bars, and cookies and cream sandwiches. **S** $ 🐭

PHOTO BY JILL SAFRO

MIN AND BILL'S DOCKSIDE DINER: A waterside walk-up window offering sumptuous, incredibly thick shakes (chocolate and vanilla), as well as frankfurters in pretzel rolls, chicken Caesar sandwiches, Italian sausage sandwiches, cookies, chips, coffee, frozen lemonade, soft drinks, and beer. **S** $

STARRING ROLLS CAFE: Baked rolls, fresh fruit, pastries, candy apples, and no-sugar-added desserts are sold at this sweet-smelling shop. This is a good place for a quick breakfast. For lunch, there's ham sandwiches, turkey on focaccia bread, yogurt, and sushi (California, spicy shrimp, and veggie rolls). Soft drinks and wine are served, too. This spot usually closes at 4 P.M. **BLS** $-$$

STUDIO CATERING CO.: Situated next to the Honey, I Shrunk the Kids Movie Set Adventure, the eatery offers Greek salad and a variety of sandwiches, including pressed Tuscan deli-style, pressed turkey club on multigrain bread, grilled veggie sandwich, and chicken Caesar wrap. With a full-service bar attached, it's possible to order just about any refreshing libation under the sun. **S** $-$$

SUNSET RANCH MARKET: Several well-stocked food stands on Sunset Boulevard offer snacking opportunities and quick bites. Umbrellas dot the outdoor seating area. *Rosie's All-American Cafe* specializes in cheeseburgers, chicken strips, and soups. *Catalina Eddie's* offers plain and pepperoni pizzas, plus sandwiches, salads, and chocolate

PHOTO BY JILL SAFRO

cake. Fruit and vegetables, juice, and soft drinks are sold at **Anaheim Produce.** The nearby **Toluca Legs Turkey Co.** offers turkey legs. **Hollywood Scoops** has a selection of creamy treats. And look no farther than **Fairfax Fare** for smoked specialties including ribs, chicken, and brisket, plus salad. **LDS** $

HOT TIP!

Hollywood Brown Derby, Mama Melrose's Ristorante Italiano, and Hollywood & Vine offer a "dinner and a show" combo (lunch is offered seasonally). General admission seating for Fantasmic! is included at no extra cost (though tax, gratuities, and alcoholic beverages carry an additional charge). For pricing information or to make arrangements, call 407-939-3463 and request the Fantasmic dinner package. Note that this package was recently tweaked and no longer offers guaranteed seating for Fantasmic. Guests are advised to arrive at the theater 30–45 minutes before showtime to snag a seat.

PIZZA PLANET: This arcade is located near the Muppets attraction. The centerpiece is a Space Crane, complete with aliens and mechanical grabber. Games line the walls (pay as you play). A good spot for children with endless energy and parents who need to rest their feet. The limited menu includes (kid-friendly) pizzas (cheese, pepperoni, and veggie), meatball subs, salads, cookies, and juice. **LDS** $-$$

Studios Mealtime Tips

- To avoid traffic jams at fast-food spots, consider eating at one of the restaurants that offer advance reservations—Hollywood Brown Derby, 50's Prime Time Cafe, Sci-Fi Dine-In Theater, Hollywood & Vine, or Mama Melrose's Ristorante Italiano. To arrange for reservations in advance, call 407-WDW-DINE (939-3463). To obtain same-day seating, go to the kiosk at Hollywood Junction (on the corner of Hollywood and Sunset) before 1 P.M. or to the restaurant itself.

- The many indoor and outdoor nooks within the Backlot Express seating area are nicely removed from the beaten path; relative quiet can frequently be enjoyed here even during prime mealtimes.

GOOD MEALS, GREAT TIMES

B breakfast **L** lunch **D** dinner **S** snacks $ under $15 $$ $15–$36 $$$ $36–$60 $$$$ $60 and up

In Animal Kingdom

Whether you eat like a bird or more like a horse, you'll have no trouble finding something to sink your teeth into at one of Animal Kingdom's eateries. The emphasis at this theme park is on fast food, though there are several table-service establishments to choose from. The quick-service options cater to carnivores and herbivores alike. Beer, including Safari Amber specialty brew, and wine are served at most restaurants.

Table Service

RAINFOREST CAFE: Like the Oasis, the region of Animal Kingdom that it borders, this cafe is a lush, soothing tropical jungle. Unlike the Oasis, any quiet moment here is merely a calm before the storm—as brief, dramatic thunderstorms occur throughout the day *inside* the restaurant. Gushing waterfalls, twisting tree trunks, and colorful fish add to the ambience. The environmentally conscious cuisine includes items like Planet Earth Pasta and the Plant Sandwich. (The Big Blue Crab Delight (creamy dip loaded with tender crab meat and served with tortilla chips—is an especially satisfying lunchtime appetizer.) There's no net-caught fish on the menu, nor beef from countries that destroy rainforest land to raise cattle.

Note: The restaurant and bar are both accessible from inside and outside the park, so admission to the park isn't necessary to enter. It is located to the left side of Animal Kingdom's entrance plaza. Reservations are recommended for breakfast, lunch, and dinner. **B L D S** $$–$$$ 🐭

TUSKER HOUSE: Harambe village sets the stage for a dining adventure at this top-notch buffet restaurant. (It was converted from a quick-service eatery in November 2007.) Seating inside is quite civilized, with cherry-wood-colored tables and carved chair backs; there's also outdoor seating under the thatched roof for a pre- or post-meal cocktail. Breakfast is a character affair known as Donald's Safari Breakfast. At press time, the characters scheduled to attend were Donald (of course), Daisy, Mickey, and Goofy (the latter three are subject to change). Reservations are highly recommended for all meals. Book breakfast as soon as possible. **B L D S** $$ 🐭

YAK & YETI: One of the few table-service eateries in the park, this place opens daily at 10 A.M. (though it doesn't serve breakfast selections). It specializes in Asian fusion cuisine. Menu items include maple tamarind chicken, crispy mahi mahi, baby back ribs, lo mein, seared miso salmon, and stir-fried beef and broccoli. Among the more tempting dessert options are fried (sweet) wontons and mango pie. Its shop offers everything from sushi plates to fine teapots. You'll find it in Asia across from Kali River Rapids. African beers and specialty drinks are available, too. **L D S** $–$$$ 🐭

Fast Food & Snacks

ANANDAPUR ICE CREAM: Cool off with a soft-serve from Asia's local ice cream truck. The refreshing snack is available by the waffle cone, cup, or in a soda float. Bottled water and a variety of soft drinks (including root beer and light lemonade) are also served. **S** $ 🐭

ANANDAPUR LOCAL FOOD CAFES: Walk-up windows adjacent to the Yak & Yeti restaurant in Asia, the cafes specialize in items with pan-Asian influences. Entrées include sweet-and-sour pork, shrimp lo mein, crispy honey chicken or pork, orange beef, Asian chicken sandwich, chicken fried rice, and Mandarin chicken salad. Egg rolls, chocolate cake, and frozen lemonade are also served. Kids choose from chicken bites or a cheeseburger. There is ample outdoor seating nearby. **L D S** $–$$ 🐭

TRILO-BITES: In DinoLand U.S.A., just inside the entrance, is a kiosk that offers smoked turkey legs, frozen lemonade, bottled water, and a variety of soft drinks throughout the day. **S** $ 🐭

FLAME TREE BARBECUE: This fast-food spot serves up a selection of barbecued sandwiches and platters, all wood-roasted. Sample the mild, tomato-based barbecue sauce or the spicy, mustard-based Carolina-style sauce with your smoked beef brisket, St. Louis ribs, and pulled pork. There's seating along the river. Located on Discovery Island, near DinoLand U.S.A. **L D S** $-$$ ♥

HARAMBE FRUIT MARKET: One healthy choice for snacking at Animal Kingdom is this refreshing fruit stand near the entrance to Kilimanjaro Safaris. Stop here for pineapple bites, fruit cups, whole fruit, bottled water, and more. **S** $

KUSAFIRI COFFEE SHOP & BAKERY: The bakery at Tusker House provides a steady stream of fresh-from-the-oven breakfast treats, yogurt, mixed fruit cup, cookies, brownies, cupcakes, muffins, and other assorted desserts, plus soft drinks, juice, cappuccino, and espresso. **B S** $

PIZZAFARI: Small pizzas are available plain and with pepperoni. Other options: Caesar salad with grilled chicken, antipasto salad, and hot Italian-style sandwiches. Colorful animal murals decorate this counter-service eatery, located on Discovery Island near the bridge to Camp Minnie-Mickey. **B L D S** $-$$ ♥

ROYAL ANANDAPUR TEA COMPANY: This hut dispenses hot and iced Asian teas in the village of Serka Zong. Light snack items round out the menu. **S** $

RESTAURANTOSAURUS: Located deep in the heart of DinoLand U.S.A., this spot is themed as a campsite for student paleontologists. It's filled with fossils, bones, and such; class notes line the walls. This eatery offers fast food at lunch and dinner: burgers, salad, veggie subs, hot dogs—plus chicken nuggets and kids' meals. Note that there is no longer a character breakfast at this eatery (though there is one at Tusker House). In fact, breakfast is no longer served here in any form. Just a heads-up. **L D S** $-$$ ♥

TAMU TAMU REFRESHMENTS: Stop by this spot in Africa's Harambe (across from Tusker House) for a light meal or a quick snack. Here you can get cheeseburgers (on multigrain buns, with apple slices or chips), turkey sandwiches, and tuna salad pitas. Dessert items include milk shakes and chocolate mousse. Soft drinks are also served. There's seating next door. Note that this spot usually opens around 10:30 A.M. **L D S** $ ♥

PHOTO BY JILL SAFRO

Animal Kingdom Mealtime Tips

- Tusker House and Rainforest Cafe are the only table-service places to offer breakfast; a handful of spots, including Pizzafari and Kusafiri Coffee Shop & Bakery, supply light breakfast options.

- At press time, the only restaurants that accepted reservations for all meals were Tusker House and Rainforest Cafe. (Yak & Yeti accepts lunch and dinner reservations.) To arrange for reservations in advance, available up to 180 days ahead for all meals, call 407-WDW-DINE (939-3463). To obtain same-day seating, go straight to the restaurant. We recommend making reservations. Rainforest Cafe may keep longer hours than the Animal Kingdom park.

- The many seating pavilions along the river near Flame Tree Barbecue provide waterside dining that's nicely removed from the hubbub of Discovery Island; it may be relatively calm here, even during prime mealtimes.

- A great place to meet Donald and pals such as Mickey, Daisy, and Goofy is at Tusker House at the daily character breakfast. (Characters appearing at the breakfast are subject to change—though Donald is always in attendance.) Don't forget to make reservations well in advance.

B breakfast **L** lunch **D** dinner **S** snacks $ under $15 $$ $15–$36 $$$ $36–$60 $$$$ $60 and up

In Downtown Disney

The region known as Downtown Disney encompasses the Marketplace, Pleasure Island, and the West Side. Downtown Disney restaurants usually operate from 11 A.M. to midnight; most snack spots are open from 11 A.M. to late into the night. For details, call 407-939-4636. It's worth noting that while the restaurants really hop at dinnertime, they are not overly crowded at lunch (except, possibly, on the weekend). Note that Pleasure Island may get a name change in 2012.

AMC DINE-IN THEATRES (West Side): Popcorn and soda are upstaged by selections such as country fried steak and mango margaritas in this in-theater dining experience known as Fork and Screen. Seat-side, table-top service (with a personal call button for the server), allows movie-goers to enjoy dinner and a movie simultaneously. The extensive menu includes appetizers, entrées, desserts, cocktails, and soft drinks—in addition to traditional movie munchies. Seating is reserved (and assigned when you purchase your movie ticket). Guests under age 18 must be accompanied by an adult. **L D S** $–$$ ❤

BONGOS CUBAN CAFE (West Side): This Gloria Estefan creation spices up the Disney dining repertoire with a menu driven by Cuban and Latin American flavors. Its slate of traditional and nouvelle Cuban dishes, such as black bean soup, plantains, steak topped with onions, and flan, tempts taste buds. Indoors, the elaborate mosaic mural and palm-leaf railings set the scene; the patio for outdoor seating wraps around a three-story pineapple. A take-out window provides snacks on the go. Reservations are not accepted. **L D S** $$–$$$

CAP'N JACK'S RESTAURANT (Marketplace): This pier house juts right out over Village Lake, providing water views. The appetizer menu is so tempting—spinach and artichoke dip, peel-and-eat shrimp, and clam chowder—that it's as good for lunch or dinner as it is for a snack. Entrées extend to pasta dishes and seafood specials. There is a variety of wines, beers, and other cocktails—and the house's special frozen margaritas are tasty. Cap'n Jack's is a nice place to chill out, especially in late afternoon, as the sun streams through the blinds and glints on the polished copper above the bar. Reservations are recommended. **L D S** $$–$$$ ❤

COOKE'S OF DUBLIN (Pleasure Island): Raglan Road's quick-service neighbor, this is the place to go for some of the freshest, most succulent fish and chips in the World. And don't ask for the recipe—it's a Cooke family secret! Other choices include battered chicken served on a skewer, beef and lamb pie, battered mini sausage, and smoked haddock pie. Save room for a fried candy bar dessert. **L D S** $$–$$$ ❤

EARL OF SANDWICH (Marketplace): The decor of this spot reflects the history of the sandwich and the family that is credited with its creation. It specializes in high-end deli cuisine, with hot and cold freshly prepared sandwiches. Breakfast sandwiches are available, too. Snacks such as ice cream sandwiches, cookies, brownies, and scones are options. Drink selections include sodas, smoothies, juices, teas, beer, and lemonade. **B L D S** $–$$ ❤

FULTON'S CRAB HOUSE (Pleasure Island): This traditional seafood house, operated by Levy Restaurants, occupies the three-deck riverboat formerly known as the *Empress Lilly*. Permanently docked on the western

PHOTO BY JILL SAFRO

edge of Village Lake (across from Saratoga Springs Resort & Spa), it is a tribute to Robert Fulton, who invented the steamboat. The place is so serious about seafood that it has hooked up with fishermen worldwide to ensure that the fish arriving daily are at their freshest.

The menu changes each day to reflect new arrivals, but is always filled with several types of crabs, oysters, and fish, plus lobster, steaks, grilled chicken, grilled vegetables, and combo platters. Signature dishes include cioppino, a savory seafood stew with a tomato broth base. Accompaniments extend to corn-whipped potatoes and grilled asparagus. Desserts, coffee, and specialty drinks are also served.

The adjoining Stone Crab Lounge has an excellent raw bar—the perfect place for lunch. Seating on the outdoor deck is sometimes available. Reservations are recommended for lunch and dinner at Fulton's. Reservations are not available at the Stone Crab Lounge. **L D S** $$$–$$$$

GHIRARDELLI SODA FOUNTAIN (Marketplace): San Francisco's famous sweet-maker finally comes east with a soda fountain extraordinaire. Stop in for a chocolatey treat, root beer float, or refreshing malt. Antique chocolate-making equipment demonstrates how the famous Ghirardelli chocolate got its start. There's no better place to please a sweet tooth. (And there's always the possibility of a free sample.) The coffee is tops, too—both the hot and iced varieties. **S** $–$$

> **HOT TIP!**
>
> Hungry for more information about WDW dining? If so, we highly (and immodestly) recommend *Birnbaum's Guide to Walt Disney World Dining 2012*.

HOUSE OF BLUES (West Side): The nightclub that Blues Brother Dan Aykroyd helped launch doubles as a Mississippi Delta-inspired dining spot. House of Blues gives Downtown Disney a culinary boost from the bayou—namely, home-style Cajun and Creole cooking. Finally, Walt Disney World has a haven for diners desperately seeking their fill of such savory things as jambalaya, étouffée, and homemade bread pudding. A gospel brunch is presented on Sundays. Reservations are recommended. **L D S** $$–$$$

PLANET HOLLYWOOD (West Side): This branch of the famed restaurant chain is a standout for its spherical silhouette. Built on three levels, this colossal globe is packed with classic movie and television memorabilia.

The creative, wide-ranging menu features first-rate salads, sandwiches, pasta dishes, burgers, appetizer pizzas, fajitas, and dessert specialties. Be sure to consider sampling the blackened shrimp, Far East chicken salad, or pasta primavera. Cap off the meal with a piece of butter rum cake. Reservations are recommended. **L D S** $$–$$$

PARADISO 37 (Pleasure Island): This lively, waterfront eatery specializes in "mangled margaritas," stocks 37 kinds of tequila, and offers the "coldest beer in the world." And they serve food, too!

The menu focuses on "street foods" of the Americas. Starters include the signature fire-roasted corn on the cob with a mild pepper sauce and cheese, mac and cheese bites, and potato pancakes. Entrées range from Argentinian skirt steak with chimichurri sauce to Chilean-style salmon, and prickly pear shrimp salad. **L D S** $$–$$$

POLLO CAMPERO (Marketplace): This wing of the international quick-service restaurant chain landed here in late 2010. Featuring fast food with a Latin flair, expect (of course) chicken, plus items such as yuca fries, sweet plantains, as well as traditional Latin soft drinks known as *horchata* and *tamarindo*. Also here is Fresh A-Peel, a counter offering all-natural burgers, salads, and wraps; and Babycakes NYC, a bake shop featuring gluten-free treats. **L D S** $–$$

PORTOBELLO (Pleasure Island): The "yacht club" decor has disappeared and this longtime favorite has been transformed into an Italian trattoria, with warm colors that match the rustic cuisine. The best seats are on the waterfront porch (when the weather cooperates), but the indoor dining spaces have much to offer. Traditional Italian cuisine includes mix-and-match antipasti, pastas, hand-crafted sausage, and fresh fish. And the wood-burning oven pizzas are a popular choice that never disappoint. At lunchtime, the menu includes sandwiches such as pesto-marinated chicken with fontina cheese, warm from the oven. For dinner, we love the ravioli gigante, filled with ricotta and spinach with tomato, basil, and toasted garlic. The full bar offers a solid wine list of Italian favorites (plus wines from other countries), cocktails, and beer. For dessert, it's tough to resist the tiramisu. **LDS** $$$

RAGLAN ROAD (Pleasure Island): As authentically Irish as you can get on this side of the Atlantic, this warm and lively establishment blends fresh ingredients to create traditional Irish fare with a modern flair. The menu comes courtesy of Kevin Dundon, one of Ireland's best-known chefs. His selections are perfectly complemented by the welcoming atmosphere, complete with antiques and bric-a-brac, free-flowing spirits, and live entertainment. Reservations are accepted for lunch and dinner. **LDS** $$–$$ 🐭

RAINFOREST CAFE (Marketplace): There's no mistaking the environmental orientation of this Amazon-emulating eatery. The atmospheric dining environs transport guests to a makeshift rainforest, complete with banyan trees, tropical fish, gushing waterfalls, and a friendly population of hand-raised parrots. A talking tree offers a constant stream of ecological insights, and animal experts are on hand to field questions.

Sophisticated special effects envelop guests in tropical storms, complete with lightning and thunder. Menu items include Planet Earth Pasta, Island Hopper Chicken, and the Plant Sandwich (portobello mushrooms, zucchini, roasted red peppers, and fresh spinach). A merchandise shop stocks logo clothing. Reservations are recommended. **BLDS** $$–$$$

T-REX: A PREHISTORIC FAMILY ADVENTURE (Marketplace): The atmosphere of this restaurant—complete with lifelike dinosaurs, waterfalls, bubbling geysers, and fossil dig site—is as family-friendly as they come. So is the fare. The menu extends from Jurassic Salad and Bronto Burgers to Primitive Pork Shank and Meteor Bites. With soup, sandwiches, pasta, seafood, steaks, and scrumptious smoothies, this place aims to please everyone—and usually succeeds. Oh, and your dino hosts? They hail from the Mesozoic era. You'll find the T-Rex eatery near the Lego store at Downtown Disney Marketplace. **LD** $$–$$$

WETZEL'S PRETZELS (Marketplace and West Side): Whether you prefer pretzels on the salty or sweet side, Wetzel's has something to satisfy. Snackers enjoy the Mexicali, the Sinful Cinnamon, and the Three-Cheese varieties. Ice cream is available, too. **S** $

WOLFGANG PUCK CAFE (West Side): Among Wolfgang's specialties are gourmet pizzas, Thai chicken satay pastas with fresh vegetables, Chinois chicken salad, and rotisserie chicken. The menu is equal parts sophisticated and straightforward—and ever so fresh. There's also an excellent sushi bar. Colorful mosaics decorate his restaurants. Reservations are recommended. **LDS** $$$ 🐭

WOLFGANG PUCK CAFE—THE DINING ROOM (West Side): The formal upstairs area in the cafe is devoted to the more elaborate of Wolfgang Puck's cuisine. Consider sampling the shrimp scampi risotto and Chinois-style lamb rack with Hunan-style eggplant stir fry. Reservations are required. **D** $$$–$$$$

WOLFGANG PUCK EXPRESS (Marketplace and West Side): Renowned chef Wolfgang Puck turns his talents to fast service and signature treats, including wood-fired pizzas, rotisserie chicken, soups, focaccia sandwiches, and fresh salads—including his famous Chinois chicken salad. The coffee here gets a big thumbs up. **LDS** $–$$ 🐭

In the WDW Resorts

Among the more pleasant surprises at Walt Disney World is the elaborate theming of the Disney hotels. Each resort sports a fanciful setting quite foreign to Central Florida, reminiscent of such places as the Pacific Northwest; the more regional-minded offer a tasty sampling of the native cuisine to complete the picture. Whereas the deluxe properties provide a variety of dining options, including at least one full-service restaurant, moderate resorts may feature a food court plus a restaurant, and the value-oriented All-Star resorts keep guests' appetites in check with food courts.

Reservations are an important part of the full-service dining circuit (call 407-WDW-DINE). Character meals are an option for breakfast, Sunday brunch, lunch, and dinner (see page 260).

All-Star Resorts

Each of these resorts features a food court. The **End Zone** food court in Stadium Hall at the All-Star Sports resort, the **Intermission** food court in Melody Hall at the All-Star Music resort, and the **World Premiere** food court in Cinema Hall at the All-Star Movies resort have similar offerings. The selections include pasta, pizza, burgers, hot dogs, sandwiches, salads, ice cream, a variety of breakfast and baked goods, plus "grab and go" selections. **B L D S** $-$$ 🐭

Animal Kingdom Lodge

BOMA—FLAVORS OF AFRICA: Big and bustling, this eatery, designed to resemble an African marketplace, has excellent buffet fare from more than 50 African countries. Breakfast features omelets, cereals, brioche, fresh fruit, sausage, biscuits, ham, corned beef, and more. At dinner, expect to fill your plate with items such as salads (including watermelon rind salad and Moroccan seafood salad), authentic African breads, soups, and stews; grilled seafood, roasted meats, couscous, and an array of vegetarian selections. For dessert, do try the decadent zebra domes—you'll regret it if you don't. Reservations are required. **B D** $$ 🐭

JIKO—THE COOKING PLACE: This sophisticated spot, which is awash in colors of a sunset, features excellent, familiar food with an African touch—seafood, steak, chicken, and

vegetarian offerings infused with the vibrant flavors and fragrant spices of Africa. The wine list is comprised of South African vintages. Reservations are required. **D** $$$-$$$$ 🐭

THE MARA: An enormous fast-food restaurant that has something for just about everyone—including a "grab and go" section for those in a hurry. **B L D S** $-$$ 🐭

SANAA: The name, pronounced *sa-NAH*, means "artwork" in Swahili, and this new 150-seat restaurant features a colorful dining room that overlooks the savanna. Animals can wander to within 20 feet of the floor-to-ceiling windows. Talk about dinner and a show! The family-friendly menu features Disney's take on African-Indian cuisine with signature dishes such as chicken, shrimp, or lamb chops slow-cooked in tandoor ovens. A full bar offers

PHOTO BY MIKE CARROLL

beer, wine, and cocktails. This stylish spot is located in the Kidani Village section of the resort. Reservations are recommended. **L D** $$-$$$ 🐭

BoardWalk

BELLE VUE LOUNGE: This cozy cocktail spot, located on the resort's second floor, offers continental breakfast each morning. **B** $ 🐭

BIG RIVER GRILLE & BREWING WORKS: Guests observe (and later sample) as the brewmaster creates three flagship ales and two seasonal brews at this working brew pub. The menu features a selection of (impressive) sandwiches and salads, plus variations on pub favorites, such as flame-grilled meatloaf. **L D S** $$-$$$ 🐭

BOARDWALK BAKERY: The aromas wafting from Kouzzina's next-door neighbor on the boardwalk reveal the fresh-baked goods therein. Display windows allow guests to watch bakers at work. **B S** $ 🐭

ESPN CLUB: A sports bar/family restaurant one-two punch, ESPN Club surrounds guests with no fewer than 100 TV monitors, so no one misses a play. The standard, reliable fare includes wings, burgers, sandwiches, and salads. There's a full bar. Reservations are not accepted, so arrive early. (We make an effort to get there at least an hour ahead to get a table or a spot at the bar on days when big games are scheduled.) **L D S** $$-$$$ 🐭

KOUZZINA BY CAT CORA: The new kid on the boardwalk occupies the space formerly filled by Spoodles. Like its predecessor, Kouzzina offers family-friendly Mediterranean-style cuisine—but, thanks to noted chef Cat Cora, it has a decidedly (and deliciously)

Greek stamp on it. Many of her family recipes—including spinach pie, oak-grilled steak and pork, and baklava—have been handed down through generations. FYI: Kouzzina (pronounced *koo-ZEE-nah*) is Greek for kitchen. For menu specifics, call 407-WDW-DINE. Reservations are recommended. **B L D** $$-$$$ 🐭

FLYING FISH CAFE: This pricey-but-worth-it eatery delivers creative seasonal menus with an obvious emphasis on seafood options. As an example of the entrées created in the open "onstage" kitchen, consider the potato-wrapped red snapper. While seafood is the house specialty, steaks are also served. Save room for dessert. The sorbets are heavenly. Reservations are recommended. Seating is available at the chef's counter—handy for solo diners. **D** $$$-$$$$ 🐭

Caribbean Beach

OLD PORT ROYALE: The food court in Old Port Royale features a large dining area and the following fast-food eateries: *Grab N Go Market* serves croissants, freshly baked rolls, pastries, ice cream, and other treats. Italian specialties are the order at the *Royale Pizza and Pasta Shop*. Soups, salads, and hot and cold sandwiches make up the selections at *Montego's Deli*. Burgers and chicken nuggets are among the offerings at *Old Port Royale Hamburger Shop*, while *Bridgetown Broiler Shop* serves made-to-order omelets for breakfast and items such as carved turkey and pork loin for dinner. **B L D S** $-$$ 🐭

SHUTTERS AT OLD PORT ROYALE: New York strip steak, pork ribs, and pasta are among the items on the menu at this inviting eatery. Reservations are recommended. **D** $$-$$$ 🐭

Contemporary

CALIFORNIA GRILL: Perched on the hotel's 15th floor, with terrific views of sunsets and Magic Kingdom fireworks, this acclaimed restaurant offers the best in West Coast cuisine in a stylish, relaxing atmosphere. (It has been named "restaurant of choice" by *Orlando Magazine*.) The ever-changing menu is defined by sophisticated use of fresh produce. Wood-fired California flatbreads, oak-fired beef filet, goat cheese ravioli, sushi, and warm Valrhona chocolate lava cake—all spectacular—are made to order in an open kitchen. Grilled pork tenderloin with polenta and balsamic vinegar-smothered cremini mushrooms suggest the chef's culinary prowess. There's even a vegetarian zone on the menu. The wine list is updated daily. Reservations are strongly recommended. All guests must check in on the resort's second floor. **D** $$$–$$$$ 🐭

PHOTO BY MIKE CARROLL

CHEF MICKEY'S: Chef Mickey and his pals host this buffet-style feast, with dramatic views of the monorail passing above. Colorful, life-size illustrations of Disney characters decorate the area. The changing menu takes advantage of seasonal offerings; a sundae bar provides a sweet finish. Be prepared to drop your fork and twirl your napkin on a moment's notice. This is a very popular eatery with an extremely loyal following. Reservations are an absolute must. **B D** $$–$$$ 🐭

CONTEMPO CAFE: After leaving its first-floor home of 35 years, the Contemporary resort snack bar has moved up in the World—all the way to the fourth floor, beside Chef Mickey's. This spot serves light fare until about midnight. Food is ordered from computer kiosks near the entrance. After doing so, proceed to the cashier. Here you'll receive cups for beverages and a beeper (which lights up when your food is ready to be picked up at the counter.) **B L D S** $–$$ 🐭

PHOTO BY MIKE CARROLL

THE WAVE . . . OF AMERICAN FLAVORS: A stellar full-service eatery, this modern establishment features healthy, creative American fusion cuisine. Think "bold cooking inspired by fresh markets." Starters of note: Wave Appetizer for Two (lump crab, Florida rock shrimp cakes, and sautéed sea scallops), and avocado and citrus salad. Main courses include grilled beef tenderloin, seasonal vegetable stew with multigrain rice, and a sustainable fish of the day. The tempting desserts include those of the no-sugar-added variety. And the Old World wine list is out of this world. It's possible to try several via flight samplers. The Wave is located on the resort's first floor, just off the lobby. We would eat breakfast, lunch, *and* dinner here without a moment's hesitation. Reservations are recommended. **B L D** $$–$$$ 🐭

Tea for Two (or Ten)

Teatime with all the trimmings—scones, tiny sandwiches, pastries, cheese plates, strawberries and jam, etc.—is from 2 P.M. until 5 P.M. in the Garden View Tea Room at the Grand Floridian resort. This elegant lounge overlooks the lovingly tended gardens surrounding the resort's main pool.

The menu here includes custom blended teas from around the world. Guests may also sip coffees and spirited drinks such as a Brandy Alexander, Champagne Cocktail, or Grand Mimosa. Note that guests must be at least 21 years of age (with valid photo ID) to consume alcohol.

The Grand Floridian offers tea parties for kids, too. For information on these special events, turn to page 216.

For details or to make reservations, call 407-WDW-DINE (939-3463).

Coronado Springs

CAFE RIX: Stop here for hot *paninis*, flat-breads, and breakfast sandwiches. There is a "grab and go" area, too. It has items such as pre-packaged sandwiches, salads, pastries, gelato, and coffee. **B L D S** $–$$ 🐭

MAYA GRILL: The only full-service restaurant at this resort, it features steak and seafood with a Latin American flair. Many items are cooked over an open-pit, wood-fired grill. Breakfast is presented as an all-you-can-eat buffet. Reservations are recommended. **B D** $$$ 🐭

PHOTO BY MIKE CARROLL

PEPPER MARKET: This colorful food court has a seating area and lots of stands where vendors sell freshly prepared pizza, sandwiches, salads, burgers, stir-fry, Mexican specialties, baked goods, margaritas, and more. Note that a ten percent gratuity is added to the bill when you eat in the dining area. We're not sure why. **B L D S** $–$$ 🐭

Disney's Old Key West

GOOD'S FOOD TO GO: Burgers, deli sandwiches, salads, ice cream, and snacks are among Good's offerings. **B L D S** $ 🐭

OLIVIA'S CAFE: An assortment of Key West favorites, including tasty shrimp dishes and conch fritters, are featured alongside contemporary Southern fare. **L D** $$–$$$ 🐭

Fort Wilderness

Many people cook their own meals here. Some supplies are available at the Meadow and Settlement Trading Posts (open from 8 A.M. to 10 P.M. in winter; to 11 P.M. in summer).

Par for the Course

The pleasant **Sand Trap Bar & Grill** in the Bonnet Creek Golf Club is a convenient dining option for golfers playing the adjacent Osprey Ridge course. It's also close to the Magic Kingdom. In addition to the traditional breakfast items, Sand Trap serves appetizers, burgers, soups, and sandwiches. There is a full bar; ice cream and milk shakes are available. **B L D S** $$ 🐭

TRAIL'S END RESTAURANT: It's a little off the beaten path for anyone but Fort Wilderness guests, but for many it's worth the trip. The informal log-walled restaurant offers a relatively inexpensive, all-you-can-eat breakfast, including grits, biscuits, gravy, and breakfast pizza. The à la carte lunch features fried chicken and waffles; sautéed catfish; and fried green tomatoes. For dinner, expect the buffet to have smoked pork ribs, peel-n-eat shrimp, fried chicken, carved meats, a salad bar, plus a variety of side dishes and desserts. There are sandwiches and a taco bar at lunch. Pizza is served nightly from 4 P.M. until 10 P.M. (until midnight on weekends). Beer and wine are served by the glass. Afterward, you can relax in a rocking chair on the front porch. It doesn't get any better than that. **B L D S** $–$$ 🐭

Grand Floridian

CITRICOS: A definite splurge, this upscale space specializes in market-fresh European cooking. The fare varies seasonally but may include items such as braised veal shank,

pan-roasted fish, and bone-in rib eye.

Restaurant sommeliers can recommend excellent wine pairings. The stunning view of the Seven Seas Lagoon is a year-round staple. A private dining room is available for parties of up to 12 people. The lounge is ideal for solo diners or those without a reservation (appetizers are served here). Reservations are recommended for the restaurant. **D** $$$-$$$$ 🎯

GASPARILLA GRILL & GAMES: Grilled chicken, burgers, pizza, hot dogs, and soft-serve ice cream are the mainstays at this 24-hour take-out restaurant near the marina. There is indoor (beside the arcade games) and outdoor seating. Breakfast selections such as scrambled eggs, waffles, pancakes, and bagels are also available. **B L D S** $-$$ 🎯

GRAND FLORIDIAN CAFE: Traditional American cooking is the specialty at this picturesque spot. Although the menu varies, selections have included pastries, sandwiches, burgers, ice cream, and vegetarian offerings. There are also salads and an assortment of more traditional entrées. Reservations are recommended. **B L** $$$ 🎯

NARCOOSSEE'S: The partially open kitchen is the focal point at this airy, octagonal dining spot on the Grand Floridian waterfront. Specialties, which vary seasonally, may include Maine lobster, grilled lamb chops, or pepper-seared

Tables In Wonderland

Attention Annual Pass-bearers and Florida residents: You are eligible for the Tables In Wonderland (T.I.W.) discount dining program. It affords members a 10- to 20-percent savings off food and beverages at many WDW table-service eateries. The discount is good for you and up to 9 members of your party. Simply present a valid photo ID and your T.I.W. card when you place an order with a server. To net the discount for the rest of the party, the check must be paid by the T.I.W. member. Membership is valid for one year and costs $75 for Annual Passholders and $100 for Florida residents. For information or to order your Tables In Wonderland card, call 407-566-5858. For a list of participating dining locations, go to: *http://disneyworld.disney.go.com/passholder-program/dining-discounts/*.

jumbo scallops. Staples include charbroiled meats, seafood, and vegetarian options. It may be possible to enjoy a cocktail on the veranda overlooking the Seven Seas Lagoon. The lounge serves 40 wines by the glass and appetizers. Reservations are recommended for the restaurant. **D** $$$-$$$$ 🎯

1900 PARK FARE: A sophisticated buffet menu and subtle decor make this the most elegant character restaurant on-property. Big Bertha, a band organ built in Paris nearly a century ago, sits 15 feet above the floor in a proscenium. Mary Poppins and friends (characters vary) mingle with guests during breakfast. Cinderella and her storybook friends visit the dining room during the dinner hours. Know that the lineup of characters does change from time to time. Dinner features seafood, salads, pastas, vegetables, breads, and carved meat. The offerings change weekly. Reservations are recommended. **B D** $$$ 🎯

VICTORIA & ALBERT'S: The intimate dining room in the only AAA 5-Diamond restaurant in Central Florida seats only 60 guests (all of whom must have already celebrated their 10th birthday). The menu is customized daily. Each night there are fish, fowl, red meat, veal, and lamb selections, which depend on the best ingredients in the market and are described in detail by your waiter. The chef may even make a personal appearance to say hello or to accommodate special requests from patrons. Guests may choose to dine in the main dining room, at the chef's table in the kitchen, or in the new Queen Victoria Room (for an additional charge).

There are also choices of two soups, two salads, and desserts, including specialty soufflés of fresh berries, chocolate, or Grand Marnier. There is an extensive wine list.

Once guests have made their selections, they are presented with a personalized menu as a souvenir of the event. A harpist provides background music. At the completion of the meal, women receive a long-stemmed rose. Jackets are required for men. Reservations are necessary. Call 407-939-3463 for current pricing. (This is one expensive spot.) **D** $$$$

Polynesian

CAPT. COOK'S: A good spot for light fare (both pre-packaged and made-to-order), this reliable snack bar is open 24 hours a day. In addition to "grab and go" items such as sandwiches, salads, sushi, fruit, and yogurt, you can order freshly prepared breakfast items, Asian noodle bowls, and more. **B L D S** $-$$ 🐭

KONA CAFE: Located on the second floor of the Great Ceremonial House, just around the corner from 'Ohana, this casual restaurant features a South Seas decor and an exotic menu. Lunch and dinner menus have Asian-influenced entrées. Possibilities include noodle bowls and macadamia-dusted sustainable fish. A variety of desserts is among the offerings. Reservations are recommended for all meals. **B L D S** $$-$$$ 🐭

KONA ISLAND: A coffee bar until noon, this is a super spot for a quick (delicious) sip on your way to the monorail. Light breakfast items are offered, too.

When 5 o'clock rolls around, so does the sushi. Roll selections include Volcano (spicy tuna, shrimp salad, and tempura crunch), California Luau (fresh jumbo lump crab, pineapple, and avocado), Tuna Poke (traditional Hawaiian poke salad), and a cucumber roll (for vegetarians).

Sashimi fans will enjoy the salmon, tuna, and chef's selection of the day. Seating is limited, but it's possible to get items to go. Beer, wine, sake, and other cocktails are served. **B D S** $-$$ 🐭

'OHANA: On the second floor of the resort's Great Ceremonial House, this restaurant features a 16-foot-long, open fire pit. Dinner choices in the all-you-can-eat, family-style feast include poultry, pork, and beef—all roasted on skewers up to three feet long. The marinated meats are served with an assortment of vegetables, salads, and potatoes

au gratin. There's no menu from which to order. Servers just deliver course after course.

The meal ends with pineapple-coconut bread pudding served à la mode with Bananas Foster sauce. Polynesian resort entertainers perform periodically at dinner, teaching songs and culture, including hula dancing and coconut-rolling contests. Kids eat it up.

Lilo, Stitch, and their good friends Mickey and Pluto host a character breakfast each morning. Keep in mind that the character line-up does change from time to time. Breakfast fare is basic and presented family-style. Reservations are strongly recommended for both meals. **B D** $$$-$$$$ 🐭

Pop Century

EVERYTHING POP: Guests of this resort dine in the food court in Classic Hall. The selection includes pasta, pizza, chicken, hot dogs, burgers, sandwiches, salads, breakfast items, and baked goods. **B L D S** $-$$ 🐭

Port Orleans French Quarter

SASSAGOULA FLOATWORKS & FOOD FACTORY: The stands at this festive food court feature pizza, pasta, gumbo, burgers, sandwiches, soups, salads, spit-roasted chicken, barbecued ribs, ice cream, and a full selection of fresh bakery products, including tempting beignets. **B L D S** $-$$ 🐭

Port Orleans Riverside

BOATWRIGHT'S DINING HALL: Be sure to notice the boat that's being built in this table-service eatery. Specialties include Southern dishes as well as American home-style favorites. Reservations are recommended. **D** $$-$$$ 🐭

RIVERSIDE MILL: This high-ceilinged food court styled in the image of a working cotton mill offers half a dozen food counters and a sprawling seating area. Collectively, the stands offer pizza; pasta; fried, grilled, and roast chicken; burgers; barbecued ribs; salads; sandwiches; and fresh baked goods.

For guests on the go, the food court's deli does double duty as a convenience store, stocking sandwiches, juices, beer, wine, snack items, and prepared salads. **B L D S** $-$$ 🐭

Saratoga Springs

THE ARTIST'S PALETTE: Fresh pizza, salads, soups, sandwiches, and desserts are among the selections at this artsy establishment. **B L D S** $–$$ ☺ ♥

THE TURF CLUB BAR & GRILL: A sporty spot offering, in addition to a lounge with pool table and big-screen TV, fare such as burgers, BLTs, salads, crab cakes, steamed mussels, grilled salmon, steak, penne pasta with shrimp, mint-crusted lamb chops, roasted chicken breast, and more. **L D S** $–$$ ☺ ♥

Swan & Dolphin

CABANA BAR & BEACH CLUB: An elegant poolside eatery, the Dolphin's Cabana serves a sophisticated selection of starters, salads, and entrées. Appetizer options include crab egg rolls, tuna tartare, and jerk spiced chicken wings. The main bites menu offers Cuban "cheese steak," grilled chicken BLT, turkey sliders, all-beef bratwurst, farm-raised, grass-fed organic burgers, and a variety of flatbreads. Should you crave a sweet finish to your meal, consider a refreshing dish of gelato. The house coffee is Starbucks, and a full bar stands at the ready. Among the signature cocktails is the Passionate Beachcomber—a high-octane mix of vodka, creme de banana, cherry brandy, maraschino liqueur, passion fruit, and fresh lime juice. For kids, Cabana serves pizza, burgers, grilled cheese, hot dogs, and chicken fingers. **L D S** $–$$

THE FOUNTAIN: A soda fountain with grown-up appeal, this is an ideal spot for a sweet snack or a satisfying meal. Homemade soft-serve ice cream is the house specialty. Be it served in a simple cone or in an elaborate sundae (the caramel apple sundae is a standout), the chilly treat is sure to please. Among the entrées from which to choose are ahi tuna burgers, cheeseburgers, vegetarian Sloppy Joe sandwiches, and a classic B.L.T. Soups and salads can augment the meal, as can fries, onion rings, or chips and salsa. Drinks-wise, this place has everything from freshly brewed iced tea and specialty coffees to impressively inventive shakes (including the chocolate raspberry torte, coco loco, peppermint, and cheesecake concoctions), plus beer and wine. The Fountain is located at the Dolphin. **L D S** $–$$

FRESH—MEDITERRANEAN MARKET: The Dolphin's airy restaurant offers salads, sandwiches, and Mediterranean-inspired dishes. The morning menu includes pastries, yogurt, homemade granola, hot cereals, eggs, pancakes, and more. Lunch here can be a Caesar salad, a sandwich (California turkey club, rotisserie chicken salad wrap, or *panini*), and/or an entrée such as pappardelle pasta, seared black bass, or chicken Marsala. Fresh offers many wines by the glass, including several organic varietals. The coffee here is Starbucks. Reservations are suggested for breakfast and lunch. **B L** $$–$$$

GARDEN GROVE: Situated in a park-like setting, this Swan spot offers hearty buffets for breakfast and dinner (as well as à la carte options). Lunch is strictly à la carte.

Disney characters are always in attendance for dinner and make appearances at breakfast on Saturday and Sunday mornings. Reservations are suggested. **B L D** $$–$$$

IL MULINO NEW YORK TRATTORIA: This Swan eatery offers upscale Italian cuisine in a trattoria setting. Specializing in *Piatti per il Tavolo*, or family-style dining, the spot is ideal for groups. The seasonal menu is characterized by blends of fresh ingredients drawn from the Abruzzi region of Italy. Signature items include *Gamberi al Mulino* (jumbo shrimp with spicy cocktail sauce), *Gnocchi Bolognese* (potato dumplings with meat sauce), and *Pollo Fra Diavolo* (chicken in a spicy red sauce with sausage). Reservations are recommended. **D** $$$–$$$$

KIMONOS: Visit this karaoke lounge for sushi and cocktails (and song). It's also possible to order miso soup, salad, edamame, tempura udon, gyoza, and kobe beef satay, among other selections. There is a full bar featuring such specialty cocktails as the Lychee Mojito and Cool Cucumber Saketini. Kimonos is located at the Swan. **D S** $–$$

PICABU: This Dolphin cafeteria is a bit above the norm. The food is usually freshly prepared—with excellent sandwiches and salads. The convenience store (open 24 hours) offers snacks and sundries. The house coffee is Starbucks (and refills are free). Note that this spot is a tad pricier than the average Disney World quick-service eatery, but the quality is appreciated by most. **B L D S** $–$$

GOOD MEALS, GREAT TIMES

SHULA'S: Like the original Shula's in Miami, this Dolphin spot specializes in generous portions of certified Angus beef, in addition to chicken and fresh fish dishes. The eatery pays tribute to the 1972 Miami Dolphins—the year coach Don Shula led his team to a perfect NFL season. Photos abound, and the menu comes on an official football. Reservations recommended. There is no kids' menu (child care may be arranged through the hotel). Business casual is the preferred attire. **D** $$$$

SPLASH TERRACE: Also known as Splash Grill, this Swan spot serves substantial fare for a pool pub. Crab cakes, tomato and mozzarella salad, and rock shrimp noodle baskets can accompany organic burgers, Cuban "cheese steak," roasted vegetable wraps, chicken club sandwiches, and "New York style" pizza. Cocktails are served. For dessert, choose from more than 15 flavors of ice cream. Soft drinks are offered, too. **L S** $

TODD ENGLISH'S BLUEZOO: This Dolphin eatery is the brainchild of celebrity chef Todd English. The menu features a selection of fresh seafood, including a tempting raw bar. The teppan-seared jumbo sea scallops take top honors in the appetizer category. All of the entrées are tempting as well, from miso-glazed mero to chilled Maine lobster to blue-zoo's dancing fish. Landlubbers can indulge in tenderloin of beef filet or pan-roasted chicken breast. Choose from a medley of desserts, including warm chocolate cake with ganache center, exotic milk chocolate bar, and pavlova. Reservations are recommended. Note that it's possible to get food service (with a full menu) at the bar. The kids' menu features chicken, spaghetti, and pizza. **D S** $$$-$$$$

Wilderness Lodge

ARTIST POINT: Housed in a cavernous dining room decorated with artwork representing painters who first chronicled the Northwest landscape, this fine-dining spot offers a creative menu that incorporates buffalo and venison, in addition to more traditional items such as beef and chicken, plus salmon and more. For dessert, many choose the famous Artist Point berry cobbler. The wine list spotlights wines from the Pacific Northwest with custom wine flights and half bottle suggestions. Reservations are recommended. **D** $$$-$$$$

ROARING FORK: Salads, burgers, fries, sandwiches, yogurt, chili, and snacks are available at this stone-walled snack bar near the main pool. This is the resort's "refillable mug" station. **B L D S** $

WHISPERING CANYON CAFE: This family-friendly (and noisy!) spot serves hearty, all-you-can-eat fare such as smoked barbecued meats with a variety of sides and salads, plus homemade desserts (for an extra charge). Assorted sandwiches and entrées are available à la carte at lunch and dinner. Reservations are recommended. **B L D** $$$

Yacht & Beach Club

BEACH CLUB MARKETPLACE: Inside the Beach Club, this spot serves breakfast items, salads, sandwiches, and desserts (including homemade gelato). It has some groceries and "grab and go" items. **B L D S** $-$$

BEACHES & CREAM SODA SHOP: This small restaurant is on the Beach Club side of the resorts. It offers sundaes, cones, floats, shakes, and sodas. Burgers, hot dogs, and fries are available, too. **B L D S** $-$$

CAPE MAY CAFE: A lovely all-you-can-eat clambake is held each evening at the Beach Club. Menu items include clams, mussels, chicken, shrimp, red-skin potatoes, and chowder. There is a character breakfast buffet each morning. Reservations are recommended. **B D** $$$

CAPTAIN'S GRILLE: This nautically themed American grill serves steak, seafood, and more. Breakfast features a buffet and a full menu; lunch and dinner are à la carte. Reservations are recommended. **B L D** $$-$$$

HURRICANE HANNA'S GRILLE: Located in the Stormalong Bay area. Hot dogs, burgers, sandwiches, salads, fries, and ice cream are on the menu. There is also a full bar. **L S** $

YACHTSMAN STEAKHOUSE: As its name implies, beef is the house specialty. Guests may watch the butcher choose cuts of meat in the glassed-in shop. The filet mignon is exceptional. Be sure to order the side of mushrooms. Seafood and chicken are available. Located at the Yacht Club. Reservations are recommended. **D** $$$-$$$$

WALT DISNEY WORLD

Name/Location	Meals	Style*	Price**	Characters	Theme
Akershus Norway Pavilion, Epcot (page 238)	Break-fast Lunch Dinner	Family style	B: $33/20 L: $35/21 D: $40/22	Belle, Jasmine, Snow White, Sleeping Beauty, and Mulan	14th-century Norwegian castle
Cape May Cafe Yacht and Beach Club resorts (page 259)	Break-fast	Buffet	$23/13	Goofy, Minnie, Donald Duck	Seaside picnic
Chef Mickey's Contemporary resort (page 254)	Break-fast Dinner	Buffet	B: $29/16 D: $36/18	Mickey, Minnie, Donald, Goofy, and Pluto	A family celebration
Cinderella's Royal Table Magic Kingdom (page 232)	Break-fast Lunch Dinner	B/L: Family style D: à la carte	B: $39/26 L: $42/27 D: $49/30	B, L, D: Princesses B, L, D: Cinder-ella greets guests in the Castle lobby	Medieval banquet
Crystal Palace Magic Kingdom (page 234)	Break-fast Lunch Dinner	Buffet	B: $23/13 L: $25/14 D: $37/18	Pooh, Eeyore, Tigger, and Piglet	Sunlit conservatory
Garden Grill Epcot (page 237)	Dinner	Family style	$35/17	Mickey, Pluto, Chip, and Dale	Home-style country cooking

* Family-style and buffet meals are all-you-can-eat dining experiences. Family-style features a set menu and table service; buffet-style meals usually present more dining options and are self-serve.

** Adult prices are followed by children's prices (diners ages 3 through 9). Prices may be higher during select "peak" times of year.

CHARACTER DINING

Featured Items	For Dessert	Tip	Wins the . . .
B: Scrambled eggs, potato casseroles, French toast sticks, bacon, sausage, fruit L/D: Norwegian fare and kid-friendly selections	Chocolate mousse cake, lingonberry cheesecake	This is the only place to have breakfast at Epcot's World Showcase. (And it's the only table-service breakfast option in the whole park.)	**It's not Cinderella's Castle, but it's still pretty cool.** (It's much easier to score reservations here, too.)
Eggs, breakfast pizza, Mickey waffles, sausage, fruit, cereal, grits	Donuts, danish, fresh berries	For guests staying in the Epcot area, Cape May is one of the best breakfast options.	**Best Chance of Getting a Table Without Reservations** (But make the arrangements, anyway!)
B: Eggs, pancakes, Mickey waffles, fruit, cereal D: Carved meats, seafood, pasta, veggies, pizza, salads	Make-your-own sundaes, cheese-cake, cookies, and pies	A celebration happens every 45 minutes. Be sure to stick around for at least one little party.	**Best All-Around Character Meal** (It has a fun and festive setting and a kid-pleasing menu.)
B: French toast, eggs, bacon, fruit L/D: Pasta al pomodoro, pan-seared salmon, herb-crusted pork tenderloin, and focaccia sandwiches	Chocolate cream cheese buckle	Payment in full is required at time of booking for all meals.	**Best Setting** (The restaurant is inside Cinderella Castle!)
B: French toast, eggs, cereal, frittata, fruit L/D: Shrimp, carved meats, pasta, veggies, pizza, salad	B: Sticky buns L/D: Cakes, pies, make-your-own sundaes, cookies	Don't be put off by this restaurant's size—the characters make the rounds surprisingly quickly.	**Best Theme Park Buffet** (Lovely setting, convenient location, and an appetizing menu.)
Catfish, beef, chicken, veggies, potatoes (mac and cheese for kids)	Freshly made desserts	The room rotates very slowly throughout the meal. It's hardly noticeable to most, but may be disorienting to those highly sensitive to motion.	**Best for Vegetarians** (Be sure to ask for the vegetarian meal—it's usually a tasty seasonal selection.)

All characters, menu items, and prices are subject to change. Prices are rounded to the nearest dollar. Call 407-WDW-DINE (939-3463) for current details or to make reservations. This listing is not comprehensive. Character meals are also presented at Buena Vista Palace (Sunday breakfast at the Watercress Cafe) and the Hilton (Sunday breakfast at Covington Mill). See pages 104 and 106 for details.

WALT DISNEY WORLD

Name/Location	Meals	Style*	Price**	Characters		Theme
Garden Grove Swan resort (page 258)	Break-fast (week-ends) Dinner (daily)	Buffet	B: $21/13 D: $30/14	B: Goofy and Pluto D: Timon and Rafiki (Monday and Friday); Goofy and Pluto (Sunday, Tuesday–Thursday, and Saturday)		Picnic in the park
Hollywood & Vine Disney's Hollywood Studios (page 244)	Break-fast Lunch	Family style	B: $25/14 L: $31/16	Handy Manny and Special Agent Oso, plus June and Leo from *Little Einsteins*		A celebration of (and with!) Playhouse Disney
Wonderland Tea Party Grand Floridian resort (page 216)	Lunch	Tea-party style	$40 (per child, ages 4–12)	Alice and the Mad Hatter		Pint-size, interactive tea party
Mickey's Backyard Barbecue Dinner show at Fort Wilderness (page 270)	Dinner	Buffet	$53/32		Mickey and friends such as Goofy, Minnie, Chip, and Dale	Backyard barbecue/ hoedown
'Ohana Polynesian resort (page 257)	Break-fast	Family style	$25/14	Lilo, Stitch, and others, such as Pluto and Mickey		Tropical hut
1900 Park Fare Grand Floridian resort (page 256)	Break-fast Dinner	Buffet	B: $21/12 D: $36/18		B: Stars like Mary Poppins and Alice D: Cinderella and friends	Turn-of-the-century circus
Tusker House Donald's Safari Breakfast at Animal Kingdom (page 247)	Break-fast	Buffet	$23/13	Donald, Daisy, Goofy, and Mickey		Safari feast

* Family-style and buffet meals are all-you-can-eat dining experiences. Family-style features a set menu and table service; buffet-style meals usually present more dining options and are self-serve.

** Adult prices are followed by children's prices (diners ages 3 through 9). Prices will be higher during select "peak" times of year.

CHARACTER DINING

Featured Items	For Dessert	Tip	Wins the . . .
B: Omelets, eggs, bacon, fruit D: Varies by day	Fresh pastries	For dinner, Sunday and Wednesday are barbecue; Monday and Friday, seafood; Tuesday, Thursday, and Saturday are Mediterranean.	**Best Variety** (You can have four dinners in one week and have a different type of cuisine each time.)
B: Mickey waffles, scrambled eggs, yogurt L: Salads, pasta dishes, fish, and chicken	Pineapple upside down cake, key lime tart	Ask for Play 'N Dine at Hollywood & Vine when you call to reserve (that's the official name!)	**Tot-Pleaser Award** (Little ones love to sing along with *Little Einsteins*.)
PB&J sandwiches, chicken nuggets, fruit, and kid-friendly "tea" (apple juice)	Cupcakes, crispy treats	Parents can stick around for the party, but kids are well supervised. Many adults choose to snooze by the pool or relax in a Grand Floridian lounge.	**Fun with Food Honor** (What's cooler to a kid than eating a cupcake? Decorating it first!)
Chicken, ribs, hot dogs, corn on the cob, baked beans	Watermelon and marble cake	Available on Tuesdays and Thursdays from March through December.	**Country Music Fan Stamp of Approval** (There is a live country band and line dancing.)
Mickey waffles, eggs, biscuits, fruit, bacon	Sweet baked goods	Don't forget your autograph book and camera. The characters spend a good amount of quality time at each table.	**Speediest Service** (Servers keep those family-style platters coming fast and frequently.)
B: Pancakes, eggs, waffles D: Prime rib, pasta, seafood	B: Sticky buns, muffins, Danish D: Key lime pie, cheesecake, bread pudding	Breakfast here is a nice way to start a Magic Kingdom day. The park is just one monorail stop away.	**Fanciest Foods** (The quality is superior to many buffets, and there's plenty to please the kids.)
Pancakes, French toast, eggs, quiche, breakfast potatoes, sausage, grits, cereal, fruit	Danish, muffins	This spot is just steps from Kilimanjaro Safaris, but it's better to take a stroll after breakfast rather than jumping right into a bumpy jeep ride.	**Best Place to Find Donald Duck** (As the host, he makes the rounds all morning long.)

All characters, menu items, and prices are subject to change. Prices are rounded to the nearest dollar. Call 407-WDW-DINE (939-3463) or visit *www.disneyworld.com/dining/* for updates or to make reservations. This listing is not comprehensive.

RESTAURANT ROUNDUP

Dining Disney style is one of the most enjoyable aspects of the vacation for many visitors. But with so many different restaurants to choose from, it can be difficult to select the spots that will best suit your family. Regulars to WDW are quick to recommend their favorites to newcomers. We, of course, are no exception to the rule. What follows is a rundown of the restaurants that we always try to include in our trips to the World and wholeheartedly recommend to those who are planning a visit. To pick these Birnbaum's Bests, we considered such factors as food quality, restaurant atmosphere, location, and overall value.

TOP WDW RESTAURANTS FOR FAMILIES WITH KIDS

TABLE SERVICE

Biergarten	Epcot (p. 238)
Boma—Flavors of Africa	Animal Kingdom Lodge resort (p. 252)
Cape May Cafe	Beach Club resort (p. 259)
Chef Mickey's	Contemporary resort (p. 254)
Cinderella's Royal Table	Magic Kingdom (p. 232)
Crystal Palace	Magic Kingdom (p. 234)
50's Prime Time Cafe	Disney's Hollywood Studios (p. 244)
Garden Grill	Epcot (p. 237)
Rainforest Cafe	Animal Kingdom and Downtown Disney (pp. 247, 251)
Sci-Fi Dine-In Theater	Disney's Hollywood Studios (p. 245)
T-Rex: A Prehistoric Family Adventure	Downtown Disney (p. 251)
Tusker House	Animal Kingdom (p. 247)
The Wave . . . of American Flavors	Contemporary resort (p. 254)

FAST FOOD

Columbia Harbour House	Magic Kingdom (p. 234)
Cooke's of Dublin	Downtown Disney (p. 249)
Earl of Sandwich	Downtown Disney (p. 249)
Everything Pop!	Pop Century resort (p. 257)
Flame Tree Barbecue	Animal Kingdom (p. 248)
Liberty Inn	Epcot (p. 242)
Pecos Bill Cafe	Magic Kingdom (p. 233)
Pinocchio Village Haus	Magic Kingdom (p. 233)
Sunset Ranch Market	Disney's Hollywood Studios (p. 246)
Sunshine Seasons	Epcot (p. 237)

BEST KIDS' MEAL PRESENTATION

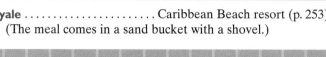

Old Port Royale . . . . Caribbean Beach resort (p. 253)
(The meal comes in a sand bucket with a shovel.)

BEST PLACE TO CELEBRATE A CHILD'S BIRTHDAY

Chef Mickey's . . . . Contemporary resort (p. 254)

RUNNER-UP

Mickey's Backyard Barbecue . . . . Fort Wilderness (p. 270)

BEST FIREWORKS VIEW

California Grill . . . . Contemporary resort (p. 254)

BEST VEGETARIAN MEALS

Jiko—The Cooking Place
Animal Kingdom Lodge resort
(p. 252)

BEST SPLURGE FOR GROWN-UPS

Victoria & Albert's . . . . Grand Floridian resort (p. 256)

RUNNERS-UP

Bistro de Paris . . . . .Epcot (p. 239)
California Grill . . . . .Contemporary resort (p. 254)
Citricos . . . . Grand Floridian resort (p. 255)
Flying Fish Cafe . . . . BoardWalk resort (p. 253)
Fulton's Crab House . . . . Downtown Disney, Pleasure Island (p. 249)
Il Mulino New York Trattoria .Swan resort (p. 258)
Jiko—The Cooking Place. . . . . .Animal Kingdom Lodge resort (p. 252)
Yachtsman Steakhouse .Yacht Club resort (p. 259)

BEST DINNER SHOW

Hoop-Dee-Doo Musical Revue: This crowd-pleasing saloon hall show
has been going like gangbusters since 1974. Kids enjoy the silly humor,
while adults eat up the bottomless buckets of ribs, fried chicken, and other
down-home dishes. Presented at Fort Wilderness (p. 270).

RUNNER-UP

Mickey's Backyard Barbecue: It's more of a big,
informal party than a show, complete with a kickin'
country band, games for the kids, and line dancing
with Disney characters. The self-serve, all-you-can-
eat barbecue fare is varied and plentiful. Presented
at Fort Wilderness (p. 270).

BEST PIZZA FOR GROWN-UPS

California Grill (flatbread) . . . . Contemporary resort (p. 254)
Via Napoli . . . . .Epcot (p. 242)

BEST PIZZA FOR KIDS

Pizzafari . . . . Animal Kingdom (p. 248)
Pizza Planet . . . . Disney's Hollywood Studios (p. 246)

BEST FIXIN'S BAR

Pecos Bill Cafe . . . . Magic Kingdom (p. 233)

BEST BUYS

Trail's End Restaurant
Pioneer Hall, Fort Wilderness (p. 255)
Boma—Flavors of Africa
Animal Kingdom Lodge (p. 252)

BEST ITALIAN FARE

Via Napoli . . . . .Epcot (p. 242)

RUNNERS-UP

Il Mulino New York Trattoria . . . . Swan resort (p. 258)
Portobello . . . . Downtown Disney, Pleasure Island (p. 251)
Tutto Italia . . . . Epcot (p. 241)

BEST ROOM SERVICE

Yacht and Beach Club resorts . . . . (p. 259)

BEST THEME

50's Prime Time Cafe . . . . Disney's Hollywood Studios (p. 244)

RUNNERS-UP

Sci-Fi Dine-In Theater . . . . Disney's Hollywood Studios (p. 245)
T-Rex: A Prehistoric Family Adventure . . . . . Downtown Disney, Marketplace (p. 251)

BEST OUTDOOR CAFE

Portobello . . . . Downtown Disney, Pleasure Island (p. 251)

RUNNER-UP

Big River Grille & Brewing Works . . . . BoardWalk resort (p. 253)

BEST SEAFOOD

Fulton's Crab House ... Downtown Disney, Pleasure Island (p. 249)

RUNNERS-UP

Coral Reef .... Epcot (p. 237)
Flying Fish Cafe .... BoardWalk resort (p. 253)
Narcoossee's .... Grand Floridian resort (p. 256)
Todd English's bluezoo .... Dolphin resort (p. 259)

BEST CRAB CAKES

Stone Crab Lounge .... Fulton's Crab House,
Downtown Disney, Pleasure Island (p. 249)
The Wave . . . of American Flavors .... Contemporary resort (p. 254)

BEST BLOODY MARY

Stone Crab Lounge .... Fulton's Crab House,
Downtown Disney, Pleasure Island (p. 249)

BEST ALL-AROUND WDW RESTAURANT

The Wave . . . of American Flavors .... Contemporary resort (p. 254)

BEST VEGGIE BURGER

Pecos Bill Cafe .... Magic Kingdom (p. 233)

BEST ICE CREAM

Plaza Restaurant .... Magic Kingdom (p. 235)
Beaches & Cream Soda Shop .... Beach Club resort (p. 259)
The Fountain .... Dolphin resort (p. 258)

BEST STEAK

Yachtsman Steakhouse .... Yacht Club resort (p. 259)

RUNNERS-UP

Le Cellier Steakhouse .... Epcot (p. 239)
Flying Fish Cafe .... BoardWalk resort (p. 253)

BEST SUSHI

California Grill .... Contemporary resort (p. 254)

RUNNERS-UP

Kimonos .... Swan resort (p. 258)
Kona Island .... Polynesian resort (p. 257)

BEST SPORTS BAR

ESPN Club .... BoardWalk resort (p. 253)

BEST COFFEE

Flying Fish Cafe .... BoardWalk resort (p. 253)

RUNNERS-UP

Kona Cafe .... Polynesian resort (p. 257)
Boma—Flavors of Africa .... Animal Kingdom Lodge resort (p. 252)
Picabu ....Dolphin resort (p. 258)
Ghirardelli Soda Fountain . .Downtown Disney, Marketplace (p. 250)

BEST MILK SHAKE

Beaches & Cream Soda Shop .... Beach Club resort (p. 259)
Min and Bill's Dockside Diner ..... Disney's Hollywood Studios (p. 246)

BEST FRESH-BAKED COOKIES

The Writer's Stop .... Disney's Hollywood Studios (p. 178)
Main Street Bakery .... Magic Kingdom (p. 235)

BEST CHARACTER MEAL

Cinderella's Royal Table .... Magic Kingdom (p. 232)

RUNNERS-UP

Akershus Royal Banquet Hall .... Epcot (p. 238)
Chef Mickey's .... Contemporary resort (p. 254)
Garden Grill .... Epcot (p. 237)
1900 Park Fare .... Grand Floridian resort (p. 256)

BEST RESORT SNACK BAR

Picabu................................Dolphin resort (p. 258)

RUNNERS-UP

Capt. Cook's .... Polynesian resort (p. 256)
Contempo Cafe .... Contemporary resort (p. 254)

GOOD MEALS, GREAT TIMES

Reservations Explained

Disney's reservation system, formerly known as "priority seating," covers most full-service restaurants on WDW property. The name may have changed, but the procedure is the same. It was designed to provide the assurance of a reservation without delays caused by no-shows and latecomers. Here's how it works: You call ahead to request a seating time; you arrive five minutes before the assigned time and check in at the podium; you receive the next available table that can accommodate your party. The system works like traditional reservations, so you will always be seated before any walk-ins.

We recommend making advance arrangements. Seating times can be secured up to 180 days ahead (see box below) by calling 407-WDW-DINE (939-3463) or visiting *www.disneyworld.com/dining/*. One notable exception to that rule is Epcot's Bistro de Paris, which accepts reservations up to 30 days ahead. The dining hotline is open daily from 7 A.M. to 10 P.M. The number of tables available in advance varies. If you are unable to book ahead of time, try to make same-day arrangements.

Most WDW resorts have at least one phone in the main lobby that provides direct contact with the Dine Line. Simply touch 55—the call is free. From other locations, dial 407-WDW-DINE. Once at the theme parks, dining reservations can be made at the restaurant itself; at City Hall in the Magic Kingdom; in Epcot at Guest Relations by Spaceship Earth; by Hollywood Junction in Disney's Hollywood Studios; and at Guest Relations in Animal Kingdom. Bookings can also be made at Guest Relations in Downtown Disney Marketplace and at the West Side.

For Disney Resort Guests *Only*

Do you have a confirmed reservation at a Disney-owned-and-operated resort? If so, you are entitled to a special perk: Call 180 days prior to the first day of your hotel reservation and you can make dining reservations for up to 10 days of your stay. That's like getting a 1- to 10-day jump on everyone else! (Stays longer than 10 days will require a second call. Inquire when you make your first set of dining reservations.) Have your confirmation number handy when you call 407-WDW-DINE.

Advance Planning

While some Walt Disney World restaurants always seem to have an available table (like Marrakesh in Epcot's World Showcase), others are booked far in advance. The restaurants for which careful planning is essential include Cinderella's Royal Table in the Magic Kingdom (call 180 days ahead and keep your fingers crossed!); Chefs de France in Epcot; Donald's Safari Breakfast in Disney's Animal Kingdom; and California Grill in the Contemporary resort.

While the Walt Disney World reservation system is often successful, there are times when the wait for a table can be unexpectedly long. This is most likely to occur during peak mealtimes at restaurants that offer buffets or family-style meals, where patrons will often opt for seconds (or thirds). For this reason, be sure to check in at the restaurant particularly early for all character-hosted meals.

HOT TIP!

At most WDW restaurants, reservations are scheduled in five- or ten-minute intervals. If they don't have a 6 P.M. availability, ask about a 6:05 P.M.

Reservations are necessary for all dinner shows—the Hoop-Dee-Doo Musical Revue, Mickey's Backyard Barbecue, and the Polynesian resort's Spirit of Aloha; they can be made by calling 407-WDW-DINE (939-3463). Reservations can be booked up to 180 days in advance. If you can't get a table for an early performance, consider a later one (they are usually less heavily booked).

Keep in mind that, with the exception of dinner shows, a WDW dining reservation is not a traditional reservation. Don't be surprised if you have to wait a bit when you arrive at your assigned time. Your party will be given the first table that opens up.

Note: Because the dining scene at Walt Disney World is ever-evolving, we advise calling 407-WDW-DINE (939-3463) to confirm current reservation policies.

GOOD MEALS, GREAT TIMES

Dinner Shows

The fact that Disney is expert in family entertainment is nowhere more readily apparent than amid the whooping and hollering troupe of singers and dancers who race toward the stage at Fort Wilderness resort's Pioneer Hall. As guests plow through ribs, fried chicken, strawberry shortcake, beer, wine, and soft drinks, these enthusiastic performers sing, dance, and joke up a storm.

The gags are groaners, but the audience eats 'em up. It's all in the course of an evening at the *Hoop-Dee-Doo Musical Revue*, presented nightly at 5 P.M., 7:15 P.M., and 9:30 P.M. Cost is about $59 per adult and $30 for children (ages 3 through 9) for Category 3 seating; about $63 for adults, $31 for kids in Category 2; and about $68 and $35 for Category 1. (The best views are in Category 1—seating is on the main floor.)

Note that the dining room in Pioneer Hall can be chilly year-round. Bring a sweater to combat the sometimes intense air-conditioning.

HOT TIP!

The Hoop-Dee-Doo Musical Revue is a popular show. Make your reservations as far in advance as possible.

Also presented at Fort Wilderness is *Mickey's Backyard Barbecue*. A country band gets guests out on the floor to kick up their heels, and Disney characters join in the fun.

Dinner consists of plenty of picnic favorites: barbecued ribs and chicken, corn on the cob, and baked beans. The seasonal dinner show costs about $45 per adult and $27 for kids. Tickets are required, so book ahead.

Disney's Polynesian luau show is called *Spirit of Aloha*. Set in the beachfront backyard of a Hawaiian house (at the Polynesian resort), the show invites guests to join in a musical celebration.

The luau experience combines traditional music as well as more contemporary ditties from the animated Disney film *Lilo and Stitch*. The performers' dancing is some of the most authentic this side of Hawaii. The *Spirit of Aloha* is presented in an open-air dining theater in Luau Cove, adjacent to the Seven Seas Lagoon.

The all-you-can-eat feast is influenced by the flavors of Polynesia and includes draft beer, wine, soft drinks, and dessert. Menu items

PHOTO BY JILL SAFRO

include roasted chicken, barbecued pork ribs, fresh pineapple, Polynesian-style rice, and vegetables. The kids' menu features PB&J sandwiches, mac and cheese, chicken nuggets, and hot dogs. Cost is about $59 for adults and $30 for kids in Category 3; about $63 and $31 for Category 2; and about $68 and $35 for Category 1 (again, the best views are from Category 1 seats).

Plan to arrive at least 30 minutes before showtime, and allow extra time for transportation and parking. (Note that prices include tax and gratuity and are subject to change.) The show may be canceled due to inclement weather (though tables are sheltered).

Reservations: Arrangements for dinner shows may be made up to 180 days in advance by calling 407-WDW-DINE (939-3463). Groups of eight or more should call 407-939-7707. *Prices include tax and gratuity and may be higher during peak seasons.*

A credit card number is required for all dinner show reservations. Full payment is required upon booking. It's also possible to redeem Disney Dining Plan credits for dinner shows. At press time all Disney dinner shows were participating in the dining plan. They are considered "signature meals" and cost two table-service meals per person. *Note that cancellations for dinner shows must be made at least 48 hours prior to showtime to avoid paying full price.*

Bars & Lounges of WDW

No one ever said the Magic Kingdom's no-liquor policy means that everyone in the World is a teetotaler. Actually, some of WDW's tastiest offerings are liquid (and spirited), and some of its most entertaining places are its bars and lounges—many of which serve things to nibble as well as sip.

Hours vary depending on the locale, but generally, watering holes at Epcot, Disney's Hollywood Studios, and Animal Kingdom shut their doors at park closing. Pool bars at the resorts keep daytime pool hours. Last call at lounges in the resorts is anywhere from 10 P.M. to midnight. Downtown Disney Marketplace spots stay open until the shops close, usually 11 P.M. Pleasure Island and the West Side may keep things going until about 2 A.M.

All-Star Movies, All-Star Music, & All-Star Sports

Silver Screen Spirits at All-Star Movies, **Singing Spirits** at All-Star Music, and **Team Spirits** at All-Star Sports serve beer, wine, and specialty drinks by the pool.

Animal Kingdom

DAWA BAR: Enjoy Safari Amber beer (among many other brews), specialty cocktails (including frozen piña coladas and strawberry daiquiris, Bloody Marys, and potent concoctions known as Lost on the Safari and Harambe Cooler), plus occasional musical entertainment under the thatched roof.

RAINFOREST CAFE: The diminutive Magic Mushroom bar serves, among other things, fruit blends and specialty drinks.

Animal Kingdom Lodge

CAPE TOWN LOUNGE AND WINE BAR: Sip African wines at this intimate spot adjacent to Jiko—The Cooking Place. In addition to a full menu, it has the largest selection of African wines in the United States.

MAJI: The appropriately named poolside bar (*maji* means "water" in Swahili) serves cool beverages when the Samawati Springs pool is open (in Kidani Village).

UZIMA SPRINGS: The bar near the resort's main pool serves beer, wine, and specialty cocktails during pool hours. The (liquor-free) Espresso Freeze—espresso blended with frozen cappuccino and ice cream—is a delightful way to counter the Florida heat.

VICTORIA FALLS: On the mezzanine level overlooking Boma—Flavors of Africa, this lounge offers coffee, wine, and other spirits—plus the soothing sounds of the falls. The real Victoria Falls, by the way, are located in Africa, between Zambia and Zimbabwe, and are nearly a mile wide.

BoardWalk

ATLANTIC DANCE: This nightclub has music, videos, and a deejay. The design is art deco, but the tunes are from the 80's through today. The club is open Tuesday–Saturday night, and guests must be at least 21 years old to enter.

BELLE VUE LOUNGE: A full bar accompanies old-time tunes from antique radios in this lobby cocktail lounge. Continental breakfast may be offered. Board games may be available for onsite use (free of charge). There's limited seating at the bar, but there are plenty of tables and comfy couches to lounge on. 🐭

BIG RIVER GRILLE & BREWING WORKS: A working microbrewery, Big River patrons may order appetizers at the bar and sample the brewmaster's flagship ales and specialty beers. They may even get to watch as a new batch is brewed. 🐭

ESPN CLUB: The ultimate sports bar provides live radio and television broadcasts along with a menu of ballpark favorites (including, of course, hot dogs). With more than 80 screens, chances are you'll find the game you're looking for. The place fills up quickly on big game days—plan to arrive at least an hour early on such occasions. Note that on NFL Sundays, the match-ups scheduled for screening are usually noted right on the TVs. If not, ask the bartender or inquire at the podium near the front entrance. 🐭

JELLYROLLS: Dueling pianos and lively sing-alongs are the draw at this club, serving beer, wine, and other drinks. There is usually a cover in the neighborhood of $10 and guests must be at least 21 years old to enter. Requests are encouraged. And don't forget to tip the piano players before you leave.

PHOTO BY JILL SAFRO

LEAPING HORSE LIBATIONS: The pool bar—designed to resemble a carousel (hence, the leaping horses)—offers cocktails, sandwiches, soft drinks, and simple snacks during pool hours.

Bonnet Creek Golf Club

SAND TRAP: Opening at about 10:30 A.M. each morning, Sand Trap offers a full bar and light menu items such as sandwiches and salads. Located at the Osprey Ridge golf course, the bar stays open until the course is clear. 🐭

Caribbean Beach

BANANA CABANA: Refreshing drinks and snack items are served at this poolside bar near Old Port Royale.

Contemporary

CALIFORNIA GRILL LOUNGE: A vast selection of California wine by the bottle (and several by the glass), plus cocktails and all items from the restaurant menu (including spectacular sushi) are offered in this tiny space inside the California Grill. Just as with the restaurant itself, all guests hoping to visit the California Grill Lounge must check in at the desk on the Contemporary's second floor. From there they are escorted to an express elevator. 🐭

COVE BAR: Set beside the pool in the resort's Bay Lake Tower, Cove Bar serves sweets (apple slices with caramel dipping sauce, fresh fruit, and frozen desserts), and light lunch items (vegetable summer rolls, five-spice chicken-lettuce wraps, and turkey club sandwiches). Wash it all down with one of their specialty drinks, such as the Strawberry Guava Sunset, Sour Apple Freeze, or Tropical Mango Mojito. 🐭

HOT TIP!

At some Walt Disney World lounges, you may order food from a neighboring or nearby restaurant's menu. Just ask.

OUTER RIM: Located on the resort's fourth floor across from Contempo Cafe, this modern lounge has about seven bar stools and an abundance of tables with cocktail service. The main draw here is not the view of the large-screen TV, but, rather the sweeping views of Bay Lake and Fort Wilderness (on the lake's far shore). Parts of this lounge host guests waiting for a table at the ever-popular Chef Mickey's restaurant, so it can be congested here at mealtimes. Beer, wine, sangria, specialty drinks, and alcohol-free kiddie cocktails are served from about 4 P.M. till 10 P.M.

SAND BAR: A full bar is offered poolside, weather permitting. Fast food is available at the adjacent counter area. 🐭

THE WAVE . . . OF AMERICAN FLAVORS LOUNGE: A sleek bar on the first floor, this is a watering hole "with a twist." The twist is the sound you'll hear when the bartender opens a new bottle of Old World wine—all feature trendy caps in lieu of the old-school corks. A full bar is available.

Coronado Springs

RIX LOUNGE: Located in the main building, this upscale lounge serves specialty drinks, beer, wine, and tapas-style appetizers. The 300-seat venue features house music and a Mediterranean-inspired atmosphere.

SIESTAS: Swimmers can take time out for burgers, sandwiches, tacos, and cocktails at this spot near the pool in the Dig Site area. 🐭

Disney's Animal Kingdom

YAK & YETI LOUNGE: A small-but-escapist space inside one of the restaurant's themed dining areas, the Yak & Yeti lounge has a fully stocked bar and seating for six. (There's standing room, too.) House specialties include the Yak Attack, Bonsai Blast, Big Bamboo, and Everest Avalanche. Beer, wine, and sake are also served.

Disney's Hollywood Studios

TUNE-IN LOUNGE: A sitcom living-room setting, with comfy stools and couches, characterizes this lounge next to the 50's Prime Time Cafe. Old TV sets play scenes from beloved sitcoms (all of which feature food). Appetizers, cocktails, beer, and wine are served.

Disney's Old Key West

GURGLING SUITCASE: This pocket-size lounge on the Turtle Krawl boardwalk serves an assortment of Key West specialties along with traditional cocktails, beer, and wine.

TURTLE SHACK: Refreshments at this poolside spot include cocktails and a small selection of fast-food items.

Downtown Disney

BONGOS: Home to two bars, Bongos' "lobby" bar has a dozen or so bongo drum stools. Mojitos are the specialty of the house, but martinis and other mixed drinks, wine, sangria, and beer are also served. This is a pleasant spot, but we prefer to relax in the big pineapple. Bongos' two-story pineapple bar has indoor and outdoor seating and offers a full bar, plus appetizers.

FUEGO: A funky cigar bar (yes, it's okay to puff away in here), Fuego features premium cigars, as well as cocktails. Guests must be at least 18 years old to smoke, 21 to drink. It gets pretty hazy here—non-smokers may want to indulge elsewhere.

HOLE IN THE WALL: Blink and you miss it, this tiny establishment is bookended (and dwarfed) by Raglan Road on the left and Cooke's of Dublin on the right. A full bar is available, but the Irish stout stands out.

HOUSE OF BLUES: Set in the back of the eatery section of H.O.B, this bar serves soft drinks and cocktails that are as cool as the atmosphere.

MAGIC MUSHROOM BAR: When the Rainforest Cafe restaurant is mobbed, we recommend taking in the thunderstorms and waterfalls from this central, mushroom-capped bar. Simply saddle a stool (all of which are shaped like animal legs) and enjoy the festive "natural" ambience. There is another Magic Mushroom Bar inside the Rainforest Cafe at Disney's Animal Kingdom.

PARADISO 37: The bar inside Paradiso 37 features an international wine list, an extensive selection of tequilas, frozen margaritas, and the "coldest beer in the world." It is possible to order items from the restaurant's menu, too.

PLANET HOLLYWOOD: Though far from the most atmospheric WDW bar, this tiny enclave within the Planet Hollywood eatery has a lot to offer a thirsty visitor. In addition to beer, wine, and champagne, the resident mixologists routinely whip up "shooter" creations known as Banana Pudding, Bubble Gum, and Grape Crush. Frozen specialties include Mama Mia!-ritas and Die Harder Daiquiris.

PORTOBELLO: In the heart of Portobello Country Italian Trattoria, the bountiful bar has an alluring ambiance and ample seating. An oenophile's dream come true, the international wine list has something for just about everyone. Italy is well-represented, with offerings from Sonoma, South Africa, Columbia, New York, and other locales. Many wines are available by the glass, bottle, and half bottle. The cordial menu boasts brandy, cognac, port, sherry, grappa, and dessert wines. There's a full bar and a selection of locally brewed, organic beers.

RAGLAN ROAD: This jovial joint, located at Pleasure Island, is an authentic Irish pub. The polished interior is a meticulously decorated Emerald Isle oasis—complete with freshly prepared Irish cuisine and live entertainment (the latter starting at about 9 P.M.). Oh, and of course, pints of stout and other spirited beverages. This place is popular and can get quite crowded on weekend evenings.

SHARK BAR: This space, inside T-Rex: A Prehistoric Family Adventure, puts the water in watering hole. Anchored under the belly of a Technicolor squid, the aqueous area serves all kinds of cocktails, plus items from the restaurant's menu. (One of our favorite things to order here is the tomato soup.) Guests must be at least 21 years of age to sit at the bar.

STONE CRAB LOUNGE: Inside Fulton's Crab House, Stone Crab is an excellent raw bar with prime water views and a honey-wheat house brew. The Bloody Marys are made from scratch and garnished with shrimp. And the bartenders here are among the friendliest at Walt Disney World. What's not to love? Hours generally run from about 11:30 A.M. till about 11:30 P.M.

CAP'N JACK'S RESTAURANT (Marketplace): Agleam with copper and right on the water, this bar's specialty is its delicious strawberry margaritas. The nibbles of steamed mussels, clam chowder, and shrimp on the appetizer menu are great for a snack or a whole meal.

Epcot

All eateries, including some fast-food spots, serve alcoholic beverages. A few other Epcot locales specialize in liquid refreshments.

LA CAVA DEL TEQUILA: A warm glow envelopes all guests who visit this little lounge inside the big pyramid at the Mexico pavilion—and that's *before* they sample any of the 70-plus tequilas on the menu. In addition to masterfully blended margaritas (many made with fresh fruit and spices), guests may sip Mexican beer, wine, cocktails, and soft drinks. Tapas-style snack selections include fresh guacamole, ceviche, and mahi mahi tostadas. This 30-seat escape is open from about noon until Epcot closing time.

ROSE & CROWN PUB: This classic pub—a veritable symphony of polished woods, brass, and etched glass—adjoins the Rose & Crown Dining Room in the United Kingdom pavilion. English, Scottish, and Irish beers are available, along with a score of specialty drinks and appetizing snacks imported from the other side of the Atlantic. If you're lucky, there will be live (and lively) piano music during your visit. Feel free to sing along. Seating indoors and out is limited and available on a first-come, first-served basis.

SOMMERFEST: Just outside the Biergarten in Germany, there's a shaded space where soft pretzels, bratwurst, frankfurters, apple strudel, and other treats may be washed down with a stein of cold German beer. They also serve German wines (red and white), Jagermeister, Goldschlager, and soft drinks.

Fort Wilderness

CROCKETT'S TAVERN: You needn't brandish a coonskin cap to belly up to the bar in this rustic saloon, merely a government-issued photo ID to prove you're not a young'un (all guests must be at least 21 years of age to drink spirits of any kind). Tucked into a corner of the Trail's End restaurant, this spot is small but cozy, and the barkeeps are as amiable as they come. Last we visited, there were a couple of domestic beers on tap, plus a full bar. Pizza and nachos are served, too. The TV is usually tuned to the big game of the moment.

Grand Floridian

CITRICOS LOUNGE: As inviting as any lounge on Disney property, this place has one stellar wine list. Old World, New World, red, white, sparkling . . . you name it, they got it. Also on tap are beer, port, sherry, specialty coffees, and creative cocktails (think along the lines of a Citropolitan or Pomegranate Splash).

Soup, salad, and appetizers may be ordered until about 10 P.M. (If it's busy, the bar may continue to serve drinks until the crowd dwindles.) Menu selections include roasted butternut squash bisque, goat cheese truffle salad, sautéed shrimp, gateau of crab, and the exquisitely crispy arancini risotto (fried balls of rice with cremini mushrooms, asiago cheese, and white truffle aioli). There are a handful of seats at the bar and roughly ten tables in the lounge. If you sit at a table, be sure to place your order with the bartender before grabbing a seat.

MIZNER'S: Named after the eccentric architect who defined much of the flavor of Florida's Gold Coast, this handsome retreat serves ports, brandies, and appetizers. Cigars may be purchased here, too (although they must be puffed elsewhere, as this, like most WDW bars, is a nonsmoking venue).

If you're in the mood for a nibble, consider the hummus and grilled flatbread, warm goat cheese flatbread, or chilled shrimp cocktail. Sweet temptations include lemon cheesecake, chocolate banana torte, and tiramisu. Food is served usually from about 5:30 P.M. until about 10 P.M., while the spirits usually flow until about midnight.

NARCOOSSEE'S LOUNGE: This upscale bar-within-a-restaurant offers a little bit of everything: appetizers, entrées, desserts, and cocktails (including dessert drinks). There is an extensive list of international wines, 40 of which are available by the glass. How serious are they about wine here? Our last bartender was a certified sommelier. Note that the dress code for this lounge is "business casual." ❤

POOL BAR: This Grand Floridian pool/beach bar stands by with beer, wine, frozen specialty drinks, soft drinks, and snacks.

Polynesian

BAREFOOT BAR: This oasis next to the swimming pool lagoon serves beer, wine, frozen tropical drinks (with and without alcohol), and soft drinks. Seasonal.

TAMBU: Adjoining 'Ohana restaurant, this bar offers Polynesian-style appetizers and specialty drinks in a tropical setting. There is seating at the bar and at nearby tables. Note that the table section serves as the waiting area for guests dining at 'Ohana, so it gets very busy at mealtimes.

Pop Century

PETALS: This poolside watering hole serves beer, wine, and cocktails.

Port Orleans French Quarter

MARDI GROGS: Beer, specialty drinks, and snacks are among the offerings at this poolside spot.

SCAT CAT'S CLUB: Next to the Sassagoula Floatworks & Food Factory, this large, informal lounge pays tribute to the uniquely American music that is jazz. In fact, live jazz music is actually presented four nights a week (Wednesday through Saturday, from 8 P.M. till about midnight). In addition to the usual brews and blends, this spot specializes in Southern drinks—including Hurricanes served in hurricane lamp shade glasses. There is a tempting appetizer menu, too.

Port Orleans Riverside

MUDDY RIVERS: The poolside bar serves beer, specialty concoctions, and snack items.

RIVER ROOST: Situated in a room designed as a cotton exchange, this spacious lounge features specialty drinks, as well as light hors d'oeuvres. Sink into a comfy chair, beside the glow of the fireplace, and sip cocktails with a Southern flair. There are stools at the bar and tables, too. Live entertainment is presented on select evenings (usually Wednesday through Saturday, from 8 P.M. until about midnight).

Saratoga Springs

THE TURF CLUB: This charming corner of the resort serves all manner of spirits. There's a pool table, too.

Swan & Dolphin

CABANA BAR & BEACH CLUB: Come for the food, stay for drinks. This Dolphin spot is a cut above the usual poolside cove. Its sophisticated air and edgy design is a definite draw for the grown-up set, yet the place doesn't take itself so seriously that it fails to please little ones (think pepperoni pizza, ice cream, and raspberry lemonade). Refined palates rave over the crab salad, tuna tartare, and rock shrimp (among other things).

Classic cocktails such as the Mai Tai, Beachcomber, and Singapore Sling share the stage with creative, original concoctions (often infused with fresh berries). Frozen libations abound, as do beer (micro- and macrobrews), rum, and tequila. Wine, scotch, cognac, and cigars are offered, too.

Soft thirst-quenchers include a variety of iced teas, lemonade, soda, chocolate milk, and specialty coffees.

IL MULINO NEW YORK TRATTORIA LOUNGE: A lovely spot (at the Swan) to sip wines and cocktails and/or enjoy the bar menu, this lounge features live music on Friday and Saturday evenings. There are seats at the bar, plus tables and comfy couches. It's usually open for business starting in the late afternoon.

JAVA BAR: Head to this Swan lobby bar for a satisfying java jolt from 6 A.M. until 11 A.M. daily. In addition to the standard cuppa Joe, Java Bar offers espresso, cappuccino, and Americano (a mix of espresso and steaming hot water)—all made with freshly ground beans. Juice and tea are served, too. Breakfast

❤ Disney Dining Plan participant at press time

items include bagels, croissants, muffins, scones, cereal, fruit salad, yogurt, and whole fruit.

KIMONOS: This Swan lounge, attractively decorated in Japanese style, has a full bar, as well as sushi and other culinary treats. It opens in late afternoon/early evening, and last call is usually between 10:30 P.M. and 1 A.M. The karaoke starts cranking at about 9:30 P.M.

LOBBY LOUNGE: This sleek Dolphin lobby bar serves beer, wine, cocktails, and soft drinks, sometimes accompanied by live piano music at night. Hours are generally 4 P.M. until about 11 P.M.

SHULA'S LOUNGE: This small, austere Dolphin saloon within Shula's Steak House features rich wood tones and plush seating— the perfect place to sip a cocktail while playing armchair quarterback.

SPLASH TERRACE: A poolside oasis near the Swan, Splash shares the menu with its Dolphin neighbor, Cabana Bar and Beach Club (see page 276).

TODD ENGLISH'S BLUEZOO BAR: The underwater mojo of Todd's bluezoo restaurant extends to the sizable bar/lounge area (booths and tables augment the bar seating, easily accommodating large parties). In addition to the liquid refreshments, this is a genuine raw bar—many guests order a cocktail with a side of something fishy.

Last call varies, depending on how crowded the place is at any given moment. Figure on getting the boot between 9 P.M. and 11 P.M.

Wilderness Lodge

TERRITORY: Located between Artist Point and Whispering Canyon Cafe, this rustic homage to the explorers of the Great West is a nice spot for a pre-dinner treat. Appetizers, beer, wine, and specialty drinks are served. The Pomegranate Sparkler is a refreshing, no-alcohol treat.

TROUT PASS: This poolside bar serves beer, wine, and frozen drinks.

Yacht & Beach Club

ALE AND COMPASS: The nautically themed Yacht Club lobby lounge boasts a drink menu complete with specialty coffees. Coffee (sans liquor) and light breakfast items are served here each morning. The lounge stays open until about midnight. ❤

CREW'S CUP: Styled after a traditional New England waterfront pub, this lounge has a seafaring feel to it. It's next door to the Yachtsman Steakhouse and has well over 30 beers. There is also a tempting menu. This is one of our favorite places to relax after a long day in the parks. Food is usually served from noon until midnight.

HURRICANE HANNA'S GRILL: This poolside spot offers specialty beverages, frozen drinks, and beer, plus fast-food items. A selection of chilly, alcohol-free concoctions is available, too. ❤

MARTHA'S VINEYARD: While a full bar is available, a small-but-satisfying selection of wines from Martha's Vineyard (and other areas) is this Beach Club bar's specialty. Appetizers and snacks are served.

INDEX

♥ Notes ♥

❤ Notes ❤

COUPONS

10% OFF
**FOOD AND BEVERAGES
FOR UP TO 4 GUESTS**
(discount excludes alcohol)

For reservations, call 407-934-2628.

Subject to terms and conditions on reverse side

Grand CAFE
WOLFGANG·PUCK

10% OFF FOOD AND BEVERAGES
(discount excludes alcohol)

**Call 407-938-9653
for reservations.**

Subject to terms and conditions on reverse side

Located at DOWNTOWN DISNEY®

10% off all curl® merchandise

* **Nixon** * **Quiksilver** * **Tom's** * **Billabong** * **Volcom**
* **Ugg** * **Reef** * **Oakley** * **Maui Jim**

For information, call 407-842-1302.

Subject to terms and conditions on reverse side

PORTOBELLO
COUNTRY · ITALIAN · TRATTORIA

10% OFF
**FOOD AND BEVERAGES
FOR UP TO 4 GUESTS**
(discount excludes alcohol)

For reservations, call 407-934-8888.

Subject to terms and conditions on reverse side

**10% OFF
MERCHANDISE**

Subject to terms and conditions on reverse side

PLANET HOLLYWOOD®

10% OFF
FOOD AND BEVERAGES
(discount excludes alcohol)
Call 407-939-3463 for reservations.

Subject to terms and conditions on reverse side

15% OFF Lunch or Dinner

for up to 8 guests in the HOB Restaurant

(discount on food only)

Enjoy distinctive Southern-inspired cuisine in an enjoyable atmosphere filled with creative folk art. Opens daily at 11:30 A.M.

For reservations, call 407-934-2623.

15% OFF Admission to the BEHIND THE SEEDS

Tour at The Land For up to 10 guests

Bring the entire family backstage for a one-hour, interactive tour of the greenhouses and fish farm at The Land.

For same-day reservations, present coupon at the Tour Desk next to the entrance of Soarin'. Or call ahead to 407-WDW-TOUR (407-939-8687) and mention the *Birnbaum Offer*. Admission to Epcot® is required.

Up to 20% OFF
Accommodations

DISNEY'S VERO BEACH RESORT
A DISNEY VACATION CLUB RESORT

- Receive 10% off most nights when arriving 3/11/12– 3/24/12; 3/25/12–3/31/12; 4/13/12–4/14/12; 5/28/12–7/2/12; 7/8/12–8/18/12.
- Receive 20% off most nights when arriving 1/1/12–2/15/12; 2/16/12–2/17/12; 2/24/12–3/10/12; 4/15/12–5/23/12; 8/19/12–8/30/12; 9/3/12–10/4/12; 10/7/12–11/19/12; 11/24/12–12/24/12.

Only 20 rooms per night have been allocated for these offers. Minimum length of stay requirements apply for Friday or Saturday arrivals. Reservations cannot be made more than 11 months prior to check-in date. For reservations, call 407-939-7652 and ask for the Birnbaum Offer.

Located at DISNEY'S CONTEMPORARY RESORT

15% OFF
ALL SAMMY DUVALL'S WATERSPORTS CENTRE ACTIVITIES

- PARASAILING
- WATERSKIING, WAKEBOARDING, AND FAMILY TUBING
- PERSONAL WATERCRAFT

RESERVATIONS ARE SUGGESTED.

CALL 407-939-0754 FOR MORE INFORMATION.

10% OFF EPCOT®
Dive Quest admission

Epcot® Dive Quest is a scuba-diving adventure open to all certified scuba divers ages 10 and up.

Call (407) 939-8687 for reservations.

10% OFF
DISNEY'S DOLPHINS IN DEPTH admission
for up to 4 guests

Disney's Dolphins in Depth is an educational dolphin interaction program open to all guests ages 13 and up.

Call (407) 939-8687 for reservations.

Valid only in the HOB Restaurant at
Downtown Disney® West Side.
Excludes alcohol, tax, and gratuity.
One offer per check for up to 8 guests.
Must present coupon to receive offer.

Expires 12/20/12

TERMS & CONDITIONS
- Must present coupon at check-in to receive discount.
- Discount does not apply to merchandise.
- Call for activity restrictions.
- All activities are subject to availability.
- We reserve the right to cancel due to inclement
  weather.
- Terms and conditions subject to change without
  notice.
- Coupon not valid with any other discount.
- Coupon cannot be copied or reproduced.
- Coupon cannot be redeemed for cash.
  For more information, visit *www.sammyduvall.com*
  or call (407) 939-0754.

Expires 12/31/12

Excludes Beach Cottages. No group rates or other
discounts apply. Advance reservations required. All
prices and other terms are subject to change
without notice. This coupon may not be redeemed
for cash in whole or in part.

© Disney

Expires 12/18/12

Up to 20% OFF Accommodations

DISNEY'S HILTON HEAD ISLAND RESORT
A DISNEY VACATION CLUB RESORT

- Receive 10% off the non-discounted rate most nights when arriving 4/13/12–4/14/12; 4/15/12–5/23/12; 5/28/12–7/2/12; 7/8/12–8/25/12.
- Receive 20% off most nights when arriving 1/1/12–2/15/12; 2/16/12–2/17/12; 2/20/12–2/25/12; 2/26/12–3/10/12; 3/11/12–3/31/12; 8/26/12–8/30/12; 9/3/12–10/4/12; 10/8/12–10/21/12; 10/22/12–11/19/12; 11/24/12–11/24/12; 11/25/12–12/24/12.

Only 20 rooms per night have been allocated for these offers. Minimum length of stay requirements apply for Friday or Saturday arrivals. Reservations cannot be made more than 11 months prior to check-in date. For reservations, call 407-939-7652 and ask for the Birnbaum Offer.

Subject to terms and conditions on reverse side

10% OFF admission for up to 4 guests

Before 4 P.M. at **Disney's Fantasia Gardens** or **Disney's Winter Summerland** Miniature Golf Course.

Subject to terms and conditions on reverse side

20% OFF
2-Hour WALT DISNEY WORLD® Guided Fishing Excursion
for you and up to four guests

Star in your own "fish out of water" story with a Walt Disney World® Guided Fishing Excursion! To make your reservation, call 407-WDW-BASS (407-939-2277) or visit *www.disneyworldfishing.com*, mention the coupon in the "Additional Comments" section of the request form, and then present the coupon upon arrival.

Subject to terms and conditions on reverse side

$10 OFF Purchase of $75 or More
at the **LEGO® Store**
at DOWNTOWN DISNEY® Marketplace

LEGO and the LEGO logo are trademarks of the LEGO Group. © 2011 the LEGO Group.

Subject to terms and conditions on reverse side

15% OFF
WILD BY DESIGN TOUR
AT DISNEY'S ANIMAL KINGDOM®

Embark on a wild adventure exploring the secrets of Disney's Animal Kingdom® park.

For more information on tours, see pages 218-220 of this book.

Call 407-939-8687 for reservations.

Subject to terms and conditions on reverse side

Enjoy special
*Cardmember perks**
during your visit to Disney.

Become a Cardmember and experience these Theme Park perks:

- ♥ Character Meet 'N' Greet at our private location
- ♥ 10% off on select merchandise purchases of $50 or more at select locations at the *Walt Disney World®* Resort
- ♥ 20% off the non-discounted price of select guided tours

For a special offer for Birnbaum Guide readers and pricing and rewards details, visit
DisneyVisaOffer.com/Birnbaum

*See back for details.

Offer is valid for 10% off one round of miniature golf before 4 P.M. Limit four guests per coupon. Not valid with any other discounts or offers. No photocopies accepted. Offer is subject to availability. Restrictions apply.

© Disney

Expires 12/31/12

Excludes Grand Villas. No group rates or other discounts apply. Advance reservations required. All prices and other terms are subject to change without notice. This coupon may not be redeemed for cash in whole or in part.

© Disney

Expires 12/24/12

Qualifying amount applies to merchandise only. Limit one coupon per transaction. Coupon must be redeemed at time of purchase. Not valid on prior purchases or gift cards. Coupon cannot be redeemed for cash or replaced if lost or stolen. May not be combined with any other offer or coupon. Offer not valid at other LEGO® stores or www.LEGO.com. Valid only at the LEGO Store in Downtown Disney® Marketplace–Orlando.

Coupon code: 999132

99913200

Expires 12/31/12

All excursions are subject to availability. Prices and terms are subject to change without notice. Offer not valid with any other discounted rate. This coupon may not be redeemed for cash in whole or in part, and may not be reproduced.

Expires 12/31/12

All tours subject to availability. Disney's Animal Kingdom® park admission is required.

Reproductions of coupon not accepted. Coupon may not be redeemed for cash in whole or in part. Offer subject to change without notice.

Ages 14 and above.

© Disney

Expires 12/31/12